Christianity in the Middle Ages

A Captivating Guide to the Tales of Templars, Trials of Faith, and the Tumult of Crusades

© Copyright 2024 - All rights reserved.

The content contained within this book may not be reproduced, duplicated, or transmitted without direct written permission from the author or the publisher.

Under no circumstances will any blame or legal responsibility be held against the publisher, or author, for any damages, reparation, or monetary loss due to the information contained within this book, either directly or indirectly.

Legal Notice:

This book is copyright protected. It is only for personal use. You cannot amend, distribute, sell, use, quote, or paraphrase any part, or the content within this book, without the consent of the author or publisher.

Disclaimer Notice:

Please note the information contained within this document is for educational and entertainment purposes only. All effort has been executed to present accurate, up-to-date, reliable, and complete information. No warranties of any kind are declared or implied. Readers acknowledge that the author is not engaging in the rendering of legal, financial, medical, or professional advice. The content within this book has been derived from various sources. Please consult a licensed professional before attempting any techniques outlined in this book.

By reading this document, the reader agrees that under no circumstances is the author responsible for any losses, direct or indirect, that are incurred as a result of the use of the information contained within this document, including, but not limited to, errors, omissions, or inaccuracies.

Free Bonus from Captivating History (Available for a Limited time)

Hi History Lovers!

Now you have a chance to join our exclusive history list so you can get your first history ebook for free as well as discounts and a potential to get more history books for free! Simply visit the link below to join.

Captivatinghistory.com/ebook

Also, make sure to follow us on Facebook, Twitter and Youtube by searching for Captivating History.

Table of Contents

PART 1: MEDIEVAL CHRISTIANITY 1
  INTRODUCTION 2
  SECTION ONE: THE GREAT EMPIRE (100-476 CE) 5
  CHAPTER 1: FROM ROYALTY...6
  CHAPTER 2: ...TO RUIN 23
  SECTION TWO: THE GREAT DIVIDE 476-1200 CE 33
  CHAPTER 3: EARLY CHRISTIAN IRELAND..34
  CHAPTER 4: THE DARK AGES IN EUROPE (476-1000 CE) 45
  CHAPTER 5: THE GREAT SCHISM (1054) 62
  CHAPTER 6: THE MAGNA CARTA (1215) 70
  SECTION THREE: THE GREAT OPPOSITION 1095-1400 CE 77
  CHAPTER 7: THE FIRST AND SECOND CRUSADES 78
  CHAPTER 8: POWER STRUGGLE (1180S-1310S) 104
  CHAPTER 9: THE RECONQUISTA (722-1300S)..131
  CHAPTER 10: THE RISE AND FALL OF THE TEMPLARS 143
  CHAPTER 11: THE OPPOSITION: ISLAM, ZENGI & SALADIN 149
  SECTION FOUR: THE GREAT REFORMATION 1510-1640 CE 154
  CHAPTER 12: WHAT WAS THE REFORMATION?..................................155
  CHAPTER 13: THE GREAT REFORMERS...165
  CHAPTER 14: CORRUPTION AND CHRISTIANITY 185
  CHAPTER 15: THE REFORMATION IN EUROPE.....................................212
  CHAPTER 16: THE COUNTER-REFORMATION (1545-1700)..................220

CONCLUSION 229
PART 2: MEDIEVAL KNIGHTS 231
   INTRODUCTION 232
   CHAPTER 1: A GLIMPSE INTO THE MIDDLE AGES 234
   CHAPTER 2: THE CRUSADES: A BRIEF OVERVIEW 240
   CHAPTER 3: THE JOURNEY TO KNIGHTHOOD 254
   CHAPTER 4: THE KNIGHTS HOSPITALLER 260
   CHAPTER 5: THE KNIGHTS OF THE HOLY SEPULCHRE 270
   CHAPTER 6: THE ORDER OF ST. LAZARUS 277
   CHAPTER 7: THE TEUTONIC KNIGHTS 281
   CHAPTER 8: THE KNIGHTS TEMPLAR 291
   CONCLUSION 318
PART 3: THE INQUISITION 320
   INTRODUCTION: ASKING TOO MANY QUESTIONS 321
   CHAPTER 1: LA CONVIVENCIA—RELIGIOUS TOLERANCE
   AND COEXISTENCE BEFORE THE INQUISITION 323
   CHAPTER 2: THE HUNTERS AND THE HUNTED: THE ROLES
   ARE ESTABLISHED, AND THE INQUISITION TAKES SHAPE 329
   CHAPTER 3: THE SPANISH INQUISITION 336
   CHAPTER 4: THE PORTUGUESE INQUISITION 346
   CHAPTER 5: THE ROMAN INQUISITION 353
   CHAPTER 6: CRIME AND PUNISHMENT DURING THE
   INQUISITION 362
   CHAPTER 7: PAPAL INVOLVEMENT 374
   CHAPTER 8: THE END OF THE INQUISITION 380
   CHAPTER 9: IMPACT AND LEGACY OF THE INQUISITION 388
   CHAPTER 10: AN INTERMISSION OF THE INQUISITION:
   HISTORIOGRAPHY THROUGH MULTIPLE LENSES 392
   CONCLUSION: MAKE WAY FOR THE GRAND INQUISITOR 395
HERE'S ANOTHER BOOK BY CAPTIVATING HISTORY THAT
YOU MIGHT LIKE 397
FREE BONUS FROM CAPTIVATING HISTORY (AVAILABLE FOR
A LIMITED TIME) 398
BIBLIOGRAPHY 399

Part 1: Medieval Christianity

A Captivating Guide to Christian History, Starting from the Fall of the Western Roman Empire through the Great Schism and the Crusades to the Reformation

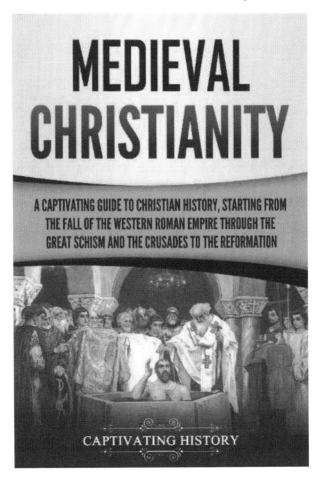

Introduction

Many theologians would cite the beginning of Christianity with Jesus Christ's death around 30 AD. However, the roots of Christianity are much older. Jesus Christ was a Jewish man, which is part of the reason Christianity and Judaism share so much with each other, even today.

Jesus Christ originally preached in Israel, in the modern-day Middle East.[1] He was later crucified, in part because of his teachings. Soon after, his former followers (disciples) began to spread his teachings around the Middle East and Europe. This new religion was called Christianity. Outside of Israel, it first caught on in Rome. Once it had made its mark in Europe, the religion changed European history forever.

From about 30 AD onward, small communities began to adopt Christianity when Jesus's followers started to spread his word. One of the most famous spreaders of the Gospel was the Apostle Paul, who is credited with bringing Christianity to Rome. Previously, many European countries and ethnic groups followed pagan religions. Many of these were polytheistic, believing in many gods, which have now been mythologized. Christianity was monotheistic, believing in only one infallible, all-seeing God. This was a huge change for Europeans, and it did not always go smoothly.

One war after another scourged Europe for centuries after the arrival of Christianity. While many of these were purely political, there was also

---

[1] Wieja, Estera. "10 Places Where Jesus Walked in Israel from Scripture." Fellowship of Israel Related Ministries, October 22, 2020, https://firmisrael.org/learn/10-places-where-jesus-walked/.

an element of religious strife. This became more apparent whenever a "Christian" country wanted to take land from non-Christian countries. Once the land was taken, the population would often be forced (or at least heavily encouraged) to convert.

Missionary efforts, mostly by the Catholic Church between the first and fifteenth centuries, also helped spread the Word of God to people living outside of mainland Europe. One of the earliest missions took place in Ireland. Later missions would take place in Africa and Asia.

Some of the biggest wars sired in the name of the faith were the Crusades. These battles began around 1100. They were religious wars in nature but also wars for land and simple attrition. The Catholic Church allied themselves with several European monarchs. They fought against armies "invading" the Holy Land in and around Jerusalem. Heavy losses on both sides forever changed the religious and political landscape of the Middle East.

The Crusades and other political issues happening around the same time added conflict between Christians and Muslims. Over the centuries, they took turns trying to slaughter or convert each other. Both sides had their fair share of wins and losses. The pain from these times is so prevalent that there is still discord between some Christians and Muslims to this day.

So, with the aid of conquest and conversion, Christianity quickly spread around the world. For over 1,000 years, the Church was a single entity—the Catholic Church. Then, around 1300, the Catholic Church split. This event was called The Great Schism, which forever broke the Catholic Church in two: the Roman Catholic Church and the Eastern Orthodox Church.

The Church broke even further around 1500 with the coming of the Reformation. During this period, which lasted roughly 200 years, several groups splintered from the Catholic Church, forming the Protestant (non-Catholic Christian) sects, many of which are still around today. Some of the biggest names in the Reformation include John Calvin, Martin Luther, and even King Henry VIII. All of these men had different reasons for splitting from the Catholic Church.

Both Luther and Calvin saw corruption in the Catholic Church. At first, their goals were not to create a new sect of Christianity but to change the Catholic Church to rid it of scandal and corruption. Some of the corruptions they opposed included the sale of indulgences, the concept of purgatory, and nepotism and bribery in the Church offices and roles. King Henry VIII, on the other hand, broke his country (England) from the Church because he wanted a divorce.

The Catholic Church lost thousands, if not millions, of members during the Reformation. It tried to counter the efforts of the Reformation with its own, aptly called the Counter-Reformation. During this time, the Catholic Church tried to fix its errors and assess what the Protestants saw as scandalous or corrupted in the Catholic Church. While the Church did make some changes after the three sessions of the Council of Trent, the Church as a whole remained mostly unchanged.

This book will cover the events listed in this short introduction in great detail, as well as several other topics not mentioned. This book, will give readers a glimpse of how Christianity grew and changed over its almost 2,000-year history. While some parts of Christianity have remained the same as they were over 1,000 years ago, much of it has changed in line with the ever-changing European political landscape.

While religion is a tricky subject to write about without bias, this book is meant to be a pure history book without taking sides. Any information in this book should be taken as historical. This book makes no claims about whether Christianity or any other religion is valid. This book also does not serve as a means to convert readers to or from Christianity.

With that said, please enjoy this book on Christianity in Europe, starting with its formation and ending with the Counter-Reformation.

Section One:
The Great Empire (100-476 CE)

Chapter 1: From Royalty...

The Roman Empire officially formed around 31 BCE with Augustus Caesar as the first emperor. Before this point, the people who occupied the land that would make up the Roman Empire were not under one form of unified leadership. Augustus Caesar ruled for decades, along with an elected Senate, before he was succeeded by his heir, Tiberius, and others. The time from the beginning of the Roman Empire to about 305 CE is commonly referred to as the High Empire.[2] During this era, Rome expanded its territory more than it would in any other.

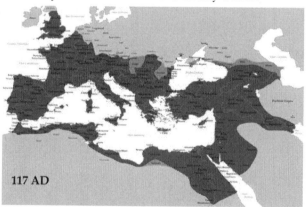

Roman Empire Trajan 117 AD
Tataryn, Wikimedia Commons, CC BY-SA 3.0, May 28, 2012,
https://commons.wikimedia.org/wiki/File:Roman_Empire_Trajan_117AD.png.

---

[2] "Roman Empire (27 BC-476 AD)." Rome.net. *Civitatis*, n.d., https://www.rome.net/roman-empire.

During the first hundred or so years of the Roman Empire, the government went through several emperors. The change in leadership occurred when an emperor died. While the Senate members were elected, the emperor was not. Who would become the next emperor was not directly based on heredity, although many of the emperors were descendants or adoptive relatives of previous emperors. However, there was a Roman civil war around 68 CE because various would-be emperors fought for power after Emperor Nero died. Ultimately, the next ruler was Vespasian, who started the Flavian dynasty.[3] However, this dynasty would not last long.

Vespasianus
Shakko. Wikimedia Commons, CC BY-SA 3.0, November 1, 2007,
https://commons.wikimedia.org/wiki/File:Vespasianus01_pushkin.jpg

The Flavian dynasty began in 69 CE. While Vespasian's rise to power was preceded by a civil war, the successions after him were peaceful. He

---

[3] "Roman Empire (27 BC-476 AD)."

was first succeeded by his son Titus in 79 CE. He ruled for two years before being succeeded by his brother, Domitian. Throughout the family's reign, the government focused on improving cities through artwork and architecture. However, Domitian also upset the Senate by giving Equestrian Officers the same or similar powers as the Senate. Eventually, this led to Domitian's assassination and the end of the Flavian dynasty in 96 CE.[4] In all, the Flavian dynasty only lasted about thirty years and did not have a lasting impact on Roman history. However, it did pave the way for the Antonine dynasty and everything that came with it.

The time of the "Five Good Emperors" began around 96 CE and lasted for about 100 years before the Age of the Antonines began. Emperor Nerva was the first leader of this dynasty. Six more men would become emperors before the dynasty ended.[5] Some of the leaders throughout the Age of the Antonines are known as the "Five Good Leaders," who would make a lasting impact on Roman history. These leaders include Nerva, Trajan, Hadrian, Antoninus Pius, and Marcus Aurelius.[6] This dynasty covers about a quarter of the time that will be discussed in this section, setting the foundation for both the Roman government and the empire's general thoughts and feelings towards religious tolerance.

Western Roman Empire History 100-285 CE

The Roman Empire flourished under the Five Good Emperors. These emperors were popular with both the common people and the Senate. Unlike previous emperors, most of these men had been military leaders and common people who had earned their roles rather than being born into them.[7] Because of this, succeeding emperors did not need to be related or adopted by the previous emperor to gain power. During this time, the Roman government began to act more like a proper democracy instead of a disguised monarchy.

---

[4] Lightfoot, Christopher. "The Roman Empire (27 BC-393 AD)." Department of Greek and Roman Art. *The Metropolitan Museum of Art,* October 2000, https://www.metmuseum.org/toah/hd/roem/hd_roem.htm.

[5] "Roman Empire (27 BC-476 AD)."

[6] Lightfoot, Christopher. "The Roman Empire (27 BC-393 AD)."

[7] Lightfoot, Christopher. "The Roman Empire (27 BC-393 AD)."

Of course, the rich members of society still held some power, but they tended to use their riches to improve their cities. Along with improving architecture within cities and founding entirely new cities, the aristocrats supported philosophers, writers, and artists. Some of the most famous Romans who lived during this time included Pliny the Younger and Tacitus.[8] At this time, Christianity was still very new and had not made much of an impact on Roman culture and society.

The Age of the Antonines began in 138 when Antoninus Pius gained power. This new era gave more power to the Senate and other government leaders, making the government more centralized. It was also during this era that new emperors again gained power due to being related to or adopted by the previous emperor.[9] Common people living in the Roman Empire during this time may not have enjoyed these changes, but since the Senate had regained more power, little was done to undo the changes, whether the common people liked them or not.

Bust of Antonius Pius (Reign 138-161 CE), Ca. 150
https://commons.wikimedia.org/wiki/File:Antoninus_Pius_Glyptothek_Munich_337_cropped.jpg.

---

[8] Lightfoot, Christopher. "The Roman Empire (27 BC-393 AD)."
[9] Lightfoot, Christopher. "The Roman Empire (27 BC-393 AD)."

Following the end of the reign of Antonius Pius in 161, his adoptive son Marcus Aurelius rose to power. However, this was a co-leadership, with Lucius Vernus (Antonius Pius's other adoptive son) sharing the emperorship.[10] While the two brothers reigned together and were supposed to have equal powers, it did not work out that way in practice, as Marcus Aurelius held more power in the end.[11] To this day, Marcus Aurelius is still the most famous of the two brothers.

Busts of the Co-Emperors Marcus Aurelius (left) and Lucius Verus (right), British Museum
https://commons.wikimedia.org/wiki/File:Co-emperors_Marcus_Aurelius_and_Lucius_Verus,_British_Museum_(23455313842).jpg.

The Marcus Aurelius-Lucius Verus reign is most notably marked by the series of wars the brothers started and ended. From 162 to 166, the Romans fought with the Parthians, Armenians, and others in Mesopotamia. Eventually, the Romans won and conquered all these

---

[10] Lightfoot, Christopher. "The Roman Empire (27 BC-393 AD)."
[11] Britannica, T. Editors of Encyclopedia. "Lucius Verus." *Encyclopedia Britannica*, January 1, 2022. https://www.britannica.com/biography/Lucius-Verus.

areas.[12] This greatly grew the Roman Empire's size and population. The people living here would have had a mix of cultures and religions.

The joint reign ended in 169 when Verus died of illness.[13] Marcus Aurelius ruled alone until 177 CE, when Commodus, his son, joined him as joint emperor. The two ruled together until Marcus Aurelius died in 180. Following this, Commodus ruled alone for the remainder of his life, until 192.[14] This would also mark the end of the Age of the Antonines.

Following Commodus's death, Rome fell into another series of civil wars that lasted several months. In the end, Septimius Severus declared himself the new emperor in 193. This would begin the Severan rule, which lasted until 284. During this time, the government gave more powers to the military and more general authority to military leaders. The Severans also replaced many members of the Senate with their own favorites.[15] This strengthened the empire's power and drastically changed the way the government was run—mostly by changing who had the power to run it.

Bust of Septimius Severus
https://commons.wikimedia.org/wiki/File:Septimius_Severus_Glyptothek_Munich_357.jpg

---

[12] Britannica, T. Editors of Encyclopedia. "Lucius Verus."

[13] Britannica, T. Editors of Encyclopedia. "Lucius Verus."

[14] Lightfoot, Christopher. "The Roman Empire (27 BC-393 AD)."

[15] Lightfoot, Christopher. "The Roman Empire (27 BC-393 AD)."

For various reasons, none of the emperors ruling during the Severan dynasty, except Septimius Severus, lasted long (compared to the emperors in the other dynasties). Septimius Severus ruled for about twenty-five years. His next three successors reigned for less than ten years each: Caracalla, Macrinus, and Elagabalus. Alexander Severus, the last of the Severans, reigned from 222 to 235.[16] All these changes in leadership brought unsteadiness to the Roman government and the people. Around this time, many Romans began questioning their leadership, faith, and values.

However, the Severan dynasty wasn't the most tumultuous era in Roman history. Between 235 and 284, the Roman Empire went through sixteen different emperors. At times, more than one emperor was ruling at a time. Even with this, sixteen emperors in about fifty years was unheard of. Most of these men were previously military members with little to no political experience. The reigns never lasted long, partly because of this lack of experience and the fact that many were murdered by other government members or those who wanted to steal the emperorship.[17] Needless to say, there was little stability in Rome during this time.

Things changed again in 284 when Diocletian took power. He worked to re-establish stability in the empire by creating provinces within Rome.[18] This didn't mean the country was split into independent nations but broken up so that areas were governed by both local and federal establishments. This is similar to how countries with city-states or states functioned throughout history and today.

Diocletian took things a step further in 286, only two years into his reign, when he split the Roman Empire—creating the Western and Eastern Roman Empires. This wasn't caused by civil war or another major conflict. Instead, it was done so the empire would be easier to manage. Each half was ruled by its own emperor.[19] The two emperors would work together on some things, which kept the empire united, but

---

[16] Lightfoot, Christopher. "The Roman Empire (27 BC-393 AD)."
[17] Lightfoot, Christopher. "The Roman Empire (27 BC-393 AD)."
[18] Lightfoot, Christopher. "The Roman Empire (27 BC-393 AD)."
[19] "Dividing the Roman Empire into Each & West." Students of History, 2022, https://www.studentsofhistory.com/division-of-the-empire#:~:text=In%20286%20CE%2C%20the%20Emperor,Roman%20life%20and%20government%20forever.

they did not work as closely together as when joint emperors were ruling over the entire Roman Empire.

Emperor Maximian (also called Maximilian or Marcus Valerius Maximianus) was the first emperor of the newly formed Western Roman Empire. During his reign, he was always subordinate to Diocletian but still did much of the governing of the West on his own. He is famous today for crushing local revolts within the Roman Empire and keeping German invaders out of Gaul.[20]

Diocletian made another serious change in 293 when he established the Roman Tetrarchy. With this system, two main (head) emperors continued to control the Eastern and Western Empires. Diocletian and Maximian were the head emperors when the Tetrarchy was established. Next, two subordinate (junior) emperors were appointed. The junior emperors would control two smaller parts of the empire. The first two junior emperors were Galerius and Constantius.[21] This system would change how the government functioned, from who was in charge to how the people were taxed. However, this system did not last long.

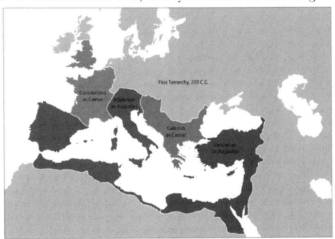

The Organization of the Empire Under the Tetrarchy
*Nacu, Andrei, Wikimedia Commons, CC BY-SA 3.0, n.d.,
https://commons.wikimedia.org/wiki/File:Wars-of-the-Tetrarchy.gif.*

---

[20] Britannica, T. Editors of Encyclopedia. "Maximian." *Encyclopedia Britannica*, January 1, 2022, https://www.britannica.com/biography/Maximian.

[21] Woolf, Greg. "The Tetrarchy." Wellesley College, 2012, http://omeka.wellesley.edu/piranesi-rome/exhibits/show/basilica-of-maxentius-and-cons/the-tetrarchy#:~:text=The%20Tetrarchy%20was%20established%20in,districts%20and%20each%20ruled%20separately.

Five Other Notable Emperors Between 306-476

The pattern of going through emperors quickly continued in both the Western and Eastern Empires. This section includes five of the arguably most important emperors from 305 to 476. These include Honorius, Constantine, Majorian, Julius Nepos, and Romulus Augustus.

Constantine

Constantine is one of the most famous Roman emperors involved in facilitating Christianity in Rome. He was made one of the four joint emperors of Rome in 306.[22] He first served under Emperors Diocletian and Galerius. Throughout his time as joint emperor, he also ruled alongside Maxentius, Maximian, Licinius, and Maximinus II.[23] This shared rule was not peaceful. Within about ten years, the empire would find itself lost in civil war—with Constantine mostly to blame.

Constantine's Head at Capitoline
King, Camille. Flickr, CC BY-SA 2.0, December 17, 2004, https://www.flickr.com/photos/spotsgot/3362379/.

---

[22] Baird Rattini, Kristin. "Who was Constantine?" National Geographic, February 25, 2019, https://www.nationalgeographic.com/culture/article/constantine?loggedin=true.

[23] Gibbon, Edward. *The History of the Decline and Fall of the Roman Empire*. Edited by David Womersley. London, England: Penguin Classics, 1996.

In 313, Constantine worked with the Eastern Roman emperor, Licinius, to pass the Edict of Milan. This edict allowed Christians and non-Christians alike to practice whichever religion they wanted without fear of persecution.[24] Before this, it was not uncommon for people to be killed or otherwise punished for their beliefs.

In 324, Constantine became the sole emperor of Rome after going through a series of civil wars, effectively uniting the empire. The next year, Constantine brought together the Council of Nicaea. This council was established to define what Roman Christians believed. The main question within the Church related to the status of Jesus's divinity. Some said Jesus was entirely divine, while others said he was fully human. In the end, the council decreed that God was a three-part entity, consisting of God the Father, Jesus the Son, and the Holy Spirit. Jesus was also determined to be part-divine, even though he was born human.[25] All these beliefs were written in the Nicene Creed, which many churches today still use in their services:

> "We believe in one God, the Father almighty, Maker of heaven and earth, and of all things visible and invisible. And in one Lord Jesus Christ, the Son of God, the only-begotten, begotten of the Father before all ages. Light of Light, true God of true God, begotten not made, of one essence with the Father by whom all things were made; who for us men and for our salvation, came down from heaven, and was incarnate of the Holy Spirit and the Virgin Mary and became man. And He was crucified for us under Pontius Pilate, and suffered, and was buried. And the third day He rose again, according to the Scriptures; and ascended into heaven, and sits at the right hand of the Father; and He shall come again with glory to judge the living and the dead; whose Kingdom shall have no end. And in the Holy Spirit."[26]

Shortly after, he commissioned the construction of a new capital in what had previously been known as Byzantium. In 330, the new capital of Constantinople (now Istanbul) was completed. He encouraged men to

---

[24] Baird Rattini, Kristin. "Who was Constantine?"

[25] History.com Editors. "Council of Nicaea Concludes." History. A&E Television Networks, July 28, 2019, https://www.history.com/this-day-in-history/council-of-nicaea-concludes.

[26] "The (Original) Nicene Creed of 325." Christ the Savior OCA, 2020, https://christthesavioroca.org/files/2020-Resurrection-Classes/The-Nicene-Creed-of-325.pdf.

move to the city by offering citizenship and free food.[27] This offer, as well as the size of the city, lured in many people from all areas of Rome and some surrounding areas.

Constantine ruled until his death due to illness in 337. Shortly before his death, he clung harder to his Christian beliefs and was baptized in the River Jordan by the Bishop Eusebius of Nicomedia. He was buried in the Church of the Holy Apostles.[28] This would make Constantine the first Roman Emperor to be baptized and buried in a church.

Honorius

Honorius became emperor in 395, succeeding Theodosius, who died in the same year. He had been raised to take on this position when the time came but was only twelve years old, so he was still inexperienced. However, he did not rule the whole empire, just the Western Empire; his brother, Arcadius, ruled the Eastern Empire. Until he was of age, Honorius was watched over by a guardian, Flavius Stilicho. Stilicho would take power for most of Honorius and his brother's "reign." This time was marked almost entirely by war until Stilicho surrendered in 408 and was executed.[29] It wasn't until after Stilicho's death that Honorius had any real ruling power.

Honorius shared power with Alaric at first. In 410, Alaric's camp was attacked by a Visigoth leader, who may have attacked because Honorius asked him to. However, this is under debate. Alaric survived this attack but turned on Honorius and began a march on Rome. This made the city susceptible to other attacks, and it was also sacked by the Visigoths. Honorius enlisted the help of Constantius, a military leader, in 411.[30] Following this, the Visigoths and Romans were at war for almost a decade, taking land and rights from each other back and forth. Honorius died of illness in 423.

Majorian

Emperor Majorian, also known as Julius Valerius Majorianus, became emperor in 457. By this time, the empire was again split, with Majorian controlling the Western half. Leo I became the Eastern emperor in the

---

[27] Baird Rattini, Kristin. "Who was Constantine?"
[28] Pohlsander, Hans A. *The Emperor Constantine*. New York, NY: Routledge, 2004.
[29] Cavazzi, Franco. "Emperor Honorius." The Roman Empire, 2022, https://roman-empire.net/people/honorius/.
[30] Cavazzi, Franco. "Emperor Honorius."

same year. Shortly after their joint reign began, Gaul proved to be troublesome. By quelling several rebellions, Majorian became known as a great leader.[31] Both Emperor Majorian's contemporaries and modern-day historians tend to view him positively.

Regarding his religious influence, Majorian was a Christian but also valued his pagan citizens. During his reign, he passed an edict that protected former and current pagan temples. This was a concern, as most of the temples were falling into disrepair, whether from old age or people breaking them to steal building materials.[32] While paganism was falling out of vogue during the time of his reign, pagan temples were seen as a part of Roman culture and history, which was to be respected.

Other religion-related edicts focused more on how Christians were treated or were allowed to be treated by each other. There were laws preventing families from forcing women to become nuns and men into the clergy.[33] All in all, this was important to many areas of Roman life. Having laws to protect Christians and pagans showed that Roman society saw both parties as equals.

Julius Nepos

The last of the emperors in this section, Julius Nepos, became the emperor of the Eastern Roman Empire in 474. During the six short years of his reign, the Romans fought on and off with the Visigoths in Gaul and parts of modern-day Spain. The Visigoths won these wars and claimed land that had previously belonged to Rome.[34] While Emperor Julius Nepos wasn't necessarily to blame for these wars, losing them did not make him popular with the Roman people. His reputation only got worse as he continued to do things viewed as unfavorable to the Roman people.

One of the last things Julius Nepos did as emperor was to appoint Romulus Augustus as Eastern Roman Emperor in 475. In the same year, Julius Nepos fled Rome to rule over Dalmatia. Although he technically

---

[31] Cavazzi, Franco. "Emperor Majorian." Roman Empire, 2022, https://roman-empire.net/people/majorian/.

[32] Bhullar, Julian. "The Roman Emperor Majorian on Protecting Pagan Temples in Late Antiquity." Medium, March 26, 2022, https://medium.com/flavius-claudius-julianus/the-roman-emperor-majorian-on-protecting-pagan-temples-in-late-antiquity-20686bbceb85.

[33] Bhullar, Julian. "The Roman Emperor Majorian on Protecting Pagan Temples in Late Antiquity."

[34] Cavazzi, Franco. "Emperor Julius Nepos." The Roman Empire, 2022, https://roman-empire.net/people/julius-nepos/.

remained the Western Roman Emperor until his death in 480, he did not hold any real political power.[35] Shortly after this, the empire would go through a period commonly referred to as the "Fall of the Roman Empire."

Romulus Augustus

This leaves Romulus Augustus, also called Romulus Augustulus, as arguably the last emperor of the Western Roman Empire. All of Romulus Augustus's rule was destined for failure from the beginning. First, he was only twelve when he became emperor. His father, Orestes, gave him this power.[36] It is still unclear why Orestes didn't take power for himself after "encouraging" Julius Nepos to leave Rome. However, it is likely that the father, more than the son, was doing more of the actual running of the government.

Romulus Augustus's reign was extremely short. He was made emperor on October 31, 475, and was forced to abdicate on September 4, 476. This occurred after a series of events in which mercenary armies tried to take land in the Roman Empire. Orestes fought back but was captured and killed in August 476. The leader of mercenaries, Odoacer, then captured Romulus, forcing him to abdicate.[37] Unlike other Roman emperors who were deposed, Romulus Augustus was not murdered but left alone to live his life. To this day, historians are not certain when or how he died. Common consensus says that he lived an unimpressive life and died between middle and old age.

Christianity in the Fourth Century CE

As touched on in the introduction, Christianity was established in the first century CE in Judea (modern-day Israel). It is based on the teachings of Jesus of Nazareth, a Jewish man. His followers, commonly called disciples in Christian circles, were the ones who spread his teachings and officially established Christianity as a religion.[38] Christianity was fairly unorganized, decentralized, and deregulated in the beginning. It was not

---

[35] Cavazzi, Franco. "Emperor Julius Nepos."

[36] "Romulus Augustulus." Imperium Romanum, June 9, 2019, https://imperiumromanum.pl/en/biographies/romulus-augustulus/.

[37] "Romulus Augustulus."

[38] Schroeder, Steven. "Christianity in the Roman Empire." Khan Academy, n.d., https://www.khanacademy.org/humanities/world-history/ancient-medieval/christianity/a/roman-culture#:~:text=Rome%20becomes%20Christian&text=The%20result%20of%20this%20council,religion%20of%20the%20Roman%20Empire.

until much later that there were standard rules and beliefs that Christians followed.

Jesus Christ Pantokrator - Byzantine Mosaic, Years 817-824 - Santa Prassede Church in Rome
https://www.flickr.com/photos/70125105@N06/23242789821.

The Apostle Paul, also known as Saul of Tarsus, is generally credited by Christians as spreading Christianity to Rome. However, this is under debate. It is well-known that there were Jews in Rome before Christianity was founded. Most of the population of Rome were (what Christians would call) pagans. These pagans were polytheistic, worshiping the old Roman gods. Jews and other religious groups made up a small part of the population.[39] Jewish people who may have traveled to Judea in the early first century CE could have converted and brought Christianity back to Rome. Paul simply spread it on a larger scale.

The Christianity that Paul brought to Rome may not have been the same Christianity practiced in Judea. For one, Paul never met Jesus. Sometime after Jesus died, Paul is said to have had a vision that encouraged him to convert to Christianity and spread Jesus's gospel. He first started preaching in Damascus around 33 CE but had to flee due to the persecution of Christians in 36 CE. It was then he went to Jerusalem

---

[39] O'Neil, Sam. "Earliest Days of the Roman Christian Church." Learn Religions. Dotdash Meredith, June 25, 2019, https://www.learnreligions.com/the-early-church-at-rome-363409.

and met with the apostles who had known Jesus.[40]

> "But when God, who had set me apart before I was born and called me through his grace, was pleased to reveal his Son to me, so that I might proclaim him among the Gentiles, I did not confer with any human being, nor did I go up to Jerusalem to those who were already apostles before me, but I went away at once into Arabia, and afterward I returned to Damascus."[41]

Within the Bible, it is well-documented that the other apostles and Paul did not always get along. Many may not have approved of Paul's teachings because he had never met Jesus. The two groups also taught different things. This could be considered the first division in Christianity.

> "But when Cephas (Peter) came to Antioch, I opposed him to his face, because he stood self-condemned; for until certain people came from James, he used to eat with the Gentiles. But after they came, he drew back and kept himself separate for fear of the circumcision faction. And the other Jews joined him in this hypocrisy, so that even Barnabas was led astray by their hypocrisy. But when I saw that they were not acting consistently with the truth of the gospel, I said to Cephas before them all, 'If you, though a Jew, live like a Gentile and not like a Jew, how can you compel the Gentiles to live like Jews?'"[42]

To remedy this, the apostles teaching Jesus's original message sent Barsabbas and Silas with Paul and Barnabas to Antioch. This was meant to "correct" the differences between what Paul had been teaching to the Gentiles (non-Jewish people) and what the apostles had been teaching to Jewish Christians.

> "Then the apostles and the elders, with the consent of the whole church, decided to choose men from among their members and to send them to Antioch with Paul and Barnabas. They sent Judas called Barsabbas, and Silas, leaders among the brothers, with the following letter: 'The brothers, both the apostles and the elders, to the believers of Gentile origin in Antioch and Syria and Cilicia,

---

[40] Meyer Everts, Janet. "The Apostle Paul and His Times: Christian History Timeline." *Christianity Today*, 1995, https://www.christianitytoday.com/history/issues/issue-47/apostle-paul-and-his-times-christian-history-timeline.html.
[41] Galatians 1:15-17, New Revised Standard Version Bible: Anglicized Edition.
[42] Galatians 2:11-14, NRSVB: AE.

greetings. Since we have heard that certain persons who have gone out from us, though with no instructions from us, have said things to disturb you and have unsettled your minds, we have decided unanimously to choose representatives and send them to you, along with our beloved Barnabas and Paul, who have risked their lives for the sake of our Lord Jesus Christ."[43]

Even so, the apostles and Paul did not teach the same things. The Apostle Peter is commonly referred to as the head of the "Church," with the original apostles. For this reason, we will refer to the original teachings as Peter's teachings. For the most part, Peter focused on converting Jews, while Paul focused on converting Gentiles. Peter still saw Jews and Gentiles as different groups, with Jews being God's chosen people. Paul believed Jews and Gentiles, were no longer Jews or Gentiles but a new entity, once taught about in Jesus's messages.[44] There were also various smaller differences between the two men's teachings.

Eventually, Paul was arrested, taken to Rome, and put under house arrest. This was about the time he wrote several books that would later be added to the Bible, including Colossians, Ephesians, and Philippians. He was eventually released and continued to do missionary work. After being arrested and returned to Rome again in 64 CE, Paul was martyred.[45] This was "allowed" to happen because Christians were still being persecuted in Rome at this time.

As discussed, most of the major changes in religious tolerance in Rome happened in the 300s CE. Emperor Constantine passed the Edict of Milan in 313 and assembled the Council of Nicaea in 325. Both were huge steps forward for Christians to be able to live without fear of persecution. The next big change came in 380 when Emperor Theodosius passed the Edict of Thessalonica. This made Nicene Christianity, which followed the beliefs stated in the Nicene Creed, the official religion of Rome.[46]

While this was a major win for Nicene Christians, it was a loss for everyone else. Other Christian groups were then seen as heretical, and all

---

[43] Acts 15: 22-26, NRSVB: AE.

[44] "Differences Between Peter and Paul's Message." Grace Ambassadors. Grace Ambassadors Ministry, 2022, https://graceambassadors.com/midacts/list-petervspaul.

[45] Meyer Everts, Janet. "The Apostle Paul and His Times: Christian History Timeline."

[46] Schroeder, Steven. "Christianity in the Roman Empire."

other religions were frowned upon. This began a new age of persecution. Shortly after this, the Roman Empire fell, but Christianity continued to spread, mostly throughout Europe, in the coming centuries.

Chapter 2: ...To Ruin

The time immediately following the deposition of Romulus Augustus is commonly referred to as the Fall of the Roman Empire. However, this is a misnomer, as it describes the fall of the *Western* Roman Empire, not the entire Roman society. The timeline used in this chapter will overlap slightly with what was discussed in chapter one. This section will focus on how both inside and outside forces led to instability in the Western Roman Empire.

Invasions by the Goths

The Goths were roving bands of nomadic people who were of Germanic descent. These peoples were not as united as the Romans, as they were composed of many tribes constantly on the move. The Goths from western areas were called Visigoths, while the Goths from the east were the Ostrogoths.[47] Of these two, the Visigoths proved to be the bigger threat to Rome.

The Visigoths first attacked Rome in 251 CE, successfully sacking Nicopolis and Philippopolis. After several battles, the Romans lost and were forced to pay tribute to the Visigoths. The Visigoths returned to Rome less than twenty years later, but the Romans successfully kept them away.[48] This was the start of a tumultuous relationship between the two

---

[47] History.com Editors. "Goths and Visigoths." History. A&E Television Networks, April 3, 2019, https://www.history.com/topics/ancient-rome/goths-and-visigoths#:~:text=The%20Thervingi%20were%20the%20Gothic,the%20next%20decade%20or%20so.

[48] "Visigoth Wars." Heritage History, 2020, https://www.heritage-

groups that would last for hundreds of years. In this chapter, we will only cover about 200 years of the history between the Romans and the Visigoths.

The next major Visigoth invasion started as a plea for sanctuary and ended with battle. Around 376, the Huns invaded Germanic land, which threatened the Gothic peoples. The Visigoths asked the Roman government for permission to relocate and settle on Roman land. The Roman government agreed but only allowed them to live on land under the Danube River, which was not up to the standards of the Visigoths. Rightly upset about this, the Visigoths began to riot. This eventually turned into the Battle of Marcianopolis, led by the Visigoth chief, Fritigern. The Visigoths won this battle,[49] leading to a full-fledged war that would last for years.

The Battle of Adrianople was arguably the most important battle between the Goths and Romans in recorded history. This battle started on August 9, 378 CE. Again, Chief Fritigern led the Goths, while Emperor Valens led the Roman military. During this single battle, over 10,000 Roman soldiers died, including Valen.[50] Needless to say, this was a major loss for the Romans. It allowed the Goths to take more land and motivated them to keep invading. The Gothic wars continued for decades after this event.

Throughout the next several decades, the Goths and Romans continued fighting. While the major players in the war changed as time went on, the primary motive for the war stayed the same. The Goths wanted to take Roman land, and the Romans wanted to take Gothic land. From 378 to 408, there were several important battles. These include the Battle of Adrianople, Battle of Verona, Battle of Pollentia, Siege of Florence, and Siege of Rome. For the most part, Fritigern continued to lead the battles for the Goths, along with Alaric the Visigoth.[51] Honorius would have been the Western Roman Emperor for most of these battles. In the East, Theodosius I, Arcadius, and Theodosius II were the emperors, in turn.[52]

---

history.com/index.php?c=resources&s=war-dir&f=wars_visigoths.

[49] "Visigoth Wars."

[50] Wasson, Donald L. "Battle of Adrianople." *World History Encyclopedia*, August 26, 2019, https://www.worldhistory.org/Battle_of_Adrianople/.

[51] "Visigoth Wars."

[52] Cameron, Averil, and Peter Garnsey. *The Cambridge Ancient History*. Vol. 13. Cambridge

One of the last major conflicts between the Goths and the Romans during this period took place in 410. The event is most commonly known as the "410 Sack of Rome." At this time, Alaric was king of the Goths; he led his army into Rome and sacked the city. This task was made easy by the fact that Rome had been weakened by previous battles and famine.[53] By this point, the Goths and Romans had been at war with each other on and off for decades. While both sides were weaker than they had been at the beginning of the wars, the Romans had faced more losses and were considerably worse off.

During the sacking of Rome, the Goths destroyed pagan temples and Senate buildings. However, they did not destroy the Christian churches.[54] This is notable in a religious aspect. The Bible texts, which were mostly written in Greek as Christianity spread throughout Rome, were only translated into Gothic runes by Ulfilas in 350. (Sadly, this Bible has since been lost to history.) Ulfilas also did some missionary work during his lifetime. Before this, the Goths had been primarily pagan, having a Germanic polytheistic religion. However, some Goths saw Christianity as a Roman religion that was a threat to their Germanic heritage, so they tried to slow the spread of Christianity throughout the Germanic tribes.[55] With Christianity so recently introduced to the Gothic tribes, it is interesting that they already showed respect to the churches but did not respect Roman pagan temples.

By the end of the sack, Alaric had also attacked Cremona and Ariminum. He surrounded Rome, forcing the city to ration food and making it difficult for the citizens to do so much as dispose of waste properly. Eventually, the Huns and a reserve of extra Goths came to Rome, which sped up its destruction. Later, Rome decided on a truce in which the Goths would lift their siege once they were paid several tons of gold, silver, and other expensive items. After leaving Rome, the Goths settled in Gaul.[56] While 410 did not see the end of the Western Roman Empire (which would fall in 476), it weakened the city enough that it

---

University Press, 1970.

[53] Wasson, Donald L. "Sack of Rome 410 CE." *World History Encyclopedia*, September 23, 2019, https://www.worldhistory.org/article/1449/sack-of-rome-410-ce/.

[54] Wasson, Donald L. "Sack of Rome 410 CE."

[55] Mark, Joshua J. "The Goths." *World History Encyclopedia*, October 12, 2014, https://www.worldhistory.org/Goths/.

[56] Wasson, Donald L. "Sack of Rome 410 CE."

would never recover, making the eventual fall possible.

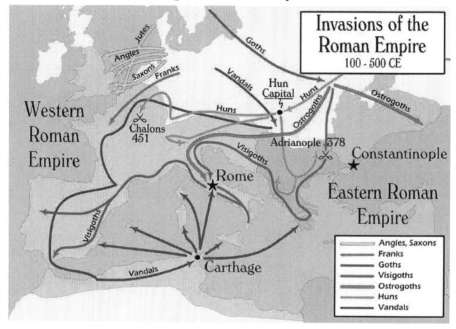

Invasions of the Roman Empire
MapMaster. World History Encyclopedia, CC BY-SA 4.0, October 16, 2015,
https://www.worldhistory.org/image/4131/invasions-of-the-roman-empire/

Invasions by the Huns

The Huns were another nomadic tribe that traveled throughout Europe. (They are not to be confused with the Mongols, a nomadic group that traveled mostly throughout Asia, led by Khan.) The Romans often referred to the Huns as Barbarians, which is how they are referred to in some scholarly sources. The Huns were first mentioned in Roman records in 91 CE but were not seen as much of a threat at this time.[57] It wasn't until a few hundred years later that they became a major issue for the Romans.

The most notable Hun the Romans would have been in contact with was Attila the Hun, who reigned over the Huns from 434 to 453. During this time, he built up a strong military.[58] Rulers all over Europe feared the Hun army, and with good reason.

---

[57] Mark, Joshua J. "Huns." *World History Encyclopedia*, April 25, 2018, https://www.worldhistory.org/Huns/.

[58] Mark, Joshua J. "Huns."

Before the Huns attacked the Romans, they began their reign of terror by conquering land near present-day Hungary. In 370, they moved on to conquer the Alans; they attacked the Visigoths in 376, which led the Goths to head towards Rome. About twenty years later, from 395 to 398, the Huns started seizing Roman territories in Thrace and Syria. While they destroyed everything in their path, they did nothing else on the land—they remained an unsettled people. During this time, the Huns attacked seemingly randomly. Armies were more likely to come across roving bands of Huns than Huns working unified under one leader.[59] For this reason, it was almost impossible for nations to know where the Huns would strike next or how often they would attack. With so many separate groups of fighters, one city could be sacked many times over.

Fast-forward a few decades to 439 when Attila and his brother Bleda made the Treaty of Margus with the Roman Empire. This was less of a peace treaty and more "Rome needs to pay the Huns not to attack them." Once the treaty was signed, the Romans stopped focusing on fighting the Huns and moved their attention (and armies) to other matters.[60] Or, at least they thought they could.

The Huns went back on the treaty in 441 and began sacking cities on the Roman border as the Roman armies focused their attention on other areas. Attila and Bleda first sacked cities in Illyricum, a Roman province and trade hub. The Huns more or less destroyed the cities in this area. After these rampages, the Western Roman Emperor Theodosius II declared the treaty broken and sent the Roman armies to fight the Huns.[61] Needless to say, this did not go well for the Romans, whose armies were already stressed.

In 451, the Huns invaded Gaul, which began the Battle of the Catalaunian Plains. This time, the Romans didn't have to fight alone. They formed an alliance with the Visigoths and other smaller Barbarian tribes. Together, they defeated the Huns.[62] This would be the Romans' first victory against Attila—and their only one.

---

[59] Mark, Joshua J. "Huns."

[60] Mark, Joshua J. "Huns."

[61] Mark, Joshua J. "Huns."

[62] History.com Editors, "Huns." History. A&E Television Networks, April 5, 2018, https://www.history.com/topics/ancient-china/huns.

A few years later, in 453, Attila died, making his oldest son, Ellac, the new leader of the Huns. However, this distracted the Huns from attacking Rome, as they threw themselves into civil war. By 459, the Hun Empire ended.[63] This, in turn, ended its reign of terror over the Roman Empire. However, the reign had lasted long enough that the mark of the invasions would scar the empire forever.

Theodosius I and Roman Civil War

Moving back on the timeline slightly, Emperor Theodosius I gained the emperorship in 379 CE and reigned for about fifteen years, until 395. Theodosius's career was ravaged by war from the beginning. Almost as soon as he rose to power, he was faced with the problem of invasions, mostly by the Goths and their allies.[64] (Remember, during this time, Rome took part in the Battle of Adrianople, which took a toll on the empire's military.)

Theodosius I took various measures to revamp the Roman army, including recruiting Barbarians. He sent many of the new Barbarian troops to Egypt, where other Roman troops were already stationed. However, in 380, many of the new troops defected to the enemy's side.[65] This left the Roman military in worse straights than before.

Military strain and other factors encouraged Theodosius I to leave Thessalonica and move to Constantinople. Once there, he asked another Roman Emperor, Gratian, for help fighting off the newest Gothic invasion in Illyricum. While Gratian helped, he did so more for his own gain.[66] Even though the Romans eventually beat back the Goths, they continued to be a threat to Rome on and off for decades.

---

[63] History.com Editors, "Huns."

[64] "Theodosius I (378-395 AD)," Roman Emperors - An Online Encyclopedia of Roman Rules and Their Families,

[65] "Theodosius I (378-395 AD)."

[66] "Theodosius I (378-395 AD)."

Theodosius I
https://picryl.com/media/theodosius-i-romischer-kaiser-fd1550

Outside forces were not the only thing Theodosius I had to worry about. Throughout his reign, he made many enemies within the Roman Empire, especially the Eastern Roman Empire, by passing laws against pagans and the pagan religion. Theodosius was one of the first Christian emperors, which is all the motivation he needed to persecute pagans. However, many Romans were still pagan at this time, and the Eastern Roman Emperors did not approve of his actions.[67] Over time, the resentment of the emperors, along with other factors, built up, leading to a civil war between the Eastern and Western Roman Empires.

One of the major points of Theodosius I's civil war was the Battle of the Frigidus on September 6, 394. The battle lasted for about two days. In this short time, Theodosius lost about 10,000 men to the Eastern Roman Empire, including General Feodosiya.[68] Even with this loss, Theodosius I was not deterred.

---

[67] Chakra, Hayden. "Battle of the Frigidus 394 AD - Clash Between the East and West." About History, September 14, 2021, https://about-history.com/battle-of-the-frigidus-394-ad-clash-between-the-east-and-west/.

[68] Chakra, Hayden. "Battle of the Frigidus 394 AD - Clash Between the East and West."

Shortly after the main battle, some of Emperor Eugenius's troops committed treason. This allowed Theodosius's troops to break into Eugenius's camp. Soon after, Eugenius was captured and beheaded. Some troops loyal to Eugenius fled the area.[69] This allowed Theodosius I to win the war.

While a few-day battle might not seem like it would have much of an impact, Theodosius's victory would shape the rest of Roman history. After his win, he made his son, Honorius, the new Emperor of the Western Roman Empire (to succeed him after his death in 395). He also influenced the spread of Christianity throughout Rome.[70] This would go on to symbolize the victory of Christianity over paganism. As paganism and the old gods began to die out in Rome, Christianity rose.

Odoacer

Odoacer, also known as Flavius Odoacer, Odovacar, and Flavius Odovacar, is commonly recognized as the first king of Italy. He took power after Romulus Augustulus's forced abdication in 476. His early life was fraught with fighting, as he joined the Roman army at a young age. He quickly rose through the ranks and gained fame by fighting against the Visigoths.[71] He gained infamy by fighting against the Western Roman Empire and disposing of Romulus Augustulus.

Romulus Augustus Surrenders the Crown in the Year 476 [to Odoacer].
https://commons.wikimedia.org/wiki/File:Romulus_Augustulus_and_Odoacer.jpg.

---

[69] Chakra, Hayden. "Battle of the Frigidus 394 AD - Clash Between the East and West."
[70] Chakra, Hayden. "Battle of the Frigidus 394 AD - Clash Between the East and West."
[71] Mark, Joshua J. "Odoacer." World History, September 20, 2014, https://www.worldhistory.org/Odoacer/.

Even though Romulus Augustulus was disposed of, the Roman Senate still existed. The Senate "approved" of Odoacer and wrote to the Eastern Roman Emperor, Zeno, that the Western Roman Empire did not need its own emperor. Instead, it could be ruled by the Eastern Roman Emperor and a new king.[72] This new king would be Odoacer.

Odoacer began his reign as the first King of Italy in 476. However, not everyone was pleased with this. What remained of the Roman army fought against Odoacer in the Battle of Ravenna on September 2, 476. Eventually, Odoacer won and proved himself worthy of his new kingship. Odoacer also used this victory to show that he didn't need Emperor Zeno's or the Eastern Roman Empire's approval.[73] This would contribute to the final separation of the Eastern and Western Roman Empires, leaving the disconnected Eastern Roman Empire and newly-formed Italy.

Odoacer's reign focused on improving the Italian military and taking land through both treaties and force. In October 476, only a few months after becoming king, Odoacer made a treat with the Vandals to add Sicily to Italy. In the next year, he annexed Dalmatia.[74] With each new land grab, Italy deviated further from the Roman Empire and became more of its own power.

Map of Odoacer's Italy in 480 CE.
Thomas Lessman. Word History, CC BY-SA-4.0, September 20, 2014,
https://www.worldhistory.org/image/3059/map-of-odoacers-italy-in-480-ce/.

---

[72] Mark, Joshua J. "Odoacer."

[73] Mark, Joshua J. "Odoacer."

[74] Mark, Joshua J. "Odoacer."

With Odoacer's reign came a change in the area's religious views. While Odoacer was a Christian, he was an Arian.[75] Arian Christians believed that Jesus and God were not one and the same. Instead, God was the original deity, and he created Jesus later on. This made the two entities separate and unequal.[76] Most Romans at the time would have believed in Trinitarianism, which held that God, Jesus, and the Holy Spirit were one and the same. Thinking otherwise would have been seen as heresy in the Church. Luckily for Trinitarians, Odoacer allowed them to keep practicing in tune with their religious views. The biggest change was, with Odoacer as king, the Arians were free to practice their religion without fear of persecution, as they could not do before.[77] So, while some former Romans saw Odoacer as a heretic, others saw him as a tolerant Christian leader.

Conclusion

In just a few hundred years, Rome went from being almost entirely pagan to Christian. The Greek and Roman pantheon of gods and goddesses filled the temples prior to the first century CE. Once Christianity was introduced to Rome, it quickly spread. Within about 300 years of Christianity's conception, it had become the official religion of the Roman Empire. Slowly, paganism became the minority religion.

Throughout this time, Christians, Jews, and pagans were alternately persecuted. Which religion was tolerated or hated was primarily determined by the Roman emperor at the moment and his personal religious preference. However, after the fourth century CE, Christianity became the norm. Soon after it was prevalent in Rome, it began to spread all over Europe and beyond.

---

[75] Mark, Joshua J. "Odoacer."

[76] Carr, K. E. "Who were the Arians?" Early Medieval Christianity, Quatr.us Study Guides, October 22, 2022, https://quatr.us/romans/arians-early-medieval-christianity.htm.

[77] Mark, Joshua J. "Odoacer."

Section Two:
The Great Divide 476-1200 CE

Chapter 3: Early Christian Ireland

While Ireland has always been a small country, it played a big part in the Christianization of Europe around the same time as the fall of the Western Roman Empire. As with the Christianization of most areas, this was done initially through missionary work. The famous St. Patrick was one of the largest contributors early on. Later, the Catholic Church, as an institution, promoted Christianity through its church services and monasteries.

St. Patrick

St. Patrick, whose real name is believed to have been Maewyn Succat, was born in Britain around 386. Both his father and grandfather were members of the clergy at some point in their lives, yet Patrick was not raised in an especially religious manner.[78] However, not much is known about his life before he was a teenager.

Patrick became much more religious once he was kidnapped and enslaved by pirates when he was about sixteen. During his enslavement, he tended sheep under the high Druid priest, Milchu. Even though much of Ireland was pagan at this time, Patrick did not convert. He saw his enslavement as a test from God, which encouraged him to cling more fervently to his Christian upbringing.[79] This would also influence Patrick later in life, inspiring him to convert Irish pagans to Christianity.

---

[78] Biography.com Editors. "Saint Patrick Biography." A&E Television Networks, Biography, April 20, 2021, https://www.biography.com/religious-figure/saint-patrick.
[79] Biography.com Editors. "Saint Patrick Biography."

In 408, after about six years of enslavement, Patrick escaped aboard a ship. He soon landed in France. He wandered around the country for about a month before he reunited with his family. Soon after, he moved to Auxerre, France, to formally study theology. He was officially ordained a deacon in 418. Throughout his deaconhood, he continued his studies, becoming a bishop in 432. It was at this time the pope gave him the name Patrick.[80] Being a bishop would mean that Patrick could never marry or have children. He was entirely devoted to his religion.

Later in 432, Pope Celestine I sent Patrick to Ireland to do missionary work. Many pagans were resistant to converting.[81] Several stories written by the Irish bishop Muirchu Maccu Machteni in the biography *The Life of Saint Patrick* tell of Patrick's attempts to convert devoted pagans. In one of these stories, Patrick attempted to convert his old slaver, Miliucc. Miliucc did not want to be "forced" to convert, so he burned himself to death. Patrick saw his old slaver's suicide as depressing since Miliucc would rather die than devote himself to the Christian God.[82] This could indicate pagans knew there was a possibility they could be forced to convert. Some people would rather die than give up their faith.

While Miliucc may have feared conversion, there is little evidence that Patrick was forceful or violent in his conversations. Having been in Ireland before and having experience with pagans, he knew being condescending or threatening people wouldn't help. He also realized that, as both a foreigner and a Christian, there was a high chance someone might kill him if he did so. Instead, he simply introduced the concept of Christianity to many people.[83] His approach to conversion and what missionaries do today are different. Patrick did not require people to fully convert, and he would rarely spend enough time with a group of people to ensure they understood Christianity in the way the Catholic Church might have wanted them to.

Instead of completely converting to Christianity and ridding themselves of their ancient traditions and beliefs, many "converted"

---

[80] Biography.com Editors. "Saint Patrick Biography."

[81] Biography.com Editors. "Saint Patrick Biography."

[82] Da Silva, Bridgette. "Saint Patrick, the Irish Druids, and the Conversion of Pagan Ireland to Christianity." *Strange Horizons,* July 27, 2019, http://strangehorizons.com/non-fiction/articles/saint-patrick-the-irish-druids-and-the-conversion-of-pagan-ireland-to-christianity/.

[83] Da Silva, Bridgette. "Saint Patrick, the Irish Druids, and the Conversion of Pagan Ireland to Christianity."

pagans kept their original belief systems while incorporating Christian ideologies and practices.[84] Over hundreds of years, paganism was slowly phased out. This would have happened long after Patrick was dead.

St. Patrick died in 461, but the exact date can only be guessed. Some say he died on March 17, which is why St. Patrick's Day is celebrated on that day.[85] Even though St. Patrick has "saint" as part of his title, he was never officially canonized by the Catholic Church. This is primarily due to when he died, as there was no official canonization process in the 400s.[86] Even though he is not officially a saint by Catholic standards, he is still reserved as one in Ireland and in other countries where Irish people have emigrated over the centuries.

Saint Palladius

Another famous missionary working in Ireland around the same time as St. Patrick is Saint Palladius of Ireland, not to be confused with Saint Palladius of Assyria. The timeline around him is uncertain, but historians guess he was born around 408 into a Gallo-Roman family. Like St. Patrick, he did not aspire to join the clergy from an early age. In fact, he married and had a child before making his decision. Afterward, he left his wife, put his daughter in a convent, and officially joined the priesthood.[87] The exact year this happened is unknown.

Later in his priesthood, Palladius was made a bishop and sent to Ireland by the pope. He first settled near Wicklow and soon founded at least three churches.[88] Rumor also has it that Palladius brought relics from saints Peter and Paul to Ireland, which were given to him by Pope Celestine.[89] Despite this, he was not very successful in Ireland. Even so, he is often referred to as the First Bishop of Ireland.

---

[84] Da Silva, Bridgette. "Saint Patrick, the Irish Druids, and the Conversion of Pagan Ireland to Christianity."

[85] Biography.com Editors. "Saint Patrick Biography."

[86] History.com Editors. "Who Was St. Patrick?" A&E Television Networks, History, March 15, 2022, https://www.history.com/topics/st-patricks-day/who-was-saint-patrick#:~:text=St.-,Patrick%20Was%20Never%20Canonized%20as%20a%20Saint,the%20era%20he%20lived%20in.

[87] "Saint Palladius." Newman Ministry, 2022, https://www.newmanministry.com/saints/saint-palladius.

[88] "Saint Palladius."

[89] Cusack, Margaret A. "Mission of St. Palladius." Library Ireland, 1868, https://www.libraryireland.com/HistoryIreland/Mission-St-Palladius.php.

There is debate as to why Palladius left Ireland and went to Scotland. Some say he was simply unsuccessful in converting the Irish and wanted to go somewhere he might have more success. Other sources say he was banished from Ireland by the King of Leinster. Either way, Pallidus entered Scotland sometime around 430.[90] Unlike St. Patrick, he spoke out fervently against paganism (which was likely part of the reason he was not as successful as St. Patrick in Ireland). He was much more successful in Scotland, as the native Scots were generally more accepting of his teachings.[91] This could be partly because some Scots had already been introduced to Christianity by their British neighbors.

Historians do not know the exact date or even year that Palladius died. Most suspect he died around 450, but it was possibly as late as 463. However, historians agree he died in Scotland and was buried there.[92] Soon after his death, some of his relics were stored in the monastery at Fordun, Scotland. Almost 1,000 years later, the relics were enshrined. St. Pallidus is still celebrated with his feast day on July 6 in Ireland.[93] While he may not have been as influential or as well remembered as St. Patrick in Ireland, he helped spread Christianity throughout modern-day Ireland and the United Kingdom.

Establishment of the Monasteries

While some of the earliest Christian missionaries began working in Ireland in the 300s, it wasn't until the 500s that the Catholic Church seriously invested in building monasteries in Ireland. The monasteries were usually built on the outskirts of towns or on small islands so the monks would have privacy and separation from the population. This was meant to give the monks a quiet place to study, worship, and do their other duties and protect the monasteries from raiders. Large stone walls around the monasteries also helped to protect them from raids.[94] The monasteries were not usually single buildings but more like little villages. They would have several buildings to worship, farms to sustain themselves, and even a graveyard sometimes.

---

[90] Butler, Alban, Rev. *The Lives of the Fathers, Martyrs, and Other Principal Saints.* James Duffy, Dublin, Ireland, 1866.

[91] "Saint Palladius."

[92] "Saint Palladius."

[93] Butler, Alban, Rev. *The Lives of the Fathers, Martyrs, and Other Principal Saints.*

[94] O'Nell, Brian. "Monasteries in Ireland." Your Irish Culture, March 2, 2020, https://www.yourirish.com/history/christianity/monasteries-in-ireland.

One of the reasons monasteries were such a target for raiders was that it was well-known that monasteries usually held valuable items and food. The Vikings were one of the biggest threats to the monasteries. Sometimes, the Vikings would leave a monastery in ruins; other times, they would simply sack them.[95] Although the monasteries had physical protections, like their walls and towers, monks were not usually fighting men. Whoever got past their fortifications could usually get away with stealing whatever they wanted.

Clonmacnoise Monastery is one of the most famous and oldest monasteries still (somewhat) standing in Ireland. Saint Ciaran founded the monastery in 550 when he placed a small wooden church in the area. Soon, a small community grew around the church. The monastery and its surrounding settlement continued to expand for several hundred years. By about 750, it contained seventeen churches, trade buildings, blacksmiths, farms, and over ten acres of land. The monastery was famous for the manuscripts the monks here produced, especially in the eleventh and twelfth centuries, the most famous of these being *The Book of the Dun Cow*. Like other monasteries of the time, Clonmacnoise was raided dozens of times throughout its history by Vikings, pagan Irish, and the Normans. The monastery was finally destroyed and defunded in 1552 with Henry VIII's dissolution of the monasteries.[96] Today, the ruins of Clonmacnoise Monastery are open as a tourist site.

Skellig Michael is another famous Irish monastery. It was founded sometime during the sixth century, most likely under the direction of St. Fionán. The first two hundred or so years of its operation were quiet, as the rocky island proved a great natural defense. However, the Vikings found a way to attack, robbing the monastery and killing its abbot in the 820s. It was rebuilt in the 860s.[97] Pilgrims and monks have inhabited and used it as a place of pilgrimage ever since.

Monk's Duties

By 600, there were more monasteries per capita in Ireland than most other Christianized countries. Monks living in these monasteries had to live with a strict set of rules and uphold certain responsibilities. Monks

---

[95] O'Nell, Brian. "Monasteries in Ireland."

[96] "Clonmacnoise - History and Significance." Enjoy Irish Culture, n.d., https://www.enjoy-irish-culture.com/Clonmacnoise.html.

[97] "Skellig Michael." Monastic Ireland, 2014, http://monastic.ie/history/skellig-michael/.

were taught to work hard serving the sick, study often, recite prayers and chants several times a day, and generally dress, eat, and live modestly.[98] All in all, they lived simple lives. They helped where they could and kept to themselves most of the rest of the time unless they were traveling to preach.

Illustrated manuscripts were one of the most cherished items a monk could make. These were handcrafted books that almost exclusively contained the Gospels or other religious texts. The Irish monks began producing illuminated manuscripts shortly after the monasteries were formed. Since the printing press would not be invented for almost another thousand years, the monks had to copy everything in a book by hand.[99] This meant making an illuminated manuscript would be tedious and take a long time. However, it also meant that no two were exactly the same. While some manuscripts might be signed by their authors, most are not.

At this time, mass, the Catholic worship service, was only held in Latin. Because of this, all of the illuminated manuscripts commissioned by the Church were also written in Latin. These books would be used primarily for study within the monastery and on religious missions.[100] So, why were they so well decorated? While all the texts were written in Latin, most Irish people could not read Latin or read at all. The pictures were a means to guide readers through the stories, much like children's books do today.[101] Even though common people would not likely own illuminated manuscripts because of how expensive they likely were, the people might see one at church or when visited by a missionary. Because of this, it was important for the text to be illustrated to ensure the average person could understand the story and make the book look interesting enough that people would want to keep "reading" it.

There are two famous Irish illuminated manuscripts. The first is the *Book of Durrow*. This book was created in the mid-600s (but the exact

---

[98] "Monasticism, Early Irish." *New Catholic Encyclopedia*. Encylopedia.com, 2019, https://www.encyclopedia.com/religion/encyclopedias-almanacs-transcripts-and-maps/monasticism-early-irish.

[99] "Illuminated Manuscripts (c. 600-1200)." Visual Arts Cork, n.d., http://www.visual-arts-cork.com/cultural-history-of-ireland/illuminated-manuscripts.htm.

[100] "Illuminated Manuscripts (c. 600-1200)."

[101] "Medieval Illuminated Manuscripts." Minneapolis Institute of Art, n.d., https://new.artsmia.org/programs/teachers-and-students/teaching-the-arts/five-ideas/medieval-illuminated-manuscripts.

date is under historical debate), making it one of the earliest surviving Irish illuminated manuscripts. Like most other illuminated manuscripts, it is a Gospel book. It is currently held at the Trinity College Library in Dublin, Ireland.[102] Another famous illuminated manuscript is the *Book of Kells*. There is a lot of historical debate about exactly when and where the book was made, which is part of what makes it so famous. The beautiful Gaelic-style artwork also makes it stand out. Unlike other illuminated manuscripts, this book contains the entirety of the New Testament of the Bible. This book is also currently on display at the Trinity College Library in Dublin, Ireland.[103] The Irish illuminated manuscripts, even as a concept, would inspire similar manuscripts to be produced in Europe in later centuries.

Trinity College Library - Book of Kells
Koester, Larry. Flickr, CC BY-SA 2.0, October 28, 2014,
https://www.flickr.com/photos/larrywkoester/15026062904

---

[102] Norman, Jeremy M. "The Book of Darrow, One of the Earliest Surviving Fully Decorated Insular Gospel Books." Jeremy Norman's History of Information, 2022, https://www.historyofinformation.com/detail.php?id=1468.

[103] King, Laura. "The Book of Kells." Virginia Commonwealth University, 2004, http://www.people.vcu.edu/~djbromle/color-theory/color04/laura/bookofkells.htm.

Irish Religious Artifacts

Lastly, let's take a look at some famous Irish religious artifacts. There are three main items we'll discuss in this section: the Bell of St. Patrick, the Cross of Cong, and Irish high crosses in general. These items have religious and historical significance that can be appreciated by Christians and non-Christians alike.

The Bell of St. Patrick is considered a religious relic. Usually, relics are relics because they belonged to a historical religious figure. However, the Bell of St. Patrick was made around 1100, hundreds of years after St. Patrick died. So, why is the bell a relic? The bell was made to be contained in a shrine to St. Patrick commissioned by the then king of Ireland, Domhnall Ua Lochlainn. It remained in the shrine until about the 1800s and is now on display at the National Museum of Ireland in Dublin.[104] So, while St. Patrick never saw this bell, it gets its relic status just by being in a shrine dedicated to him.

The Bell of Saint Patrick Shrine
Elkington & Co., CC0, via Wikimedia Commons
https://commons.wikimedia.org/wiki/File:The_Bell_of_Saint_Patrick_Shrine_MET_tem07651s1.jpg

---

[104] "Bell of St Patrick and its Shrine." National Museum of Ireland, 2022, https://www.museum.ie/en-IE/Collections-Research/Collection/Resilience/Artefact/Test-5/8e122ba9-6464-4533-8f72-d036afde12a9#:~:text=This%20bell%20is%20reputed%20to,the%20principal%20relics%20of%20Ireland.

The Cross of Cong is another Irish artifact from the 1100s. This artifact was commissioned to hold a piece of the True Cross. As the name implies, the True Cross is believed to be the cross on which Jesus was crucified. Pieces of the True Cross are said to be pieces of wood that were directly taken from that cross. The king of Ireland at this time, Tairdelbach Ua Conchobair, also known as Turlough O'Connor, brought a piece of the True Cross to Ireland in 1122. The king commissioned Mael Isu mac Bratain Ui Echach to make the cross, which is made of bronze and crystal. This relic is also displayed at the National Museum of Ireland, in Dublin.[105] It is almost impossible to know for sure if any piece of the True Cross is authentic. Even if the piece enclosed in the Cross of Cong is not authentic, it is still an important religious artifact simply because people *think* it is authentic and its historical significance as a relic brought to Ireland by a king.

Cross of Cong in the National Museum of Ireland
National Museum of Ireland, CC BY-SA 2.0 <https://creativecommons.org/licenses/by-sa/2.0>, via Wikimedia Commons
https://commons.wikimedia.org/wiki/File:Cross_of_Cong_in_the_National_Museum_of_Ireland.jpg.

---

[105] "The Cross of Cong." National Museum of Ireland, 2022, https://www.museum.ie/en-IE/Collections-Research/Irish-Antiquities-Division-Collections/Collections-List-(1)/Early-Medieval/The-Cross-of-Cong.

Irish high crosses, also called Celtic high crosses, started being crafted sometime around 750. These statues were usually made of stone. What makes them special is the combination of a traditional Christian cross and classic Celtic knot designs. Sometimes, the statues will also be engraved with scenes from the Bible or pictures of religious figures. It is a perfect marriage of the "new" Christian and "old" pagan designs and ideas. While the sculptures are scattered all over Ireland, they were mainly constructed at religious sites.[106] Many of these sculptures are still standing today outside old religious sites, in cemeteries, or in museums.

Clonmacnoise High Cross
CCharmon. Flickr, CC BY-ND 2.0, May 7, 2010,
https://www.flickr.com/photos/9439733@N02/4630502118

---

[106] "Celtic High Cross Sculptures (c. 750-1150 CE)" Visual Arts Cork, n.d., http://www.visual-arts-cork.com/irish-sculpture/celtic-high-cross-sculptures.htm.

Conclusion

While Ireland may seem secluded from continental Europe and a tangent on the Christian history timeline, the missionaries who came here made a large impact on the Irish population. This impact would lead to the construction of monasteries, and the monks at these monasteries would convert people in Ireland and on the British Isles. Outside of missionary work, the monks also made beautiful illuminated manuscripts and kept relics safe so that we can still appreciate them today.

Chapter 4: The Dark Ages in Europe (476-1000 CE)

The Dark Age goes by many names, including the Early Middle Ages and the Migration Period. No matter what it is called, this period is often represented in media as dark, dirty, and filled with illiterate people. No progress was made, and for hundreds of years, time only marched slowly forward. As with most things the media portrays, this telling is not exactly true of the Dark Ages.

Most historians will agree that the Dark Ages began after the Fall of Rome in the late fifth century CE. However, there is much debate about when it ended. For the sake of this chapter, we will go with the argument that the Dark Ages ended in 1000. During the 500 or so years of the Dark Ages, time did not stand still. People didn't stop inventing things, going to war, and generally living their lives. The Dark Ages are full of many important historical events that shaped European and Christian history. This includes the crowning of Holy Roman Emperors, mass conversions on continental Europe, the introduction of Islam, and more.

Dark Ages Major Events

The Dark Ages is a historical misnomer if there ever was one. The term was originally coined by Francesco Petrarch, a scholar who lived in 1300s Italy. He made his term to simply describe the lack of high-brow literature produced during this period. In later centuries, other scholars would expand on this idea and choose other factors that added "darkness" to these times.[107] However, living in the 1300s, Petrarch had no experience with the Dark Ages. The term confused people about the period for centuries—and to this day. This section will cover some of the major events in Europe between the Fall of Rome and 1000 CE. These events will be summarized, and we may skip some lesser events entirely, as a whole book could be written about the events of the Dark Ages. The events below are listed in chronological order.

Founding of Islam: Beginning in 610

Religious factions have often interacted with each other throughout history. We could not give an accurate story of Christianity in Europe during the Dark Ages without mentioning the formation and rise of Islam, the religion that Muslim people follow. Islam was founded by the prophet Mohammad, a young man living in Saudi Arabia in the late 500s to mid-600s.[108] While Mohammad likely followed some monotheistic religion before founding Islam, no one is sure what it might have been.

According to traditional religious legend, Muhammad was visited by the angel Gabriel in 610. The angel told him about Allah and how Allah wanted to be worshipped. Muhammad was continuously visited by angels and more throughout his life. Even though the first visit was in 610, he did not start preaching until 613. He started collecting followers. His next major milestone came in 622 when he traveled to Medina from Mecca. This year has also been established as the first year in the Islamic calendar.[109] From this point forward, Mecca and Medina were important religious sites often used for pilgrimages. Muslims still revere these places today.

---

[107] Sullivan, Nate. "The Dark Ages: Definition, History & Timeline." Study, September 7, 2015, www.study.com/academy/lesson/the-dark-ages-definition-history-timeline.html.

[108] History.com Editors. "Islam." A&E Television Networks. History, March 11, 2022, https://www.history.com/topics/religion/islam.

[109] "Islam Timeline." *World History Encyclopedia*, 2022, https://www.worldhistory.org/timeline/islam/.

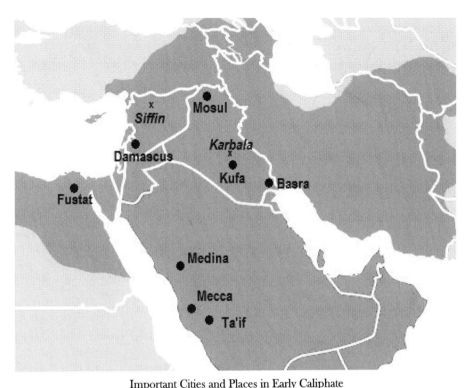

Important Cities and Places in Early Caliphate
AhmadLX. Wikimedia Commons, CC BY-SA 4.0, March 14, 2019,
https://commons.wikimedia.org/wiki/File:Important_cities_and_Places_in_Early_Caliphate.png.

Muslims then and now have the Quran, also known as the Qur'an or Koran, the Muslim holy book. It contains many stories also told in the Jewish Torah and Christian Bible. On top of this, it includes works directly related to Muhammad's teachings.[110] While no one knows for sure when the Quran was written, many Muslims agree that it was compiled shortly after Muhammad's death.

Five main pillars of Islam influence Muslim beliefs, as follows:

Profession of Faith. Muslims must profess that they believe in one God, often called Allah. The phrase from the Quran attached to this goes, "There is no god but God, and Muhammad is the Messenger of God."

Prayer. Muslims must pray five times a day at specific times. When they pray, they bow on a prayer rug and face Mecca.

---

[110] History.com Editors. "Islam."

Alms. Muslims must give a percentage of their income to charity or to the mosque (Islamic place of worship). This money is often used for public works projects, to maintain the mosque, or to help Muslims in need.

Fasting. During the religious holiday of Ramadan, which lasts for about a month, most Muslim adults must fast during the day. Some members of the community are exempt from this requirement.

Pilgrimage. Every able Muslim is supposed to take a pilgrimage to Mecca at least once in their lifetime.[111]

Western civilizations often record in their histories that Islam was "spread by the sword." While this doesn't sound pleasant and seems discriminatory against Muslims, it's not exactly incorrect. From 624 through the 630s, Muhammad and/or his followers fought battles and conquered lands throughout the Middle East.[112] Below is a short timeline of some of the major battles, land acquisitions, and peace treaties.

- **624:** Battle of Badr - Muslim forces win against the Quraysh tribe.
- **625:** Battle of Uhud - Muslim forces lose against the Quraysh tribe.
- **627:** Battle of the Trench - Muslim forces win against a Quraysh invasion of Medina.
- **627:** Siege of Bani Qurayzah - Muslim forces capture a Jewish stronghold at this location.
- **628:** Treaty of Hudaybuyyah - Muslim forces and the people of Mecca sign a peace treaty.
- **629:** Battle of Mu'tah - Muslim forces lose to Byzantine forces while trying to capture land near the Jordan River.
- **630:** Conquest of Mecca - Muslim forces and the Quraysh tribe come to an agreement. The Muslims "earn" the city of Mecca without a battle.
- **630:** Battle of Hunayn - Muslim forces win against the Bedouin tribe.

---

[111] "The Five Pillars of Islam." The MET, 2022, https://www.metmuseum.org/learn/educators/curriculum-resources/art-of-the-islamic-world/unit-one/the-five-pillars-of-islam.

[112] "Islam Timeline."

- **630:** Siege of Ta'if – Muslim forces attempt (but fail) to capture Ta'if.[113]

Muhammad died in 632 in Medina, solidifying the site as a place of religious pilgrimage in later years. However, Muhammad's passing left the fate of Islam's leadership in debate. Eventually, Abu Bakr became the first caliph, marking the beginning of the Rashidun Caliphate, which lasted until 661, followed by the Umayyad and Abbasid caliphates.[114] During all this, there were more battles and religious and political strife between the Muslims and over countries, tribes, and religious groups.

As Christians would face much later, Islam would also face a religious schism. People who followed the original caliphate were called Sunnis. People who believed that Ali and his descendants were the true leaders are called Shiites.[115] These two factions exist to this day. About 90 percent of practicing Muslims are Sunnis to this day; Shiites make up the next-largest faction. Several smaller sects with their own beliefs also fall under the Islamic umbrella.

The Feudalism Economic System Takes Hold in Europe (Beginning in the 700s)

Historians debate on when exactly feudalism, a type of economic system, began in Europe. Some say it didn't become popular until the tenth century, while others say the eighth. For this section, we will say it began in the eighth century in the Frankish Kingdom.[116] From the Franks, feudalism would spread across Europe. Of course, other countries around the world had their own systems of feudalism. However, we will only focus on feudalism in European countries.

The word "feudalism" comes from the Latin words *feudalis* and *feodum,* which roughly translate to "fee" and "fief" (a type of land). Feudalism began when a king started giving out land to his nobles and other favorites to reward their support or good deeds. The nobles could work the land, but more often, they would rent out the land to others. People who worked the land would pay the landowner either in money or

---

[113] "Islam Timeline."

[114] "Islam Timeline."

[115] History.com Editors. "Islam."

[116] Cartwright, Mark. "Feudalism." World History Encyclopedia, November 22, 2018, https://www.worldhistory.org/Feudalism/#:~:text=Origins%20of%20Feudalism&text=The%20system%20had%20its%20roots,and%20receive%20service%20in%20return.

in farmed or created goods, like food or cotton.[117] The landowner would set the rental price just as landlords do today, so rent prices could vary largely depending on the location, quality of the land, or the landlord's mood.

William the Conqueror of England is largely credited with popularizing feudalism and encouraging its spread. When he became King of England in 1066, he declared all the land in England was his. That also meant it was his to take or give away. Like the Frankish kings before him, he mainly gave land to nobles and favorites. However, he also began giving land in exchange for military service, encouraging people to sign up for the military. Nobles still often "earned" more land than the military did.[118] Because of this, nobles were more likely to be rich landowners who rented out their land, whereas ex-military members were more likely to keep and farm their land.

Outside of nobles and military men, bishops and other members of the clergy were some of the wealthiest landowners in Europe. Many of these bishops came from rich families, which only compounded the land they owned.[119] Like any other landowner, bishops could charge their tenants whatever they wanted. Bishops could keep the money for themselves, invest it in a monastery, or donate it to the Church.

Since the king was free to give and take land, sometimes he would take it back. This practice was less than favorable to everybody except the king. It didn't change in England for ages but changed in modern-day Germany and France. There, some land was considered an "allod," land the government could not be forcibly take back.[120] Of course, there were likely some exceptions to this rule.

Unless stated otherwise by the government, all owned land was also included in inheritances. If someone's father owned land and died, it would most often go to one son or be divided among his sons. It was unlikely that land would be passed down to a daughter, as women were not allowed to own property in many places in Europe at this time. Tenants could also be inherited. The same tenants, and sometimes their

---

[117] Cartwright, Mark. "Feudalism."

[118] Cartwright, Mark. "Feudalism."

[119] Barraclough, Geoffrey. "History of Feudalism." History World, n.d., http://www.historyworld.net/wrldhis/PlainTextHistories.asp?ParagraphID=env#:~:text=Although%20feudalism%20develops%20as%20early,the%20entire%20continent%20is%20Christian.

[120] Cartwright, Mark. "Feudalism."

descendants, would pay rent to generations of the same landowning families.[121] This would lead to a cycle of generational wealth—and generational lack of wealth.

With the rise of feudalism came a mightier wealth disparity problem—aka, the rich got richer, and the poor got poorer. The landlords could charge whatever they wanted in rent, and the tenant farmers were forced to pay or become homeless. Often, tenants would become indebted to their landlords, which would only cause more problems.

Moors Invade Spain (Iberian Peninsula): Beginning in 711

Before Spain was Spain, it was often called the Iberian Peninsula. While people today think of Europe and Africa as separate entities, they are close geographically. That's why it was easy for a group of African, Arab, and Muslim soldiers to cross the Straits of Gibraltar in 711 to enter the Iberian Peninsula of Europe.[122] Collectively, this group was known as the Moors.

Much earlier in European history, the Moors had controlled land on the Iberian Peninsula, but it was taken by the Visigoths. One reason the Moors invaded the Iberian Peninsula was to take this land back. Beginning when they first entered the peninsula in 711 until about 732, the Moors successfully took land in modern-day Spain and Portugal.[123] As the invasion continued, the Moors moved eastward, taking even more land.

Tariq ibn Ziyad led the Moorish forces, while King Roderick led the Visigoths.[124]

Encouraged by Tariq ibn Ziyad's victory, Musa ibn Nusayr brought another Moorish army to the Iberian Peninsula in 712. The two joined forces to capture more land to the north and west. As they went, they spread Islam.[125] Within a few years, most of the Iberian Peninsula was under Moorish/Muslim control. However, this does not mean everyone living in the Iberian Peninsula was Muslim. Many people were still

---

[121] Cartwright, Mark. "Feudalism."

[122] Murphy, Michael. "The Moors - 711 CE." History Tree, 2022, https://www.historytree.net/world-history/the_moors_711_ce.

[123] Murphy, Michael. "The Moors - 711 CE."

[124] Nutter, Nick. "Muslim Invasion of Hispania 711 AD." Visit Andalucia, March 18, 2022, https://www.visit-andalucia.com/muslim-invasion-hispania-711ad/.

[125] Nutter, Nick. "Muslim Invasion of Hispania 711 AD."

Christian, Jewish, or pagan/ polytheistic.

In 732, the Moors reached an area near modern-day France. Here, they came face-to-face with the Francs, a Barbarian tribe. The Francs won, stopping the Moors in their tracks.[126] Even though the Moorish military was defeated, Moorish people continued to live in the Iberian Peninsula, sharing their religion and culture and encourage the spread of Islam into Europe. However, a larger portion of the European population practiced Christianity.

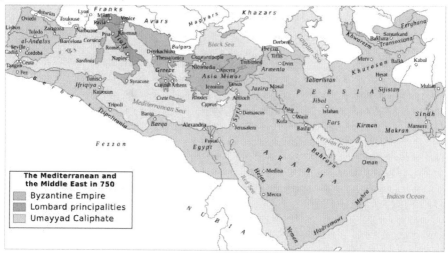

Caliphate 740

Constantine Plakidas, CC BY-SA 4.0 <https://creativecommons.org/licenses/by-sa/4.0>, via Wikimedia Commons, https://commons.wikimedia.org/wiki/File:Caliphate_740-en.svg.

Holy Roman Emperor Charlemagne (r. 768-814, 800-814)

Charlemagne, also known as Charles the Great, was the king of the Franks, a Germanic tribe. He was born around 748 in either modern-day Belgium or Germany. Historians also know little about his upbringing besides that he was highly educated, which allowed him to become a powerful leader later in life. After the death of his father in 768, Charlemagne became co-king with his brother. However, his brother died in 771, leaving Charlemagne the only king of the Franks.[127] In the late 770s, Charlemagne's forces continued to spread into modern-day Spain. There, he came across the Moors, whom he battled for several years

---

[126] Murphy, Michael. "The Moors - 711 CE."

[127] History.com Editors. "Charlemagne." A&E Television Networks. History, July 22, 2022, https://www.history.com/topics/middle-ages/charlemagne.

before finally proclaiming victory and dominance in the Iberian Peninsula.[128] These battles only continued as his reign went on.

Charlemagne Engraving
Theodoro Matteini, CC BY-SA 4.0 <https://creativecommons.org/licenses/by-sa/4.0>, via Wikimedia Commons https://commons.wikimedia.org/wiki/File:Charlemagne_engraving.jpg.

In the 780s, Charlemagne began sending his armies on military campaigns around Europe with the goal of expanding his kingdom. He soon conquered the Lombards and Avars. Often, after he took land, he forced all of the people to convert to Christianity. If they did not agree to convert, they could be penalized with a death sentence.[129] Even with this,

---

[128] "Charlemagne: King of the Franks." Students of History, 2022, https://www.studentsofhistory.com/charlemagne-the-holy-roman-empire.
[129] History.com Editors. "Charlemagne."

there were likely many people in the kingdom who continued to practice their native religions in secret.

While he was busy murdering and pillaging, he was also giving money and land to the Catholic Church. Needless to say, the pope loved his, no sarcasm intended. On December 25, 800, Pope Leo III crowned Charlemagne as the first Holy Roman Emperor. With this designation, Charlemagne could control more land and have more influence. He used much of this influence to make religious and economic reforms.[130] All the while, he continued his wars and gave money and lands to the Church.

Pope Leo III Crowing Charlemagne as Emperor on Christmas Day 800; From Chroniques de France ou de St Denis, 14th Century
https://www.flickr.com/photos/levanrami/22690436826

Charlemagne ruled his lands independently until 813 when he made his son, Louis the Pious, his co-emperor. Louis was also the King of Aquitaine (an area of modern-day France). Charlemagne died in 814, likely of old age. Over the next several decades, what had been Charlemagne's land was divided among his descendants until it was nothing like the vast empire that had once existed. Charlemagne was unofficially canonized in 1165 by Emperor Frederick Barbarossa, but he has not been officially canonized by the Catholic Church.[131] Members of the Catholic Church today have varied opinions about Charlemagne's rule and his efforts to spread Christianity, even if he did so violently at times. With all this in mind, it is not likely the Catholic Church will ever officially canonize him.

---

[130] History.com Editors. "Charlemagne."

[131] History.com Editors. "Charlemagne."

Debate on the Dark Ages Timeline

While most historians will agree that the Dark Ages ended around 1000 CE, some say the period lasted until about 1400. There are a few reasons for this. One is that Europe went through the Middle Ages between 1000 and 1500, so the two eras are often combined and referred to as the Dark Ages.[132] This doesn't mean that people who combine the two eras are wrong, just that they see the two eras as more closely related than other historians might.

It is also important to remember that Petrarch, who lived in the 1300s, coined the term "Dark Ages" because he did not think there was enough high-quality literature being produced. By this definition, high-quality literature started to be produced again in Europe during the Renaissance, which started in Europe around the 1400s.[133] Using this logic, it makes sense that some historians would say the Dark Ages ended when the Renaissance began. Overall, the Dark Ages timeline depends on who you ask and what you think caused and carried the Dark Ages.

Treatment of Christians During the Dark Ages

Unlike many other religious groups in Europe during the Dark Ages, Christians were not often persecuted or otherwise punished for their belief in God. Most Christians, unless nobility or clergy, were often poor farmers. They were as loyal to the Church as they were to the monarchy.[134] Overall, Christians were some of the best-treated groups during the Dark Ages, even if they were poor.

The Catholic Church During the Dark Ages

The Catholic Church arguably grew the most during the Dark Ages, both in size and power. This led to the Church doing both good deeds for the common person and abusing its power and committing various atrocities. The Church could both help and hurt for two main reasons—it was rich and had a large following.

A few things the Church set up near the beginning of the Dark Ages helped it to do more or less whatever it wanted. The most (literally) damning thing the Church did was declare that the Catholic Church was

---

[132] Becker, Rachel and Sullivan, Nate. "The Dark Ages - Definition, Causes, & History." Study, October 11, 2021, https://study.com/learn/lesson/the-dark-ages.html.

[133] Becker, Rachel and Sullivan, Nate. "The Dark Ages - Definition, Causes, & History."

[134] The Editors of Give Me History. "Christianity in the Middle Ages." Give Me History, November 17, 2022, https://www.givemehistory.com/christianity-in-the-middle-ages.

the only "true" church. People could not be granted salvation or entry into Heaven unless they were a practicing Catholic. Those who disagreed with the Church were at risk of excommunication—getting kicked out of the Church.[135] If this happened, a person would be damned and sent to Hell after their death for the rest of eternity. As most people did not want to burn for the rest of forever, they were apt to choose to worship within the confines of the Catholic Church.

Not every "bad" or sinful thing a person did would get them excommunicated. Excommunication was saved for severe acts against man or God. For minor sins, a person would need to give penance. For men, this might include doing manual labor or other acts to "work off" their sins or to "prove" their faith. Women and children were more likely to have to pray, confess, or fast.[136] Most often, a person would confess their sins to a priest and then be told what to do for penance and to be forgiven for their sins.

Several Church reforms and new "rules" were also made during the Dark Ages. In the late 500s, Pope Gregory I established the "Doctrine of Purgatory."[137] This doctrine basically stated that purgatory was a physical place a sinner would go to after death, assuming they had unforgiven sins. Purgatory was similar to Hell in that a person would burn to "cleanse" themselves. However, unlike Hell, sinners would only be in purgatory for a set amount of time, not for eternity. While this idea is wild in itself, what is even crazier is that *nothing* in the Bible describes purgatory or a place like it. The general Protestant thought (which did not exist during the Dark Ages) was that Jesus died to forgive all of our sins and that, after death, a person would go to Heaven or Hell.[138] All in all, purgatory did not "exist" until Pope Gregory I said it did.

---

[135] Arnold, Jack L. "The Roman Catholic Church of the Middle Ages: Reformation Men and Theology, Lesson 1 of 11." *IIIM Magazine Online* 1, no. 1 (March 1, 1999), https://www.thirdmill.org/newfiles/jac_arnold/CH.Arnold.RMT.1.html.

[136] Arnold, Jack L. "The Roman Catholic Church of the Middle Ages: Reformation Men and Theology, Lesson 1 of 11."

[137] Arnold, Jack L. "The Roman Catholic Church of the Middle Ages: Reformation Men and Theology, Lesson 1 of 11."

[138] "Is Purgatory Mentioned in the Bible?" Watch Tower Bible and Tract Society of Pennsylvania, 2022, https://www.jw.org/en/bible-teachings/questions/is-purgatory-in-the-bible/.

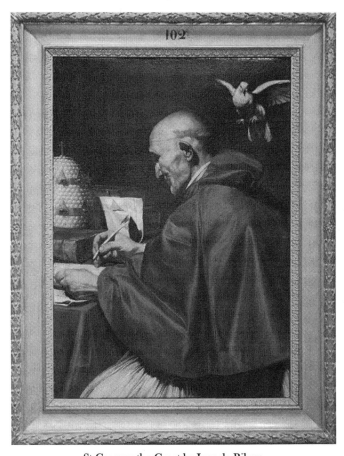

St Gregory the Great by Jose de Ribera
Livioandronico2013, CC BY-SA 4.0 <https://creativecommons.org/licenses/by-sa/4.0>, via Wikimedia Commons
https://commons.wikimedia.org/wiki/File:St_Gregory_the_Great_by_Jos%C3%A9_de_Ribera.jpg

 Tithing was another concept that wasn't exactly new but brought change to the Church. Tithing, the act of donating part of a person's income or harvested foodstuff, was voluntary. However, in 567, at the Council of Tours (followed by the Council of Macon in 585), the Church started to require tithing. If the government and Church worked together, tithing and taxes were so similar that they could have been one and the same.[139] Tithing was mostly still related to giving foodstuff until after the Dark Ages, when giving money became more common.

---

[139] Renee, R. "When Was Tithing Instituted in the Church?" The Tithing Hoax, 2022, https://thetithinghoax.com/when-was-tithing-instituted-in-the-church/.

In 600, Pope Gregory I passed another new standard. All church services must be conducted in Latin rather than the common language of the people in the area.[140] This would cause some problems within the Church. Namely, most people could not speak Latin. So, while people would sit in church listening to the priest, they would not usually understand anything. It was very much a "smile and nod" service, with the occasional mutterings of memorized chants and hymns. However, the Church made the language rules knowing this was the case. The Church believed that the Word of God (anything in the Bible) was too complicated for the average person to understand.[141] If the Gospels were written in Latin and the masses were also conducted in Latin, the common person wouldn't have the knowledge to interpret the text as anything other than what the priest said to be true.

Around the same time, the pope also allowed people to begin praying to Mary, saints, and angels. Previously, people would have prayed to God, Jesus, or the Holy Spirit—all one and the same in the Catholic Church. The veneration of relics and holy images was officially allowed through the authorization of Pope Adrian in 786.[142] Catholics were likely praying to figures other than God and venerating objects before the papacy allowed it, but now it would not have to be done in secret.

Below are some of the other new rules/developments in the Catholic Church from 850-1000 CE:

- 850 - Holy Water is introduced
- 927 - The College of Cardinals is established
- 995 - Pope John XV makes the first official canonization of a saint
- 998 - Fasting is implemented during Lent
- 1000s - Attendance of mass is made mandatory by the Church[143]

In all, the Catholic Church was a central part of life in Dark Ages Europe. At this point, the Reformation or the Great Schism (both of

---

[140] Arnold, Jack L. "The Roman Catholic Church of the Middle Ages: Reformation Men and Theology, Lesson 1 of 11."

[141] Mark, Joshua J. "The Medieval Church." *World History Encyclopedia*, June 17, 2019, https://www.worldhistory.org/Medieval_Church/.

[142] Arnold, Jack L. "The Roman Catholic Church of the Middle Ages: Reformation Men and Theology, Lesson 1 of 11."

[143] Arnold, Jack L. "The Roman Catholic Church of the Middle Ages: Reformation Men and Theology, Lesson 1 of 11."

which are discussed in detail later) had not happened yet. There was only one official, uniform Catholic Church. There were likely other fringe Christian sects, but these would have been considered heretical and not given merit by the Catholic Church.

Missionary Work and Conversion Across Europe

Missionary work did not stop during the Dark Ages. On top of this, many European leaders had converted to Christianity by 700 and either directly (and lawfully) or indirectly (voluntarily) encouraged the people in their kingdoms to do the same. Like Islam, Christianity was spread through the sword and by conquest, but not always.

Going back to Ireland, some of the most impressive missionary work in the Dark Ages was completed by Irish monks. Beginning in 563, they went on a series of missions, commonly referred to as the Hiberno-Scottish missions, and continued for hundreds of years. During these missions, monks would travel throughout the British Isles. As the years went on, they expanded their range, going into modern-day Belgium, Germany, France, and Switzerland. While traveling and converting individuals, the monks also set up monasteries and other religious buildings.[144] This missionary work continued throughout the Dark Ages and afterward.

Starting around 800, Europe began to see vicious attacks from the Vikings. The Vikings from history are different than the Vikings commonly portrayed in popular media. The Vikings included people from all over Scandinavia, many of whom spoke a Germanic language (different from German). They traveled most often by sea. While they fought harshly, they were also willing to make alliances and compromises. As they invaded their way throughout much of Europe, they also intermarried (whether willingly or by force) with the people living in these countries. Many of the wives would have been raised Catholic and brought their religion with them. This is one of the main reasons early Catholicism spread to Scandinavia.[145]

---

[144] McIntosh, Matthew A. "The Early Medieval Hiberno-Scottish Missions." Brewminate, January 31, 2021, https://brewminate.com/the-early-medieval-hiberno-scottish-missions/.

[145] Hamilton, Bernard. "Spreading the Gospel in the Middle Ages." *History Today* 53, no. 1, January 2003, https://www.historytoday.com/archive/spreading-gospel-middle-ages.

Viking Age [790-1100] Trade Routes in Northwest Europe
MacAmhlaidh, Brianann. *World History*, CC BY-SA, September 28, 2018,
https://www.worldhistory.org/image/9284/viking-age-trade-routes-in-north-west-europe/.

Christianity spread further east in the 900s. During this century, St. Cyril and St. Methodius helped create a written Slavic language and translated some Biblical texts. Of course, this would have been frowned upon by the Catholic Church, which was still operating entirely in Latin. Either way, Russia was officially made Catholic when Prince Vladimir of Kyiv was baptized in 988.[146]

Conclusion

After all we have learned in this chapter, it's clear that the Dark Ages weren't all that dark. While Petrarch may not have thought much of this

---

[146] Hamilton, Bernard. "Spreading the Gospel in the Middle Ages."

period and given us the misnomer, modern historians have proven him wrong. The Catholic Church expanded exponentially during these few hundred years. During the medieval period, the basis of the Catholic Church was built —including some of the foundational doctrines Catholics still believe and follow to this day.

Chapter 5: The Great Schism (1054)

The Catholic Church prospered throughout the Dark Ages. Sure, it had its struggles, but it made it through. That all changed in 1054, around the time the Dark Ages ended. Up to this point, there had been heated conflicts, both religious and political, within the Church. These differences were mostly between the Western Roman Church (later renamed Roman Catholic) and the Eastern Byzantine Church (later renamed Orthodox Catholic). The differences within the Church came to a head, causing what would be known as the Great Schism. This would divide the Church, creating two new branches of Catholicism—with neither branch seeing the other as valid.

Lead-up to the Great Schism

By 1054, the Catholic Church had been around for hundreds of years. Within any institution that old, there was bound to be disagreements. For the most part, the Church made rules and declarations about what the religion as a whole believed. Eventually, some issues either could not be resolved or were resolved by establishing official doctrines within the Church, but not everyone believed in them. Some of the main issues included what breads were acceptable to use for Communion, whether clergy members had to be celibate, and how strictly the Nicene Creed should be taken.[147] These were minor issues, but as smaller issues popped

---

[147] *National Geographic Society.* "Jul 16, 1054 CE: Great Schism." *National Geographic Society,*

up, they compounded on each other and were taken more seriously as time went on.

Next were the problems with politics. At this time, there was no separation of church and state. They were intertwined so thoroughly that they could have been one and the same. In the 1000s, the bishop of Rome, also known as the pope, was the leader of the Western Roman Church. The patriarch was the leader of the Eastern Byzantine Church. Some people, mostly Romans, thought the pope should have more authority than the patriarch or even authority *over* the patriarch.[148] Needless to say, this made the current patriarch, Michael Cerularius, very upset. In turn, his followers were upset—upset enough to divide the Catholic Church as the medieval world knew it.

In the end, Michael Cerularius was excommunicated from the Catholic Church, which meant he could never enter Heaven. It also gave the pope complete control over the Catholic Church. Soon after, Cerularius, not accepting his excommunication, excommunicated Pope Leo IX from the Church as well.[149] Believe it or not, Pope Leo IX also did not recognize his excommunication as legitimate.

Key Players

As you might have guessed, the main players in the Great Schism were Pope Leo IX and Michael Cerularius. While others also played their part in the Schism, it would not have happened at all (at least when it did) if not for these two men. Let's look at their lives before and during the Schism to better understand them.

Pope Leo IX

Born Bruno von Egisheim-Dagsburg, Pope Leo IX entered the clergy early in life, becoming a bishop at twenty-five. He worked within the Church for about twenty years before formally becoming the new pope on February 12, 1049. Once on the "throne," Pope Leo IX was ready to make dramatic reforms.[150] This would eventually lead to some of the arguments that would cause the Great Schism.

May 20, 2022, https://education.nationalgeographic.org/resource/great-schism.

[148] *National Geographic Society.* "Jul 16, 1054 CE: Great Schism."

[149] *National Geographic Society.* "Jul 16, 1054 CE: Great Schism."

[150] "Pope St. Leo IX." Pope History, 2022, https://popehistory.com/popes/pope-st-leo-ix/.

Many of the things Pope Leo IX wanted to change were things the Church had been debating for years. He wanted to rid the Church of simony (buying leadership positions), disallow clergy members from marrying, and more. To get these things done, he brought in some of his favorites as cardinals. These men included Frederik of Lorraine, Humbert of Moyenmoutier, and the future Pope Gregory VII.[151] Having all of this concentrated power working as one, Pope Leo IX passed most of his reforms by or around the time of the Easter Synod of 1049.

Pope Leo IX was "excommunicated" on April 19, 1049. Since he and the rest of the Western Roman Church did not recognize the excommunication as legitimate, Leo IX continued to be pope until his death (due to illness) on April 19, 1054.[152] When exactly Pope Leo IX was canonized is under debate. Some sources say he was canonized immediately after his death, while others say he was canonized in either 1082 or 1083 by Pope Gregory VII.[153] No matter when he was canonized, the current Roman Catholic Church respects and accepts his sainthood.

Michael Cerularius

Considerably less is known about Michael Cerularius (also known as Michael I Cerularius, Michael Keroularios, and Patriarch Michael I) than Pope Leo IX. Historians know he was born in 1000 in Constantinople. He became the Patriarch of Constantinople in 1043. He "ruled" more or less peacefully until just before the Great Schism, as the pope hadn't paid him much attention until this point.[154]

---

[151] "Pope St. Leo IX."

[152] "Pope St. Leo IX."

[153] Wooden, Cindy. "Heavenly Hosts: Popes Aren't Automatically Saints." Catholic News Service, May 3, 2011, https://web.archive.org/web/20130518205656/http://www.catholicnews.com/data/stories/cns/1101685.htm.

[154] "Michael I Cerularius." Hellenica World, n.d., https://www.hellenicaworld.com/Byzantium/Person/en/MichaelICerularius.html.

Enthronement of Patriarch Michael Cerularius
https://commons.wikimedia.org/wiki/File:Michael_Keroularios.jpg.

Michael Cerularius wasn't doing anything especially blasphemous to upset the pope. One of the largest reasons Pope Leo IX argued with him was that he used unleavened bread during Communion. However, this wasn't new, as the Byzantine Church had been doing this for centuries.[155]

Over the next few years, Pope Leo IX and Cerularius kept butting heads. In 1054, the Pope sent a representative to negotiate with Cerularius. However, Cerularius refused to meet with them. Later that same year, Cardinal Humbert of Silva Candida went to the Hagia Sophia to excommunicate Cerularius. Shortly afterward, Cerularius held a Holy Synod and excommunicated all the legates.[156] This was more of a symbolic move than anything else, reflecting Cerularius's lack of respect for the legates. As Pope Leo IX had sent the legates to Cerularius, the Roman Catholic Church would not recognize these excommunications.

---

[155] "Michael I Cerularius."

[156] Editors of Encyclopedia the Britannica. "Michael Cerularius." *Encyclopedia Britannica*, January 17, 2022. https://www.britannica.com/biography/Michael-Cerularius.

None of this deterred Cerularius. He eventually asked the city of Constantine to support him. However, it was led by Emperor Isaac I Komnenos at the time, who supported the pope more than the patriarch. Komnenos exiled Cerularius in 1058. Cerularius died a few months later on January 21, 1059.[157] Hundreds of years later, in 1965, the Roman Catholic Church rescinded his excommunication.[158] However, he was never canonized.

Catholic vs. Orthodox Churches

After the Great Schism, the Orthodox and Roman Catholic Churches began to govern themselves independently. The Roman Catholic Church stayed the same as it was before the Great Schism. However, the Orthodox Church was free to make the reforms it wanted without having to pass anything by the pope, whom they ignored in favor of the patriarch. Below are some of the most notable differences between the two churches as they stand today. Some of these changes were made shortly after the Great Schism, while others took longer to develop and put in place.

One of the first changes after the Schism was who was the head of the Church—at least as the Orthodox saw it. The pope remains the head of the Roman Catholic Church. The pope is above all other religious figures, possessing divinity or direct communication with God. The Orthodox consider Jesus Christ the head of their Church. However, the patriarch still heads the Church on Earth. The Orthodox respect clergy members but do not believe they have more direct contact with God than anyone else.[159]

In the Roman Catholic Church, priests and other higher members of the clergy cannot be married and must remain celibate. Orthodox leaders, on the other hand, can still become priests or higher if they are married. However, priests cannot get married, and if their wives die, they cannot remarry.[160] For these reasons, it is possible for an Orthodox priest to have a wife and children, while a Catholic priest cannot do so unless he renounced his priesthood—which is generally frowned upon.

---

[157] Editors of Encyclopedia the Britannica. "Michael Cerularius."

[158] "Michael I Cerularius."

[159] *Russia Beyond.* "7 Main Differences Between Catholicism and Orthodox Christianity." *Russia Beyond,* June 1, 2022, https://www.rbth.com/lifestyle/335081-7-main-differences-orthodoxy-catholicism.

[160] *Russia Beyond.* "7 Main Differences Between Catholicism and Orthodox Christianity."

Some of the biggest differences between the Churches come in how Holy Communion is done, who can take it, and what is used for the Eucharist (the bread used in Communion). Orthodox Christians can begin taking Communion as soon as they are baptized, usually shortly after birth. Roman Catholic children cannot take Communion until after their first confession, usually around age eight. Interestingly enough, Orthodox children also do not have their first confession until they are about eight. As far as the Eucharist goes, Roman Catholics usually use unleavened bread, while Orthodox Christians can use leavened bread.[161]

Even with these differences, both Churches can still agree on at least one thing—that they are the one "true" Church. People can only get to Heaven by worshiping in their religious sect.[162] Before the Schism, any Catholic would have been in the "right" sect, but not so much after the split.

Controversies Caused by the Great Schism

There can't be a good schism without some controversies to follow. These were related to the general differences between the two Churches, and more heat surrounded them. While no one would fistfight over what kind of bread was used during Holy Communion, people were more likely to argue over serious matters. Two major controversies that came out of the Great Schism were the Iconoclastic Controversy and the Filioque Controversy.

Iconolatry is the worship of religious images or icons. People who rejected the practice of worshipping these items and images were called iconoclasts.[163] Oddly enough, people who practiced iconolatry did not have a name. Before further investigating this topic, we need to know some important background information.

In the early days of the Church, most Catholics were vehemently opposed to revering images and holy objects. They saw it as a form of idolatry—worshiping something other than God. However, as the Church continued to grow in size (and wealth), the Church and artists began producing more religious icons and items. As these got more popular,

---

[161] *Russia Beyond.* "7 Main Differences Between Catholicism and Orthodox Christianity."

[162] Chery, Fritz. "Catholic vs Orthodox: 14 Major Difference to Know." Bible Reasons, November 12, 2022, https://biblereasons.com/catholic-vs-orthodox/.

[163] Editors of *Encyclopedia Britannica.* "Iconoclastic Controversy." *Encyclopedia Britannica,* September 4, 2020, https://www.britannica.com/event/Iconoclastic-Controversy.

people started to revere them. Icons hit their peak of popularity, mostly in Byzantine, between the seventh and eighth centuries.[164] People who liked the icons argued that they were mostly symbolic and that venerating them was not a form of idolatry. Most people who were against the practice stuck to their idolatry arguments.

As the practice of iconolatry became more popular, the Church began to make official rules about how religious art could be made. In the 690s, the Quinisext Council determined that buildings could not have crosses on floors, as then people could walk on them, which would be disrespectful. This council also said that Jesus must be drawn as a human rather than symbolically depicted as another creature.[165] These and other rules were mostly made to keep the art respectful.

Eventually, things got weird. Some priests would encourage the worship of icons. This led to superstitious beliefs about some items, especially statues. Some people even thought the religious icons could become animated! However, these beliefs had more of a (literal) cult following than anything else. Pope Leo III officially prohibited the worship of icons in 726, and people caught worshiping icons would be severely punished.[166] These bans would be issued on and off until modern times.

The next most important controversy was the Filioque Controversy. This controversy cropped up due to some of the wording in the original Nicene Creed. There was an addition to the creed that changed "I believe ... in the Holy Ghost which comes from the Father ..." to "in the Holy Ghost which comes from the Father and the Son."[167] This led to the debate, did the Holy Spirit come only from God the Father or from both God and Jesus Christ, the Son?

At this point, there was no question about Jesus's divinity. The Catholic Church agreed that Jesus was both human and divine. The Church also believed that the Holy Trinity (God, Jesus, and the Holy Spirit) were one and the same. Now, it was a matter of whether the Holy

---

[164] Editors of *Encyclopedia Britannica*. "Iconoclastic Controversy."

[165] Freeman, Evan. "Byzantine Iconoclasm and the Triumph of Orthodoxy." Khan Academy, 2013, https://www.khanacademy.org/humanities/medieval-world/byzantine1/beginners-guide-byzantine/a/iconoclastic-controversies.

[166] Editors of *Encyclopedia Britannica*. "Iconoclastic Controversy."

[167] "What is the Filioque Clause/Controversy?" Compelling Truth, n.d., https://www.compellingtruth.org/filioque-clause.html.

Spirit could be sent down to Earth by Jesus or not. Roman Catholics believed that, since Jesus and God were the same (in a sense), both could send the Holy Spirit. However, the Orthodox kept to the original writing of the Creed, asserting that only God could send the Holy Spirit.[168] As things usually go within the Church, the Orthodox Church changes its opinion on this every once in a while, but the Roman Catholic Church has clung firm to their beliefs over the years.

Conclusion

While it can be argued that the Great Schism was an event—as it took place in a specific place and time—there is no debate that it was not an isolated event. This one event, and everything that led up to it, divided a Church that had been whole for hundreds of years. The Roman Catholic and Orthodox Churches are still separated to this day. With all their differences, it is unlikely they will ever reconnect. Ultimately, the Great Schism changed the Catholic Church forever. It leaves the question—was this a good change or not?

---

[168] "What the Early Church Believed: Filioque." Catholic Answers, August 10, 2004, https://www.catholic.com/tract/filioque.

Chapter 6: The Magna Carta (1215)

Similar to the Great Schism, the signing and implementation of the Magna Carta was an event that took place in a single moment of history. Unlike the Great Schism, the Magna Carta was an item rather than an event. The Magna Carta is a government charter. While it is often compared to the Constitution of the United States, it is not the same thing. However, it does include laws, clauses, and other governmental jargon. Interestingly, it did affect religion in England. Remember, at this point in history, there was little, if any, separation of church and state, and this shows in the Magna Carta.

Reasons for the Magna Carta's Creation

In 1199, King John became the new King of England after his brother Richard's death. While King John was not unanimously hated, it is fair to say that few people liked him, partly because of his high taxes and almost constant wars with France. It didn't help that he seemed to have a personal vendetta against the pope at a time when England was still Catholic (and would be for several hundred more years).[169]

King John and Pope Innocent III's fighting came to a head in 1208. In short, the position of Archbishop of Canterbury was unfilled after the previous title holder had died. King John wanted one man for the job, while the pope wanted another. Each claimed he had more right to put whoever he wanted in place. While this may or may not have been true,

---

[169] History.com Editors. "Magna Carta." A&E Television Networks. History, October 21, 2021, https://www.history.com/topics/european-history/magna-carta

the pope excommunicated King John in November 1209. This was the first time an English monarch would be excommunicated. As we might imagine, this did not make the English people confident in his rule. After a few years, King John agreed to pay the Church 1,000 marks, and his excommunication was annulled in 1213.[170] Of course, there were other struggles in the middle of all this, but these were the main points of contention between the pope and King John.

To pay off the Church, King John raised taxes in 1209. At the same time, he was still sending the military to war with France. He lost a major fight in 1214. All of this eventually led to his people growing sick and tired of him, starting the First Barons' War (also called the Barons' Rebellion) in 1215. The rebels put up an amazing fight against King John's army and won quickly. However, unlike most rebels, the barons didn't have anyone in mind to take over the government if they deposed King John. Instead, they forced the king to write a charter that would put some limits on his powers. After months of negotiations and the barons re-declaring their allegiance to King John, the first version of the Magna Carta was signed in July 1215.[171] Several revisions were made over the next few decades. For the purposes of this book, we will focus on the causes and impacts of the first version.

Clauses of the Magna Carta

There are about sixty clauses in the original Magna Carta. In this section, we will only cover the most important of these clauses. The clauses were only granted to "all free men of our kingdom."[172] This means the Magna Carta applied to, firstly, men. Secondly, it did not apply to slaves, no matter their race or gender. This did not mean women and slaves did not have to follow the laws, but they may not have had the same protections as free men did.

Below are some of the most important clauses, copied from its original modern English translation:

1. "The English Church shall be free, and shall have its rights undiminished, and its liberties unimpaired."

---

[170] Holt, James. "Quarrel with the Church of John." The *Encyclopedia Britannica*, n.d., https://www.britannica.com/biography/John-king-of-England/Quarrel-with-the-church.

[171] Johnson, Ben. "The History of the Magna Carta." Historic UK, n.d., https://www.historic-uk.com/HistoryUK/HistoryofEngland/The-Origins-of-the-Magna-Carta/.

[172] Davis, G. R. C. *Magna Carta*. London, British Museum. January 1, 1985.

13. "The city of London shall enjoy all its ancient liberties and free customs, both by land and by water. We also will and grant that all other cities, boroughs, towns, and ports shall enjoy all their liberties and free customs."

16. "No man shall be forced to perform more service for a knight's 'fee,' or other free holding of land, than is due from it."

20. "For a trivial offense, a free man shall be fined only in proportion to the degree of his offense, and for a serious offense correspondingly, but not so heavily as to deprive him of his livelihood."

25. "Every county, hundred, wapentake, and tithing shall remain at its ancient rent, without increase, except the royal demesne manors."

40. "To no one will we sell, to no one deny or delay right or justice."

41. "All merchants may enter or leave England unharmed and without fear, and may stay or travel within it, by land or water, for purposes of trade, free from all illegal exactions, in accordance with ancient and lawful customs. This, however, does not apply in time of war to merchants from a country that is at war with us."

49. "We will at once return all hostages and charters delivered up to us by Englishmen as security for peace or for loyal service."

61. "The barons shall elect twenty-five of their number to keep, and cause to be observed with all their might, the peace and liberties granted and confirmed to them by this charter. If we, our chief justice, our officials, or any of our servants offend in any respect against any man, or transgress any of the articles of the peace or of this security, and the offense is made known to four of the said twenty-five barons, they shall come to us - or in our absence from the kingdom to the chief justice - to declare it and claim immediate redress."[173]

---

[173] Davis, G. R. C. *Magna Carta*.

On top of these are many clauses about repaying debts, how law enforcement can or cannot take property, how inheritances work, and how women are allowed to marry.[174] Many of these clauses were meant to limit the power of the government (both the king and local law enforcement) and increase the power of the Church and barons.

Impacts on the Government and Religious Institutions

It is difficult to say who was affected more by the Magna Carta—the government, the Church, or the common people. The government lost some of its authority, the Church gained more authority over itself, and the common people got some trickle-down benefits. This section will focus on the impact on the government and the Church.

One of the main goals of the Magna Carta was to insist that no one was above the law—not the lawmakers, the law enforcement, or even the king.[175] Several clauses in the Magna Carta aimed to restrict the government's power, most referencing which lands the king could or could not take and how people could be taxed.[176] These were clauses meant to make payments and punishments more equal for people of different classes and levels of wealth.

Perhaps one of the things that limited the government (the monarchy, specifically) was Clause 61. While the text of this clause is above, it can be complicated to understand. Clause 61 essentially states that the barons were allowed to set up a voting board with twenty-five members. If the king went against the rules in the Magna Carta, these barons would have the right to punish him. The punishment could be as severe as deposing the king and installing a new leader.[177] This clause was added to give the barons a voice and give the king a threat. With the barons' new permissions, the king was permanently in check. If he didn't move the right way and stick to the rules, it could be a checkmate for him.

Moving on to religion, many people misunderstand the Magna Carta in thinking it gave the people of England total religious freedom. However, that's not the case. People could still be prosecuted for their beliefs (and were) for hundreds of years after the Magna Carta was signed.

---

[174] Davis, G. R. C. *Magna Carta*.
[175] "Magna Carta: Muse and Mentor." Library of Congress, 2014, https://www.loc.gov/exhibits/magna-carta-muse-and-mentor/executive-power.html.
[176] Davis, G. R. C. *Magna Carta*.
[177] Davis, G. R. C. *Magna Carta*.

In reality, the Magna Carta gave the Church the right to govern itself without interference from the government.[178] This didn't mean the churches in England could do whatever they wanted. Like all other Catholic churches, they were still governed by the pope and the rules of the Catholic Church.

Along with the Church being allowed to govern itself, it was also given special protections *by* the government. Clauses 22 and 27 gave the Church special rights to have lower fines on its lands and to sell them at whatever prices it saw fit. Clause 62 cleared clergy members of charges associated with the struggles that led up to the creation of the Magna Carta.[179] All in all, the Church did not lose anything from the signing of the Magna Carta, as the government had, but instead gained rights and powers.

Impacts on the Common People

Almost all of the Magna Carta's impacts on the common people had to do with protections against law enforcement and unlawful seizures and general inheritance laws. These laws would have mostly affected free men but could also include women and minors. None of these laws were likely to impact slaves.

Clauses 3-5 protected land inherited by a minor. The land could not be taxed excessively before the owner was of age. A guardian would protect the land until the landowner was of age, but they could not sell or cause damage to the land. The land could not be sold without the landowner's permission or unless the landowner needed to pay off debts.[180] Once the landowner came of age, he would have as much power as any other adult landowner.

Clauses 7 and 8 apply to women, specifically widows. A widow would receive her "marriage portion" and inheritance as soon as her husband died. She would be allowed to stay in the marriage home for at least forty days before having to move if the deceased husband's family wanted her to move. Widows would not be forced to remarry. However, widows who had inherited land would have to ask the Crown or their governing lords

---

[178] Wilson, Stephen D. "The Magna Carta & the Rise of Religious Liberty." Baptist Press, June 15, 2015, https://www.baptistpress.com/resource-library/news/the-magna-carta-the-rise-of-religious-liberty/.

[179] Wilson, Stephen D. "The Magna Carta & the Rise of Religious Liberty."

[180] Davis, G. R. C. *Magna Carta.*

if they wanted to remarry.[181] These laws may seem to reach a low bar compared to today's standards, but they would have been quite an improvement over the norms at the time.

There were also several clauses having to do with Christians taking loans from Jews. At this time, if a person died before paying off his debts, his inheritors would need to pay off the debts. If underage family members inherited the debt, the lender was not allowed to put interest on the loan until the inheritor was of age. If a woman inherited the debt, she would get her dowry without having to pay any of it towards the debt.[182] It is never clarified within the Magna Carta why there are specific clauses for dealing with money lending from Jews specifically. Other groups were allowed to give loans, so it is odd that the Jews were called out.

Impacts Beyond the British Isles

When the Magna Carta was first signed, it only impacted people living in England. As the years went on, Britain began to establish colonies around the world. Many of these territories and colonies would have had the protections promised in the Magna Carta. However, some of these same colonies would use the clauses in the Magna Carta to justify their independence or use wording similar to that of the Magna Carta to create their own constitutions.

The United States of America is the country that draws most heavily from the Magna Carta. Britain began sending colonists to the United States in the 1600s, but by the 1700s, Americans were tired of being governed by a king who lived across the sea. They also saw themselves as being unfairly taxed. Even the famous Benjamin Franklin cited the Magna Carta when arguing about taxation. After the Revolutionary War, the United States became its own country but kept many laws it had used under British rule. According to historian Matthew Shaw, both the Declaration of Independence and the Bill of Rights (the first ten amendments to the Constitution) are heavily influenced by the Magna Carta.[183]

Many former Commonwealth Nations that left British rule (usually less violently than the Americans did) also used the Magna Carta when

---

[181] Davis, G. R. C. *Magna Carta*.
[182] Davis, G. R. C. *Magna Carta*.
[183] McClintock, Alex. "8 Ways Magna Carta Still Affects Life in 2015." *ABC News*, October 9, 2016, https://www.abc.net.au/news/2015-06-15/magna-carta-800-years/6538364.

forming their own constitutions. These included Australia, New Zealand, Canada, South Africa, India, and Hong Kong.[184] It is equally likely that other non-Commonwealth countries have taken inspiration from the Magna Carta when making their own constitutions.

Relevance Today

The Magna Carta wasn't just used hundreds of years ago when countries were forming. It has been cited as recently as the 1900s to form government groups and create laws. Both the Universal Declaration of Human Rights (1948) and the European Convention on Human Rights (1950) were influenced by the Magna Carta.[185] Both of these were influenced by the terror seen during World War II. Even after such a modern war, governments from all over the world agreed that a then 700-year-old document still had some redeeming qualities.

Even without looking at historical documents, the average person can still see the Magna Carta hard at work in England today. The monarchy still has limited power, and the common people have protections. Would this have been possible without the Magna Carta? Sure, but it would have taken a lot longer without it.

Conclusion

While the Magna Carta has had new amendments added and some original clauses deleted, the document has kept the same values over the centuries. It works to limit the power of the government and give more protection to the common people. Nowadays, the religious protections aren't the same, but this has more to do with the modern separation of church and state than anything else.

Similar to the Great Schism, the signing of the Magna Carta was a one-off event. Even so, it has affected England—and its colonies—from the time it was signed to today. Without it, medieval Christian history, and history in general, would have gone much differently.

---

[184] McClintock, Alex. "8 Ways Magna Carta Still Affects Life in 2015."

[185] Favorito, Rebecca. "The Magna Carta and Its Legacy." *Origins*, January 2015, https://origins.osu.edu/milestones/january-2015-magna-carta-and-its-legacy?language_content_entity=en.

Section Three:
The Great Opposition
1095-1400 CE

Chapter 7: The First and Second Crusades

The Crusades were a series of religious wars during the medieval period. These wars were started by the Catholic Church, usually directed by the pope. All in all, there were over a dozen Crusades. The goal of most of these was to "take back" the Holy Land (usually the land in and around Jerusalem).[186] This chapter will cover the first two Crusades, as they are arguably the most important.

What control did the pope have over the Holy Land? In reality, none. In his head, all of it. The Holy Land was the land around Jerusalem, which included parts of many Middle Eastern countries such as Palestine, Jordan, Syria, Lebanon, and Israel.[187] These were considered the Holy Land because many of the events in the Bible took place there. However, it wasn't just Christians who revered these places. Both Jews and Muslims also had holy sites within the "Christian" Holy Land. Because of this, the area was filled with locals and pilgrims from several religious groups. While most common people coexisted well with this melting of cultures, the pope did not like it. In the Catholic world at this time, what the pope said mattered more than anything else.

---

[186] Jones, Terry, and Alan Ereira. *Crusades.* Facts on File, 1995.
[187] Beck, Elias. "What is the Holy Land in the Crusades?" History Crunch, June 22, 2021, https://www.historycrunch.com/what-is-the-holy-land-in-the-crusades.html#/.

Lead-up to the First Crusade

Christians, Jews, and Muslims had coexisted in the Holy Land for centuries before the First Crusade. The common people were peaceful with each other, but there were wars between differing powers in the area over the centuries. Remember, from the 600s onward, Islam was spreading outward from the Middle East. This occurred both peacefully and through conquest.[188] So, if all this was going on for centuries, why was the pope suddenly concerned about it? Well, a lot of it had to do with the Seljuks.

First, we have to rewind a bit. Much of the Middle East, Northern Africa, and Crete had been controlled by (what we would now call) Arabs since about 970. However, in the late 900s to about 1025, the Arabs were driven away from more "European" areas, causing them to centralize themselves around Jerusalem (although they still had some holdings in Anatolia and Crete). In 1053, Pope Leo IX rallied an army to start a holy war.[189] This war was not considered a Crusade, partly because there wasn't much of a concept of what an "official" religious Crusade was yet.

The Seljuks came into the picture about two years later, in 1055. The Seljuks were a Turkish tribe, primarily Muslims. They were first centralized in Baghdad but quickly spread their territory through warfare.[190] Around 1070, the Seljuks came into contact with the Byzantine armies and won—and kept winning. By 1090, the Seljuks had taken control of several major cities/regions in and around the Holy Land, including Manzikert, Edessa, Antioch, and, of course, Jerusalem.[191] This would not affect the average European much. Then again, the pope and kings of Europe rarely saw themselves as "average." If they were bothered by this, *everyone* had to be bothered by it, whether they wanted to or not.

---

[188] "Islam Timeline."

[189] Jones, Terry, and Alan Ereira. *Crusades*.

[190] Jones, Terry, and Alan Ereira. *Crusades*.

[191] Cartwright, Mark. "First Crusade." *World History Encyclopedia.* July 9, 2018, https://www.worldhistory.org/First_Crusade/.

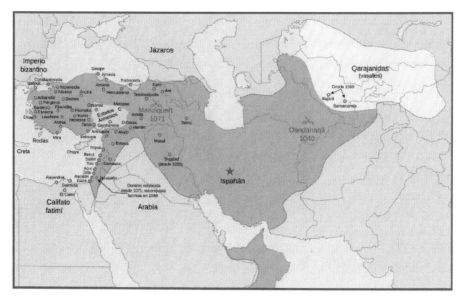

Seljuk Empire (1070s)

Seljuk Empire locator map-pt.svg: MapMaster (talk · contribs)derivative work: rowanwindwhistler, CC BY-SA 4.0 <https://creativecommons.org/licenses/by-sa/4.0>, via Wikimedia Commons https://commons.wikimedia.org/wiki/File:Seljuk_Empire_locator_map-es.svg.

During the Seljuk expansion, the Catholic Church went through a few popes. In 1088, Pope Urban II became the newest pope and brought a world of trouble along with him. The Byzantine Emperor, Alexios I Komnenos, tried to take advantage of Urban's obvious hatred of the Seljuks. The emperor asked for the pope's assistance in battling the Seljuks in Asia Minor. Urban II sent troops in 1091 and repeatedly throughout the following years to "protect the Holy Land"—meaning he wanted to keep them under Christian control. He also wanted to bring fame to himself, as he knew a religious Crusade would be something history would never forget.[192] All he had to do now was make the Crusade official.

Pope Urban II made the Crusade official on November 27, 1095, at the Council of Clermont in France. This council wasn't specifically called to form the Crusade—it was already scheduled, and the Crusade was just part of the agenda. Think of it as a lengthy business meeting, just with excommunications and calls to war.[193] However, before the Crusade could

---

[192] Cartwright, Mark. "First Crusade."

[193] Cartwright, Mark. "Council of Clermont." *World History Encyclopedia*, October 22, 2018, https://www.worldhistory.org/Council_of_Clermont/.

be launched, the pope had to plead his case for it.

Urban did plead his case at the council and did so well, but he also lied and exaggerated what was going on in the Holy Land to get his point across. One quote goes like this: "They have circumcised the Christians, either spreading the blood from the circumcisions on the altars to pouring it into the baptismal fonts ... They tie some to posts and shoot at them with arrows, they order others to bare their necks and they attack them with drawn swords, trying to see whether they can cut off their heads with a single stroke."[194] All of this was almost definitely not true. Still, the council believed him. After all, a pope wouldn't lie, would he?

Of course, these were religious men at the council. Murder was a sin—one of the Ten Commandments. Having a Crusade would inherently be sinful, right? Well, the pope had already figured out his argument for that, too. He declared the Crusade to be a "just war" in the name of God. This meant the war was a fight to save all of Christendom (at the very least, a half-lie, as the Seljuks were not a threat to most of the Christian world), and killing people who were killing Christians (still not entirely true) was God's work. God's work could not be a sin. The pope went on to say, "Whoever for devotion alone, not to gain honor or money, goes to Jerusalem to liberate the Church of God can substitute this journey for penance."[195] In other words, whoever went on the Crusade would not only *not* be committing sin by murdering but would have all their previous sins forgiven by the pope. Soldiers would most often be paid, which gave men a dual motive for joining the Crusade.

Once the Crusade was agreed to, the pope outlined the new primary objectives. Firstly, the main goal would be to run the Seljuks out of Jerusalem. After all, Christians were suffering there. The quicker this was done, the better. If successful, the Crusaders would also help the Byzantine army with their fight against the Seljuks.[196]

Soon after the council was concluded, the Crusade was made official. The Church and various European leaders began organizing troops from the rest of 1095 to the middle of 1096.[197] Then, it was time for war in the Middle East. But first, there was a fight to be had at home in Europe.

---

[194] Jones, Terry, and Alan Ereira. *Crusades*.

[195] Jones, Terry, and Alan Ereira. *Crusades*.

[196] Cartwright, Mark. "Council of Clermont."

[197] Cartwright, Mark. "Council of Clermont."

Crusaders vs. Jews in Europe

The Crusaders needed to travel hundreds of miles from wherever they originated in Europe (any one of several eastern European countries) to the Holy Land. To get there, they would spend much of their time traveling through Europe. What better way for a Crusader to pass the time than by murdering innocents? There's no way to tip-toe around it—it was awful.

Before the Crusaders were anywhere near the Holy Land, they were determined to "purify" Europe, or at least the parts of Europe they happened to be passing through. Since history rhymes but never exactly repeats, one of the places the Jews were hit the heaviest was in nearby modern-day Germany. Many of the Crusaders who did this did so simply because the Jews were not Christians. If they were not Christians, they must be enemies of God.[198] It did not seem to matter to anyone that the Jews worshiped the same God or saw Jesus as an important religious figure (even if he was not considered a deity). They didn't worship in the same ways Christians did, which meant they had to be eliminated. The same logic was also applied to the Muslims.

While the average Crusader might have been okay with killing Jews, members of the clergy weren't. Several bishops defended the Jews and explained why they shouldn't be killed. One such example comes from Spier in 1096. The bishops there tried to protect the local Jews. Soon, Count Emich of Leiningen invaded the bishop's palace, drove out the archbishop, and killed about 500 Jews.[199] Events such as these had varied effects on both the clergy and the Crusaders. Some members of the clergy were more likely to help Jews, while others were afraid to. Some kings were fine with the slaughter, while others started to grow resentful against the Crusaders.

Count Emich and others like him continued to lead their troops through Europe, killing Jews along the way simply because they were Jews. The Jews weren't building up armies to fight back. They were simply civilian casualties. Eventually, some of these armies were stopped in Hungary, as the Hungarian king had his army scatter the Crusaders.[200] This would not stop the Crusaders from killing Jews everywhere but

---

[198] Jones, Terry, and Alan Ereira. *Crusades*.
[199] Jones, Terry, and Alan Ereira. *Crusades*.
[200] Jones, Terry, and Alan Ereira. *Crusades*.

helped remove them from Hungary. After this point, the Crusaders focused on going to the Holy Land to kill Muslims.

The First Crusade (1096-1099)

Before we take a look at the events of the First Crusade (described below in chronological order), it's important to know *who* was fighting in the Crusades. With the promise of money and penance, but also the threat of a grizzly death, who would join the cause? As it turns out, everyone and their fathers. This included royalty and nobility as well as commoners. Some of the famous men who joined the fights included Hugh of Vermandois (brother to the King of France), Godfrey de Bouillon (duke and count), Baldwin of Boulogne, and the Duke of Normandy.[201]

One seemingly random character who played a large part in the Crusades was Peter the Hermit. At the beginning of the First Crusade, he was a forty-something Catholic priest from France. He lived a simple life and had very little money. However, this didn't stop him from somehow forming an army of over 40,000 men.[202] This group would later be referred to as Peter's Army or the People's Crusade.

Peter the Hermit and the Patriarch of Jerusalem
https://www.flickr.com/photos/136041510@N05/24209601033.

---

[201] Jones, Terry, and Alan Ereira. *Crusades*.

[202] "Peter the Hermit: 1050-1115." Heritage History, 2023, https://www.heritage-history.com/index.php?c=resources&s=char-dir&f=hermit3.

Peter's Army was, in all senses of the word, unofficial. While the group was collected by a priest, it was not organized by the pope. The people in this group were likely not getting paid. While Peter might have been seen as a leader to other armies, he had very little control over the army. Still, he managed to somehow march his men through Europe. Around July 1096, they ran through Belgrade, killing, pillaging, and burning parts of the city. They committed similar atrocities on their way down to Constantinople, which they reached in August 1096.[203] Other armies would later meet them there. Peter's Army joined forces with these armies and moved across the Asiatic to fight the Turks. Peter became a member of the emperor's council in 1097.[204] Peter and his army continued to fight throughout the First Crusade, but after joining up with the other Crusaders, Peter and his army became more of a footnote in the Crusade than anything else.

By September 1096, the Crusaders reached Nicaea. There were many problems with this. Namely, most of the people living here were already Christians, not that the Crusaders could tell them apart from members of any other religious group in the area. Because of this, they ended up killing (often in nasty ways) many Christians as they made their way through the area.[205] However, the citizens of Nicaea were not about to go down without a fight.

The citizens knew things the Crusaders didn't. Namely, the city's water supply didn't come from within the city. The Crusaders went without water for eight days, surviving by drinking their own urine and the blood from their animals before surrendering. Of course, there were terms to their surrender. The Crusaders could either convert to Islam—or die.[206] The Crusaders were split on what to do. In the end, some converted, and others chose to be murdered/martyred.

Later in 1096, some Crusader forces reached Byzantium. They were welcomed by the local government. Byzantine Emperor Alexius Komnenos even offered the position of liege man to Hugh of Vermandois. Soon after, the Boulogne brothers and their armies, along with other groups of Crusaders, joined Hugh in Byzantium. They were

---

[203] Jones, Terry, and Alan Ereira. *Crusades*.
[204] "Peter the Hermit: 1050-1115."
[205] Jones, Terry, and Alan Ereira. *Crusades*.
[206] Jones, Terry, and Alan Ereira. *Crusades*.

less thrilled with the emperor and did not want to become liege men.[207] The emperor, Hugh, and the Boulogne brothers were supposed to be on the same side. In reality, it didn't work out that way.

The Boulogne brothers wanted to stay in the Byzantine Empire until other crusading armies could meet up with them. However, that's the last thing the emperor wanted. To convince the brothers and their armies to leave, he tried to starve them out by cutting off their food supply. This didn't work right away, so he cut off even more supplies in March 1097. Needless to say, the brothers were not happy about this. They led their armies against the city. The emperor fought back and claimed victory by Easter. He then shipped the brothers and their armies out of the city and into Asia—but not before making them pledge allegiance to him and give him any lands they took from the Turks.[208] While the brothers did what they were told, they were not happy about it. Neither were their allies and friends.

Soon after, in April 1097, Bohemond I (also known as Marc de Tarente, Bohemond de Tarente, Bohemond of Otranto, and Bohemond I Prince of Antioch)[209] and his forces landed in Constantinople.[210] Bohemond had been involved with the Crusades from the beginning and had long been working with various military groups. Bohemond hadn't gone to Constantinople so much to fight but to strike a deal. After weeks of talks, he and the emperor came to terms that would allow Bohemond to have significant military power in Asia. Getting what he wanted, Bohemond left Constantinople. Other armies, made up of Franks and Normans, also later used Constantinople as a rest and meeting spot.[211]

---

[207] Jones, Terry, and Alan Ereira. *Crusades*.
[208] Jones, Terry, and Alan Ereira. *Crusades*.
[209] Hill, J. H. and Hill, Laurita L. "Bohemond I." *Encyclopedia Britannica*, June 10, 2020. https://www.britannica.com/biography/Bohemond-I.
[210] Jones, Terry, and Alan Ereira. *Crusades*.
[211] Jones, Terry, and Alan Ereira. *Crusades*.

Bohemund the Norman
https://www.worldhistory.org/image/9036/bohemund-the-norman/

Just a few months later, in June, the Crusaders made their way to Nicaea, which had been a "Christian" place not long before. They quickly took the city. While not much was special about the fight itself, capturing Nicaea was crucial for the Crusaders. The city had a prime location on the way to Jerusalem: the Crusader's final destination.[212] Once Nicaea was captured, the Crusaders could use it as an ensured safe spot, and other crusading armies could rest there.

The next major victory for the Crusaders came in March 1098. Baldwin I (also known as Baldwin of Boulogne, Baudouin de Boulogne, or Baldwin I of Jerusalem) had been a part of the Crusades since 1096.[213] On the way to Edessa, Baldwin's armies passed through Constantinople and helped take Tarsus.[214] Victory seemed to follow him almost everywhere he went.

---

[212] Jones, Terry, and Alan Ereira. *Crusades*.

[213] Lock, Peter. *The Routledge Companion to the Crusades*. Routledge, 2006.

[214] Ashbridge, Thomas S. *The First Crusade: A New History*. Oxford University Press, New York, 2004.

Baldwin I of Jerusalem
https://picryl.com/media/baldwin-i-of-jerusalem-c6c513

Surprisingly, Baldwin was welcomed in Edessa. The local Armenian population saw him as a sort of liberator for what he had done in Tarsus and for his other victories against the Seljuk Turks. Several Armenian leaders joined Baldwin in his fights, including Thoros, the Lord of Edessa.[215] They worked together well, and Thoros eventually adopted Baldwin even though he was an adult.[216] This practice was odd for the time but not unheard of; it would pay off for Baldwin when Thoros was murdered on March 9, 1098. The next day, Baldwin was named the Count of Edessa, allowing him to formally recreate Edessa as the first Crusader state.[217]

---

[215] Lock, Peter. *The Routledge Companion to the Crusades.*

[216] MacEvitt, Christopher. *The Crusades and the Christian World of the East: Rough Tolerance.* University of Pennsylvania Press: Philadelphia, USA, 2010.

[217] Maalouf, Amin. *The Crusades Through Arab Eyes.* Schocken Books: New York, USA, 1984.

In the summer of 1098, the Crusaders captured Antioch by fighting and starving the people out. However, once the Crusaders claimed the city, they learned they had starved the city a little too effectively, leaving no food for themselves. Weeks went by as they struggled to find food. Many Crusaders returned home, while many more starved to death.[218] Sure, they had captured a major city, but was the cost of victory worth it?

Near the end of summer/beginning of autumn 1098, everything seemed to be falling apart even though the Crusaders were so close to reaching their goal of capturing Jerusalem. The Bishop of Le Puy, who had been appointed by the pope to help lead the Crusade, died in August. This left the Crusade without official religious leadership—and the Crusaders to fight for leadership among themselves.[219] No one knew who was in charge, but they knew the plan was still to go to Jerusalem. So, that's what they did. They decided to choose the leader of Jerusalem once they got there.

Within two weeks of various armies reaching Jerusalem, the Crusaders took the town. The whole affair was grossly violent. False promises, sieges, and even cannibalism played a part in the events that followed.[220] At this point, the Crusaders were more motivated by bloodshed than by religious glory. They slaughtered anyone who got in their way, including Orthodox Christians as, often, they could not tell the difference between the Orthodox, Muslims, and Jews. Other times, they did not care enough to ask questions first before killing.

With Jerusalem secured, the Crusade was more or less over. There was still fighting in many areas, but the main goal was accomplished. Many Crusaders called it a day and went back home. The ones who stayed voted on who would be the leader of this "new" Jerusalem. Eventually, Godfrey of Bouillon took the helm, becoming the Advocate of the Holy Sepulchre.[221] However, he only held this post for about a year, as he died in 1100.[222]

---

[218] Jones, Terry, and Alan Ereira. *Crusades*.

[219] Jones, Terry, and Alan Ereira. *Crusades*.

[220] Jones, Terry, and Alan Ereira. *Crusades*.

[221] Jones, Terry, and Alan Ereira. *Crusades*.

[222] Britannica, T. Editors of Encyclopedia. "Godfrey of Bouillon." *Encyclopedia Britannica*, July 14, 2022. https://www.britannica.com/biography/Godfrey-of-Bouillon.

Bronze Statue of Godfrey of Bouillon in the Hofkirche of Innsbruck
Dralon, CC BY-SA 2.5 <https://creativecommons.org/licenses/by-sa/2.5>, via Wikimedia Commons https://commons.wikimedia.org/wiki/File:Gottfried_von_Bouillon_%28Hofkirche_Innsbruck%29_2006_0931_C.jpg.

To add one last hint of irony to the First Crusade, the man who called it never lived to see it completed. Pope Urban II died on July 29, 1099, in Rome.[223] While Jerusalem was officially taken while he was still alive, the news reached Rome after his death. With one order to begin the Crusades, Pope Urban II was indirectly responsible for the deaths of thousands, if not millions. His quest for Jerusalem had been completed successfully but not without paying the price of thousands of Christian and pagan souls.

---

[223] Britannica, T. Editors of Encyclopedia. "Urban II Summary." *Encyclopedia Britannica*, March 5, 2003. https://www.britannica.com/summary/Urban-II.

Baldwin: Crusader King of Jerusalem

When Godfrey of Bouillon took control of Jerusalem, he was not a king in name but had the power of one. When he died in 1100, the throne had to be taken by someone, and that ended up being his brother, Baldwin.[224] After hearing of his brother's death, Baldwin left Edessa and arrived in Jerusalem around November 1100. However, he did not take the title "Advocate of the Holy Sepulchre" but "prince." About a month later, on Christmas Day 1100, Baldwin was officially crowned as King of Jerusalem in the Church of the Nativity in Bethlehem.[225] This coronation also made it clear that Baldwin was the indisputable heir of Godfrey. His reign could not, and would not, be challenged.

Within the next two decades, Baldwin spent most of his time in Jerusalem or at war. (The First Crusade ended before his reign began, and the Second Crusade would not begin until decades after his death.) The battles he participated in were efforts to gain more land than anything else. He succeeded in this goal, taking lands in Arsuf and Caesarea in 1101. Over the next decade, he continued to take lands, mostly in the coastal regions near Jerusalem.[226]

Of course, there were some loose ends to tie up. After leaving Edessa in 1100, he named his cousin Baldwin of Bourcq the new Count of Edessa to rule in his place. This would prove useful when Baldwin I died in 1118 (due to illness)[227] without any heirs. Baldwin of Bourcq was crowned as the new King of Jerusalem, becoming King Baldwin II.[228] He, too, would continue to reign as King of Jerusalem until his death in 1131.[229]

---

[224] Barber, Malcolm. *The Crusader States.* Yale University Press: New Haven, Connecticut, USA, October 23, 2012.

[225] Murray, Alan V. *The Crusader Kingdom of Jerusalem: A Dynamic History 1099-1125.* Occasional Publications of the Unit for Prosopographical Research: Oxford, UK, 2000.

[226] Britannica, T. Editors of Encyclopedia. "Baldwin I." *Encyclopedia Britannica*, March 29, 2022. https://www.britannica.com/biography/Baldwin-I-king-of-Jerusalem.

[227] Barber, Malcolm. *The Crusader States.*

[228] Britannica, T. Editors of Encyclopedia. "Baldwin I."

[229] Britannica, T. Editors of Encyclopedia. "Baldwin II." *Encyclopedia Britannica*, July 28, 2022. https://www.britannica.com/biography/Baldwin-II-king-of-Jerusalem.

Baldwin II
https://commons.wikimedia.org/wiki/File:Balduin2.jpg.

Aftermath of the First Crusade Summary

The gap between the First and Second Crusades lasted about thirty years. During this time, there were no official crusading armies sent off to war by the pope or any kings. However, that does not mean this was a peaceful time. In the aftermath of the Crusades, the native people of Jerusalem and other areas captured by the Crusaders needed to regroup and rebuild—and sometimes take revenge.

Shortly after the First Crusade ended, many refugees from conquered areas fled to Damascus, Baghdad, and other nearby cities still controlled by Islamic governments. Many of these refugees were Muslims. However, not all Muslim refugees were united or agreed on what they should do next.[230] Some turned on each other, some turned on other nearby leaders (related to the Crusades or not), and others wanted to live their lives as peacefully as possible and avoid any more bloodshed.

For Muslims who wanted to fight, some of their main enemies were the Turks and the Franks. The Turks were often Muslim themselves but of another religious sect. The Franks were directly related to the Crusades in one way or another. With both parties, the main message the Muslim fighters were trying to send was clear: "Get out." The bulk of the major battles began in the 1110s and continued until the Second Crusade.[231]

Even with so many groups battling it out, the majority of people lived as peacefully as they could, even after Baldwin I's death. Baldwin II ruled as any other European king would rule over a feudal country. The main difference was that most of the people in the country were not of European descent. However, by Baldwin II's reign, there was a new generation of people living in and around Jerusalem. This new generation of Europeans had been born and raised in the Middle East or at least spent much of their life in it.[232] In this way, their cultures had begun to slowly blend together.

Lead-up to the Second Crusade

For most of the time the Muslims were fighting back and trying to reclaim the lands that had been theirs historically, they were not unified under one leader or even one plan of action. That changed in the 1120s when Imad al-Din Zengi (Zangi) was granted power.[233] In 1126, Mahmud II, the Seljuk Sultan, made Zengi the governor of Basra.[234] The same year, he also put down an uprising in Baghdad.[235] This helped to cement him as a leader for the Muslim armies.

---

[230] Jones, Terry, and Alan Ereira. *Crusades*.
[231] Jones, Terry, and Alan Ereira. *Crusades*.
[232] Jones, Terry, and Alan Ereira. *Crusades*.
[233] Jones, Terry, and Alan Ereira. *Crusades*.
[234] Britannica, T. Editors of Encyclopedia. "Zangī." *Encyclopedia Britannica*, January 1, 2022. https://www.britannica.com/biography/Zangi-Iraqi-ruler.
[235] Jones, Terry, and Alan Ereira. *Crusades*.

Imad al-Din Zengi
https://commons.wikimedia.org/wiki/File:Imad_al-Din_Zengi.jpg.

Over the next decade or so, Zengi led his armies to take lands for the Sultanate. However, for most of this time, he did not attack lands held by the Crusaders or Baldwin II. This changed when he attacked King Fulk of Jerusalem (heir to King Baldwin II) in 1137.[236] To combat Zengi's forces, King Fulk made an alliance with the Byzantines. The two armies fought on and off for years, mostly over Damascus. Zengi and his armies were eventually driven away from Damascus in 1140.[237]

Accepting his defeat in Damascus, Zengi moved his attention to Edessa—but not before a few years of political changes. In 1143, King Fulk died (due to a hunting accident).[238] He was succeeded by his oldest son, who would become King Baldwin III. However, Baldwin III was only a teenager at the time, so his mother, Queen Melisende of Jerusalem, co-ruled with him for almost a decade.[239] Baldwin III would

---

[236] Jones, Terry, and Alan Ereira. *Crusades*.

[237] Britannica, T. Editors of Encyclopedia. "Fulk." *Encyclopedia Britannica*, October 28, 2022. https://www.britannica.com/biography/Fulk.

[238] Britannica, T. Editors of Encyclopedia. "Fulk."

[239] Britannica, T. Editors of Encyclopedia. "Baldwin III." *Encyclopedia Britannica*, February 6, 2022. https://www.britannica.com/biography/Baldwin-III-king-of-Jerusalem.

have been about 14 in 1143 when Zengi made his way towards Edessa, meaning Queen Melisende likely would have had more sway over the political situation than most historians give her credit for.

Baldwin III
https://commons.wikimedia.org/wiki/File:Baldwin_III.jpg.

With the change in leadership and unrelated political turmoil in Edessa, Zengi saw the city as a weak point in the Crusader states. In 1144, he and his armies attacked Edessa, both armed defenders and religious leaders. Within no time, he had won control over the city.[240] The Islamic takeback of the Crusader states had begun.

The Second Crusade (1145-1149)

There is debate as to when the Second Crusade began. For the sake of this chapter, we are considering the beginning of the Second Crusade as the moment Pope Eugenius III called for it. (As mentioned, there was a great deal of fighting between various nations and religious groups

---

[240] Jones, Terry, and Alan Ereira. *Crusades.*

between the two Crusades, but these were not "official" Crusade battles as they were not directed or approved by the pope.)

Pope Eugenius III was elected in February 1145, and he wasted no time beginning the Second Crusade. Like much of the Christian West, he was extremely angered by the fall of Edessa, which took place just a few months before he became the newest pope.[241] Even though he may have wanted to call for a Crusade right away, he was wise enough to know that no one would agree to a war ordered by a brand-new pope. So, he enlisted the help of St. Bernard of Clairvaux, a highly respected and charismatic preacher whom crowds would literally line up to listen to. Pope Eugenius III commissioned St. Bernard to preach about the merits of a new Crusade, giving the same promises that came with the last one: anyone who participated in the Crusade would have their sins on Earth pardoned and receive heavenly rewards after death. St. Bernard continued to preach even after the Crusade started to rally new Crusaders to the cause.[242] It only took a few months for this advertisement campaign to pay off. The pope was ready to declare a new Crusade.

Eugenius III
Praefcke, Andreas. Wikimedia Commons, CC BY-SA 4.0, March 13, 2020,
https://commons.wikimedia.org/wiki/File:Eugenius-III.jpg.

---

[241] Loughlin, James. "Pope Blessed Eugene III." New Advent LLC, 1909, https://www.newadvent.org/cathen/05599a.htm.

[242] Gildas, Marie. "St. Bernard of Clairvaux." New Advent LLC, 1907, https://www.newadvent.org/cathen/02498d.htm.

On December 1, 1145, Pope Eugenius called for the Second Crusade at the papal court in Viterbo. He did this through a papal bull, which had no name at the time but is now referred to as the *Quantum praedecessores*. In this papal bull, he talked about the events of the First Crusade and how the Second Crusade was needed to reclaim Edessa and take other areas in the Holy Land.[243] All of this is interesting in itself, but remember that Pope Urban II did not call for the First Crusade in a papal bull. This was new, exciting, and had the potential to become a dangerous precedent.

Around the same time, Louis VII of France was also trying to start his own Crusade without papal approval. However, his attempts were not very successful. After the papal bull was announced, he asked for the pope's blessing (and support). Because of this and other factors, Pope Eugenius reissued the papal bull on March 1, 1146, to bring more attention to the cause.[244]

Even with the papal bull and its reissue, people were not exactly lining up to sign up for the Second Crusade. Pope Eugenius III later issued two more papal bulls. The first of these, the *Divina dispensatione*, was issued on October 5, 1146. It specifically called for Italians to join the Second Crusade.[245] The second, *Divina dispensatione II*, was issued about six months later. This bull called for the Crusaders to attack the Wends, a group of several Slavic tribes that lived in the Baltics and were primarily pagan.[246] The second of these papal bulls was more successful in recruiting people, but neither would do much to impact the fighting going on in the Holy Land. Instead, the second papal bull set off the Wendish Crusade, which focused its efforts in the Baltics.

In the end, the pope managed to recruit many soldiers to his cause—but not nearly as many as had been a part of the First Crusade. While the previous Crusade had fighters from all over Europe, these new Crusaders were mostly French and German.

---

[243] Runciman, Steven. *A History of the Crusades, Vol. II: The Kingdom of Jerusalem and the Frankish East, 1100-1187*. Cambridge University Press: Cambridge, UK, 1952.

[244] Runciman, Steven. *A History of the Crusades, Vol. II: The Kingdom of Jerusalem and the Frankish East, 1100-1187*.

[245] Constable, Giles. "The Second Crusade as Seen by Contemporaries." *Traditio 9* (1953): 213-79. http://www.jstor.org/stable/27830277.

[246] Taylor, Pegatha. "Moral Agency in Crusade and Colonization: Anselm of Havelberg and the Wendish Crusade of 1147." *The International History Review* (2000): 772.

The German forces left home in May 1147, and the French followed quickly after in June. Some of the travel was peaceful—but not for long. Turmoil began before the forces even made it out of Europe. As in the last Crusade, the Crusaders murdered many of the Jews they came across, usually for the simple reason that they were Jews.[247] The leaders were losing control of their Crusaders faster than expected.

Things only got worse as the Crusaders continued towards the Holy Land. As they fought the Jews and random other groups along the way, their armies lost numbers. A flood in early September killed several German troops before the forces finally reached Constantinople on September 10, 1147.[248] However, Emperor Manuel of Constantinople was not comfortable having a large army on his lands. He suggested the German Crusaders split their army in half and leave his lands without bothering to wait for the French armies. King Conrad III eventually agreed to these terms and sent half of his army to the coastland and the other half to Anatolia.[249]

Manuel I Komnenos
https://commons.wikimedia.org/wiki/File:Manuel_I_Comnenus.jpg

---

[247] Jones, Terry, and Alan Ereira. *Crusades*.

[248] Nicolle, David. *The Second Crusade 1148: Disaster Outside Damascus*. Bloomsbury USA: New York, January 20, 2009.

[249] Jones, Terry, and Alan Ereira. *Crusades*.

By the time the French reached Constantinople, they had been joined by other French nobility, as well as armies from Normandy, Provence, Aquitaine, Brittany, Burgundy, and Lorraine.[250] The French were treated considerably better than the Germans when they reached Constantinople. At least, the French king was. The French people and other countrymen they had picked up along the way were infuriated that the Emperor of Constantinople had made a truce with the Seljuks. The armies wanted to fight the emperor's army, but the king would not allow it.[251] Instead, the French army and its joiners peacefully left Constantinople to continue its journey and meet up with the German army.

The two armies met again in Lopadion in late November or early December 1147. However, it wasn't long before King Conrad of the German army fell ill and returned to Constantinople. This left his armies under the care of the French, for better or worse. It is difficult to say whether it really was better or worse, as the armies were attacked by the Turks on December 24 in what would later be called the Battle of Ephesus. Only a few days later, they were attacked again by the Turks at the Battle of the Meander. Luckily, the Crusader army won both battles.[252] From there, the Crusader armies continued south towards Jerusalem.

As the Crusader army continued to travel, they also continued to be attacked by the Turks. Eventually, King Louis decided it would be better to travel by ship and ordered several to meet the armies at Adalia and bring them to Antioch. However, not enough ships arrived, so the king and his favorites took the ships while the rest of the army marched to Antioch. On the way, most of the marching army died, either by attacks from the Turks or by illness.[253] This was surprising to King Louis but probably should not have been, as illness was a common reason for wartime death.

King Louis reached Antioch on March 19, 1148, while most of the other armies arrived sometime in April.[254] Next, the Crusaders headed towards Damascus. The regent of the area, Mu'in ad-Din Unur, was none

---

[250] Runciman, Steven. *A History of the Crusades, Vol. II: The Kingdom of Jerusalem and the Frankish East, 1100-1187.*

[251] Runciman, Steven. *A History of the Crusades....*

[252] Runciman, Steven. *A History of the Crusades....*

[253] Runciman, Steven. *A History of the Crusades, Vol. II: The Kingdom of Jerusalem and the Frankish East, 1100-1187.*

[254] Riley-Smith, Jonathan. *Atlas of the Crusades.* Facts on File: New York, 1991.

too happy about this. He asked for help from the rulers of Aleppo and Mosul as a last-ditch effort to keep the Crusaders from taking Damascus, even though these rulers were usually the regent's enemies. Either way, the troops did not arrive in time to help.[255] This begs a question, though. If the Crusade had been called because Edessa fell to the Muslims, why were the Crusaders going after Damascus?

Louis VII of France
https://commons.wikimedia.org/wiki/File:Decaisne_-_Louis_VII_of_France.jpg.

The attack on Damascus was anything but impulsive. On June 24, 1148, the Crusaders held the Council of Palmarea (also called the Council of Acre). Here, the Crusaders talked about which city was the most valuable to take from the Muslims. A few cities were discussed, but it eventually came down to Ascalon and Damascus.[256] In the end, the Crusaders decided to take Damascus because it would add to the political

---

[255] Nicolle, David. *The Second Crusade 1148: Disaster Outside Damascus.*
[256] Britannica, T. Editors of Encyclopedia. "Zangī."

power of King Baldwin II and take power from Nur ad-Din (the successor to Zengi).[257] With the council over, the Crusading army, in all its forces—around 50,000 men—left to fight in Damascus.[258]

Siege of Damascus, Second Crusade
https://commons.wikimedia.org/wiki/File:Siege_of_Damascus,_second_crusade.jpg

The last battle of the Second Crusade, the Siege of Damascus, began on July 24, 1148. Things began to go south for the Crusaders right away. Within four days, the battle was lost. Some historians say the battle ended when the Templars (who will be discussed in detail later in this book) took a bribe from the Turks, while others say it was simply due to heavy losses and the Crusaders' lack of organization and teamwork.[259] Either way, after the battle, the Crusaders planned to attack Ascalon instead, but

---

[257] Mayer, Hans E. *The Crusades*. Oxford University Press: Oxford, UK, 1972.
[258] Runciman, Steven. *A History of the Crusades, Vol. II: The Kingdom of Jerusalem and the Frankish East, 1100-1187*.
[259] Davies, Norman. *The Isles: A History*. Pan Macmillan: London, 2008.

this plan never went through for various reasons.[260] Instead, the Crusaders needed to accept that it was time to go home. With the defeat at the Siege of Damascus, the Second Crusade was over, all without the Crusaders trying to retake Edessa.

Wendish Crusade

Before we can finish with the Second Crusade, we must go back to 1147 to discuss an often-forgotten part of the Second Crusade—the Wendish Crusade. The Wendish Crusade, which put the Crusaders against western Slavic pagans (the Wends), was approved in the *Divina dispensatione,* discussed briefly earlier in this chapter.[261]

As with most of the Second Crusade, St. Bernard was charged with preaching about the benefits of crusading against the Wends. Anyone who joined this fight would also have all their sins forgiven and be given the same indulgences as the Crusaders who went to the Holy Land.[262] Even with these promises, considerably fewer men signed on for the Wendish Crusade than the Holy Land Crusade. Oddly enough, the Wendish Crusade attracted different people to the cause, as well. Most of the men who signed on were either Danish, Polish, or Saxon.[263] Few Germans or Frenchmen joined the Wendish Crusade. This is especially odd, considering that the Germans were, in part, led by Saxon families.[264] Either way, by mid-1147, the troops were assembled and ready to go on their holy Crusade.

While the official start date of the Wendish Crusade is debatable, historians know that one of the first major battles occurred when the Slavic leader, Niklot, invaded Wagria and destroyed several Fleming and Frisian villages, beginning in June 1147. Niklot remained a problem for the Crusaders throughout the summer of '47. Battles spread across the Baltic, with some of the biggest battles in Dobin.[265] The two sides continued fighting and alternately winning battles. After losing one battle in Dobin, Niklot agreed to have all of his troops in the area baptized as

---

[260] Runciman, Steven. *A History of the Crusades, Vol. II: The Kingdom of Jerusalem and the Frankish East, 1100-1187.*

[261] Taylor, Pegatha. "Moral Agency in Crusade and Colonization: Anselm of Havelberg and the Wendish Crusade of 1147."

[262] Murray, Alan V. *Crusades: An Encyclopedia.* ACE-CLIO: Santa Barbara, 2006.

[263] Davies, Norman. *The Isles: A History.*

[264] Herrmann, Joachim. *Die Slawen in Deutschland.* Akademie-Verlag GmbH: Berlin, 1970.

[265] Christiansen, Eric. *The Northern Crusades.* Penguin Books: London, 1997.

Christians. In the end, the Crusaders won more battles than they lost, taking Havelberg and Malchow, but losing a siege on Demmin and some battles in Pomerania.[266]

The Capture of the Wends
https://commons.wikimedia.org/wiki/File:Wojciech_Gerson-Oplakane_apostolstwo.jpg.

The winner of the Wendish Crusade depends on how each historian chooses to look at it. The "official" goal of the Wendish Crusade was to convert the majority of the Wends, which did not happen.[267] In this way, the Crusaders lost. However, the Crusaders received tributes from Niklot as part of the terms to end the fighting. The Crusaders also gained much land in the Baltics. The monarchs were pleased—especially the Danes, who gained control of most of the new land.[268] All in all, the Wendish Crusade serves as a footnote in the history of the Second Crusade. Still, it has enough historical and religious value to earn more than a few footnotes in this book.

Aftermath of the Second Crusade Summary

After the Second Crusade ended in defeat for the Crusaders, they had little choice but to go home, tails between their legs. The failure was felt

---

[266] Christiansen, Eric. *The Northern Crusades*.
[267] Christiansen, Eric. *The Northern Crusades*.
[268] Murray, Alan V. *Crusades: An Encyclopedia*.

heavily by the rulers who joined the campaign, as they believed they could no longer trust each other.[269] No one European monarch had done anything to purposefully sabotage the other, but resentment held strong.

The biggest loss for the Crusaders was their loss of Damascus. In 1154, the city was handed over to the Turks to be ruled by Nur ad-Din.[270] This was one of the last things the Crusaders could have wanted to happen. The Christians were losing their hold over the Holy Land. Now, the Church had to regroup and decide what to do next. Should they continue crusading or try something new?

Conclusion

The first two Crusades are marked as the most important. It's fair to say that the Crusaders won the First Crusade but lost the Second Crusade, even though they certainly won and lost battles in both. The Crusades were a violent means of "saving" the Holy Land and converting pagans and Muslims. The Crusaders did win and lose lands and convert some pagans. However, many more people died and suffered for the Christian cause. The same Christians who claimed Islam was spread by the sword were trying to convert with the same weapons.

---

[269] Riley-Smith, Jonathan. *Atlas of the Crusades*.

[270] Runciman, Steven. *A History of the Crusades, Vol. II: The Kingdom of Jerusalem and the Frankish East, 1100-1187*.

Chapter 8: Power Struggle (1180s–1310s)

Picture it—Europe in the 1150s. The Second Crusade is over. For better or worse, the Crusaders have lost and have made their way back home. The heads of several monarchies across the continent are upset at each other because of their loss in the Second Crusade. Tensions between the European nations are high due to suspicion more than anything else. What did Europe gain from all this? In short, nothing good. In this chapter, dozens more Crusades.

Between 1150 and 1310, there were about twenty Crusades. Not all of these were called for or even sanctioned by whoever the current pope was at the time. Many of these were started and led by various members of the European monarchy.[271] For the sake of this chapter, we will cover the ten most important Crusades that occurred during this period. Some of these Crusades were to regain land in the Holy Land, to spite the Byzantine Empire, to fight other Christians, or because a king was having a particularly bad year.

Between Crusades (1150-1180)

In the roughly thirty years between the Second and Third Crusades, the politics in Europe and the Holy Land did anything but pause. Kings and queens died and were replaced. *The king is dead. Long live the king!* These changes in leadership led to changes in how the countries were

---

[271] Murray, Alan V. *Crusades: An Encyclopedia.*

run. Depending on who was in charge, alliances and enemies could switch in the blink of an eye.

First, let's look at the Holy Land. In 1154, Nur al-Din took Damascus. Before this, he held the title of the ruler (atabeg) of Aleppo. In just a few decades, he made allies with the Abbasid Caliph (Baghdad) and annexed parts of Egypt.[272] By the time he died in 1174 due to illness, he had held control over much of the Holy Land, in addition to Syria and Egypt. His son, As-Salih Ismail al-Malik, was made his legal heir. However, he was only eleven at the time, and many others wanted to see him off the throne.[273]

One of the men who wanted the throne for himself was Saladin (also known as Salah ad-Din). In 1174, Saladin began to lay siege to al-Malik's lands in Baalbek. After four months of battle, Saladin captured the lands and made his way towards Damascus. It took another two years for Saladin to defeat the troops defending the city. He then cemented his claim to the throne of Syria by marrying Ismat ad-Din Khatun, the daughter of the regent of Damascus.[274] With this, al-Malik's reign came to an end. He died just a few years later due to illness, before reaching age twenty.[275]

---

[272] Britannica, T. Editors of Encyclopedia. "Nūr al-Dīn." *Encyclopedia Britannica*, May 11, 2022. https://www.britannica.com/biography/Nur-al-Din.

[273] Brill, E.J. *Encyclopedia of Islam: A Dictionary of the Geography, Ethnography, and Biography of the Muhammadan Peoples.* Ed 1., Vol. 1. BRILL, 1913.

[274] Gibb, H. A. R. *The Damascus Chronicle of the Crusades: Extracted and Translated from the Chronicle of Ibn Al-Qalanisi.* Dover Publications: Garden City, NY, November 24, 2011.

[275] Gibb, H. A. R. *The Damascus Chronicle of the Crusades: Extracted and Translated from the Chronicle of Ibn Al-Qalanisi.*

Saladin
https://www.worldhistory.org/image/9138/saladin/.

Saladin continued to hold power into the Third Crusade. He would soon become one of the Crusaders' biggest and most famous enemies—whether he wanted to or not. Saladin will be discussed in greater detail throughout this chapter as we get to the Crusades.

Now, let's look back at Europe. For the purpose of this chapter, we'll look at some of the countries that played the biggest parts in the first two Crusades or took center stage in the upcoming Crusades. The changes in government and religious leadership are in no particular order below.

Between the Crusades, power in England changed drastically. During the Second Crusade, England was ruled by the Normans, namely King Stephan. In 1154, power shifted to the Plantagenets.[276] Like most shifts in

---

[276] Department of European Paintings. "List of Rulers of Europe." In Heilbrunn Timeline of Art History. New York: The Metropolitan Museum of Art, 2000-. (originally published October

power, this did not happen without bloodshed. King Stephen was brought to the throne in 1135 after his uncle, King Henry I, died. However, he was not Henry's first choice for a successor. Henry had a daughter, Matilda, who was meant to inherit the throne. In short, the English nobility did not trust a woman with the throne, so they chose Stephen to become the new king. Matilda was none too pleased. Just three years after Stephen took the throne, Matilda and her half-brother, the Earl of Gloucester, assembled troops to invade England. She took a considerable amount of land, and her troops captured King Stephen at one point. These battles went on until 1148.[277] This timeline explains why England did not do more in the Crusades—it had its own struggles to deal with.

Painting of King Stephen of England
https://www.worldhistory.org/image/11535/painting-of-king-stephen-of-england/

2003, last revised April 2007).

[277] Britannica, T. Editors of Encyclopedia. "Stephen." *Encyclopedia Britannica*, December 23, 2022. https://www.britannica.com/biography/Stephen-king-of-England.

Empress Matilda of England
https://www.worldhistory.org/image/11550/empress-matilda-of-england/

The fighting ended around 1148 when Matilda left England after one too many losses in battle. However, in January 1153, Matilda's son, Henry of Anjou, invaded England. He wanted to take back the throne, which he believed was rightfully his. King Stephen wanted the throne to pass to his own son, Eustace. The battles waged on for months until Eustace died in August. With the king's one hope for succession dashed, he signed a treaty to end the war. The treaty stated that, once he died,

Henry of Anjou would become king.²⁷⁸ Henry II ascended to the throne in 1154 and remained king into the Third Crusade.²⁷⁹

Henry II of England
https://www.worldhistory.org/image/11597/henry-ii-of-england/

In France, King Louis VII was king for several years before and throughout the Second Crusade. He ruled until the Third Crusade in 1180, when he died due to illness. His son, Philip II Augustus, was named his successor. Later in the same year, the new King Philip II married Isabella of Hainaut, who was the daughter of King Baldwin V. With this marriage, Philip also gained the territory of Artois (in modern-day France) as part of the dowry.²⁸⁰ Talk of the Third Crusade began during his first year as king. This would no doubt have some influence on the king's actions throughout the upcoming Crusades.

---

²⁷⁸ Britannica, T. Editors of Encyclopedia. "Stephen."
²⁷⁹ Department of European Paintings. "List of Rulers of Europe."
²⁸⁰ Pacaut, M. "Philip II." *Encyclopedia Britannica*, August 17, 2022. https://www.britannica.com/biography/Philip-II-king-of-France

Louis VII of France
https://picryl.com/media/decaisne-louis-vii-of-france-96ded3.

King Conrad II of Germany ruled until his death in 1152. However, he also ruled alongside his son, Henry Berengar, from March 1147 to August 1150. He would have become the sole king of Germany after his father's death but sadly died before he got the chance to.[281] Conrad III had to pick a new heir. Knowing he was not long for this world, Conrad did not want to choose his young son, who was not yet a teenager, to become the next king. Instead, he chose his nephew, Frederick I Barbarossa, to succeed him. Frederick became the new king in 1152 and reigned for the next several decades.[282] Throughout his reign, Frederick faced both internal and external conflict. This likely influenced his actions throughout the next few Crusades, as he would be one of the biggest European players.

Life only got more interesting for Barbarossa when he was named Holy Roman Emperor in 1155. This was not only significant because he

---

[281] Fuhrmann, Horst. *Germany in the High Middle Ages: c. 1050-1200.* Cambridge University Press: Cambridge, UK, 1986.

[282] Görich, Knut. *Friedrich Barbarossa: Eine Biographie.* Germany: C. H. Beck, 2011.

gained power but because it had been almost twenty years since there had been a Holy Roman Emperor, which had been Lothair II from 1133 to 1137.[283] Pope Innocent II had made Lothair II the Holy Roman Emperor. However, neither Celestine II, Lucius II, Eugenius III, nor Anastasius IV named anyone as the Holy Roman Emperor during their reigns.[284] There may have been many reasons these popes did not name a new Holy Roman Emperor.[285] The Crusades and their aftermath likely had something to do with it. Either way, Pope Adrian IV broke the pattern when he made Barbarossa the newest Holy Roman Emperor, a position he would hold until his death.[286]

Lastly, let's look at the popes. While the popes did not reign over a specific geographic location, they did hold a lot of power in Europe. In the 1100s, the only way to get to Heaven was to be a good Catholic. This meant listening to the pope.

Pope Eugenius III called for the Second Crusade and lived to see it started and finished. After him, there were Anastasius IV, Adrian IV, and Alexander III.[287] Talks of a new Crusade were in the works in the 1180s, but Alexander III took no formal action to call for a Crusade. It took three more popes before Gregory VIII officially called for the Third Crusade in 1187.[288]

Europe and the Holy Land went through more changes than can be counted in the roughly thirty years between the Second and Third Crusades. Even with all the ever-changing monarchs and various problems in Europe, the pope and several heads of state in Europe agreed on one thing—it was once again time to retake Jerusalem.

---

[283] Comyn, Robert B. *The History of the Western Empire: From Its Restoration by Charlemagne to the Accession of Charles V.* W.H Allen & Company: Oxford, 1841.

[284] Kelly, J. N. D., and Michael J. Walsh. *A Dictionary of Popes.* Oxford University Press, 2010. https://www.oxfordreference.com/view/10.1093/acref/9780199295814.001.0001/acref-9780199295814.

[285] Duggan, Anne J. *Queens and Queenship in Medieval Europe.* The Boydell Press: London, 2002.

[286] Comyn, Robert B. *The History of the Western Empire: From Its Restoration by Charlemagne to the Accession of Charles V.*

[287] Kelly, J. N. D., and Michael J. Walsh. *A Dictionary of Popes.*

[288] Cartwright, Mark. "Third Crusade." *World History Encyclopedia*, August 27, 2018, https://www.worldhistory.org/Third_Crusade/.

Third Crusade: The King's Crusade (1189-1192)

As with the Second Crusade, the Third Crusade was prompted by non-Christians taking back land in the Holy Land. This time, instead of Edessa, the "victim" was Jerusalem. The perpetrator was Saladin, who took Damascus in 1174, Aleppo in 1183, and finally Jerusalem in 1187. After taking these lands and others, Saladin would hold European soldiers for ransom or sell them into slavery.[289] This was more than the conquerors of Edessa had done. The pope and much of the European monarchy were quickly upset and ready to take up arms against Saladin and his troops.

Pope Gregory VIII officially called for the Third Crusade in October 1187. The main goal of this Crusade was to take back Jerusalem. The pope also wanted the Crusaders to bring back religious relics from Jerusalem—some that may or may not have existed there, like the True Cross.[290] However, it took another two years before any monarchs agreed to join the cause.

The first monarch to join was Frederik Barbarossa, by this time the King of Germany, the King of Italy, and the Holy Roman Emperor. He and his army (which totaled between 10,000 and 20,000 men) left for the Holy Land from Germany in Mary 1189.[291] Other smaller armies would later join them, adding a few thousand more men to the fight.[292] Modern-day historians do not know exactly how many men were in the army by the time they reached the Holy Land.

Frederick's army traveled through mainland Europe (primarily the Balkans) before reaching the Byzantine Empire. Along the way, they were given more troops and supplies from various European leaders. They did not face much conflict. The army's biggest battles, which only lasted a few days at most, were perpetrated by Europeans who thought the army had disrespected them in one way or another.[293] The real problems came when the army finally reached Turkish territory.

---

[289] Cartwright, Mark. "Third Crusade."

[290] Cartwright, Mark. "Third Crusade."

[291] Loud, G. A. *The Crusade of Frederick Barbarossa: The History of the Expedition of the Emperor Frederick and Related Texts.* Ashgate Publishing: Surrey, 2010.

[292] Kongstam, Angus. *Historical Atlas of the Crusades.* Facts on File: New York, USA, 2002.

[293] Freed, John. *Frederick Barbarossa: The Prince and the Myth.* Yale University Press: New Haven, CT, 2016.

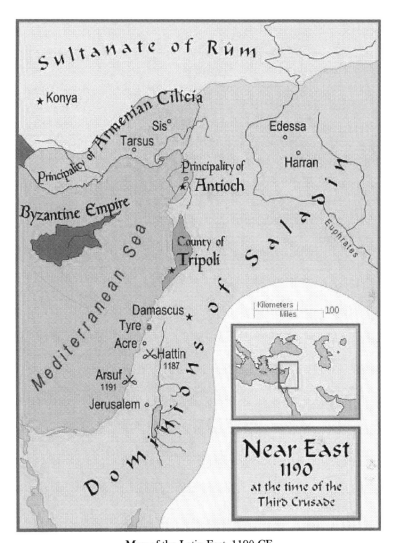

Map of the Latin East, 1190 CE
Mapmaster. World History Encyclopedia, CC BY-SA, August 27, 2018,
https://www.worldhistory.org/image/9121/map-of-the-latin-east-1190-ce/.

The Battle of Philomelion was the first major battle of the Third Crusade. This battle pitted about 10,000 Turks against 2,000 Crusaders. Unbelievably, the Crusaders won, taking light losses and killing about half of the Turkish army. Next, the Crusaders went to the Turk's capital city of Iconium. Barbarossa sacked the city for its supplies and killed another several thousand Turks.[294] Things were set to continue to go well for the

---

[294] Loud, G. A. *The Crusade of Frederick Barbarossa: The History of the Expedition of the*

Crusaders before tragedy struck.

On June 10, 1190, Barbarossa died after either falling from his horse, drowning, or both. Historians dispute the cause of death but not when it happened or what happened afterward. After Barbarossa's death, many members of his army felt disheartened and left the Crusade. Only about 5,000 men stayed to travel to Antioch in the Holy Land, led by Barbarossa's son, Frederick of Swabia. However, once in Antioch, many of the troops died due to illness.[295] The few remaining men continued to travel through the Holy Land.

Eventually, the army made it to the Seljuk capital. They sacked it and killed almost 10,000 Turks through various battles.[296] However, the goal of the Third Crusade was to take Jerusalem. Neither of the Fredericks were able to do so. This left the rest of the Third Crusade up to two other monarchs.

These two monarchs were Richard I of England (Richard the Lionheart) and Philip II of France. Around the same time Barbarossa had left on the Third Crusade, England and France were at war with each other. This war did not end until January 1188. Almost immediately after this war was done, Philip II and the then-king of England, Henry II, agreed to go on a Crusade.[297] However, Henry II died in July before either party could do much to organize an army.[298]

Richard I of England
https://picryl.com/media/richard-i-of-england-7636dd.

Emperor Frederick and Related Texts.
[295] Loud, G. A. *The Crusade of Frederick Barbarossa....*
[296] Loud, G. A. *The Crusade of Frederick Barbarossa....*
[297] Freed, John. *Frederick Barbarossa: The Prince and the Myth.*
[298] Oehring, Chris. "King Henry II." Historic UK, n.d., https://www.historic-uk.com/HistoryUK/HistoryofEngland/King-Henry-II-of-England/.

Philip I of France
https://commons.wikimedia.org/wiki/File:Saint-%C3%689vre_-_Philip_I_of_France.jpg

Richard I began raising funds for the Third Crusade once he was coronated. Philip II did the same, calling it a "Saladin Tithe."[299] Richard I and his troops left to fight in early 1190, meeting up with Philip II in July 1190 and joining forces. The two stayed together for only a short time before the English army left for Sicily and the French to Genoa.[300] These places were more or less pit stops on the way to the Holy Land.

In May 1191, Richard's army took the island of Cyprus, which was technically a part of the Byzantine Empire being ruled by rebels under the command of Isaac Komnenos. Even though this was a great land grab, it was not a major battle. The first major battle for Richard and Philip was the Siege of Acre in June 1191. The two armies captured the city within a month and executed about 2,000 prisoners of war.[301]

Around the same time, Richard sold Cyprus to the Knights Templars to support the cause. The island was then ruled by Guy of Lusignan. After the battle, in August, Philip returned to France to deal with more personal political problems.[302] This left only one king to finish the King's Crusade.

---

[299] Freed, John. *Frederick Barbarossa: The Prince and the Myth.*

[300] Painter, Sidney. "II. THE THIRD CRUSADE: RICHARD THE LIONHEARTED AND PHILIP AUGUSTUS" In A History of the Crusades, Volume 2: The Later Crusades, 1189-1311 edited by Robert Lee Wolff, Harry W. Hazard and Kenneth Meyer Setton, 45-86. Philadelphia: University of Pennsylvania Press, 1962. https://doi.org/10.9783/9781512819564-009.

[301] Cartwright, Mark. "Third Crusade."

[302] Cartwright, Mark. "Third Crusade."

In September, the remains of the crusading armies attacked Arsuf, followed by a brief rest in Jaffa. Jaffa was an important port city that supplied Jerusalem with everything their defending armies would need. Richard's army was in view of Jerusalem—but did not fight. Richard was a great military strategist and figured he would not be able to win because of the heavy hits the crusading armies had taken recently.[303] However, the Crusade wasn't over yet.

A Muslim army attacked Jaffa in July 1192 and successfully took the city. Richard went to fight and won back the city again in August. However, in October, Richard was also forced to leave the Crusade to deal with political problems in England.[304] With no more kings left in the King's Crusade, the battle was over. The Crusaders had gained Jaffa but had never so much as attacked Jerusalem. Once again, the Crusaders had failed their mission.

Fourth Crusade: The Unholy Crusade

There were about ten years of relative peace between the Third and Fourth Crusades. Several shifts in leadership in Europe occurred during these ten years, as Barbarossa had died in the Third Crusade. Henry II of Champagne was also made the new King of Jerusalem. As king, he extended a truce with the Sultan of Egypt, Al-Aziz Uthman.[305] This gave certain protections to both Christians and Muslims in the area.

There were also some shifts in leadership in the Holy Land. About a year after the Third Crusade ended, Saladin died. He had several heirs, so his lands were divided five ways via various relatives. This was done peacefully without any interference from the Europeans until 1197 when there was a minor German Crusade.[306] This was not considered the Fourth Crusade, as it was called for by the Holy Roman Emperor, not the pope.[307]

This German Crusade only lasted about a year, starting in 1197 and ending in mid-1198. Its goal was to take back land and kill as many Muslims as possible while doing so. In the end, the Germans took back

---

[303] Cartwright, Mark. "Third Crusade."

[304] Cartwright, Mark. "Third Crusade."

[305] Kedar, Benjamin Z. *Urbs Capta: The Fourth Crusade and its Consequences.* Lethielleux: Paris, 2005.

[306] Kedar, Benjamin Z. *Urbs Capta: The Fourth Crusade and its Consequences.*

[307] Norwich, John J. *A Short History of Byzantium.* Vintage Books: New York, 1997.

some land near Gibelet and Tripoli. However, they never took Jerusalem or any of the major cities of the first three Crusades.[308] They did, however, ruin the truce between the King of Jerusalem and the Sultan of Egypt.

While this seems like it would have called for another Crusade, there was a new pope with bigger issues in Europe weighing him down. Pope Innocent III began his papacy in 1198. At this time, France and England were back at war with one another, and turmoil was building in the Holy Land.[309] So, on August 15, 1198, the new pope issued the *Post miserabile,* a new papal bull that would call for a Crusade. This Crusade was meant to take back land in the Holy Land and bring the European leaders back together by turning their forces to helping God and giving them a common enemy outside of Europe.[310]

Pope Innocent III
https://picryl.com/media/innocent-iii.

---

[308] Loud, G. A. "The German Crusade of 1197-1198." White Rose Research Online, 2015, https://eprints.whiterose.ac.uk/82933/.

[309] Runciman, Steven. *A History of the Crusades: The Kingdom of Acre and the Later Crusades, Volume III.* Cambridge University Press: Cambridge, 1954.

[310] Madden, Thomas F. *The Fourth Crusade: Event, Aftermath, and Perceptions: Papers from the Sixth Conference of the Society for the Study of the Crusades and the Latin East in Istanbul, Turkey.* Routledge: London, 2008.

As with the other Crusades, it took years for the pope and various monarchs to assemble an army. Crusaders were collected from all over Europe, but a majority were from France. These troops started their campaign in October 1202. The plan was to head to Cairo, Egypt, the capital of the Ayyubid Sultanate.[311] If all went as the pope hoped, the European monarchs would befriend each other and take Cairo along the way.

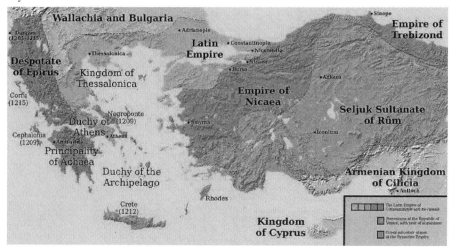

Byzantine Empire 1204
LatinEmpire. World History Encyclopedia, CC BY-SA, January 30, 2018, https://www.worldhistory.org/image/8048/division-of-the-byzantine-empire-1204-ce/.

One of the first major battles of the Fourth Crusade was at Zara in November 1202. The Crusaders won this battle and took the city. Reinforcements arrived in May 1203. They then continued to Constantinople and began to sack the city in April 1204. Soon after, the Crusaders won this battle and made Count Baldwin IX of Flanders the new Emperor of Constantinople.[312] The pope was unaware that this was happening and was shocked when he heard the news. However, he eventually came to terms with it and recognized Baldwin IX as a true leader.[313] Baldwin IX would from then on be known as Baldwin I, the first

---

[311] Hughes, Philip. *History of the Church: Vol. II: The Church in the World: The Church Created: Augustine to Aquinas.* A&C Black: London, 1979.

[312] "Fourth Crusade Timeline." *World History Encyclopedia*, 2023, https://www.worldhistory.org/timeline/Fourth_Crusade/.

[313] Britannica, T. Editors of Encyclopedia. "Baldwin I." *Encyclopedia Britannica*, January 1, 2023. https://www.britannica.com/biography/Baldwin-I-Byzantine-emperor

Latin emperor of Constantinople.

King Baldwin I created a new local government for Constantinople to Westernize it, replacing the government that was previously set up.[314] So, with Constantinople under the leadership of a good Christian king, the Fourth Crusade was over.

The Crusaders once again failed their original objective of taking Cairo, not getting militarily or even geographically close. To make things hurt even more, Jerusalem was still under the control of the Muslims. But the Crusaders' takeover of Constantinople softened the blow. With the quest for Jerusalem and the fact that Muslims lived in other lands the pope wanted, another Crusade was always around the corner.

Children's Crusade

The Children's Crusade is probably the most famous of the non-numbered Crusades. However, it's not famous for its success but for the fact that it was allowed to happen in the first place. The Children's Crusade is exactly what it sounds like. Tens of thousands of adults and children went on a crusade to the Holy Land. The general thought was, "Who would attack children?" As it turns out, sending children to fight in a war is not a good idea.

In 1212, Stephen of Cloyes claimed to be divinely inspired. God had given him the idea that children should be allowed to fight in the Crusades. To spread the word and collect children fighters for his cause, Stephen preached his message far and wide. Eventually, he assembled upwards of thirty thousand children and adult Crusaders. Stephen was many things: charismatic, a leader, and twelve years old.[315]

Around the same time Stephen was assembling his army, another boy named Nicholas in Germany was doing the same. Eventually, these boys and their armies came together. Historians are not sure exactly how many children were between the two armies, but most estimates suggest around 30,000.[316] As far as historians know, this Crusade was not organized by any clergy members. The Crusade was also not sanctioned by the pope, which

---

[314] Britannica, T. Editors of Encyclopedia. "Baldwin I." *Encyclopedia Britannica*, January 1, 2023.

[315] Blakemore, Erin. "The Disastrous Time Tens of Thousands of Children Tried to Start a Crusade." History. A&E Television Networks, April 8, 2019, https://www.history.com/news/the-disastrous-time-tens-of-thousands-of-children-tried-to-start-a-crusade.

[316] "Children's Crusade 1212: The Strange & Confusing Children's Crusade 1212." *Medieval Chronicles*, 2023, https://www.medievalchronicles.com/the-crusades/childrens-crusade/.

is why it is not a numbered Crusade.

Around July, the children left on their Crusade. Various sources say they stopped at different towns, visited with different adults, and more. However, historians can agree that when the children reached Genoa in August, all but 7,000 children had either died or gone back home.[317] The children were not met with enemies. They never even made it to the Holy Land. They simply died because it was an army of children led by other children—which was bound to result in failure.

The children continued to travel for several months before finally giving up and agreeing to head home. Two seemingly helpful merchants from Marseilles offered the children a ride home on their seven ships. Sadly, two of these ships sank, killing all the children onboard. Maybe even sadder, the other five ships landed in Northern Africa, where the surviving children were sold into slavery.[318] This saw the end of the Children's Crusade. From then on, children were not allowed to go on a Crusade.

Fifth Crusade

Unlike the previous two, the Fifth Crusade does not have an extra title that makes it sound like an action movie. Like the previous Crusades, the goal of the Fifth Crusade was to take back the Holy Land by capturing Jerusalem and defeating the Ayyubid Sultanate. Spoiler alert: things didn't go well for the Crusaders again.

So, what got the pope so heated this time? Well, after Saladin's death, his land was divided among several family members. In the roughly fifteen years between Crusades, some of these family members also died and left their lands to others. Fast forward to 1200 when Saladin's brother, al-Malik al-Adil Sayf ad-Din Abu-Bakr Ahmed ibn Najm ad-Din Ayyub, more commonly called Al-Adil I, inherited land and became the new Sultan of Egypt. Several years before this, he was also made the Emir of Damascus.[319] Pope Innocent III, who had called the Fourth Crusade, was less than happy to see the Holy Land continuously led by non-Christians.

---

[317] Smitha, Frank E. "More Crusades and Heretics, 1144 to 1212." F. Smitha, 2018, http://www.fsmitha.com/h3/eu09.htm.

[318] Smitha, Frank E. "More Crusades and Heretics, 1144 to 1212."

[319] Petry, Carl F. *The Cambridge History of Egypt, Vol I: Islamic Egypt, 640-1517.* Cambridge University Press: Cambridge, 1997.

Pope Innocent III called for the Fifth Crusade in 1215. The main goal of this Crusade was still to get Jerusalem "back" under Christian control. However, the plan of attack was different. Instead of capturing totally unrelated cities like Cairo or going straight for Jerusalem, the Crusaders were supposed to sack Muslim-led countries in the Near East and Northern Africa.[320] The hope was that, by attacking many cities, the Ayyubid Sultanate would weaken and would be more likely to give up Jerusalem to the Crusaders.

The pope sent out preachers to once again recruit Crusaders by promising forgiveness of sins and indulgences for the Crusader's participation. After the outcome of the Children's Crusade, the pope only wanted adult men to fight. However, he allowed any adult man to join, whether or not he had military experience (so long as he wasn't a clergy member). If men did not want to join the fight, they could instead give money to the Church as a way to contribute to the Crusade. This would also lead to a remission of sins. The recruitment efforts worked well this time. Most of the fighters came from Germany, England, Italy, the Holy Roman Empire, and Hungary.[321] As with the other Crusades, the recruitment took about two years to complete.

Pope Innocent III could not give the troops his send-off, as he died on July 16, 1216. Luckily (or not), he was succeeded by Pope Honorius III, who was ready to kick the Crusade into full gear.[322] He sent the troops on their way shortly after he took command, and the Fifth Crusade officially began in 1217.

The Fifth Crusade did not strike the Ayyubid Sultanate by surprise. Beginning in 1216, merchants left large cities. Al-Adil I began to collect his own forces in Syria and Egypt and near Damascus and Jerusalem.[323] After so many Crusades where the goal was to capture sites in either Egypt or Jerusalem, the Ayyubids knew where to best place their troops.

---

[320] Cartwright, Mark. "Fifth Crusade." *World History Encyclopedia*. September 6, 2018, https://www.worldhistory.org/Fifth_Crusade/.

[321] Cartwright, Mark. "Fifth Crusade."

[322] Cartwright, Mark. "Fifth Crusade."

[323] Setton, Kenneth. *A History of the Crusades, Vol. VI.* University of Wisconsin Press: Madison, 1969.

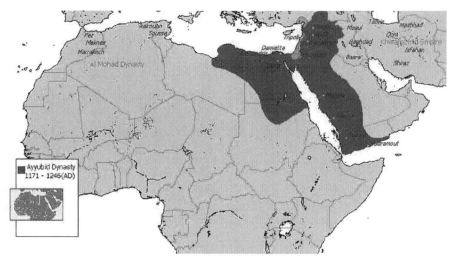

Map of the Ayyubid Empire
https://www.worldhistory.org/image/9203/map-of-the-ayyubid-empire/

The Crusaders crossed the Jordan River in November 1217, only a short distance from Damascus. However, the Crusaders didn't attack right away. Instead, they made camp in Acre, which was still held by the Christians. In December, the battles finally started. Both sides were competent and well-matched, but in the end, the Crusaders were defeated and forced to return to Acre to save their remaining troops.[324]

In May 1218, the first Crusaders made their way to Damietta, a port city in Egypt. These first troops were met with others soon after, and enough men were ready to fight by June. However, since the Crusaders came in waves but did not attack right away, the Egyptians had time to prepare. They set up defenses as well as they could around Damietta, including the famous Tower of Damietta.[325] The Siege of Damietta began in June 1218 and continued for years, with heavy losses on both sides. In November 1219, the Crusaders finally conquered the city.[326]

---

[324] Fulton, Michael S. *Artillery in the Era of the Crusades*. Brill Publications: Paderborn, Germany, 2018.

[325] Runciman, Steven. *A History of the Crusades, Vol. III: The Kingdom of Acre and the Later Crusades*.

[326] "Fifth Crusade Timeline." *World History Encyclopedia*, 2023, https://www.worldhistory.org/timeline/Fifth_Crusade/.

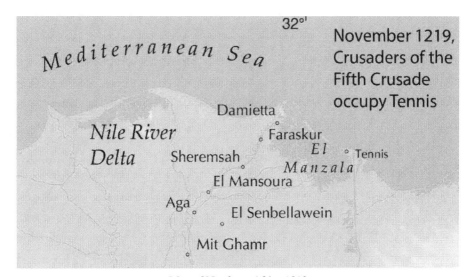

Map of Northern Africa 1219
Wikimedia Commons, n.d., CC BY-SA 4.0,
https://commons.wikimedia.org/wiki/File:TennisEgypt1219.png.

The Crusade was far from over after the capture of Damietta. For months, the Crusaders were attacked by Muslims. All the while, both sides lost hundreds or thousands more people. Even with all this, the soldiers got bored and rowdy. They needed something else to do. The next target was Mansoura, another city in Egypt. The attacks here began in late summer 1221. However, the Crusaders were quickly defeated when they faced the known enemy (the Muslims) and a surprise enemy— the flooded Nile River. Faced with heavy losses, the army was forced to surrender on August 28, 1221.[327] With that, the Fifth Crusade was over.

In the end, the Crusaders still held Damietta, something of a consolation prize. However, they again failed to take any other major cities in Egypt or even get close to Jerusalem. The Crusades were not paying off. When would the popes stop calling for them? Well, not for at least 100 more years, bringing us to the Sixth Crusade.

Sixth Crusade: The Crusade of Emperor Frederick II

As the title suggests, this Crusade was led by the Holy Roman Emperor Frederik II. As most Crusades went, the goal was to take back Jerusalem, which had now been under Muslim control for decades.[328]

---

[327] "Fifth Crusade Timeline."
[328] "Sixth Crusade Timeline." *World History Encyclopedia*, 2023, https://www.worldhistory.org/timeline/Sixth_Crusade/.

Would this Crusade work out? Stay tuned to find out.

Some historians see the Sixth Crusade as an extension of the Fifth Crusade, while others do not. Either way, it hinged on Frederick II's involvement. He was involved with the Sixth Crusade but not the Fifth, as he was focusing on his power in Europe. With the Fifth Crusade proving to be an absolute failure and having gained more power in Europe, Frederick II was more ready to fight in the Sixth Crusade.[329] Besides, as the Holy Roman Emperor, many— including the pope—saw it as his duty to fight in the Crusades.

Before Frederick started with a new Crusade, he wanted to solidify his power in the Holy Land. In August 1225, he married Isabella II, the daughter of John of Brienne. She was made Queen of Jerusalem later that month, making Frederick II the new King of Jerusalem. However, this was a marriage by proxy, which meant the couple hadn't actually met. They did not have a wedding together until November 1227, after the Sixth Crusade had already begun.[330] Even though the couple had not met, the marriage by proxy still made Frederick II a valid King of Jerusalem, for better or worse.

For most of the 1220s, Frederick II had been talking about going on a Crusade but never made much of a move to organize any troops. In 1227, he was motivated to assemble an army, as the pope threatened to excommunicate him if he did not. So, by the summer, he was ready to travel. However, many of his men died of disease, and Frederick II himself became ill before they made it anywhere. Even though he had tried to go on a Crusade, he was still excommunicated.[331] He remade his plans for a Crusade to win back favor with the pope.

Frederick II finally set off successfully by ship in June 1228, reaching Acre in September. He was still excommunicated at this time. Even worse, his wife, the Queen of Jerusalem, had died in childbirth just months earlier. This made their son the new King of Jerusalem, stripping Frederick II of the title.[332] Both the loss of his title and excommunication

---

[329] Cartwright, Mark. "Sixth Crusade." *World History Encyclopedia*, September 10, 2018, https://www.worldhistory.org/Sixth_Crusade/.

[330] Van Cleve, Thomas C. *The Emperor Frederick II of Hohenstaufen, Immutator Mundi*. Clarendon Press: London, 1972.

[331] Schrader, Helena P. "The Knights Templar and the Emperor: The 6th Crusade." Defender of Jerusalem, n.d., https://www.defenderofjerusalem.com/kt---6th-crusade.html.

[332] Schrader, Helena P. "The Knights Templar and the Emperor: The 6th Crusade."

ruined his reputation. The people in Jerusalem were less likely to see him as a leader. People left his army in droves due to this and other political factors. By the time he was ready to fight, he didn't have an army large enough to be much of a threat to the Muslims.

Instead of fighting, he wanted to negotiate. The Crusaders had previously proposed a truce with Al-Kamil, the Muslim leader. Frederick II referenced this and made threats (bluffing all the way) to strike a deal. Somehow, this worked, and Frederick II and Al-Kamil made a treaty that was finished in February 1229.[333] Even though the treaty was not signed there, it would be referred to as the Treaty of Jaffa. This is because Jaffa was one of the cities the Crusaders earned in the treaty. The Crusaders (and Frederick II) also got Bethlehem, Nazareth, Toron, and parts of Jerusalem. However, the Muslims kept the Temple Mount in Jerusalem and the Dome of the Rock. A ten-year truce was also included. There may have been other land deals involved with this treaty. However, historians do not know, as there are no surviving copies of the treaty.[334]

With the signing of the treaty, the Sixth Crusade was over. The Crusaders didn't exactly win this Crusade, but they did not lose, either. Ultimately, the Sixth Crusade ended in a compromise. On the bright side, this was the least violent and bloody of all the Crusades so far. With several more Crusades left to go, the peace could not or would not be forever.

Seventh Crusade: King Louis IX's Crusade

Historians debate on when the Seventh Crusade began. Plans for the Crusade began in 1244, but no battles occurred for several years after. However, historians can agree on why it happened and who was involved. By the 1240s, the ten-year truce written in the Treaty of Jaffa was well over. The members of the Ayyubid Sultanate, led by Al-Salih starting in 1245, began taking back lands in the Holy Land. This upset not only the pope but also King Louis IX of France. In 1244, the king vowed to go on a Crusade to attack Egypt.[335] However, like the other Crusades, it took

---

[333] Van Cleve, Thomas C. "The Crusade of Frederick II." Library at the University of Wisconsin-Madison, 1969, https://images.library.wisc.edu/History/EFacs/HistCrus/0001/0002/reference/history.crustwo.i0026.pdf.

[334] Van Cleve, Thomas C. "The Crusade of Frederick II."

[335] "Seventh Crusade Timeline." *World History Encyclopedia*, 2023, https://www.worldhistory.org/timeline/Seventh_Crusade/.

several years to assemble a large enough army to leave Europe.

King Louis IX took serious measures to fund his Crusade. For years, he raised taxes to collect money. However, that wasn't enough. Already known for hating the Jews, he commanded that all Jews leave France in 1248. When they left, he took their property and anything they left behind. He also prepared for the journey by collecting and storing goods on the island of Cyprus, which would be a mid-point for the traveling army.[336] After all this, the army was ready to head off in the summer of '48.

About 10,000 Crusaders set off by ship in August 1248 towards Egypt and Northern Africa. They soon stopped in Cyprus to collect supplies and wait for more troops to join them, staying there for almost a year. In the meantime, Louis IX wrote threatening letters to the Sultan of Egypt, Al-Salih, warning him that he wanted to take Muslim-held cities in Egypt and Northern Africa and eventually retake Jerusalem.[337] This was a petty move on Louis IX's part and an all-around bad idea. It let the Sultan know the Crusaders were coming and gave them months to prepare for an attack.

The Crusaders finally landed in Egypt in June 1249. By waiting in Cyprus, they had amassed another 10,000-plus fighters. However, in that time, the Egyptians had made fortifications in Damietta. As it turned out, Damietta was one of the first places the Crusaders attacked. They captured the city within a month, showing the Egyptians' fortifications had been in vain, as they would now stand to help the Crusaders.[338] With one city down and many more to go, the Crusade was far from over.

Louis IX waited for more reinforcements before taking on another major battle. The only problem was that it took months for these reinforcements to arrive. When they finally arrived in October, the Nile was a bit flooded. His advisors told him not to press forward until after the waters fully receded, but he did not listen. His troops left Damietta for Cairo in November 1249. Conveniently or not, Al-Salih died due to illness in the same month. He was replaced by the Bahri commander

---

[336] Cartwright, Mark. "Seventh Crusade." *World History Encyclopedia*, September 12, 2018, https://www.worldhistory.org/Seventh_Crusade/.
[337] Cartwright, Mark. "Seventh Crusade."
[338] Cartwright, Mark. "Seventh Crusade."

Fakhr al-Din, who continued the fight against the Crusaders.[339]

After about a month of travel, the Crusaders made it to their next destination, a camp near Mansoura. This place had natural and man-made fortifications meant to keep them at bay—not to mention angry Egyptians. The two sides battled for weeks, with much progress on either side. The Crusaders tried to go behind the camp. One of the Crusade leaders, Robert of Artois, attacked too early. While they killed Fakhr al-Din, the Crusaders faced much heavier losses than the Muslims.[340]

Soon after, the Muslims went on the counterattack, hitting the Crusaders while they were down. The attacks came in waves. This would have given the Crusaders the time to resupply—if they had been able to get any supplies. Threatened with disease and starvation, the Crusaders retreated to Damietta. However, not all of them made it, including Louis IX, who was captured in April 1250. He was released a month later after paying a ransom of 400,000 livre tournois and agreeing to give up Damietta.[341] With this, the Seventh Crusade came to an end, proving to be a serious loss for the Crusaders and Louis IX personally, both with his physical health and the bankbook of France.

Eighth Crusade

The Eighth Crusade was a long-awaited extension of the Seventh Crusade. This one was also led by King Louis IX. However, it was now 1270—twenty years after the Seventh Crusade.[342] By this time, Louis IX was fifty-six and had much more experience in warfare. He had also spent years in Northern Africa and the Holy Land after the Seventh Crusade.[343] Louis IX was much more prepared for this Crusade, but would that mean it would go better than the last?

Louis IX officially recommitted to the Crusade in 1267 but took several years to amass the forces to fight. Because of this, the troops did not leave until July 1290. The goal of this Crusade was to take Tunis, a city in Northern Africa. The plan was to sail there, set up camp, and wait

---

[339] Cartwright, Mark. "Seventh Crusade."
[340] Cartwright, Mark. "Seventh Crusade."
[341] Cartwright, Mark. "Seventh Crusade."
[342] "Eighth Crusade Timeline." *World History Encyclopedia*, 2023, https://www.worldhistory.org/timeline/Eighth_Crusade/.
[343] Levron, J. "Louis IX." *Encyclopedia Britannica*, January 13, 2023. https://www.britannica.com/biography/Louis-IX.

for other European reinforcements. However, while waiting, many French soldiers came down with dysentery, including Louis XI himself.[344]

Shortly after falling ill, Louis IX died on August 25, 1270. Since he was the one leading the Crusade, his death led to the end of the Seventh Crusade.[345] All in all, the Eighth Crusade was a complete failure. So many Crusaders died without any major battles or breakthroughs—all because of disease. One would think the kings and pope would begin to lose the allure of the Crusades, but not before one more major endeavor.

Ninth Crusade: Lord Edward's Crusade

The Ninth Crusade was the last of the major Church-endorsed Crusades. Some historians see it as an extension of the Eighth Crusade, as it started shortly afterward. However, others do not count it as an extension because it was organized and led by different people, namely Lord Edward of England (future King Edward I).

King Edward I
https://commons.wikimedia.org/wiki/File:EdwardI-Cassell.jpg

---

[344] Beck, Elias. "Eighth Crusade." History Crunch, November 17, 2019, https://www.historycrunch.com/eighth-crusade.html#/.
[345] Beck, Elias. "Eighth Crusade."

Lord Edward assembled his troops, left Europe, and arrived in Acre in May 1271. However, he only had about 1,000 troops. This was one of the lowest-populated Crusades, even compared with "unofficial" Crusades. The goal was to fight the Muslims in the area. He first fought them by sea and later moved to land battles.[346]

To help with the land battles, Edward attempted to ally with the Mongols. By September 1271, the alliance had been made, and the Mongols agreed to strike the Muslims in the Holy Land. In October, Crusader-Mongol forces attacked Qaqun, areas in Syria, and land near Aleppo. With the help of the Mongols, the Crusaders won many of these battles. Sometime near the end of October/early November, the Mongols left to get back to their own business.[347]

After a few more battles, with the Crusaders winning more than they lost, Edward moved to naval battles. He won one major naval battle. With his spirits boosted from the recent win, he began making a truce with the Muslims who controlled the Holy Land. A truce was made and a treaty completed in May 1272.[348] Even though the fighting was over and the Crusaders had won many of the battles, the Crusaders did not complete the goal of the Crusade. They did not take Jerusalem, and Edward had given up hope that they could, as his army was simply not big enough.[349] With this truce and treaty, the Ninth Crusade was more or less done.

Shortly after the truce was made, Edwards was forced to leave the Holy Land and return to England after news that his father had died. He arrived in England much later and was not crowned King of England until August 1274.[350]

Conclusion

Altogether, the nine major Crusades took about 200 years to complete. The battles spanned all over Europe, the Near East, the Middle East, and Northern Africa (including Egypt). Pope after pope had their own agendas. The wars were both politically and religiously

---

[346] Beck, Elias. "Ninth Crusade." History Crunch, June 22, 2021, https://www.historycrunch.com/ninth-crusade.html#/.

[347] Runciman, Steven. *A History of the Crusades, Vol. III: The Kingdom of Acre and the Later Crusades.*

[348] Beck, Elias. "Ninth Crusade."

[349] Baldwin, Philip B. *Pope Gregory X and the Crusades.* The Boydell Press: Suffolk, UK, 2014.

[350] Beck, Elias. "Ninth Crusade."

motivated. Of course, the Crusaders weren't the only hostile party, with the Muslims starting their fair share of battles. One noticeable difference is that the Muslims did not invade mainland Europe during this time. In this way, they were nearly always the defenders.

None of the later Crusades were especially successful. While treaties and truces were made and broken, the Crusaders never took back Jerusalem or any other major areas in the Holy Land. The Church eventually accepted their losses and focused their efforts elsewhere. In the upcoming chapters, we'll look at some of what the Church was doing shortly before, during, and after the Crusades.

Chapter 9: The Reconquista (722–1300s)

For this chapter, we must go back a little in Europe's history. We discussed how, throughout the Crusades, Europeans went into Muslim-held lands to fight. However, one exception to this was the Iberian Peninsula (modern-day Spain and Portugal). Beginning in the eighth century CE, Muslim invaders, mostly Moors from Northern Africa, began fighting and taking lands in the Iberian Peninsula. This continued for about 700 years, from before the First Crusade to after the last Crusade. The Reconquista, then, was an attempt to reconquer the lands that the Europeans (mostly Visigoths) had lost to the invading Muslims.[351] Because the Reconquista period lasted for so long, this chapter will gloss over the timeline, focusing on important battles, main players, and how Christians were treated during it all.

Muslim Interest in the Iberian Peninsula

The Europeans wanted to fight for control of the Iberian Peninsula because it was their homeland. They had lived on the land for centuries. The Muslims seemingly came from nowhere. So, why did the Muslims come to the Iberian Peninsula in the first place?

It all started in the late 600s. (Remember, this was before the Crusades when the Muslims controlled much of Northern Africa and some parts of

---

[351] Cartwright, Mark. "Reconquista." *World History Encyclopedia*, October 5, 2018, https://www.worldhistory.org/Reconquista/.

the Holy Land.) By the early 700s, Musa ibn Nusayr was made governor of the western Muslim lands. During his leadership, he annexed most of North Africa, spreading Islam along the way. Throughout this time, he met with Count Julian, the leader of Ceuta. The two agreed to invade the Iberian Peninsula to take land and spread their respective religions. Count Julian was a Christian, just not the same type of Christian as the Visigoths living in the Iberian Peninsula.[352] The difference was that the Visigoths believed in the Trinity (Trinitarian), while Count Julian and the Muslims did not.

Visigothic Hispania and its divisions from 625 to 711
https://commons.wikimedia.org/wiki/File:Hispania_700_AD.PNG.

In 711, these combined forces entered the Iberian Peninsula. Most of the army was made up of Muslims. The battles against the Visigoths were usually quick, with the Muslims winning most often. It took about seven years for the invaders to conquer the Iberian Peninsula.[353] The Christians

---

[352] Vernet Gines, Juan and Viguera, Maria J. "Muslim Spain." The *Encyclopedia Britannica*, 2023, https://www.britannica.com/place/Spain/The-Almoravids.

[353] "Muslim Spain (711-1492)" BBC, September 4, 2009, https://www.bbc.co.uk/religion/religions/islam/history/spain_1.shtml#:~:text=In%20711%20Muslim%20forces%20invaded,1492%20when%20Granada%20was%20conquered.

lived under Muslim rule for several years before putting a full-force effort into fighting back and reclaiming their land.

The Beginning: The Battle of Covadonga (722)

Many historians point to the Battle of Covadonga as the beginning of the Reconquista. First, we need some background information to understand how the Muslims and Christians got to this point.

As noted, before the Muslims arrived in the Iberian Peninsula, the area was primarily controlled by the Visigoths.[354] These people were sometimes called Berbers or Moors. By the early 700s, the Muslims had almost total control over the Iberian Peninsula and had established the Al-Andalus Emirate.[355]

Umayyad Hispania at its Greatest Extent in 719
Al-Andalus732.jpg:Q4767211492~commonswiki (talk · contribs)EmiratoDeCórdoba910.svg:rowanwindwhistler (talk · contribs)derivative work: rowanwindwhistler, CC0, via Wikimedia Commons
<u>https://commons.wikimedia.org/wiki/File:Al-Andalus732.svg</u>

---

[354] Cartwright, Mark. "Reconquista."

[355] Beuck, Charles. "718/722: The Battle of Covadonga as the Beginning of the Reconquista in the Iberian Peninsula." *Medium*, January 3, 2021, <u>https://medium.com/traveling-through-history/718-722-the-battle-of-covadonga-as-the-beginning-of-the-reconquista-in-the-iberian-peninsula-e3fae9a8942b</u>.

When the Muslims took control, the Visigoth civilians were given two options: submit to the Muslims and live under their rule or leave.[356] Non-Muslims were taxed at a higher rate than Muslims. This was an annoyance the non-Muslims had dealt with for years, but the issue came to a head when the Emir Anbasa ibn Suhaym al-Kalbi raised taxes again.[357] This encouraged rebellions throughout the peninsula that would last for several years, eventually resulting in the Battle of Covadonga.

The leadership of this battle and the preceding rebellions is attributed to Don Pelayo, the King of Asturias. While the Muslims and Europeans (mainly Visigoths) had been fighting for years, the Battle of Covadonga was the first major victory against the Muslims. After the battle, many Muslims retreated, only to be killed by Visigoth forces in the surrounding areas.[358] This win encouraged the Visigoths to keep fighting against the Muslims—which they would continue to do for the next 800 years.

Don Pelayo, King of Asturias
Luis de Madrazo y Kuntz, CC BY-SA 4.0 <https://creativecommons.org/licenses/by-sa/4.0>, via Wikimedia Commons
https://commons.wikimedia.org/wiki/File:Don_Pelavo,_rey_de_Asturias.jpg.

---

[356] Britannica, T. Editors of Encyclopedia. "Al-Andalus." *Encyclopedia Britannica*, July 9, 2019. https://www.britannica.com/place/Al-Andalus.

[357] Beuck, Charles. "718/722: The Battle of Covadonga as the Beginning of the Reconquista in the Iberian Peninsula."

[358] Beuck, Charles. "718/722: The Battle of Covadonga as the Beginning of the Reconquista in the Iberian Peninsula."

The following are some of the most important events of the Reconquista. During the years that are not listed, the Christians and Muslims were fighting on and off with each other, with no major wins or losses on either side. The following events are in chronological order.

Barcelona (985)

Barcelona was an important city to the Visigoths for hundreds of years before the Muslims arrived on the Iberian Peninsula. In 801, the Carolingian Franks gained control of the city and held it for almost 200 years before the Moors came to attack it.[359] Barcelona was an important port city, so having control over it would have given the Moors an advantage.

The Moors, led by al-Mansur (Chief Minister of the Caliphate of Cordoba), attacked the city in 985.[360] The Frankish king did little to help during or after the attack. Local leaders were left to protect Barcelona and other local areas. Even after the sack, the city was not ruled by the Moors. However, the people lived under the constant threat of attack for hundreds of years.[361]

It wasn't until the mid-900s that emissaries began to work with the caliphate to get protection for Barcelona and other cities in the Iberian Peninsula. Leaders from other cities tried to raid the Moors in the spirit of revenge; some raids worked, and some did not. Finally, in 1010, an agreement was made in Cordoba that the people of Barcelona would pay tribute to the Muslim princes.[362] These payments ensured the safety of the city and also set a precedent for how things would work for the Christians living in the Muslim-held territories from then on.

The Taifa Kingdoms

The Taifa kingdoms were small Muslim-ruled areas primarily located in the Iberian Peninsula. The periods in which the Taifa kingdoms held power are often referred to as the Taifa periods. There were three main Taifa periods within the Reconquista timeline.[363]

---

[359] Connell, Timothy J. and Rodriguez, Vicente. "History of Barcelona." The *Encyclopedia Britannica*, n.d., https://www.britannica.com/place/Barcelona/History.

[360] Connell, Timothy J. and Rodriguez, Vicente. "History of Barcelona."

[361] Armistead, Samuel G. and Gerli E. M. *Medieval Iberia*. Taylor and Francis: London, 2003.

[362] Armistead, Samuel G. and Gerli E. M. *Medieval Iberia*.

[363] Abbey, Ian. "Taifa." *World History Encyclopedia*, May 16, 2022, https://www.worldhistory.org/Taifa/.

The first Taifa period/kingdom started around 1031. In recent years, the Umayyad Caliphate had been in decline—fragmenting itself through infighting and arguments over succession. The Taifas were mainly territories that had once been fiefdoms or city-states. By 1030, there were somewhere between thirty to fifty Taifas in the Iberian Peninsula.[364] These Taifas had loose control over the people living in the Iberian Peninsula but control nonetheless.

The First Taifa Period

The first Taifa period lasted fifty to sixty years. Christian Europeans fought against the Taifas as hard as they had against previous Muslim-led governments. The Siege of Toledo in 1085 marked one of the Taifas' most serious defeats against Christian Spaniards, left by the King of Castile and Leon. The Taifas called for help from the Almoravids and successfully defeated the Castilians. However, the Almoravids decided to claim dominant rulership and absorbed the Taifas in the area. They had complete control by 1090.[365] With this, the first Taifa period ended.

The Second Taifa Period

The Almoravids ruled for about fifty years before the second Taifa period began around 1144. This time, it wasn't so much that the Taifas were independent but that they were conquered/absorbed by a new group—the Berber dynasty (also known as the Almohads).[366]

Beginning in the 1140s, the Berbers started to take over the Almoravids. Over the course of about thirty years, the Berbers took over more and more Taifas. By the 1170s, they controlled most of them.[367] However, like the last Taifa period, this one was not to last. The Christians were back and ready to fight again.

The battles started to ramp back up in the 1210s. In 1211, al-Nasir and his army fought against the European Christians. He eventually took Salvatierra, an important military location.[368] This posed another threat to the Church. (Remember, around this same time, the Children's Crusade

---

[364] Abbey, Ian. "Taifa."
[365] Abbey, Ian. "Taifa."
[366] Abbey, Ian. "Taifa."
[367] Abbey, Ian. "Taifa."
[368] Holt, Edward L. "Out of Many, One?: The Voice(s) in the Crusade Ideology of Las Navas de Tolosa." Medievalists, 2010, https://www.medievalists.net/2011/05/out-of-many-one-the-voices-in-the-crusade-ideology-of-las-navas-de-tolosa/.

was being assembled and getting ready to fight.) The pope had a lot on his plate, and al-Nasir wasn't making things any easier for him.

In response, Alfonso VIII of Castile and Pedro II of Aragon joined forces to fight against the Muslim armies in the Iberian Peninsula. They began assembling their forces in late 1211 and were ready to fight by May 1212. The Muslim army was prepared and tried to block passages to make travel more difficult for the Christian Europeans.[369]

Finally, on July 16, 1212, the two sides converged in the Battle of Las Navas de Tolosa. The battle was quick, with the Christian Europeans winning by a considerable margin. This single battle made way for the Christians to take back power in the Iberian Peninsula. The Almohad Taifa was defeated.[370]

The Taifas did not last long after the Battle of Las Navas de Tolosa. By the 1250s, most of the Taifas were under the control of Christian Europeans. Castile and Aragon held control over most of them. The only major remaining Taifa was Granada.[371]

The Third Taifa Period

By the 1230s, the Taifa of Granada had rebranded to the Emirate of Granada, also known as the Nasrid of Granada.[372] By this time, the rest of the Taifas had been destroyed, taken over, or otherwise disbanded. Granada was the last Taifa, and its power was the source of the third Taifa period. However, since it was one nation, historians rarely refer to Granada as a Taifa.

Muhammad ibn al-Ahmar established the Nasrid dynasty in about 1230. During the next two decades, he and his armies took more land. Eventually, they owned land covering the modern-day areas of Granada, Almeria, and Malaga.[373] The empire had its fair share of battles and more, but for the most part, it faced no major threats. This period of relative

---

[369] Holt, Edward L. "Out of Many, One?: The Voice(s) in the Crusade Ideology of Las Navas de Tolosa."

[370] Holt, Edward L. "Out of Many, One?: The Voice(s) in the Crusade Ideology of Las Navas de Tolosa."

[371] Abbey, Ian. "Taifa."

[372] Holt, P.M., Lambton, Ann K. S., et al. *The Cambridge History of Islam: Volume 2A: The Indian Sub-Continent, South-East Asia, Africa, and the Muslim West.* Cambridge University Press: Cambridge, 1977.

[373] Garcia-Arenal, Mercedes. "Granada." *Encyclopedia of Islam, Three.* Union Academy International: Brill, 2014.

peace lasted for about 200 years.

Muhammad I of Granada (in the red tunic).
https://commons.wikimedia.org/wiki/File:Muhammad_I_Granada_cropped_CSM_185_(187).jpg.

Things changed when the Christians began to conquer the area in the 1480s.[374] Starting in 1482, Isabella I of Castile and Ferdinand II of Aragon combined forced to attack the Emirate of Granada. This attack was provoked by smaller infighting between local Christians and Muslims.[375] However, once the monarchy got involved, the Iberian Peninsula was thrown into a full-blown war.

It all began when Granada attacked the Christian-held city of Zahara in December 1481, capturing the town and enslaving the people living there. In retaliation, the Christian Europeans, led by Aragon of Castile, took Alhama in April 1482.[376] With that, the Granada War began. It would continue for about ten years, with battles on and off.

---

[374] "Muslim Spain (711-1492)."

[375] Hillgarth, J.N. *The Spanish Kingdoms: 1250-1516. Volume II: 1410-1516, Castilian Hegemony.* Clarendon Press, Oxford University Press: Oxford, 1978.

[376] Hillgarth, J.N. *The Spanish Kingdoms: 1250-1516. Volume II: 1410-1516, Castilian Hegemony.*

Not all was peaceful in Granada before the war with the Spanish began. The area already faced power struggles as various groups and individuals fought for leadership. One of the people who made the most progress in his quest for power was Boabdil, the son of Abu'l-Hasan Ali, the Sultan of Granada. After many battles between Christians and Muslims, Boabdil named himself the new leader of Granada. This caused more instability in the area and eventually led to a civil war.[377] The civil war created even more instability, making it easier for the Christians to move in.

Boabdil of Granada
https://commons.wikimedia.org/wiki/File:Boabdil_de_Grenade.jpg

---

[377] "The Conquest of Granada." *The Spanish War History*, 2012, https://www.spanishwars.net/15th-century-conquest-of-granada.html.

The Christians took advantage of the distraction caused by the civil war. During the Battle of Axarquía, the Spanish captured Boabdil. While captured, he converted to Christianity and joined the Spanish side. He was eventually released and returned to Granada to fight for the Spanish.[378] Cities began to fall to the Spanish, and the conquest of Granada was well underway. Soon, the Spanish had total control over the Iberian Peninsula.

Once Granada was conquered, the Spanish agreed to give Boabdil lands. However, these were not in his old homeland but in Castile. Boabdil returned to Granada and turned on the Spanish. He tried to ally with other Muslim countries, but his efforts made little difference. The Spanish re-seized and held Granada in April 1491.[379] The conquest of Granada and the Iberian Peninsula was complete. The Christians had regained control, and the Reconquista was over.

Christianity in the Iberian Peninsula Under Muslim Control

In this section, we'll look at how Christians were treated during the Reconquista. The following statements and facts are generalizations from large swatches of time, not one specific year or even century.

Before we can get into how the Muslims changed the way Christians lived in the Iberian Peninsula, we need to understand how Christians were treated *before* the Muslims landed in the Iberian Peninsula.

The Visigoths, at least from the sixth to eighth centuries, were primarily Catholic. With the Catholics in charge, Christians were treated just as well in the Iberian Peninsula as anywhere else in Europe.[380] The Jews, however, were another question.

The Visigoth Catholic rulers were heavily anti-Semitic. While it was not illegal to be Jewish, fines and other penalties were much worse for a Jewish person than for a Christian. Some Jewish traditions were made illegal in parts of the Iberian Peninsula, including circumcisions or refusing to eat pork. Breaking a law or angering the wrong Catholic could leave a Jew faced with exile, physical punishments (beating),

---

[378] "The Conquest of Granada."
[379] "The Conquest of Granada."
[380] Claxton, Miguel A. III. "The Islamic Iberian Peninsula: Cultural Fusion and Coexistence." *Young Historians Conference,* February 29, 2016, https://pdxscholar.library.pdx.edu/cgi/viewcontent.cgi?article=1082&context=younghistorians.

property/item confiscation, and even death.[381] Catholic rule brought in one of the many periods of history in which Jews were persecuted so heavily that, if Catholic power had lasted much longer, the Jews in the area may have been eradicated entirely.

When the first Muslims came into the Iberian Peninsula and took power, they were still a minority and did little to affect the Christians living there.[382] (Remember, the Muslims conquered the Iberian Peninsula not so much because they came in large numbers but because the Visigoth government was weak, unorganized, and disconnected.)

Under Islamic law, most people who followed some kind of Abrahamic religion, such as Islam, Christianity, or Judaism had a measure of religious freedom. So, while the Christian community was largely unaffected in the way they practiced their faith, the Jewish community was finally free of (serious) persecution.[383]

Both Christians and Jews were now allowed to hold positions in local government and could elevate their family status in the community more easily than under Visigoth rule.[384] Christians and Jews were treated equally and regarded as slightly less than their Muslim neighbors.

The longer the Muslims stayed in their area, the more their culture spread. More and more non-Muslims learned how to speak Arabic. Muslim literature, arts, and fashion became more popular. In the same way, some Christian and Jewish customs spread throughout the Muslim communities in the area. This was due, in part, to living so closely together but also because intermarriage between the religions was allowed during this period.[385] Even after the Muslims lost power, some level of equality between members of the Abrahamic faiths remained. In a way, this was one conquest that led to more life than bloodshed.

Conclusion

The Reconquista only lasted for a fraction of the time as the Crusades. Yet, it was much less bloody, and the "conquered" people in the Iberian Peninsula kept a relatively stable lifestyle. The Muslims did not persecute

---

[381] Bachrach, Bernard S. "A Reassessment of Visigothic Jewish Policy, 598-711." *Oxford University Press,* February 1973, https://www.jstor.org/stable/1853939.

[382] Claxton, Miguel A. III. "The Islamic Iberian Peninsula: Cultural Fusion and Coexistence."

[383] Claxton, Miguel A. III. "The Islamic Iberian Peninsula: Cultural Fusion and Coexistence."

[384] Claxton, Miguel A. III. "The Islamic Iberian Peninsula: Cultural Fusion and Coexistence."

[385] Claxton, Miguel A. III. "The Islamic Iberian Peninsula: Cultural Fusion and Coexistence."

the Christians and Jews as the Christians often did when they invaded during the Crusades. This stark difference shows that a conquest doesn't need to end in annihilation. It can end in compromise and cultures melting together.

Chapter 10: The Rise and Fall of the Templars

The Knights Templar, also simply known as the Templars, were a famous Christian martial force. There are countless myths surrounding the Knights Templar featured in many books and movies over the years. One of the most famous myths is that they worked to find and protect the Holy Grail, which was the cup Jesus Christ and his disciples drank out of at the Last Supper. While there is no proof of this, historians do know that the Templars were established to help during the Crusades. This chapter will work on separating fact from fiction.

Most of the Templar's history takes place during the Crusades. So, once again, we will go back in time a bit. This section will give more context to the Crusades.

The Formation of the Templars

Historians debate on when exactly the Knights Templar was formed, but most can agree it was sometime between 1118 and 1120. Hugh de Payns (Hugues de Payens),[386] a French knight, founded the Knight's Templars. The men who joined this group, mostly Payn's friends and relatives, had to take monastic vows and follow a strict code of conduct

---

[386] History.com Editors. "Knights Templar." History, A&E Television Networks, August 23, 2022, https://www.history.com/topics/middle-ages/the-knights-templar#:~:text=Around%201118%2C%20a%20French%20knight,simply%20as%20the%20Knights%20Templar.

agreed upon by the Templars. All the men had to swear to protect Christian pilgrims in the Holy Land, with a focus on Jerusalem.[387]

The new group quickly became popular with the local Christian government. King Baldwin II of Jerusalem gave the Templars his palace to use as their headquarters in 1120. The building was then called the Temple of Solomon, which is why the Knights are sometimes called the Order of the Knights of the Temple of Solomon.[388]

Only men could join this organization, and the Templars preferred to accept men who had no debts. Most of the men who joined were in their twenties, but sometimes parents would send teenagers, or old men would join as a last act of penance. However, while they were referred to as the Knights Templar, very few of the members were knights.[389] While they were not officially knighted, most still had some military experience.

There was a strict hierarchy within the Templars, with the Grand Master at the top, knights and sergeants in the middle, and non-military members at the bottom. With as many members as they had, the Templars did not have one center. Instead, each group was assigned to a priory.[390] These were areas where the Templars were needed to protect Christians in and around the Holy Land, like the Levant.

Rise to Power

The Templars claimed they were a group dedicated to fighting for Christianity and the Holy Land. However, they were not given papal recognition until 1129—almost ten years after the Templars were formed. Pope Honorius II gave this recognition at the 1129 Council of Troyes.[391] Along with papal recognition, the Templars were also given a code of rules to follow. All members had to abide by these rules to become/stay a member of the Templars. Some of these rules included taking a vow of chastity and poverty, agreeing to wear plain clothing, and agreeing to many of the same terms of service as monks at the time did. Additionally, the pope and other high-ranking Catholic officials would have a say in

---

[387] Cartwright, Mark. "Knights Templar." *World History Encyclopedia,* September 28, 2018, https://member.worldhistory.org/Knights_Templar/.

[388] Cartwright, Mark. "Knights Templar."

[389] Cartwright, Mark. "Knights Templar."

[390] Cartwright, Mark. "Knights Templar."

[391] Cartwright, Mark. "Knights Templar."

how the Templars operated.[392] The official requirements for joining would change over the centuries. However, these standards stayed the same for most new recruits.

Money and prestige were not the only reasons a man would want to join the Templars. Like joining to fight one of the many Crusades, anyone who joined with the Templars, even if he didn't fight, would have guaranteed entry to Heaven from the pope.[393]

Having official papal recognition worked as free advertising, enabling the Knights to recruit more members.[394] At its peak, there were about 20,000 Templars. Of course, it's not cheap to employ this many fighting men. The members were paid mostly through donations given by Catholics. Some of the donations were in the form of cash, but some richer benefactors donated horses, weapons, and even land.[395] The Templars could then rent the land to increase revenue.

However, even with these numbers, the Templars did not see much real action in combat until 1147, during the Second Crusade. After the Second Crusade, the Templars began taking part in more and more battles. They fought in both the Baltic Crusades and in many battles during the Reconquista.[396]

Land Acquisition and the Crusader States

Along with getting land through donations, the Templars also "acquired" new lands through their conquest of various cities, usually in and around the Holy Land.[397] As with the lands donated to them, the Templars rented out this land and otherwise made money from it.

Owning more land in more places again worked as free advertisement: the Templars could make their presence known in more places. This, in turn, allowed them to recruit even more members.[398]

Many of these newly acquired lands were later known as Crusader states. The first Crusader states were established after the First Crusade.

---

[392] Phillips, Jonathan. "Troyes, Council (1129)." *World History Encyclopedia*, February 9, 2015, https://www.worldhistory.biz/middle-ages/23710-troyes-council-1129.html.
[393] Cartwright, Mark. "Knights Templar."
[394] Phillips, Jonathan. "Troyes, Council (1129)."
[395] Cartwright, Mark. "Knights Templar."
[396] Cartwright, Mark. "Knights Templar."
[397] Cartwright, Mark. "Knights Templar."
[398] Cartwright, Mark. "Knights Templar."

These were the Kingdom of Jerusalem, the counties of Edessa and Tripoli, and the Principality of Antioch.[399] Most of the Templar's involvement with the Crusades was fighting to defend the Crusader states. Throughout the Crusades, they had their fair share of wins and losses.[400]

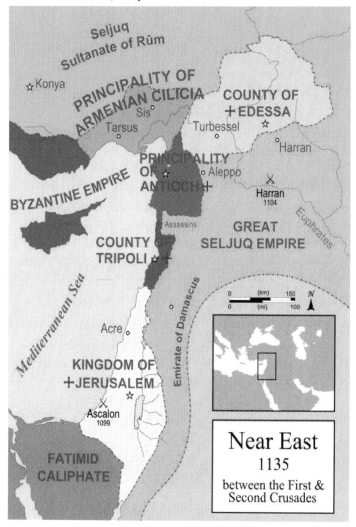

The Near East Crusader States (1135)
MapMaster, CC BY-SA 3.0 <http://creativecommons.org/licenses/by-sa/3.0/>, via Wikimedia Commons https://commons.wikimedia.org/wiki/File:Map_Crusader_states_1135-en.svg

---

[399] Cartwright, Mark. "Crusader States." *World History Encyclopedia,* November 1, 2018, https://www.worldhistory.org/Crusader_States/.
[400] Cartwright, Mark. "Knights Templar."

Trade and Treasure

The Templars may have been earning piles of gold and other treasures, but they were not allowed to keep all of it. For the first years of their service, Templars were required to pay taxes and give donations to the Church. As a self-proclaimed charitable organization, they also donated food and alms to the poor.[401] However, in 1139, Pope Innocent II signed a papal bull that allowed the Templars to be exempt from paying taxes.[402] That being said, the Templars likely kept most of their money, which helped make them a large and rich group. This gave the average man even more incentive to join the Templars.

Fall of the Templars

As the Templars grew in numbers, land, and riches, European rulers began to feel more and more uncomfortable with their presence in the Holy Land and elsewhere. As the decades went on, the Templars became their own military power. Their large land holdings made them almost a nation of their own. However, they were still accountable to the pope—or at least they were supposed to be.

The European leaders began to lose faith in the Templars as they began to lose more fights in the Crusades. In 1291, the Templars lost Acre to the Muslim forces. By 1303, they had lost most of their influence in Muslim-held lands.[403]

Adding to all this were rumors of corruption within the Templars. They were abusing their powers, hoarding money, and killing more than converting. Many of these rumors had some truth to them. The Templars were rich and had power in many countries. However, some rumors had less foundation in truth. These included rumors that the Templars did not believe in Jesus, practiced homosexuality, and worshipped idols. Whether these rumors were true or not, the consequence was the same—the Templars were put on trial.[404]

Late in the first decade of the 1300s, Pope Clement V ordered the arrest of all the Templars in Europe. The Templars fought back, sometimes in literal battle, but enough Templars were collected by 1310 to hold a trial. The trial was held in Paris that year. The Grand Master

---

[401] Cartwright, Mark. "Knights Templar."
[402] History.com Editors. "Knights Templar."
[403] History.com Editors. "Knights Templar."
[404] Cartwright, Mark. "Knights Templar."

and other leaders were treated more harshly than lower-ranking Templars. In the end, over fifty Templars were burned at the stake.[405] This was the beginning of the end for the Templars.

The 1311 Council of Vienne put another nail in the Templars' coffin as more investigations into the order took place. Many Templars were arrested and tortured into confessing to various charges. Shortly after, on April 3, 1312, the pope officially called for the "termination" of the Templars. Not all Templars were put on trial after this. However, many of the Templars' military fighters were banned from joining any country's military. The Templars' lands and other acquired wealth were taken by the Church.[406] Some stragglers of the Templars likely held on to their ways for a few years after this. However, the 1312 demand of the pope ended the Templars as a formal, legal group.

Conclusion

With the formal end of the Knights Templar in the 1300s, the Templars lost their power and prestige. There are rumors they went looking for the Holy Grail and other relics, but these are unfounded. The Templars moved into obscurity and legend, leaving behind more questions than answers.

---

[405] Cartwright, Mark. "Knights Templar."
[406] Cartwright, Mark. "Knights Templar."

Chapter 11: The Opposition: Islam, Zengi & Saladin

In Chapter 8, we mentioned the years between the third and fourth Crusades and the part that Saladin and Imad al-Din Zengi played in the power struggle between Christians and Muslims. This chapter will take a more in-depth look at these two key players and some of their biggest battles against the Crusaders and Templars, discussing the tensions between Muslims and Christians during the twelfth century.

Imad al-Din Zengi

As mentioned in Chapter 6, Imad al-Din Zengi began to rise to power in the 1120s. However, his family had been important in what we would now call the Middle East since before he was born. His father was the governor of Aleppo until 1094 when he was murdered. Zengi and his family had to flee the city, forcing them to start all over in Mosul. However, this would prove advantageous for Zengi, as he was raised by the governor of Mosul and later served under Mahmud II of the Seljuks. His faithful service earned him the governorship of Basra in 1126.[407]

In 1127, the Abbasid Caliph, Al-Mustarshid, rebelled against Mahmud II. While Zengi could have joined his side, he stayed by Mahmud II. After the rebellion was swiftly crushed, Zengi was rewarded by obtaining the governorship of Mosul. So, while Zengi was never a sultan or king, he

---

[407] Britannica, T. Editors of Encyclopedia. "Zangī."

held considerable power over many cities in the Holy Land.[408]

Battles in Damascus and Edessa

Zengi's battles with the Crusaders began in 1130. At this point, the Crusaders were trying to take Damascus, which was under the control of Taj al-Muluk Buri. Zengi allied himself with Buri to increase his chances of winning. However, the alliance was for personal gain, as he would later take Buri's son captive and ransom him and other captives back to Buri.[409]

The next few years of Zengi's life were tumultuous. In 1131, Mahmud II died, leading to several drastic changes in government. While power switched hands, Zengi used the time to his advantage and tried to seize Damascus. His attempts to take the city were combated by the Iraqi government. Years went by without Zengi taking control of the city. However, his actions led the rulers in Damascus to ally with the Crusaders.[410]

Zengi knew that he could not defeat the Crusaders in Damascus, so he set his sights on an army from Jerusalem, which he fought and defeated in the Battle of Ba'rin in 1137.[411] His victory here encouraged him to aim for Damascus again, which he tried to conquer several times between 1137 and 1140. He continued to try to take Damascus unsuccessfully until his death.[412]

Instead of capturing Damascus, Zengi led a siege of Edessa in 1144. At the time, Edessa had little protection from the Crusaders, making it especially vulnerable to attack. The battle began in the autumn of 1144; by the end of the year, Zengi captured the city.[413] This was his most famous victory over the Crusaders and directly led to the Second Crusade.

---

[408] Britannica, T. Editors of Encyclopedia. "Zangī."

[409] Markseken, Susan F., Surgone, Lambert M., and Timpledon, Miriam T., ed. *Zengi*. ZDM Publishing, 2010.

[410] Markseken, Susan F., et al. *Zengi*.

[411] Smail, R. C. *Crusading Warfare 1097-1193*. Barnes & Noble Books: New York, 1995.

[412] Maalouf, Amin. *The Crusades Through Arab Eyes*. Schocken Books, Germany, 1985.

[413] Markseken, Susan F., et al. *Zengi*.

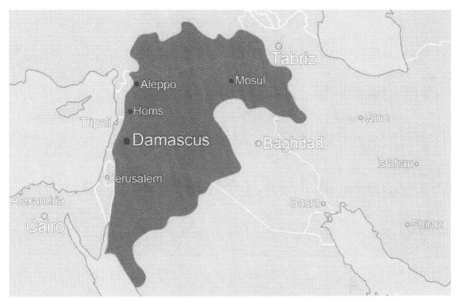

Zengid Dynasty 1127-1150
MoeyElan, CC BY-SA 4.0 <https://creativecommons.org/licenses/by-sa/4.0>, via Wikimedia Commons https://commons.wikimedia.org/wiki/File:Zengid_-_Without_Theme.png.

Zengi's reign as governor—and his life—ended just a few years after the Siege of Edessa. In 1146, he went to quash another rebellion in modern-day Iraq. However, he was murdered by one of his servants.[414] He was succeeded as the governor of Aleppo by his son, Nur al-Din.[415] After some debate as to who would take the governorship of Mosul, the title was given to Sayf al-Din Ghazi I.[416] Neither of his two successors ever gained the same level of success, prestige, or remembrance as Zengi.

Saladin

Salah ad-Din, better known as Saladin in the West, was born in 1137. By the time he was an adult, the first two Crusades were already over and done. He was raised in a world where the Crusades were the new normal. When he became the new Sultan of Egypt and Syria in 1174, he was primed to fight in the Third Crusade. In fact, he had gained support throughout the decades by promising his people another holy war.[417]

---

[414] Britannica, T. Editors of Encyclopedia. "Zangī."
[415] Britannica, T. Editors of Encyclopedia. "Nūr al-Dīn."
[416] Grousset, Rene. *History of the Crusades and the Frankish Kingdom of Jerusalem II.* L'equillbre, Paris, 1935.
[417] Cartwright, Mark. "Saladin," *World History Encyclopedia*, August 30, 2018,

As a young man, Saladin was in the military. He campaigned with various family members for decades.[418] This gave him the skills he would later use when fighting the Crusaders. He also had several battles against various Muslim groups. His battles were not only for religious reasons but also for land grabs.

One of Saladin's first major wins that gave his empire more land was the capture of Aleppo in 1183. Throughout the 1180s, he continued to take more "Latin" lands, like Mosul. By this time, Saladin's son, al-Afdal, was old enough to join the fight to help his father claim more lands.[419]

The Battle of Hattin

Saladin's most famous battle against the Crusaders was the Battle of Hattin in 1187. At the beginning of the battle, the Franks held control of Hattin. Saladin fought in waves, attacking and retreating over and over again. Over the next several weeks, both sides pitted over 10,000 soldiers against each other. However, Saladin had more men and supplies. Soon after the battle began, Saladin's forces captured the King of Jerusalem, Guy of Lusignan. The Franks did not last long once their leader was captured. Saladin claimed his victory and the city of Jerusalem in September 1187.[420]

Saladin held Guy of Lusignan for ransom after the battle. However, he executed other Frankish leaders. Perhaps even more barbaric, many of the other prisoners of war were sold into slavery. The people living in the captured city did not fare much better than the soldiers who had fought to defend it. Many of the Christians living in Jerusalem were ransomed, sold into slavery, or executed. Christianity in the city was erased, and the churches were converted to mosques.[421] As awful as it all sounds, this type of warfare and religious intolerance was common during this period. It would have been unusual for Saladin to leave the Christians alone and free his enemies.

Third Crusade Onward

Saladin and his forces held Jerusalem without much competition for several years. However, the Crusaders struck back with the Third

---

https://www.worldhistory.org/Saladin/.
[418] Cartwright, Mark. "Saladin."
[419] Cartwright, Mark. "Saladin."
[420] Cartwright, Mark. "Saladin."
[421] Cartwright, Mark. "Saladin."

Crusade. (Read previous chapters to learn more about the Third Crusade.) In brief, the Crusaders tried to take Jerusalem back, resulting in full-scale battles in September 1191. Saladin and his forces won most of these battles, but he lost Jaffa to the Crusaders.[422] Overall, it can be argued that Saladin and his Muslim allies won the Third Crusade, as the Crusaders could not take Jerusalem back.

Even though Saladin was instrumental in his people's victories against the Crusaders, he did not get to enjoy the spoils of war for long. He died in March 1193, likely from illness or pure strain.[423] He was succeeded by two men. Al-Aziz Uthman, Saladin's son, took control of Egypt.[424] Al-Afdal, one of Saladin's other sons, took Syria.[425] Neither reign lasted long before the lands were ruled by other men. Still, Saladin's legacy lived on.

Conclusion

Zengi and Saladin were a couple of the most formidable Muslim enemies the Crusaders faced in the twelfth century. Their battles dominated the 1100s, which would have greatly affected everyday life in the Holy Land for both the average Christian and Muslim, who would have little say in their fates. With the ever-changing political and religious landscape of the Holy Land, it is no wonder things got so violent so quickly.

This concludes our study on the Crusades. Next, we'll look at how the Catholic Church changed in the 1300s, leading to the Catholic Reformation.

---

[422] Cartwright, Mark. "Saladin."

[423] Cartwright, Mark. "Saladin."

[424] Lyons, M.C. and Jackson, D.E.P. *Saladin: The Politics of the Holy War*. Cambridge University Press, Cambridge, UK, 1982.

[425] Dhahabui, Muhammad A. *The Lives of Notable Figures: Volume 21*. Al Resala Publishers, Beirut, 2014.

Section Four:
The Great Reformation
1510–1640 CE

Chapter 12: What Was the Reformation?

For most of Christian history, the Church was unified. There was the one Holy Catholic Church with few official offshoots or sects. Any sects that existed likely would have been considered heretical. These churches would have been condemned by the Catholic Church, so they were not very popular. This is how the story went for about 1,500 years, with some minor disputes and separations. This chapter will look at how Martin Luther's work changed the Catholic Church in a major way in the 1500s. Martin Luther wasn't the only Reformer or even the first, but he was one of the most popular then and one of the most famous reformers to this day. Therefore, this chapter will focus on his work, with succeeding chapters discussing some of the other reformers.

Martin Luther and the 95 Theses

Martin Luther did not set out to start a new Christian sect; instead, his goal was to "fix" some of the issues he found in Catholicism. While Catholicism has remained relatively unchanged throughout its history, it used to be much more corrupt. Church leaders would sell indulgences (which would allow a person to buy time out of Purgatory), use the Church's money on various vanities, and write and hold services in Latin—which most people could not understand. All in all, Martin Luther wanted to increase the accessibility of Catholicism to the common person while reducing the amount of money the Church took in and spent on nonessentials.

Martin Luther by Lucas Cranach the Elder
Lucas Cranach the Elder, CC0, via Wikimedia Commons
https://commons.wikimedia.org/wiki/File:Martin_Luther_%281483%E2%80%931546%29_MET_DP159769.jpg.

Luther, like most people living in Europe at the time, grew up a Catholic. He was a part of a poor working-class family and lived in Germany. He became a monk around 1505, in his early twenties. He thoughtfully served the monastery for over a decade before beginning to make his issues with the church known.[426] Again, he was not voicing his concerns to abolish Catholicism but to change the Church to be more in tune with his idea of what Christianity should look like in regards to his interpretation of the Bible.

The most famous of these vocal concerns was made in 1517, when he posted his famous *Ninety-Five Theses* on the door of a church in Wittenburg, Germany. This document contained ninety-five items he

---

[426] Logos Staff. "How Martin Luther Accidentally Sparked the Reformation." Word by Word, Logos, October 8, 2021, https://www.logos.com/grow/luther-how-he-accidentally-sparked-the-reformation/.

believed the Catholic Church should change to be more in line with the teachings of the Bible. The theses were originally written in Latin. Luther did this on purpose so the clergy could read them but the common person could not.[427] Doing this was not "bad" in the eyes of the Catholic Church. In fact, he had posted a similar thesis in a similar way just a few months earlier that did not garner much attention. What made this thesis stand out (and Luther a threat to the Catholic Church) was the actions of others.

Shortly after Luther posted his theses, some of his followers devoted themselves to translating the document from Latin into German, which more of the common people could read. The translation was then printed in multiples, which was made possible by the new invention of the printing press.[428] The combination of the theses being translated into the common vernacular and being printed made Luther's message easy to spread among the general public—and easy for them to read. The spread started in Germany and soon reached other nearby countries.

The Catholic Church could have ignored Luther's complaints to them in Latin. The clergy could have discussed it among themselves. No, the problem was that the common people were made aware of what Luther thought the problems in the Catholic Church were, and now they were discussing it outside of the church. Even worse, they could form their own ideas about it.

The Church was furious with Luther. In 1520, the Church passed the *Exsurge Domine* papal bull, which gave Luther sixty days to recant what he had written in the Ninety-Five Theses. He refused. As a direct result of this, he was excommunicated by the Church in 1521 with the *Decet Romanum Pontificem* papal bull.[429]

After his excommunication, Luther was "kidnapped" and hid at Wartburg Castle to avoid further persecution. While there, he worked on translating the New Testament of the Bible. He came out of hiding in 1522 but continued writing religious essays and texts, including a

---

[427] Mark, Joshua J. "Martin Luther." *World History Encyclopedia*, November 30, 2021, https://www.worldhistory.org/Martin_Luther/.

[428] Mark, Joshua J. "Martin Luther."

[429] Schurb, Ken. "Martin Luther's Early Years: Christian History Timeline." Christian History Institute, Originally published in *Christian History*, Issue 34, 1992, https://christianhistoryinstitute.org/magazine/article/martin-luthers-early-years-timeline.

complete translation of the Bible into German in 1534.[430] His followers read his writings, and eventually, the Christian branch of Lutheranism was formed. This branch would later break off into many other sects. Lutheranism and several of its sects are still alive and well to this day.

Now that we've briefly summarized Luther's life, let's take a deeper dive to understand some of the details.

Diet of Worms

In 1521, Roman Emperor Charles V brought the Diet of Worms to session. The goal of this meeting was to convince Luther to recant his writings in the *Ninety-Five Theses,* as the emperor and the Catholic Church at large saw the writings as heretical.[431] (Remember, by this time, Luther's *Ninety-Five Theses* had been in circulation for about three years, and he had been recently excommunicated.) Whether he wanted it or not, he was getting attention from clergy members and laymen alike. He was amassing a following of people looking for reform in the Catholic Church and only finding it through Luther's writings.

Luther at the Diet of Worms by Anton von Werner (1877)
https://commons.wikimedia.org/wiki/File:%D0%9B%D1%8E%D1%82%D0%B5%D1%80_%D0% B2_%D0%92%D0%BE%D1%80%D0%BC%D1%81%D0%B5.jpg

The Diet of Worms was Luther's last formal chance to recant, but he chose not to. Because of this, he was officially charged with the crime of

---

[430] Schurb, Ken. "Martin Luther's Early Years: Christian History Timeline."
[431] Mark, Joshua J. "Diet of Worms." *World History Encyclopedia*, December 8, 2021, https://www.worldhistory.org/Diet_of_Worms/.

heresy.[432] Shortly after this, he was taken to Wittenberg, where he wrote many of his works.

After Luther was officially made a heretic, several Church leaders ordered all of Luther's writings to be burned in mass book burnings. Two of the main players in this event were Bishop John Fisher and the famous Cardinal Thomas Wolsey, who worked under King Henry VIII.[433] This by no means eliminated all of Luther's prints, but it did limit the number his followers could get their hands on. Those who kept copies of his work would likely need to hide them, lest they be found and the owners charged with minor heresy.

Luther's Writings and Changes

Once Luther could comfortably come out of hiding, he began to make his own religious reforms, text translations, and other writings. Over the years, he gained a large following. Lutheranism became most popular in Europe, starting in Germany and spreading to other Germanic language-speaking countries. Part of the reason Lutheranism became so popular was the changes Luther made. Overall, the Lutheran churches had their background and bones from the Catholics but made the church more people-oriented instead of strictly clergy-oriented.

Translating the Bible and other religious texts into German paved the way for the common person to read the Bible and make their own interpretations of the text. The Catholic Church was against this because its line of thinking was that the clergy should tell the common people what the Bible meant. Lutheranism, on the other hand, encouraged people to read the Bible. Eventually, songs and prayers were also translated, making the services easier for the average person to understand.[434] (A population's native language is called the "vernacular.")

Some of Luther's most historically significant writings were his catechisms. Luther published several editions of these books in the 1520s.[435] These catechisms, with some edits and forewords by modern pastors, are still in print today. These books explained some of the rules,

---

[432] Mark, Joshua J. "Diet of Worms."

[433] The Anne Boleyn Files and Tudor Society. "May 12 - Martin Luther's Books are Burned in London." May 11, 2019, video, https://www.youtube.com/watch?v=bI9d8GhvZMo&t=186s.

[434] "Martin Luther and the Protestant Reformation." Trinity Lutheran Church, n.d., https://trinitylutheranchurch.360unite.com/martin-luther.

[435] "Martin Luther and the Protestant Reformation."

beliefs, and religious sacraments Lutherans were supposed to take part in. Lutheran churches still follow what was first written in Luther's catechisms today.

Luther's Catechism

The following changes in belief from Catholicism to Lutheranism are taken from *Dr. Martin Luther's Catechism with Explanation and Bible History*, published by the Apostolic Lutheran Church of America in 1951, with the most recent edition in 1996. Apostolic Lutheranism is just one sect of Lutheranism; other sects may have slightly different beliefs. These beliefs may not be exactly what Luther was preaching in the 1500s, but they provide a good example of the overall ideas Luther was spreading in Europe.

One of Luther's biggest changes that irked the Catholic Church (but that most common people enjoyed) was his answer to the question, "How do I get into Heaven?" The Catholics had determined that good Christians needed to both believe in Jesus Christ (God and the Holy Spirit), do good works, and sometimes pay indulgences. Luther, on the other hand, taught that it was faith (believing in the Holy Trinity) and faith alone that earned someone a spot in Heaven.[436] This meant that all someone had to do to get into Heaven was to believe in the Holy Trinity. They did not need to do any of the sacraments, pay any money to the Church, or do good works. These were still things that Lutherans should do, but they would not be damned if they did not.

On the topic of sacraments, Luther believed there were two basic kinds of sacraments— the Old Testament and the New. The ones that were the most important to Luther were the ones from the New Testament. These included baptism, Confirmation, and Communion. One of the Old Testament sacraments that was no longer required under Luther was circumcision (the removal of the foreskin of the penis).[437]

Baptism was the earliest sacrament a person could go through. This required being blessed with holy water. Infant baptism is common in Lutheranism. Luther believed that even little children could believe in Jesus, so they should be allowed to be baptized.[438] This belief was based

---

[436] Luther, Martin. *Dr. Martin Luther's Catechism with Explanation and Bible History*. The Apostolic Lutheran Church of America, 1996.
[437] Luther, Martin. *Dr. Martin Luther's Catechism with Explanation and Bible History*.
[438] Luther, Martin. *Dr. Martin Luther's Catechism with Explanation and Bible History*.

on the Bible verse Mark 10:14: "Suffer the little children to come unto me and forbid them not: for of such is the kingdom of God."

Anyone who believed could be baptized at any time in their life. Baptism was said to remove the "original sin" from the soul, which had been inherited from Adam and Eve when they first sinned in the Garden of Eden. From there, the person would be a blank slate. However, Luther also knew that no person, apart from Jesus, could remain sinless.[439] As baptism was a sacrament, Lutherans would be encouraged to be baptized, but it would not be required for entry into Heaven. Many Catholics believed that people had to be baptized to go to Heaven, unless they died in infancy or without ever learning about Jesus's teachings.[440]

However, just because a person is baptized does not automatically mean they will get into Heaven no matter how they live their life. A person must be baptized *and* believe in the Holy Trinity to go to Heaven.[441] Again, believing without baptism will result in salvation, but baptism without belief will not.

Luther also changed the concept behind Holy Communion. Holy Communion is the sacrament based on Jesus's Last Supper with his disciples before he was hung on the cross. Lutheran churches will serve Holy Communion regularly, usually once a week or once a month, depending on the church. Bread and wine make up the physical aspects of Holy Communion,[442] but these may be switched with wafers, grape juice, crackers, or water. What was most important to Luther were the spiritual elements of Holy Communion, which are the body and blood of Jesus Christ.

---

[439] Luther, Martin. *Dr. Martin Luther's Catechism with Explanation and Bible History.*
[440] Broussard, Karlo. "Is Baptism Necessary for Salvation or Not?" Catholic Answers, 2023, https://www.catholic.com/qa/is-baptism-necessary-for-salvation-or-not
[441] Luther, Martin. *Dr. Martin Luther's Catechism with Explanation and Bible History.*
[442] Luther, Martin. *Dr. Martin Luther's Catechism with Explanation and Bible History.*

Detail of the Holy Communion Window in St. Matthew's Lutheran Church by Franz Mayer & Co. (1966)
Cadetgray, CC BY-SA 3.0 <https://creativecommons.org/licenses/by-sa/3.0>, via Wikimedia Commons https://commons.wikimedia.org/wiki/File:Communion_Closeup.jpg.

The Catholic Church conducted its version of Holy Communion the same way. The main difference between the two was the spiritual belief behind them. The Catholic Church believed (and still believes) that once consumed, the bread and wine used in Holy Communion would literally transform into the body and blood of Christ.[443] This transformation is called "transubstantiation." Luther argues against the Catholic way of thinking in his *Catechism*, in which he answers the question, "Does transubstantiation take place in the elements of Communion?"[444]

"No. Because of its false doctrine concerning the Lord's Supper, the Roman Catholic Church has fallen into these additional errors: (1) The sacrifice of the Mass, in which the priest, by blessing the bread and wine, is supposed to turn them into the body and blood of Christ, thus offering an unbloody sacrifice of Christ supposedly as effective as Christ's death on the cross. (2) The *withholding* of the Cup from the laity. (3) The Elevation of the Host, in which the wafer (or host) is adored as the body of Christ."[445]

However, not everyone can partake in Holy Communion. Only those who are willing to receive the sacrament "worthily" may do so. Luther defines "worthy" as follows:

"The worthy are they who examine themselves whether they are acceptable to God: 1. Whether they have truly repented of their sins. 2. If they firmly believe that God for Christ's sake forgive them their sins and confirms it in His Holy Communion. 3. If their hearts are right with their neighbor. 4. If they have a true and firm intention to do better. The unworthy are they who disregard the importance of Communion, and partake thereof because it is customary so to do, for outward show, and with hypocrisy, having no contrition whatsoever, and thus drink unto themselves damnation and destruction."[446]

Both the Catholic and Lutheran churches keep the sacrament of Confirmation. People who have been baptized can choose to become confirmed. Going through the process of Confirmation basically means that a person is declaring their faith in the Holy Trinity. This usually requires some Sunday School classes for Catholics and Confirmation classes for Lutherans. If baptized as infants, Catholic children can become confirmed as early as age seven. Adults and people who are

---

[443] Luther, Martin. *Dr. Martin Luther's Catechism with Explanation and Bible History*.
[444] Luther, Martin. *Dr. Martin Luther's Catechism with Explanation and Bible History*, p. 117.
[445] Luther, Martin. *Dr. Martin Luther's Catechism with Explanation and Bible History*, p. 117.
[446] Luther, Martin. *Dr. Martin Luther's Catechism with Explanation and Bible History*, p. 118.

baptized later in life can become confirmed shortly after the baptismal service.[447]

While Luther agreed with the sacrament of Confirmation, he did not agree with the age range for becoming confirmed. In modern Lutheran churches, most people need to be at least fifteen to start Confirmation classes. This is usually a two-year process. Luther's *Catechism* states:

> "Confirmation is not commanded in the Scriptures, but is a useful ordinance of the Church. It does not make us members of the Church, for we become members by baptism; but it admits us to *communicant* membership in the Church. We believe that they have reached the age of discretion when they are confirmed and are then admitted to the Lord's Supper. They are also entitled to be sponsors at the baptism of children, and are considered to be adult members of the congregation."[448]

In short, Luther thought teenagers were old enough to decide whether they truly believed in the Holy Trinity and wanted to be full-fledged church members. By being "admitted to the Lord's Supper," Luther means that people who have been confirmed can take part in Communion. By saying they can be "entitled to be sponsors at the baptism of children," he means they can be godparents.

Lutheran Creeds

The Lutheran Church follows three main creeds (listed in order of importance): the Apostles' Creed, the Nicene Creed, and the Athanasian Creed.[449] Most Lutheran adults will have memorized the Apostles' Creed but not the others.

Conclusion

While this chapter does not cover the entire scope of Lutheranism, it gives an idea of how Lutheranism differed from Catholicism at the start and today. Luther's speaking out against the Catholic Church helped to inspire other Reformers to begin their own Christian sects, many of which are still around today.

---

[447] Petruzzello, Melissa. "The Seven Sacraments of the Roman Catholic Church." *Encyclopedia Britannica*, February 6, 2018. https://www.britannica.com/list/the-seven-sacraments-of-the-roman-catholic-church.

[448] Luther, Martin. *Dr. Martin Luther's Catechism with Explanation and Bible History*, p. 120.

[449] Luther, Martin. *Dr. Martin Luther's Catechism with Explanation and Bible History*.

Chapter 13: The Great Reformers

Martin Luther is arguably the most famous Reformer, partly because he helped kick off the Reformation and begin the formation of Protestant churches around Europe. As Protestantism (non-Catholic but still Christian) grew, it spread outside Europe, to the Americas, and eventually around the world. This section will give brief biographies and faith overviews of other famous Reformers and those who in some way contributed to the Reformation. Martin Luther is omitted from this list only because his background was so thoroughly covered in the last chapter. The Reformers below were mostly active in the 1500s. They are listed in no particular order.

John Calvin

John Calvin, also known as Jean Calvin, was born in 1509 in France. He contributed to the Reformation around the same time as Luther but primarily practiced his teachings in France. He was raised in a highly religious (Catholic) household, as his father worked for a local bishop. Calvin's parents had originally planned for him to go into the priesthood, but he eventually switched from studying theology to studying law in the 1530s.[450]

---

[450] Bouwsma, W. J. "John Calvin." *Encyclopedia Britannica*, July 6, 2023. https://www.britannica.com/biography/John-Calvin.

Portrait of John Calvin (1509-1564)
https://picryl.com/media/portrait-of-john-calvin-15091564-by-anonymous-museum-catharijneconvent-4a06f1.

Even though he switched his official area of study to law, he still had an interest in religion. He began studying it himself and eventually published papers on his thoughts about religion, called *Institutes*, in 1536. While Calvin had not tried to preach at this point, his writings caught other Reformer's attention, namely, Guillaume (William) Farel.[451] Farel worked under Guillaume Briçonnet, a Reformist bishop living in France. In 1536, he convinced Calvin to work with him as his assistant. However, the two were expelled from Geneva by 1538. Through their work, they influenced each other. For the first two years, before leaving Geneva, they were equally important to the Reformation movement, but Calvin soon outshone Farel.[452]

---

[451] Bouwsma, W. J. "John Calvin."

[452] Britannica, T. Editors of Encyclopedia. "Guillaume Farel." *Encyclopedia Britannica*, January 1,

While living outside of Geneva, Calvin continued writing and began preaching for Protestant churches. After participating in this line of work for several years, he crafted a theory on how the church should be ordered. This included a hierarchy, with pastors at the top to teach, deacons to administer charity, and so on.[453] Calvin returned to Geneva once it was safe enough for Protestants to live there, around the mid-1550s, and would stay for most of the rest of his life.

During his years of preaching, he started his own religious sect known as Calvinism. This sect had much in common with Lutheranism but was more systematic in a way. Calvinists believed in salvation through faith alone. However, Calvin emphasized Jesus's divinity over his humanity. God was infallible and had predetermined everything that would ever happen on earth.[454]

The concept that God has predetermined everything that will ever happen is called "predestination." In line with this, Calvin believed that God had already decided who would be saved and who would not before people were even born. Calvin argued that there might be signs someone was chosen to be saved, such as God granting blessings on them in life. However, a person could never be entirely sure they were chosen, not until after death. He also sustained that humans could not do anything to change God's decision.[455] Their acts did not matter. All that mattered regarding salvation was whether God chose to save a person in his divine plan.

Calvin had a major influence on Protestant churches both during and after the Reformation. While he was alive, Calvinism spread throughout Western Europe, becoming most popular in France, the Netherlands, and Scotland. After his death in 1564, the main branch of Calvinism stayed united, but other branches broke off to form their own sects; these include Presbyterianism, which became popular in North America.[456] Many of these branches still survive to this day, as does Calvin's influence.

2023. https://www.britannica.com/biography/Guillaume-Farel.
[453] Bouwsma, W. J. "John Calvin."
[454] Bouwsma, W. J. "John Calvin."
[455] "John Calvin on Predestination." Theologians & Theology, 2013, https://www.theologian-theology.com/theologians/john-calvin-predestination/.
[456] Bouwsma, W. J. "John Calvin."

Henry VIII

Henry VIII did not set out to become a Reformer. He was raised Catholic and stayed in the faith for most of his life. Unlike Luther and Calvin, who were making changes to Catholicism in their own sects, Henry VIII was making changes for personal gain.

King Henry VIII of England was born in 1491 and became king in 1509 after his father, Henry VII, died. Soon after, he married his first wife, Catherine of Aragon. Oddly enough, she happened to be his older brother's widow. Arthur, Henry's brother, was only married to Catherine for a short time before he died. Rumor has it that they never consummated their marriage. While this may seem like a trivial detail, it would one day be brought up in court, around the same time Henry VIII broke from the Catholic Church to start his own church.[457] This church would later be known as the Church of England, which still exists today, but let's not get ahead of ourselves just yet (which is something Henry VIII should have said to himself).

Henry VIII's desire to break from Catholicism had more to do with his wife than religion. By the 1520s, Henry VIII had been married to Catherine of Aragon for over a decade, and they only had one surviving child—a girl—to show for it. Henry VIII wanted sons to succeed him on the throne after he died, and Catherine was proving unable to provide them.[458] As it was the sixteenth century, neither Henry VIII nor anyone else knew the science that goes into making a male heir and that it likely had nothing to do with Catherine. It was more likely that the problem was on Henry's end or that it was just bad luck that they only had one surviving child.[459] Nevertheless, Henry blamed Catherine, which loosened his affection for her and eventually led to the end of their marriage.

---

[457] Morrill, J. S. and Elton, Geoffrey R. "Henry VIII." *Encyclopedia Britannica*, June 30, 2023. https://www.britannica.com/biography/Henry-VIII-king-of-England.

[458] Morrill, J. S. and Elton, Geoffrey R. "Henry VIII."

[459] MacMillian, Amanda. "What Influences a Baby's Sex?" *Health*, June 9, 2023, https://www.health.com/condition/pregnancy/do-these-5-things-really-influence-a-babys-gender.

Catherine of Aragon
https://picryl.com/media/portrait-of-katherine-of-aragon-74025d.

"Conveniently," around the same time Henry was getting tired of Catherine, he met a new, twenty-something lady at court, Anne Boleyn. She caught the king's attention, and he would not give it up. He wanted more than anything to woo her, but rumors say that she refused to have sex with him unless they were married, likely part of the reason Henry wanted to divorce Catherine so badly.[460] After all, he had many affairs while married to Catherine, but none of the women could stand up to Anne in his eyes.[461]

---

[460] Starkey, David. *Six Wives: The Queens of Henry VIII.* Harper Perennial, New York, 2004.
[461] Morrill, J. S. and Elton, Geoffrey R. "Henry VIII."

Anne Boleyn
https://picryl.com/media/anne-boleyn-a3dabx.

Needless to say, there were a few problems with Henry's newfound infatuation. Firstly, he was still very much married to Catherine. Secondly, the Catholic Church did not grant divorces lightly. Henry tried a few tactics to get the divorce approved, such as saying that it was against the Bible to be married to your brother's widow (which really is in the Bible). He claimed that God's withholding of male heirs was part of his punishment for living a sinful life with Catherine. The only way to remedy this was to get a divorce. However, the pope at the time, Pope Clement VII, threw out this reasoning, as Henry had been given a special papal dispensation to marry Catherine in the first place![462] Going back on this would mean the pope would have to admit the papacy was fallible, which was not going to happen.

Henry fought with Rome for years verbally and in writing, trying to get his divorce. Eventually, he accepted that the Church would not grant his divorce. The only way to get the divorce was to break with Rome and seek out a new religion that would allow a divorce. He broke with Rome in 1532 and created his own church—the Church of England. He then annulled his marriage to Catherine and married Anne Boleyn soon after, in January 1533.[463] This would be the start of both a new religious sect and Henry's problems with Rome.

As Henry created the Church of England, he also named himself the leader of the Church.[464] In the Catholic faith, the pope was the leader of the Church, no matter which country a person lived in. The pope, in a way, was above the king. With Henry's reformation, he was the head of both the country and the Church. There was no one above him but God.

The English people, who until this moment were (mostly) all Catholics, did not all agree with the king's decision. But the king did not care much what others thought about his decision to break with Rome. The pope even excommunicated him, but Henry gave little attention to that.[465] Breaking from the Church continued to prove beneficial to Henry. He not only got his new wife but also began raking in money that had previously gone to the Catholic Church. Before the break with Rome, part of the country's taxes went to the Catholic Church in Rome. Now, that percentage went directly to the Crown. Shortly after he founded the Church of England, he also dissolved the monasteries. This also put more money, land, and buildings back into the king's pocket.[466] This would later cause welfare-related problems in the country, but again, that wasn't Henry's highest concern.

Of course, Henry changed the way the Church itself was run. This originally started with the Six Articles of the Church of England. These

---

[462] Morrill, J. S. and Elton, Geoffrey R. "Henry VIII."
[463] Morrill, J. S. and Elton, Geoffrey R. "Henry VIII."
[464] Morrill, J. S. and Elton, Geoffrey R. "Henry VIII."
[465] Morrill, J. S. and Elton, Geoffrey R. "Henry VIII."
[466] Ames, Tom. "6 Key Changes During the Reign of Henry VIII." History Hit, January 11, 2021, https://www.historyhit.com/key-changes-during-henry-viiis-reign/.

articles served as the outlines for the rules of the Church.[467] The articles were changed over time, but for the purpose of this section, we will look at what the articles were when Henry VIII was alive. The articles supported the following:

> "(a) The catholic doctrine of the transubstantiation of the substance of the eucharistic elements into the body and blood of Christ, in its most exclusive form; (b) the view that one need not receive both bread and wine in the communion; (c) the obligation of priests to remain celibate; (d) the binding character of vows of chastity; (e) private masses; and (f) auricular confession."[468]

In short, these rules were what the Catholic Church had already been asking its parishioners to do and believe. Very little changed other than where the money was going and who was in charge of the Church. Henry had consolidated power for himself and was not likely to let it go easily.

Older Henry VIII by Hans Holbein the Younger
https://picryl.com/media/portrait-of-king-henry-viii-of-england-14911547-by-hans-holbein-the-younger-799cad.

---

[467] Cameron, Euan. "Six Articles, Act Of." Oxford University Press, 2019, https://www.encyclopedia.com/history/encyclopedias-almanacs-transcripts-and-maps/six-articles-act.

[468] Cameron, Euan. "Six Articles, Act Of."

England remained under the Church of England for the rest of Henry's reign until shortly after his death in 1547. His son and heir, Edward VI, kept with the religion, as he was raised Protestant. However, he was only king for a few years before he died at age fifteen in 1553.[469] During this time, in part because of his age, he did not have much real power, so it is not likely he could have done much to change England's religion even if he had wanted to.

King Edward VI by William Scrots
https://picryl.com/media/portrait-of-king-edward-vi-of-england-15371553-attributed-to-william-scrots-79258a.

The country's official religion returned to Catholicism when Queen Mary I succeeded her brother after his death. Her mother, Catherine of Aragon, had raised her to be a Catholic. As queen, she wanted her country to follow what she believed to be the "true" religion. She reigned until her death and had many English Protestants killed. The country's official religion was changed back to the Church of England when Queen Elizabeth I, Anne Boleyn's Protestant daughter, took the throne after Mary's death.[470]

---

[469] Morrill, J. S. "Edward VI." *Encyclopedia Britannica*, July 2, 2023. https://www.britannica.com/biography/Edward-VI.

[470] Simkin, John. "Mary and Elizabeth: Catholics and Protestants." Spartacus Educational, January

While the history of the changes back and forth is more complicated than the short paragraph above contains, the point is that Henry VIII, whether he intended to or not, kicked off a religious reformation in England. From the reign of Elizabeth I onward, the country slowly became more religiously tolerant of other Christian sects.

St. Francis de Sales

Before we get started with St. Francis de Sales, it is important to know that (in Christian sects) it is mainly Catholics who canonize people, giving them the title of saint. While it may sound confusing, Francis de Sales, also known as Francis of Sales, was both a Catholic and instrumental in the Reformation.

Francis de Sales was born in 1567, and it didn't take him long to become involved with the Catholic Church. It is likely he was raised in the Church, and he joined the Jesuit college in Paris and later in Italy to study law. In 1593, he returned his focus to religion and was ordained as a priest.[471]

St. Francis de Sales

Rojosfscollege, CC BY-SA 4.0 <https://creativecommons.org/licenses/by-sa/4.0>, via Wikimedia Commons https://commons.wikimedia.org/wiki/File:Saint_Francis_de_Sales_.jpg

2020, https://spartacus-educational.com/U3Ahistory12.htm.

[471] Britannica, T. Editors of Encyclopedia. "Saint Francis of Sales." *Encyclopedia Britannica*, December 24, 2022. https://www.britannica.com/biography/Saint-Francis-of-Sales

If there was one thing in this world that de Sales hated more than anything, it was Calvinism. While working as a priest and later as a bishop of Geneva (1602), he focused on trying to convert Calvinists back to Catholicism. He focused on the town where he worked, in Chablais, France. History says he succeeded in converting the "bulk" of Calvinists in the town back to Catholicism through his sermons and writings against Calvinism.[472] Since he worked to fight against Reformation efforts, he would be considered part of the Counter-Reformation, which we will discuss in more detail in later chapters.

Besides fighting against Calvinism, de Sales also tried to make Catholicism better. He did this by focusing on women in the Church, particularly nuns. In 1610, he founded the Visitation Order. Today, this group is also referred to as "the Order of the Visitation of Holy Mary," Filles de Sainte-Marie, Visitandines, and the Salesian Sisters. Before establishing this order, most nuns would stay in their cloisters and work from within in. The Visitandines were instead allowed to leave the cloister to help others. They often left the nunnery to help the sick and the poor.[473] This order of nuns is one of de Sales's most influential works, as the order still operates to this day.

Francis de Sales died in 1622. He was later canonized by Pope Pius XI in 1923 and made the Patron Saint of Writers.[474]

John Wycliffe

John Wycliffe, our next Reformer, lived hundreds of years before the formal Reformation began, but his work was instrumental in making it happen. Wycliffe is most famous for creating the first English translation of the Bible.

Wycliffe was born in 1330 in Yorkshire, England. He spent much of his life either learning at or working in colleges, including Oxford. He eventually became a vicar for the Catholic Church in 1361.[475] There were no such things as Reformers yet, just heretics and blasphemers.

---

[472] Britannica, T. Editors of Encyclopedia. "Saint Francis of Sales."

[473] Pernin, Raphael. "Visitation Order." *The Catholic Encyclopedia,* Vol. 15, New York: Robert Appleton Company, 1912. Accessed August 14, 2023. https://www.newadvent.org/cathen/15481a.htm#:~:text=The%20nuns%20of%20the%20Visitation,Jane%20de%20Chantal.

[474] Britannica, T. Editors of Encyclopedia. "Saint Francis of Sales."

[475] Stacey, John. "John Wycliffe." *Encyclopedia Britannica,* August 4, 2023. https://www.britannica.com/biography/John-Wycliffe

The Church saw some of Wycliffe's ideas as radical. For example, he believed that people should be able to have direct access to the Word of God, not just through priests. He both wrote and preached about this concept. This was likely one of his motivations for translating the Bible into English, which he completed in 1381.[476]

Wycliffe's other radical ideas included his belief that the church was taking too much money, transubstantiation wasn't true, and the Church and its clergy members had more power than they should have.[477] The Catholic Church cared for none of these teachings. However, it did not do much to stop him other than refuse to give him more prominent roles in the Church.

Oddly enough, it was not until forty years after Wycliffe's death (1384), in 1415, that he was declared a heretic by the Church. His works were declared heretical and burned. Years later, in 1428, his body was dug up and burned, and the ashes were spread in the River Swift. This was done to remove his body from consecrated ground.[478]

While the Catholic Church did not appreciate Wycliffe, he was more popular with Protestants after his death. His works became more appreciated during and after the Reformation. Today, there are several colleges and churches named after him, and the Wycliffe Global Alliance works to translate the Bible into every language.[479]

Johannes Gutenberg

Johannes Gutenberg is another character from history who influenced the Reformation even though he was not alive when it happened. Unlike the other people in this chapter, he wasn't directly involved with the Catholic Church at all. Instead, his invention tied him into the Reformation.

Gutenberg was born around 1400 (the exact year is unknown) in Mainz. Not much is known about his early life. Most of what historians know about him has to do with his invention in 1450. What did he invent? The printing press.[480] The printing press was a miraculous

---

[476] Stacey, John. "John Wycliffe."

[477] Stacey, John. "John Wycliffe."

[478] Conti, Alessandro. "John Wycliffe." *Stanford Encyclopedia of Philosophy*. Retrieved June 3, 2019.

[479] "Who We Are." Wycliffe Global Alliance, 2023, https://www.wycliffe.net/about-us/.

[480] Mark, Joshua, J. "Johannes Gutenberg." *World History Encyclopedia*, July 25, 2022,

invention that changed the way books were published. As the name implies, the printing press "pressed" out words. It did this by using metal blocks that contained letters or words. These were pressed against ink and paper to make text appear on pages.

Gutenberg Printing Press
Dronpicr, Gutenberg Museum, Mainz. World History Cyclopedia, CC BY-SA, July 18, 2022, https://www.worldhistory.org/image/16159/gutenberg-printing-press/.

https://www.worldhistory.org/Johannes_Gutenberg/.

The printing press was, without exaggeration, revolutionary. Before the printing press was invented, all books had to be handwritten. If a person wanted a copy of a book, they needed access to an original and someone to copy from it. Because of this, making books was an extremely expensive process. Only the richest of the rich, or the Church, could afford books. For this reason, most books were made in monasteries and were religious in nature.[481] Because books were individually made, they could also contain errors, which could lead to misinterpretations of the text.

Once the printing press was invented, printing became much faster, which in turn made books considerably less expensive.[482] Whereas before, people might have been able to write a page or so an hour, the printing press could turn out as many as 250 pages in the same amount of time! This meant the common person could now afford books and other readings. In turn, this led to an increase in the literacy rate of the common people in Europe. As the printing press became more famous, the invention spread around the world, allowing people in various countries to print text in their own languages. This, too, increased literacy rates in other countries across the globe.[483]

One of the first major projects that Gutenberg and his company worked on was a copy of the Bible in the mid-1450s. Once the Bible was completed, Gutenberg turned over the project to artists who added pictures so that the printed Bible looked like an illuminated manuscript that the monasteries were famous for producing.[484] By printing the Bible, even if it would have likely been in Latin at first, more people would have had access to the scriptures.

---

[481] Mark, Joshua, J. "Johannes Gutenberg."

[482] Mark, Joshua, J. "Johannes Gutenberg."

[483] "Discover how Johannes Gutenberg's printing press increased the literacy and education of people in Europe." Encyclopedia Britannica, Inc., n.d., video, https://www.britannica.com/video/171689/history-printing-press-work-discussion-Johannes-Gutenberg.

[484] Mark, Joshua, J. "Johannes Gutenberg."

Gutenberg Bible in the Beinecke Library, Yale University
*Adam Jones from Kelowna, BC, Canada, CC BY-SA 2.0
<https://creativecommons.org/licenses/by-sa/2.0>, via Wikimedia Commons
https://commons.wikimedia.org/wiki/File:Gutenberg_Bible_in_Beinecke_Library_-_Yale_University_-_New_Haven_-_Connecticut_-_USA_%28413900148949%29.jpg*

When Luther began publishing his works, he took full advantage of everything the printing press had to offer. It was a direct result of Gutenberg's work that Luther and other Reformers after him could print translations of the Bible and other works. Without the wide-spread texts, the Reformation would have been a more lengthy and likely less successful venture.

Huldrych Zwingli

After Luther and Calvin, Huldrych (Ulrich) Zwingli is the third most famous Reformer from the standard Reformation period. Like Luther, Zwingli had no plans of creating a new Protestant branch at first. However, some of his ideas were too radical for the Catholic Church, eventually forcing him out and encouraging him to create the Reformed Church.[485]

---

[485] Mark, Joshua J. "Huldrych Zwingli." *World History Encyclopedia*, January 13, 2022, https://www.worldhistory.org/Huldrych_Zwingli/.

Huldrych Zwingli
https://picryl.com/media/zwingli-ulrich-9a0039.

Zwingli was born in 1484 in Switzerland. Like our other Reformers, he was raised in a very religious Catholic household, with several of his relatives involved in the Church in some way. In 1486, he joined them, becoming an ordained priest. However, he did not only preach; he was also sent to war as a military chaplain in 1513. While on campaign, he saw the brutalities of war firsthand and began reading more philosophy and the works of other Reformers, namely Luther.[486] It was no doubt partly due to Luther's writings that Zwingli was inspired to take to the pen himself.

Like Luther, Zwingli believed that the Catholic Church was taking in too much money, and his largest disagreement was with indulgences. He did not believe the Church should be selling indulgences that supposedly allowed people to literally pay off the amount of time they would be in

---

[486] Mark, Joshua J. "Huldrych Zwingli."

purgatory after death.[487] (Remember, purgatory is not in the Bible. However, the common people, most of who could not read Latin, likely would not have known this. Zwingli, able to read in Latin, would have known this.)

Zwingli also did not believe in transubstantiation as the Catholics did. Instead, he saw Communion as more symbolic than literal. However, he still performed Communion and believed it was an important sacrament. The only other sacrament he preached in favor of was baptism. He also believed that priests should be allowed to marry and suggested there was no Biblical reason they should not. He himself was married in 1524.[488]

Most importantly, he believed that the Bible was the highest authority in the Church, even above the pope. He argued that only the Bible could give Christians the laws and rules they should live by. In line with this, he rejected all religious leadership roles. He believed people should be able to interpret the Bible as they saw fit.[489] If their ideas were correct, they would be supported by the Bible. If the views were incorrect, they would not.

Eventually, Zwingli was forced to leave his home because of Protestant persecution. He met with Luther, with whom he hoped to form a religious alliance against the Catholic Church. They agreed on most of their teachings but could not agree on Communion. Because of this disagreement, the two stopped working together.[490]

In 1481, the Catholic cantons officially declared war on Zurich, where Zwingli did most of his work. Zwingli was killed in battle.[491] Of course, his teachings lived on. Today, he is remembered as the leading Reformer in Switzerland.

Katharina von Bora

Last but not least on our list of people who influenced the Reformation is Katharina von Bora. She is most famous for simply being Luther's wife. She is also the only female Reformer in this chapter, and there is good reason for that.

---

[487] Mark, Joshua J. "Huldrych Zwingli."
[488] Mark, Joshua J. "Huldrych Zwingli."
[489] Mark, Joshua J. "Huldrych Zwingli."
[490] Mark, Joshua J. "Huldrych Zwingli."
[491] Mark, Joshua J. "Huldrych Zwingli."

In the 1500s, and in the Catholic Church to this day, women were not allowed to be priests or members of the clergy, excluding nuns. The Catholic Church, in particular, did not allow this in part because Jesus had no female apostles. The Church saw this as meaning that women, while they could believe in Jesus, pray, and spread the gospel, could not preach in an official capacity.[492] The Catholic Church still does not allow women to preach. Some Protestant sects allow women preachers, while others do not; whether women are allowed to preach depends on the denomination and sometimes the specific church in question.

Katherina von Bora (Luther) by Lucas Cranach I
https://picryl.com/media/katharina-von-bora-04-ac11d0.

---

[492] Evert, Jason. "Why Can't Women Be Priests?" Catholic Answers, January 1, 2002, https://www.catholic.com/magazine/print-edition/why-cant-women-be-priests.

So, while Katharina von Bora did not preach in her own right, her ideas likely influenced Luther to create Lutheranism as we know it today. Like many of our other Reformers, Katherina spent much of her life involved with the Catholic Church. As a child, she went to live in a nunnery, and she took her vows to become a full-fledged nun at age fifteen. However, life at the nunnery was anything but ideal. That's why Katherina and some of her Sisters reached out to Luther to ask for his help in escaping from the nunnery, This was both highly dangerous and illegal. If caught, she and her Sisters could be jailed.[493] This is not to mention what could have happened to Luther if he had been caught.

Luther took pity on the women and agreed to help, and the women finally escaped the convent in 1523. Once the women were rescued, Luther helped find husbands for all of them. However, Katherina stood out. She didn't want to marry just anyone. She said she would only marry if she could have either Luther or Nicholas von Amsdorf as her husband. Eventually, Luther agreed to be her husband, despite their ten-plus year age gap, and the couple wed in 1525. The marriage was fruitful, producing six children.[494]

However, not everyone was thrilled about the marriage at first. Some of Luther's colleagues thought the marriage would prove to the Catholic Church that Luther had only left the monastery so he would no longer have to be celibate. However, Luther ignored this, as he had believed priests should be allowed to marry before he wed von Bora.[495] To this day, Lutheran pastors are allowed to marry and have children.

As far as reports show, Katherina was a loyal and helpful wife and supported Luther in his teachings. They remained married for the rest of his life, with Katherina dying six years after him, in 1546.[496]

Conclusion

This short list of influential Reformers helped to shape the Reformation and modern-day Protestantism as we know it. Of course, this list does not contain every person who helped the Reformation efforts, simply the most famous ones. They helped do everything from

---

[493] Kilcrease, Jack. "Katharina von Bora Luther." Lutheran Reformation, December 20, 2016, https://lutheranreformation.org/history/katharina-von-bora-luther/.

[494] Kilcrease, Jack. "Katharina von Bora Luther."

[495] Kilcrease, Jack. "Katharina von Bora Luther."

[496] Kilcrease, Jack. "Katharina von Bora Luther."

making reading materials more accessible to the common person to starting new religious groups. Without them, Christianity would be very different today. Who knows? Protestantism may not have gained the traction and popularity it has today without the help of these people who lived over 500 years ago.

Chapter 14: Corruption and Christianity

The Reformation didn't begin on the whim of some disgruntled nuns, monks, and clergy members. No, the Reformation happened because countless people could see the Catholic Church was facing internal problems. Many of these problems were brought on because of greed—the Catholic Church wanted more money. This directly led to indulgences and other complications the Reformers did not agree with.

In this chapter, we will look at the popes who served during the Reformation from 1510 to 1650. However, as there were twenty different popes throughout these 150 years, some will have more detailed biographies than others. After our pope review, we will take a deeper look at some of the Church's most common corruptions, including simony, nepotism, and more.

Popes of the Reformation

All of the popes below are listed in chronological order of their papacy.[497] As most popes take the throne when they are fairly old, many of their reigns lasted a decade or less. This is part of the reason the Catholic Church went through popes so quickly.

---

[497] "The List of Popes." *The Catholic Encyclopedia.* Vol. 12. New York: Robert Appleton Company, 1911. Accessed 17 Aug. 2023 <http://www.newadvent.org/cathen/12272b.htm>.

Julius II (1503-13)

Pope Julius II was the first pope of the Reformation, one who rose through the ranks in part on merit but also on family ties. His uncle became Pope Sixtus IV in 1471 when Julius (then known as Guiliano della Rovere) was in his twenties. Not long after Sixtus took the papal throne, Guiliano became a cardinal.[498] This obvious nepotism was the first strike against Guiliano. However, it was also an extremely common practice for clergy members, nobility, and laymen alike. In the sixteenth century, much like today, getting work sometimes had to do more with *who* you knew than *what* you knew.

Pope Julius II by Raffaello Sanzio, 1545
https://picryl.com/media/titian-portrait-of-pope-julius-ii-wga22961-6402d8.

Soon after, in 1474, Guiliano went into battle in Umbria for the Papal States. However, during this time, his relationship with the next pope,

---

[498] "Julius II Ca. 1445-1513 Pope." Encyclopedia.com, 2019, https://www.encyclopedia.com/humanities/encyclopedias-almanacs-transcripts-and-maps/julius-ii-ca-1445-1513-pope.

Alexander VI, grew bitter. Because of this, Guiliano did not feel like he could safely return to Rome.[499] He had been trying to get himself elected as pope since as early as the 1480s.[500] However, these dreams were not realized, and other men continued to take on the papacy instead of him. So, he hid in France until Alexander VI's death in 1503. After returning to Rome, he was almost instantly voted in as the new pope. He had gained fame during his time with the military, and as the Papal States were still in danger, the cardinals thought him the best man for the job.[501]

As pope, Guiliano (now Julius II) worked tirelessly to win back lands for the Papal States. He allied with the other members of the League of Cambrai in 1509. With this alliance, he defeated the Venetians and fought off the French, who were threatening to invade Italy. Pope Julius II and his allies were finally successful in 1512, winning their battles.[502] Along with these victories, he added the cities of Piacenza, Parma, and Reggio to the Papal States.[503]

Outside of warfare, Pope Julius II is also famous for being a patron of the arts. He hired the now-famous Michelangelo to paint the ceiling of the Sistine Chapel, which retains his artwork to this day. He also hired the famous artist Raphael for several commissions.[504]

Such a fantastic life came to a mundane end. In 1513, he came down with a fever and died on February 21. He was buried under the floor in St. Peter's Basilica in present-day Vatican City.[505]

Leo X (1513-21)

Pope Leo X is one of the longest-reigning popes of the Reformation period. Like many popes of the time, Giovanni de Medici, the future Pope Leo X, grew up in an extremely religious household. He entered the Church in an official capacity in 1482, at less than ten years old. He became the Abbot of Dont Fouce the year after. It was unusual for

---

[499] "Julius II Ca. 1445-1513 Pope."

[500] Ott, Michael. "Pope Julius II." *The Catholic Encyclopedia*. Vol. 8. New York: Robert Appleton Company, 1910. 17 Aug. 2023 <http://www.newadvent.org/cathen/08562a.htm>.

[501] "Julius II Ca. 1445-1513 Pope."

[502] "Julius II Ca. 1445-1513 Pope."

[503] Ott, Michael. "Pope Julius II."

[504] "Julius II Ca. 1445-1513 Pope."

[505] "Death of Pope Julius II." Italy On This Day, February 21, 2016, https://www.italyonthisday.com/2016/02/death-of-pope-julius-ii-san-pietro-in-vincoli-rome.html.

someone so young to have an official placement in the Church. It became even more odd when Pope Innocent VIII made him a cardinal when he was only thirteen years old.[506] Part of Giovanni's quick rise in rank was because he belonged to the famous de Medici family, who had their grip on the Catholic Church and in numerous monarchies in Europe.

Pope Leo X by Raphael, 1518
https://commons.wikimedia.org/wiki/File:Raffaello,_ritratto_di_papa_leone_X_tra_i_cardinali_luigi_de%27_rossi_e_giulio_de%27_medici,_1518,_03.jpg.

While being a de Medici helped gain Giovanni power, it also caused him serious problems. His father, Lorenzo de Medici (Lorenzo the Magnificent), died in 1492. Because of this, Giovanni's older brother, Piero di Lorenzo de Medici, took over their father's lands. Piero was only twenty-one. While he had military experience, he was not the brightest character in history. After one military-based mistake after another, Piero, Giovanni, and many other members of the de Medici family were exiled from Florence in 1494.[507] This forced Giovanni out of the range of Rome for years.

---

[506] Löffler, Klemens. "Pope Leo X." *The Catholic Encyclopedia.* Vol. 9. New York: Robert Appleton Company, 1910. 17 Aug. 2023 <http://www.newadvent.org/cathen/09162a.htm>.

[507] Britannica, T. Editors of Encyclopedia. "Piero di Lorenzo de' Medici." *Encyclopedia Britannica,* January 1, 2023. https://www.britannica.com/biography/Piero-di-Lorenzo-de-Medici.

It wasn't until 1500 that Giovanni returned to Rome. All this time, he continued his work as a cardinal. In Rome, he was more easily able to secure his promotion. In 1512, he was made a papal legate to Pope Julius II. When the pope died one year later, Giovanni took his place and became Pope Leo X.[508]

As pope, Leo X continued Julius II's art and architecture projects and commissioned artists for his own commissions. One of his most famous commissions was the *Stanza dell'Incendio de Borgo*. Like Julius II, he also continued to hire Raphael for various projects. He also helped to set up colleges in Rome and Florence and improved the roads in modern-day Vatican City. While many of these art and architecture pieces were beautiful and still stand to this day, they also came with a hefty price tag. By the time of his death in 1521, likely due to illness, he had sunk 600,000 ducats into projects.[509]

Adrian VI (1522-23)

Adrian Florensz Boeyens, one of the few popes to keep his given first name, was born in 1459. As a teenager, he was ordained as the bishop of Tortosa. One year later, in 1517, he was made a cardinal. Only a few years after that, in 1522, he became pope. Unlike other popes, his quick ascension had more to do with what he knew than who he knew. He was famous for having several years of university study under his belt and for tutoring Erasmus.[510] However, there was one problem—he wasn't Italian.

While one would think the clergy would be the last people to care about a person's ethnicity, that was not the case. Things only stacked against him, as he inherited Leo X's massive pile of debt. Because of this, he tried to reduce the Church's spending, much to the distaste of many in Rome. He reached out to the heads of European monarchies for help, but to no avail.[511]

---

[508] "Pope Leo X (Giovanni de' Medici)." The Medici Family, October 31, 2022, https://themedicifamily.com/pope-leo-x.

[509] "Pope Leo X (Giovanni de' Medici)."

[510] Britannica, T. Editors of Encyclopedia. "Adrian VI." *Encyclopedia Britannica*, February 26, 2023. https://www.britannica.com/biography/Adrian-VI.

[511] Loughlin, James. "Pope Adrian VI." *The Catholic Encyclopedia*. Vol. 1. New York: Robert Appleton Company, 1907. 17 Aug. 2023 <http://www.newadvent.org/cathen/01159b.htm>.

Pope Adrian VI, 1523
https://commons.wikimedia.org/wiki/File:Portrait_of_Pope_Adrian_VI_(after_Jan_van_Scorel).jpg.

All of this increased Adrian's health problems and put him in a quick decline. He died within a year of taking the papacy. He now has a monument dedicated to him in Rome.[512]

Clement VII (1523-34)

Next on our list of popes is Clement VII, born Giulio de Medici. This last name should sound familiar. Guilio was the grandson of Piero de Medici, the brother of Pope Leo X.[513] At this point in history, the Medici family still held important ties with the Catholic Church.

By 1513, when he was in his early thirties, Guilio had already been made archbishop of Florence and a cardinal. Both of these positions were given to him by his cousin, Pope Leo X.[514] This was proving to be another case of nepotism in the Church.

---

[512] Loughlin, James. "Pope Adrian VI."

[513] Thurston, Herbert. "Pope Clement VII." *The Catholic Encyclopedia*. Vol. 4. New York: Robert Appleton Company, 1908. 18 Aug. 2023 <http://www.newadvent.org/cathen/04024a.htm>.

[514] Britannica, T. Editors of Encyclopedia. "Clement VII." *Encyclopedia Britannica*, August 18, 2023. https://www.britannica.com/biography/Clement-VII-pope.

The family's efforts to make a name for Guilio in the Church paid off when he was chosen to become the next pope in 1523.[515] While ascending to the papacy was easy enough, keeping the Catholic Church under control during his reign was another matter. By the 1520s, the Reformation was in full swing. By this time, Martin Luther was active, and in the coming decades, other Reformers would follow in his lead.

On top of the religious scruples surrounding the Church, Clement VII also had to pick sides in a political struggle between France and the Holy Roman Empire. Throughout the 1520s, he went back and forth on which side he was supporting. Constantly switching sides put him in danger, so much so that he had to take refuge in and outside of Rome periodically for months at a time.[516]

Pope Clement VII is perhaps most famous for opposing Henry VIII's attempt to divorce his first wife, Catherine of Aragon. Of course, Clement VII could not go back on another pope's word and annul the marriage. That, and Catherine of Aragon was a staunch supporter of the Catholic Church.[517] All these things made for a terribly messy situation with England and did not help improve the pope's popularity.

One of the biggest problems Pope Clement VII faced with the Reformation was the fact that he simply didn't know what to do about it. Like any other Catholic, he did not support the Reformation and would have rather seen it end. However, he hesitated to take action. In wasting precious time, the Reformation movement had time to grow—and grow exponentially. His inaction spurred the Protestants and sowed resentment in Catholics. He became so hated in Germany that the Protestants reigned supreme more quickly than in other countries.[518]

Everything continued to go downhill for Clement in the 1530s. Henry VIII divorced Catherine of Aragon and married Anne Boleyn. In November 1534, King Henry VIII passed the Act of Supremacy, which officially broke England from the Catholic Church, formed the Church of England, and made the king the head of his new church.

No doubt, the considerable stress he was under affected his health negatively. In December 1533, he came down with a fever and stomach

---

[515] Britannica, T. Editors of Encyclopedia. "Clement VII."
[516] Britannica, T. Editors of Encyclopedia. "Clement VII."
[517] Starkey, David. *Six Wives: The Queens of Henry VIII.*
[518] Britannica, T. Editors of Encyclopedia. "Clement VII."

issues. His skin seemed to turn a shade of yellow, which could suggest that he was jaundiced.[519] He remained ill for the last year of his life, finally dying on September 23, 1534. Some suggested he was poisoned, but it is more likely that he was simply sick.[520] He is buried in the Santa Maria sopra Minerva in Rome.[521]

Paul III (1534-49)

Pope Paul III was born Alessandro Farnese in 1468. Like the Medici family, the Farnese family was also famous in Rome. More importantly, they were well-connected. From a young age, Alessandro was taught and tutored by the best money could buy. However, even all the money in the world couldn't keep him out of trouble. He landed himself in jail. His family helped get him out (likely buying his way out), but he had to stay with some Medicis to finish his education.[522]

Alessandro went to live and learn in the court of Lorenzo de Medici in Florence. He met several other Medicis around this same time, some of whom were members of the clergy. Eventually, he returned to Rome to speak to Pope Innocent VIII, who invited Alessandro to work within the Church. One thing led to another, and by 1503, he was a cardinal.[523] He served faithfully for the next thirty years before becoming pope himself.

---

[519] Strathern, Paul. *The Medici: Power, Money, and Ambition in the Italian Renaissance.* New York, Pegasus, 2016.

[520] Rodocanachi, Emmanuel. *History of Rome: The Popes Adrian VI to Clement VII.* Paris, Hacette, 1933.

[521] Visceglia, Maria A. "A Comparative Historiographic Reflection on Sovereignty in Early Modern Europe: Interregnum Rites and Papal Funerals." *Cultural Exchange in Early Modern Europe.* Cambridge University Press, 2006.

[522] "Historical Figure: Alessandro Farnese." Histouring, n.d., https://www.histouring.com/en/historical-figure/alessandro-farnese/.

[523] "Historical Figure: Alessandro Farnese."

Pope Paul III by Titan, 1543
https://commons.wikimedia.org/wiki/File:Portrait_of_Pope_Paul_III_Farnese_(by_Titian)_-_National_Museum_of_Capodimonte.jpg.

Pope Paul III received anything but a peaceful Church to mentor when he took on the papacy in 1534. England had just left the Catholic Church, Germany had all but officially rejected the Church, and now France and the Holy Roman Empire were threatening to go to war. While there was little the pope could do about England and Germany, he still had some power over the Holy Roman Empire and France. He tried to intervene to get the battles to stop, but it did little good.[524]

After the death of King Frances I, Pope Paul III stepped back. Of course, the king's death had nothing to do with him, but he had been an ally. The pope declared that he would remain neutral in any fights between France and the Holy Roman Empire.[525] After all, he had set up one council after another to try to help, especially with the religious differences between these two countries, not to mention the newly

---

[524] "Historical Figure: Alessandro Farnese."
[525] "Historical Figure: Alessandro Farnese."

Protestant countries, and none of it had made much of a difference.[526] So, what was the point in continuing?

Shortly after deciding to be neutral, Pope Paul III came down with a terrible fever. His health declined rapidly, and he died. He is buried in St. Peter's Church, Rome, in a tomb designed by the artist Michelangelo.[527]

Julius III (1550-55)

Giammaria (Giovanni Maria) Ciocchi del Monte is another future pope from a prestigious family in Rome. His father worked in law, and he went on to study the same as he grew up. By 1534, he was the legate of Bologna. He continued to rise through the ranks until he was finally voted in as the new pope after Paul III's death. He ascended to the throne of St. Peter in 1550.[528]

While taking the throne, Julius III also took over the debates between France and the Holy Roman Empire. He was more decisive than Paul and sided with the Holy Roman Empire. However, the Holy Roman Empire eventually lost, which was quite embarrassing for the pope. He stepped back from the Church and worked more behind the scenes to create reforms.[529]

Meanwhile, he was involved in a serious scandal. This event in history is often called "the Innocenzo scandal." While in middle age, Pope Julius adopted a teenage beggar boy, Innocenzo del Monte, as his nephew, meaning he had his brother adopt the boy. Soon after, the boy was brought into religious life and was called the "cardinal-nephew."[530] However, rumors soon spread that the pope's interest in his new nephew was not entirely wholesome. Long story short, many clergy members thought the pope was having sex with Innocenzo. However, he never admitted as much.

One of the best things that could have happened to Rome was England's return to the Church as Queen Mary I took the throne in

---

[526] Loughlin, James. "Pope Paul III." *The Catholic Encyclopedia*. Vol. 11. New York: Robert Appleton Company, 1911. Accessed August 21, 2023, <http://www.newadvent.org/cathen/11579a.htm>.

[527] Loughlin, James. "Pope Paul III."

[528] Ott, Michael. "Pope Julius III." *The Catholic Encyclopedia*. Vol. 8. New York: Robert Appleton Company, 1910. August 21, 2023 <http://www.newadvent.org/cathen/08564a.htm>.

[529] Ott, Michael. "Pope Julius III."

[530] Pastor, Freiherr L. *The History of the Popes*. Legare Street Press, 2022.

1553.[531] However, the pope did not live long after this. He had been suffering from gout for some time, and it finally contributed to his death on March 23, 1555.[532] However, some sources say it was more likely that he died from stomach cancer.

Marcellus II (1555)

Marcellus II, born Marcello Cervini, was one of the shortest-reigning popes in history. Born in 1501, he rose through the ranks of the clergy and became a cardinal in 1539. He continued to serve as a cardinal until he was elected pope in 1555. He ascended to the throne of St. Peter on April 9 or 10, 1555.[533] While Marcellus II had great aspirations to reform the Catholic Church, he did not live long enough to do much of anything. He died suddenly of a stroke on May 1, 1555.[534] In total, he only reigned for twenty-two days.

Paul IV (1555-59)

While Pope Marcellus II was more of a footnote in the history of the Reformation, Paul IV was one of the main players. Born Giovanni Pietro Carafa, he had strong ties to the Church. His uncle, Oliviero Carafa, was a cardinal and introduced Giovanni to the papal court in 1476 when he was about eighteen.[535]

---

[531] Ott, Michael. "Pope Julius III."

[532] "Pope Julius III (1487-1555) - a dream about the power of ... a family." Roma Non Per Tutti, n.d., https://roma-nonpertutti.com/en/article/417/pope-julius-iii-14871555-a-dream-about-the-power-of-a-family.

[533] Britannica, T. Editors of Encyclopedia. "Marcellus II." *Encyclopedia Britannica*, May 2, 2023. https://www.britannica.com/biography/Marcellus-II.

[534] Pirie, Valerie. *The Triple Crown: An Account of the Papal Conclaves From the Fifteenth Century to the Present Day.* New York: G.P. Putnam's Sons, 1936.

[535] Loughlin, James. "Pope Paul IV." *The Catholic Encyclopedia.* Vol. 11. New York: Robert Appleton Company, 1911. August 22, 2023 <http://www.newadvent.org/cathen/11581a.htm>.

Pope Paul IV by Jacopino del Conte, 1560
https://commons.wikimedia.org/wiki/File:Pope_Paul_IV_%E2%80%93_Jacopino_Conte_(Manner),_ca._1560.jpg.

Giovanni spent much of his youth traveling around Europe, doing tasks for the pope and other clergy members. In 1536, he had earned so much respect within the papal courts that he was made a cardinal. Shortly after, he was also made the Archbishop of Naples.[536]

Finally, in 1555, he was made the new pope. It didn't take him long to abuse his powers as such. He made his nephew, Carlo Carafa, a cardinal. This was especially scandalous, as Carlo had no official religious training. He also gave gifts of land to friends and family members.[537]

Perhaps worse of all, in the Church's eyes, was his fumbling of England. At the time of his papacy, England had been returned to the Catholic faith by Queen Mary I. However, with the queen's death in 1558, her sister, Queen Elizabeth I, took the throne of England and returned the country to Protestantism. He tried to fight this, claiming that Elizabeth was illegitimate and could not take the throne.[538] However, his

---

[536] Loughlin, James. "Pope Paul IV."

[537] Loughlin, James. "Pope Paul IV."

[538] Loughlin, James. "Pope Paul IV."

opinion did not seem to matter much to England, and Elizabeth kept the throne nonetheless.

Paul IV did not outlive Queen Mary I by long. His health took a turn for the worse in May 1559. This was not unexpected, as the pope was in his early eighties. After months of recurring sickness, he died on August 17, 1559.[539]

Pius IV (1559-65)

Another in a long line of Medici, Giovanni Angelo Medici was born in Milan in 1499. He always had ambitions to be someone important but not always to become a pope. He first aimed to become a lawyer before switching his field of study to theology. This turned out to be a good move for Giovanni, as he rose through the ranks quickly and began working in the papal court in 1527. During this time, he worked closely with both Pope Julius III and Paul IV.[540]

Pope Pius IV by Scipione Pulzone
https://commons.wikimedia.org/wiki/File:Portrait_of_Pope_Pius_IV,_three-quarter-length,_seated_at_a_draped_table_(Circle_of_Scipione_Pulzone).jpg

---

[539] Setton, Kenneth M. *The Papacy and the Levant, 1204-1571. Volume IV: The Sixteenth Century.* Philadelphia: American Philosophical Society, 1984.

[540] "Pope Pius IV." Pope History, 2023, https://popehistory.com/popes/pope-pius-iv/.

Eventually, Pius IV was made pope in December 1559. Like several of the popes before him, he inherited an unsteadied Catholic system. Lutheranism was growing at an alarming rate. So far, the Catholic Church had not found any way to curb this growth. However, Pius IV thought holding a council might do the trick.[541] In 1562, he took part in the 19th Ecumenical Council of Trent. This council had formally begun in 1545, long before Pius was pope. Now, in the third period of the council, Pius took on one of the bigger threats to Catholicism: Calvinism. The Church doubled down on its beliefs, giving concrete definitions of rules and laws and issuing doctrinal statements on several issues, including saints, relics, purgatory, and indulgences.[542] This was to make the Church's stance on these issues clearer, in the hope that Protestants would understand them better and return to Catholicism.

To Pius's credit, this did work a little. In the previous few decades since the beginning of the Reformation, the Catholic Church had changed some of its ways. Pointing out that they had changed brought some people back to the flock but by no means crushed the Reformation.[543]

In 1565, a conspiracy was uncovered. However, this time it was not caused by the pope. A scheme was discovered in which Benedetto Accolti was trying to murder the pope. Luckily, he was found out in time to save the pope's life.[544] The pope lived for another few years before dying of an infection in 1565. He was buried in Santa Maria degli Angeli.[545]

Saint Pius V (1566-72)

St. Pius V was born Antonio Ghislieri in 1504. He joined the order of the Dominicans of Voghera when he was in his twenties and was formally ordained in 1528. Ghislieri spent the next decade in this monastery, continuing his religious studies and living a simple life. In 1556, he was made the Bishop of Sutri. The next year, he was made a cardinal and the

---

[541] "Pope Pius IV."

[542] Britannica, T. Editors of Encyclopedia. "Council of Trent." *Encyclopedia Britannica*, July 14, 2023. https://www.britannica.com/event/Council-of-Trent.

[543] Britannica, T. Editors of Encyclopedia. "Council of Trent."

[544] Reeves, Marjorie. *The Influence of Prophecy in the Later Middle Ages: A Study in Joachimism*, Oxford University Press, 1969.

[545] Adams, John P. "Sede Vacante 1565-1655." CSUN, October 15, 2015, http://www.csun.edu/~hcfll004/SV1566.html.

inquisitor general.⁵⁴⁶

Ghislieri was elected pope in 1566, becoming Pope Pius V. In the beginning of his reign, he focused on giving to the poor—in excessive amounts. While this was generous, it put a dent in the Papal Court's bank holdings. He also visited the sick, prayed often, and tried to live as close to his previous monastic life as possible.⁵⁴⁷

Pope Pius V by Bartolomeo Passarotti, 1566
https://commons.wikimedia.org/wiki/File:Bartolomeo_Passarotti_-_Pius_V.jpg.

Outside of his personal life, Pius V tried to improve the "morality" of those around him. He worked to reform the clergy, encouraging them to live more simple lives. He also limited prostitution and made bullfighting illegal. However, like many of the popes before him, he also had the Protestants to deal with. He did his best to support the Catholic nobility. At the same time, he excommunicated the Protestant Queen Elizabeth I

---

⁵⁴⁶ Lataste, Joseph. "Pope St. Pius V." *The Catholic Encyclopedia*. Vol. 12. New York: Robert Appleton Company, 1911.
⁵⁴⁷ Lataste, Joseph. "Pope St. Pius V."

and gave overwhelming support to the Catholic Queen Mary of Scots.[548]

Pope Pius V died in 1572, in part due to bladder stones and the resulting symptoms. He was canonized in 1696 and became a saint in 1712.[549]

Gregory XIII (1572-85)

Gregory XIII was born Ugo Boncompagni in 1502. His mother came from an aristocratic line, allowing him to get the best education, which he used to get a doctorate in law from the University of Bologna. He stayed at the college for almost a decade afterward as a professor. Unlike many of the other popes, he had a son before joining the clergy, named Giacomo.[550] However, he never married Giacomo's mother.[551] Since clergy are made to take a vow of chastity but not a vow of virginity (which means they could have had sex in the past but not after being ordained), Ugo was able to join the clergy when he was in his forties. His law education helped him gain acclaim, as he was instrumental in the successes of the Council of Trent. He worked on this from 1562-63.[552]

All of this work with the council and other Church matters enabled him to win the papacy in 1572. This was shortly followed by the most tragic event in his papacy, the St. Bartholomew's Day Massacre. Over 4,000 French Huguenots (a branch of Protestantism) were murdered by the command of the French monarchy. The pope apparently had no knowledge this was going to happen. However, that didn't stop the event from tarnishing his good name.[553]

Of course, Gregory XIII did some good deeds that are still remembered today. One of his creations was the Gregorian calendar, which most countries still use to this day. He also tried to improve the training for priests and was a fan of missionary work. He sent some of the earliest successful missionaries on missions in India, Japan, and Brazil.[554]

---

[548] Lataste, Joseph. "Pope St. Pius V."

[549] Corkery, James; Worcester, Thomas. *The Papacy Since 1500: From Italian Prince to Universal Pastor*. Cambridge University Press, 2010.

[550] "Pope Gregory XIII." Papal Artifacts, 2021, https://www.papalartifacts.com/portfolio-item/pope-gregory-xiii/.

[551] "Pope Gregory XIII." Pope History, 2023, https://popehistory.com/popes/pope-gregory-xiii/.

[552] "Pope Gregory XIII." Papal Artifacts.

[553] "Pope Gregory XIII." Papal Artifacts.

[554] "Pope Gregory XIII." Papal Artifacts.

Pope Gregory VIII died on April 10, 1585. He is now buried in the Chapel of St. Peter, also called the Gregorian Chapel.[555]

Sixtus V (1585-90)

Felice Piergentile (later Peretti) was born in 1521 when the Reformation was in full swing.[556] Each of the popes before him would have been able to remember a time before the Reformation. In a way, his popehood was the start of a new era.

Felice joined the clergy as a member of the Franciscan order in 1533 when he was still a child. However, he was not ordained until 1547, when he was sixteen. He then spent the rest of his adulthood working within the Church in one capacity or another. He was made a bishop in 1566, a cardinal in 1570, and was an inquisitor general for several years. Finally, he was unanimously elected pope in 1585.[557]

The Church was more or less broke when Sixtus V took the throne. Because of this, one of his main focuses as pope was to rebuild the treasury. He set new taxes, regulated prices as well as he could, and even sold Church office positions (which only added scandal to his name). However, at the same time, his spending was immense. He set up numerous architectural plans, including rebuilding palaces in the Vatican.[558]

Outside of finances, Sixtus also made reforms within the Church regarding clergy members. With his 1586 papal bull, he set the maximum number of cardinals to seventy. This proved to be successful for about 400 years.[559]

Lastly, he put a lot of effort into the Counter-Reformation, especially in France. During this time, France was going through the Wars of Religion, which pitted French Catholics against French Huguenots (Protestants). In these efforts, he excommunicated Henry of Navarre in 1585. He also encouraged Spain to invade England.[560]

---

[555] "Pope Gregory XIII." Pape History.

[556] Ott, Michael. "Pope Sixtus V." *The Catholic Encyclopedia.* Vol. 14. New York: Robert Appleton Company, 1912, August 30, 2023 <http://www.newadvent.org/cathen/14033a.htm>.

[557] Britannica, T. Editors of Encyclopedia. "Sixtus V." *Encyclopedia Britannica*, August 23, 2023. https://www.britannica.com/biography/Sixtus-V

[558] Britannica, T. Editors of Encyclopedia. "Sixtus V."

[559] Britannica, T. Editors of Encyclopedia. "Sixtus V."

[560] Britannica, T. Editors of Encyclopedia. "Sixtus V.'

In 1590, Sixtus contracted malaria. He died within three days of showing symptoms, on August 27. His reputation was mixed at the time of his passing.[561]

Urban VII (1590)

Giovanni Battista Castagna was born in 1521. As a young adult, he went to several colleges and studied both theology and law. When he finished his studies, he began working as a lawyer for the Roman Curia.[562]

Eventually, Giovanni was chosen to be the Archbishop of Rossano. There was just one problem—he wasn't even an ordained priest. So, he became ordained in March 1533 and became the bishop shortly after. After this, he was fully invested in church work. Later, Gregory XIII made him a cardinal.[563]

When Sixtus V died, Giovanni was instated as Pope Urban VIII. However, he had one of the shortest popehoods, lasting twelve days. In those twelve days, he banned tobacco, making it an excommunicable offense.[564]

Like Sixtus, he died of malaria. He was first buried in the Vatican, but his body was later moved to the Church of Santa Maria sopra Minerva. He left his riches to the Church, which was intended to be used to support young women in the area.[565]

Gregory XIV (1590-91)

Niccolò Sfondrato was born in 1535. He was from a prominent family, as his father was a senator. As a young adult, Niccolò studied law. In his adult years, he joined the clergy and later became the Bishop of Cremona. After befriending Pope Gregory XIII, he was made a cardinal.[566]

While Gregory XIV was only pope for less than a year, he racked up all kinds of scandal. He was known to have a penchant for nepotism. He made his nephew, Ercole Sfandrato, the general of the Church, sending

---

[561] Collier, Theodore F. "Sixtus." In Chisholm, Hugh (ed.). *Encyclopedia Britannica*. Vol. 25 (11th ed.). Cambridge University Press, 1911.

[562] "Pope Urban VII." Pope History, 2023, https://popehistory.com/popes/pope-urban-vii/.

[563] "Pope Urban VII."

[564] "Pope Urban VII."

[565] "Pope Urban VII."

[566] "Pope Gregory XIV." Pope History, 2023, https://popehistory.com/popes/pope-gregory-xiv/.

him to France to fight.[567]

Pope Gregory XIV
https://commons.wikimedia.org/wiki/File:Roman_School_%E2%80%93_Portrait_of_Pope_Gregory_XIV_(16th_Century).jpg.

However, Gregory XIV did some good things for the church as well. For one, he made betting on who would become the pope illegal. While excommunication wasn't guaranteed if a person was caught doing this, it was a possibility.[568] He also donated much of his money to the poor.[569]

Then again, some things Gregory XIV did as pope could be seen as either good or bad depending on the standpoint of the person judging. Like some of the popes before him, he was also involved with the French Wars of Religion. He sided with King Philip, a Catholic, and excommunicated Henry IV of France. Unrelated to the wars, he literally rewrote the Catholic stance on abortion. Before him, abortion was a sinful stop. With his new papal bull, abortion was only a sin if the fetus was

---

[567] Frakas, Catherine. "Biography - Pope Gregory XIV - The Papal Library." Saint Mike, March 17, 2021, https://saint-mike.org/blogs/papal-library/gregoryxiv-biography.

[568] "Pope Gregory XIV." Pope History, 2023, https://popehistory.com/popes/pope-gregory-xiv/.

[569] Frakas, Catherine. "Biography - Pope Gregory XIV - The Papal Library."

animated.⁵⁷⁰ For example, it would not be a sin to abort a fetus that had already died in utero or that was too young to begin moving.

Like most popes, Gregory XIV came down with a health problem that would later lead to his demise. Complications and pain due to gallstones led to his death on October 16, 1591.⁵⁷¹

Innocent IX (1591)

Another short-lived pope, Giovanni Antonio Fachinetti, was born in 1519. He quickly rose through the Catholic ranks and was the Bishop of Nicastro by the 1560s. He also held roles as a papal ambassador and in the Roman Inquisition. He was made the patriarch of Jerusalem in 1576 and a cardinal in 1583.⁵⁷²

As pope, he continued to support Spain and work against Henry IV of France. However, he did not live long enough to accomplish much.⁵⁷³ Pope Innocent IX died on December 18, 1591, due to a feverish cold. He is buried in the Vatican Grottoes.⁵⁷⁴

Clement VIII (1592-1605)

We are finally getting back to a pope who lasted more than a year. Ippolito Aldobrandini was born in 1536. His father was a canon lawyer, so Ippolito had the benefit of growing up close to the Church. He eventually entered into the law business himself as a judge in the Holy See. It was partly because of his legal background that he was elected pope in 1592.⁵⁷⁵

Clement's politics were unlike those of the popes immediately before him. While most of them sided against King Henry IV of France, Clement reversed his excommunication and focused his armies elsewhere.⁵⁷⁶ He instead sent the Papal State's troops to fight in the Long War, also known as the Fifteen Years' War of Hungary. This war began

---

[570] "Pope Gregory XIV."

[571] "Pope Gregory XIV."

[572] Britannica, T. Editors of Encyclopedia. "Innocent IX." *Encyclopedia Britannica*, July 16, 2023. https://www.britannica.com/biography/Innocent-IX

[573] Weber, Nicholas. "Pope Innocent IX." *The Catholic Encyclopedia*. Vol. 8. New York: Robert Appleton Company, 1910. August 30, 2023 <http://www.newadvent.org/cathen/08020a.htm>.

[574] Adams, John P. "Sede Vacante 1591." SCUN, July 24, 2015, http://www.csun.edu/~hcfll004/SV1591.html

[575] "Pope Clement VIII." Pope History, 2023, https://popehistory.com/popes/pope-clement-viii/.

[576] "Pope Clement VIII."

in the early 1590s and went on throughout Clement's reign. Along with Spain, Austria, and over a dozen other nations, Clement's side fought against the Ottoman Empire and its allies. Both sides faced heavy losses, but the pope and his allies finally won in 1606.[577] However, Clement would not be alive to see it.

Pope Clement VIII
https://commons.wikimedia.org/wiki/File:Papst_Clemens_VIII_Italian_17th_century.jpg.

In the meantime, Clement passed a number of anti-Semitic papal bulls. Some of these banned Jewish people from residing in Rome and other Church-held territories.[578] Other negative things he did were to expand the list of forbidden books and increase the efforts of the Inquisition, which would lead to countless non-Catholic deaths across Europe.[579]

Eventually, Clement found his end through illness. For some time before his death, he was afflicted with gout, and complications due to this

---

[577] Csorba, Csaba; Estok, Janos; and Salamon, Konrad. *The Illustrated History of Hungary*. Magyar Konuvklub, Hungary, 1999.

[578] "Pope Clement VIII."

[579] Britannica, T. Editors of Encyclopedia. "Clement VIII." *Encyclopedia Britannica*, March 1, 2023. https://www.britannica.com/biography/Clement-VIII-pope

would lead to his death in 1605. He was buried first in St. Peter's Basilica but then moved to the Borghese Chapel.[580]

Leo XI (1605)

Once again, we are back to a pope who reigned for less than a year. Alessandro Ottaviano de Medici was born in Florence in 1535. As a member of the Medici family, Alessandro was raised in a life of privilege. He eventually joined the clergy and moved through the ranks quickly. He was made the Bishop of Pistoia in 1573, an archbishop in '74, and a cardinal in '83.[581]

After Clement's death, there was much debate as to who would be the next pope. Alessandro used his Medici connections to give him an edge in the voting. The monarchy of France donated around 300,000 ecus as a bribe to get Alessandro the popehood. It worked. He was made pope on April 1, 1604. However, he became sick soon after.[582] He died less than a month later from this illness.[583]

Paul V (1605-21)

Camillo Borghese was born in Rome in 1550. Like many of the other popes during the Reformation, he started out studying law before making a name for himself in the Church. In fact, his church career started as a canon lawyer.[584]

For years, he worked as the papal envoy to Spain under Pope Clement VIII. Clement also made him a cardinal in 1596. He served in this position until he was eventually made pope in 1605.[585]

Most of Paul's conflicts had to do with his less-than-perfect relationships with secular European leaders. This was because a precedent had been set that clergy members were allowed to hold their own courts to try other clergy members for crimes. However, once, the court in Venice tried to judge two clergy members in a secular court.

---

[580] "Pope Clement VIII."

[581] Ott, Michael. "Pope Leo XI." *The Catholic Encyclopedia*. Vol. 9. New York: Robert Appleton Company, 1910. September 1, 2023.

[582] Ott, Michael. "Pope Leo XI."

[583] Williams, George L. *Papal Genealogy: The Families and Descendants of the Popes*. McFarland & Company, 1998.

[584] "Pope Paul V." Pope History, 2023, https://popehistory.com/popes/pope-paul-v/.

[585] Britannica, T. Editors of Encyclopedia. "Paul V." *Encyclopedia Britannica*, January 24, 2023. https://www.britannica.com/biography/Paul-V

Luckily, King Henry IV of France intervened before the situation got too serious to remedy. However, this brought up the question, "Why can't secular courts try clergy members?"[586] Religious courts, sometimes called ecclesiastical courts, still operate in some parts of the world today, including in the United States. These are usually used for divorces, annulments, and similar religious matters rather than crimes.[587] However, this does not mean that priests and clergy members cannot be tried in a secular/state court. If a clergy member is accused of a crime that breaks state or federal laws, they would likely need to be tried by a state or federal court.

Paul also faced conflicts with James I of England (James VI of Scotland). While England was a blend of Protestants and Catholics, and Scotland was primarily Catholic, James still encouraged Catholics to be more loyal to their country than to Rome. The king even wanted English citizens to take an oath saying so.[588] Paul forbade Catholics from signing this oath. This divided Catholics in the country, which only led to more problems for Paul.[589]

Since things were not going well with England and Venice, Paul focused on the king of France, with whom he was on good terms. This went well enough, but it left Germany ignored. At this time, Germany had a mix of Protestant and Catholic citizens. During Paul's reign, the Thirty Years War began in Germany. Paul avoided taking sides, even though one was decidedly Catholic.[590]

Aside from conflict, Paul was also easily caught up in scandal. He was active on the nepotism scene, making his nephew Marcantonio Borghese a prince of Vivaro. He also spent large sums on architectural and artistic vanity projects in Rome.[591]

In his last years of life, Paul grew ill and began to suffer from strokes. In 1621, one final bout of strokes ended his life. He is buried in the

---

[586] "Pope Paul V."

[587] Masci, David and Lawton, Elizabeth. "Applying God's Law: Religious Courts and Mediation in the U.S." Pew Research Center, April 8, 2013, https://www.pewresearch.org/religion/2013/04/08/applying-gods-law-religious-courts-and-mediation-in-the-us/.

[588] "Pope Paul V."

[589] Britannica, T. Editors of Encyclopedia. "Paul V."

[590] Britannica, T. Editors of Encyclopedia. "Paul V."

[591] Britannica, T. Editors of Encyclopedia. "Paul V."

Borghese Cappella Paolina of Santa Maria Maggiore, a building he commissioned.[592]

Gregory XV (1621-23)

Alessandro Ludovisi was born in 1554 in Bologna. He came from a rich, noble family; because of this, he could afford the best education. He studied at the University of Bologna, where he earned a doctorate in law.[593]

He was older than most other popes when he entered the clergy, becoming an archbishop in 1612 and a cardinal in 1616.[594]

Gregory was elected as the new pope in 1621. He was pope for a little over two years, but he did many great things while he was there. Arguably, one of the most important things he did was invent a secret ballot for all future papal elections.[595] In theory, this would decrease simony, blackmail, and any other interference that could cause someone to vote for a man they did not think was right for the job.

Like many other popes, he was also guilty of nepotism. During his time as pope, he made one of his nephews and cousins cardinals. He also spent an excessive amount of money on art commissions, including paintings of himself.[596]

Gregory's popehood ended quickly due to his death. Since before he became pope, his health was failing. He died from generalized poor health on July 4, 1623. He is currently buried in the Church of Saint Ignazio.[597]

Urban VIII (1623-44)

Near the end of the Reformation, we have Maffeo Barberini. He was born to a noble father and was the heir to his wealthy uncle. He had all the advantages a person could have in the 1600s and used them to get a

---

[592] McGinness, Frederick J. "Paul V (Pope) (Camillo Borghese; 1552-1621; Reigned 1605-1621)." Europe, 1450 to 1789: Encyclopedia of the Early Modern World. Encyclopedia.com. (August 23, 2023). https://www.encyclopedia.com/history/encyclopedias-almanacs-transcripts-and-maps/paul-v-pope-camillo-borghese-1552-1621-reigned-1605-1621.

[593] Britannica, T. Editors of Encyclopedia. "Gregory XV." *Encyclopedia Britannica*, July 4, 2023. https://www.britannica.com/biography/Gregory-XV.

[594] Britannica, T. Editors of Encyclopedia. "Gregory XV."

[595] Britannica, T. Editors of Encyclopedia. "Gregory XV."

[596] "Pope Gregory XV." Pope History, 2023, https://popehistory.com/popes/pope-gregory-xv/.

[597] "Pope Gregory XV."

great education. He attended a Jesuit school and later studied at the University of Pisa, where he earned his doctorate in law.[598]

Maffeo used his family's connections to get into the clergy. Under Pope Clement VIII, he served as a papal legate to King Henry IV of France. After doing this job for several years, he became the Archbishop of Nazareth. Eventually, Pope Paul V made him a cardinal. He was officially chosen as pope in 1623.[599]

Pope Urban VIII by Gian Lorenzo Bernini
https://commons.wikimedia.org/wiki/File:Gian_Lorenzo_Bernini_-_Portrait_d%27Urbain_VIII.jpg.

As pope, Urban focused on missionary work. He sent many Jesuits throughout the Eastern world, which had previously been mostly neglected by other popes. He also sent missionaries to South America, which was still a relatively newly discovered land mass.[600] To provide training to these new missionaries, he founded the Collegium Urbanum

---

[598] "Pope Urban VIII." Pope History, 2023, https://popehistory.com/popes/pope-urban-viii/.
[599] "Pope Urban VIII."
[600] "Pope Urban VIII."

in 1627.[601]

While starting a good thing, he also started a literal war. He played the primary antagonist in the Wars of Castro, which began in 1642. He faced off against Duke Odoardo I Farnese of Parma. Oddly enough, Farnese was already excommunicated by the time the war ended. The pope's hope was to gain a larger ruling power in what is now northern Italy. However, the pope lost in 1644 after Modena, Tuscany, and Venice allied with Parma.[602]

Even with all the good he did with his missionary work, he is most infamous for his terrible control over the papal budget. Like other popes, he spent much too much on architectural and art commissions. He also spent a lot of money on the papal armies. By the time of his death, he had increased the Church's debt by 35 million scudi.[603] As part of this spending, he commissioned Forte Urbano in Castelfranco.[604]

Pope Urban VIII died shortly after the end of the Wars of Castro on July 29, 1644. Stress due to the loss of war likely contributed to his death.[605]

Innocent X (1644-55)

Finally, we come to the last pope of the Reformation—Giovanni Battista Pamphili. He was born to a rich family in Rome with connections to the papal court through Pope Alexander VI. Some of his other family members also worked closely with the Vatican. Giovanni first focused on studying law and then worked as a lawyer. It wasn't until he became an auditor and a canonist that he began his own career with the Catholic Church.[606]

Once he began working with the Church, everything seemed to go smoothly for Giovanni. Pope Clement VIII made him a judge. Pope Gregory XI made him a papal representative in Naples. Pope Urban VIII made him an ambassador to Spain and later a cardinal. With all of this,

---

[601] Britannica, T. Editors of Encyclopedia. "Urban VIII." *Encyclopedia Britannica,* July 25, 2023. https://www.britannica.com/biography/Urban-VIII.

[602] Britannica, T. Editors of Encyclopedia. "Urban VIII."

[603] "Pope Urban VIII."

[604] Britannica, T. Editors of Encyclopedia. "Urban VIII."

[605] Chinazzi, Ernesta. *Sede Vacante per la morte del Papa Urbano VIII Barberini e conclave di Innocenzo X Pamphili.* Rome, 1904.

[606] "Pope Innocent X." Pope History, 2023, https://popehistory.com/popes/pope-innocent-x/.

he was ready to take up the papal throne in 1644.[607]

One of Innocent's biggest pests during his papacy was Jansenism. This was a religious sect that had ideas about predestination and original sin that did not match Catholic beliefs. He set forth papal bulls against the sect.[608]

Innocent X had his fair share of scandals, mostly revolving around nepotism. There were rumors that he had a romantic relationship with his sister-in-law, as well.[609]

As he grew older, Innocent developed health problems, namely gout. Complications due to this eventually led to his death in 1655, when he was eighty. He is currently buried in the Church of Saint Agnes, which he commissioned in 1652.[610]

Conclusion

Well, there we have it—the twenty popes of the Reformation period. These men were as varied as the times they lived in, and their lifestyles are a reflection of this time. Nepotism ran rampant in the Church, which led to countless scandals. This, along with the Church's lack of budget control and the rise of Protestantism, brought the general esteem of the popes to the lowest level it had been in years. People were losing respect for the Church. In a way, the popes only encouraged the Reformation, even while many of them actively tried to end it.

---

[607] Britannica, T. Editors of Encyclopedia. "Innocent X." *Encyclopedia Britannica*, May 3, 2023. https://www.britannica.com/biography/Innocent-X.

[608] "Pope Innocent X."

[609] Britannica, T. Editors of Encyclopedia. "Innocent X."

[610] Adams, John P. "Sede Vicante 1655." CSUN, March 14, 2016,

Chapter 15: The Reformation in Europe

With our look at Luther and Lutheranism, we have already covered the bulk of Protestant history in Germany. The two other European countries with the most activity in the European Reformation were England and France. For this reason, we will use this chapter to take a closer look at the Reformation in these two countries. With this, we will take a deep dive into Calvinism in France and the Church of England. Because some of this has been discussed in the famous Reformers chapter, we will gloss over what has already been stated and focus on the details.

The Reformation in France

One of the biggest Protestant influences on France during the Reformation was Calvinism. However, Calvin himself wasn't the one to kick off the Reformation in France. Instead, the historian Wylie credits the beginning of the French Reformation to a man named Jacques Lefèvre d'Étaples, who first converted around 1510.[611] Lefèvre would later go on to influence Calvin.

Lefèvre was born in France in 1455. He had very little formal education in his youth but made up for it as an adult. He traveled around Europe and Asia before finally earning his Doctor of Divinity at the University of Paris in 1493. From there on, he taught as a professor and

---

[611] "France During the Reformation." Lineage, 2023, https://lineagejourney.com/read/france-during-the-reformation.

published several written works.[612]

Like Luther, Lefèvre was a Catholic. Once he realized there were errors within the Catholic Church, he did not try to start his own religion. He simply wanted to reform the Catholic Church to improve it. He wanted to go back to the original Scriptures and convince the Church to do the same thing. He was against the veneration of saints, in particular.[613]

Around 1510, William Farel (discussed in the Reformers' chapter) became acquainted with Lefèvre. As the two worked together, Farel gradually became more involved with the Reformation.[614] As we know, this would later lead to Farel meeting Calvin and teaching him about the Reformation.

Calvin began writing about religion in the 1530s, publishing his first version of *The Institutes of the Christian Religion* in 1536. For the next several years after this, Calvin and Farel moved to Geneva to focus on Reformation efforts there. They stayed there until they were exiled. Calvin went on to preach in Strasbourg for about a year before returning to Geneva, where he stayed for the rest of his life.[615]

France and the Catholic Church

Around the same time Calvin was preaching, France was going through a military crisis. Beginning in 1522, France was locked into the Anglo-French War (sometimes considered the Italian War). The French stayed locked in combat for about five years and would later battle on and off with the same opponents in the 1640s. However, the wars that mattered most to the Catholic Church were the French Wars of Religion.[616]

Officially, the Wars of Religion lasted from 1562 to 1598—over thirty years. During these wars, the French military fought against a group called the Huguenots, an overarching term used to describe French Protestants. While some could have been Lutherans, most were Calvinists by the time of the Wars of Religion. Many Huguenots were forced out of France for

---

[612] Cameron-Smith, Ray. "Jacques Lefevre: A Reformer Before the Reformation." Banner of Truth, Oct 31, 2018, https://banneroftruth.org/us/resources/articles/2018/jacques-lefevre-a-reformer-before-the-reformation/.
[613] Cameron-Smith, Ray. "Jacques Lefevre: A Reformer Before the Reformation."
[614] Cameron-Smith, Ray. "Jacques Lefevre: A Reformer Before the Reformation."
[615] "John Calvin Timeline." *World History Encyclopedia*, 2023, https://www.worldhistory.org/timeline/John_Calvin/.
[616] Britannica, T. Editors of Encyclopedia. "Wars of Religion." *Encyclopedia Britannica*, June 1, 2023, https://www.britannica.com/event/Wars-of-Religion.

their own safety, as a majority of the French rulers were still Catholics.[617]

The war kicked off as the French and Roman governments showed little favor to the French Huguenots. Things escalated when the Guise family, from Rome, massacred a Huguenot congregation in 1562. This incident caused Huguenots from all over France to rebel against their Catholic leaders. The war continued with skirmishes throughout the 1560s, with breaks in fighting every few years.[618]

There was a considerable break from fighting between 1670 and 1672. This ended with the Massacre of Saint Bartholomew's Day. The Catholics were the villains of this massacre, taking out numerous Huguenots and their leader, Gaspard II de Coligny, and setting off a war stronger than before. The unrest lasted until 1576 when the French government gave the Huguenots the freedom to practice their religion in peace. This was revoked in 1584 when Henry IV became the new heir to France. He was a Huguenot, which the Catholic Church did not appreciate. This would later lead to the War of the Three Henrys, which pitted France against Spain and Rome. This war concluded, as did the Wars of Religion, in 1598, with the Huguenots maintaining their right to practice their religion.[619]

Executions of Huguenots after the Huguenot Conspiracy of Amboise (1560)
See page for author, CC BY 4.0 <https://creativecommons.org/licenses/by/4.0>, via Wikimedia Commons
https://commons.wikimedia.org/wiki/File:Executions_of_Huguenots_after_the_Huguenot_conspiracy_of_Am b_Wellcome_V0048252.jpg.

---

[617] Britannica, T. Editors of Encyclopedia. "Wars of Religion."
[618] Britannica, T. Editors of Encyclopedia. "Wars of Religion."
[619] Britannica, T. Editors of Encyclopedia. "Wars of Religion."

All in all, the French Protestants literally had to fight for their right to practice their religion in peace. It took decades to accomplish their goal, taking up most of the Reformation period. In the end, a change in the secular leader of the country made it happen. There is no telling if the Huguenots would have been allowed to practice freely if another Catholic had ascended to the throne.

The Reformation in England

As opposed to the way France was reformed, the English Reformation was started because of, not in spite of, a secular leader. As discussed in the Reformers chapter, Henry VIII (Henry Tudor) broke from the Catholic Church because he wanted to divorce his Catholic wife, Katherine of Aragon. The divorce had little to do with Katherine being Catholic—so was Henry for most of his life—and almost everything to do with the fact that Katherine had not borne him a surviving male heir.

Since we already talked about Henry VIII in detail, let us move on to his two daughters who survived to adulthood, Queen Mary I and Queen Elizabeth I, and how they also left their mark on the English Reformation.

Mary I

Mary I ascended the throne after her brother, King Edward VI, passed away in 1553. By this time, England had been worshipping under the Church of England for about twenty years. A whole generation had grown up in this new Church. However, Mary had been raised as a staunch Catholic. Now that she was queen, she was ready to return England to Catholicism, whether the general populous of England wanted to convert or not.

One of the first things Mary did as queen was release several former Catholic nobles and bishops from the Tower of London, including Bishop Tunstall and the Duke of Norfolk.[620] This was done quickly, while the rest of her pro-Catholic initiatives were more slow-going.

Mary gave up the title of "Supreme Head of the Church of England" and instated the Catholic Church. To do this, she had to reintroduce bishops and other Catholic clergy and restore order to the monasteries.[621] The latter part of this would be more difficult, as Henry VIII had

---

[620] Simkin, John. "Mary and Elizabeth: Catholics and Protestants."
[621] "Mary I (r.1553-1558)." The Royal Household, n.d., https://www.royal.uk/mary-i.

dissolved the monasteries during his reign.

Along with restarting the Catholic Church in England, she also dug up old heresy laws— laws that made it illegal to go against the Catholic Church. As most English had converted to the Church of England decades before (willingly or not), many people were breaking heresy laws. One of the only ways to get past this was to convert back to Catholicism, which many commoners were reluctant to do. Mary did not care that her people did not want to convert. She punished those who were caught breaking heresy laws. As a result, over 300 Protestants were burned alive by the English government during Mary's reign.[622] Needless to say, this led to many commoners hating Mary. To this day, she bears the nickname "Bloody Mary."

The Death of Thomas Cranmer at the Stake, Burned for Heresy in 1566
See page for author, CC BY 4.0 <https://creativecommons.org/licenses/by/4.0>, via Wikimedia Commons https://commons.wikimedia.org/wiki/File:The_death_of_Thomas_Cranmer_at_the_stake,_burned_for_heresy_Wellcome_V0041610.jpg.

Many nobles also did not want England to revert to Catholicism. This had less to do with being religiously tied to the Church of England and more to do with being *financially* tied to the Church. This is because

---

[622] "Mary I (r.1553-1558)."

many nobles had bought land previously owned by monasteries.[623] By owning this land, they made money off it, mostly through renting it out to others. However, if the Catholic Church returned, they might lose their land, assuming the monks would take over the monasteries. In fact, Mary asked many nobles to give back the land willingly, which did not go well.[624]

Luckily for the Reformation's cause, Mary I did not live long enough to enact many of her plans. She died from an illness, possibly cancer, in 1558, after reigning for only about five years.[625] With her death, England's return to Catholicism also died.

Elizabeth I

Unlike Mary I, Elizabeth was raised as a Protestant. After all, Henry VIII had created the Church of England so he could marry Elizabeth's mother, Anne Boleyn. Elizabeth had only ever known the Church of England, except for the few short years Mary I was queen. Because of this, one of the first things she did when she inherited the throne from her late half-sister was to make it clear to the English people that she was a Protestant and that Protestantism in England was there to stay.[626]

While being queen made her all-powerful, there were more steps to take before the Church of England would be England's official state religion again. In January 1559, she held Parliament with Nicholas Bacon, proposing a new act to make Elizabeth the new official head of the Church of England. However, the new act was rejected by the majority Catholic Parliament.[627] So, while the Church of England was the official state church, Elizabeth was not initially seen as its official head.

---

[623] "Mary I (r.1553-1558)."

[624] "Mary I (r.1553-1558)."

[625] "Mary I (r.1553-1558)."

[626] "Elizabeth I's Religious Settlement." Royal Museums Greenwich, n.d., https://www.rmg.co.uk/stories/topics/elizabeth-religious-settlement.

[627] "Elizabeth I's Religious Settlement."

Sir Nicholas Bacon, Lord Keeper by Jacobus Houbraken, 1738
Jacobus Houbraken, Yale Center for British Art. Wikimedia Commons, CC0 1.0 Universal Public Domain, 1738, https://commons.wikimedia.org/wiki/File:Jacobus_Houbraken_-_Sir_Nicholas_Bacon,_Lord_Keeper_-_B1998.14.575_-_Yale_Center_for_British_Art.jpg.

Elizabeth and her Protestant allies had to regroup to think of a new way to get their religious reform successfully through Parliament. They met in Parliament again in April 1559 and presented the Act of Supremacy. They reworded the act so that Elizabeth would be the

Supreme Governor of the Church rather than the Supreme Head. Surprisingly, it passed easily.[628]

Later in 1559, Parliament passed the Act of Uniformity. This act allowed people to practice either the Catholic Communion or the Protestant. (However, the Church of England's Protestant prayer book was the official one used for the country.) It was difficult to get Parliament to agree on allowing both Communions; however, it eventually passed by three votes.[629] After this point, Christians living in England more or less had the freedom to practice Protestantism or Catholicism without worry of prejudice (at least during the 1600s).

Things would change in the next 100 or so years, taking an especially wild turn when King James I became the new leader of England. However, as that happened long after the Reformation, that is another story for another day (and book).

Conclusion

Germany was one of the biggest hot spots during the beginning of the Reformation. However, France and England also had their parts to play. While by the end of the Reformation almost all European counties had some form of Catholicism or Protestantism, many people practiced their beliefs differently. This would contribute to cultural differences that these countries and their former territories and colonies still show today.

---

[628] "Elizabeth I's Religious Settlement."
[629] "Elizabeth I's Religious Settlement."

Chapter 16: The Counter-Reformation (1545-1700)

Last but not least, we get to the Counter-Reformation. As the name implies, the Counter-Reformation's goal was to counter the effects of the Reformation. The Counter-Reformation was the efforts of the Catholic Church, popes, and other clergy members to bring followers back from Protestant sects, invalidate Protestantism, and promote Catholicism.

We have already covered many of the events of the Counter-Reformation in the chapter on the popes. In this chapter, we will spend more time focusing on the key events of the Counter-Reformation period.

Council of Trent

The Council of Trent's name can be deceiving. It was not one steady council meeting. Instead, it was many council meetings that took place between 1545 to 1563. We have already discussed parts of this council throughout other chapters. Let's take a closer look at it now.

First Session (1525-1549)

The first Council of Trent (sometimes called the First Session) was arranged by Pope Paul III in 1545. The pope and other clergy understood that something was wrong, or appeared to be wrong, with the Catholic Church. Why else would so many people be leaving the Church to worship in Protestant sects? So, the Council of Trent was set up to address some of the issues within the Church.[630] By going through these issues and perhaps solving them, the Catholic Church hoped that some of their old congregation members would return to the fold.

While the sessions were created to talk about what to do with the changes brought on by the Protestant Reformation, no Protestants were allowed to be a part of the council. However, this did not mean that they ignored Protestants entirely. Much of the First Session focused on Martin Luther and his teachings.[631] While the Church as a whole did not agree with what he said, they needed to look into it. After all, if there was not *some* validity to his claim, why would Catholics leave the Church to follow him?

One of the main points the First Session discussed was whether people are saved through faith alone (Luther) or by faith and works together (Catholic). People arguing from either side could find Bible verses to back up their points. They also discussed which Bible translations were accurate and whether infants should be baptized.[632]

By the end of the First Session, the Catholics had decided that the "Vulgate translation of Saint Jerome" was the best Bible translation. This is, in part, why the Catholic Bible has different books in it than the Protestant Bible. They also agreed that babies must be baptized, congregants should take part in the sacraments, and people are saved by both faith and good works.[633]

Second Session (1551-1552)

The First Session contained the most meetings and was the most extensive of the three sessions. Pope Julius III was still in power when the second session began. For this session, the Church was focused on the Eucharist (Communion). Some Protestant sects believed that the Eucharist being made of the body and blood of Christ was metaphorical, while the Catholic Church saw it as literal.[634] Their evidence came from the Bible:

---

[630] Mark, Joshua J. "Council of Trent." *World History Encyclopedia*, June 16, 2022, https://www.worldhistory.org/Council_of_Trent/.
[631] Mark, Joshua J. "Council of Trent."
[632] Mark, Joshua J. "Council of Trent."
[633] Mark, Joshua J. "Council of Trent."
[634] Mark, Joshua J. "Council of Trent."

"And as they were eating, Jesus took bread, and blessed it, and brake it, and gave it to the disciples, and said, Take, eat; this is my body. And he took the cup, and gave thanks, and gave it to them, saying, Drink ye all of it; for this is my blood of the new testament, which is shed for many for the remission of sins. But I say unto you, I will not drink henceforth of this fruit of the vine, until that day when I drink it new with you in my Father's kingdom. And when they had sung a hymn, they went out into the mount of Olives." (Matthew 26:26-30, King James Version)

The Church used a similar argument to justify the sacraments. They agreed that anything Jesus said in the Bible and any sacraments he encouraged should be done. By ignoring the word of Jesus/God, Catholics would be risking eternal damnation in Hell.[635]

The Second Session was interrupted and ended early by the Schmalkaldic War.[636]

The Council of Trent by Pasquale Cati, 1588

Pasquale Cati, Santma Maria in Trastvere. Wikimedia Commons, CC BY-SA 3.0 Unported, 2.5 Generic, 2.0 Generic, and 1.0 Generic, 1588.
https://commons.wikimedia.org/wiki/File:Pasquale_Cati_da_Iesi_C.ofTrent2.JPG.

Third Session (1562-1563)

The Third Session was held under Pope Pius IV beginning in January 1562. This session continued to focus on reformation within the Catholic

---

[635] Mark, Joshua J. "Council of Trent."
[636] Mark, Joshua J. "Council of Trent."

Church, with a focus on fixing what the Protestants saw as abuses.[637] Again, all these changes would be coming from within the Church. While some Protestant theories and opinions would be discussed, no Protestants would be working within the Church to make these changes.

One of the issues the Church worked on was educating priests and other clergy members more. The Church set up several schools around Europe that specialized in educating clergy members/those who wanted to go into the clergy.[638] The hope was that more educated clergy members would be less susceptible to scandal.

The Third Session also made the firm decision that priests and higher clergy members (all but deacons) could not get married. The Church would also stop selling indulgences but would occasionally give them out for free or for donating to the Church. Protestant saints were rejected, and the veneration of Catholic saints continued. The Church did not cut down on spending dramatically, either.[639] It continued to commission art projects and buildings. Many of these reforms still apply in the Catholic Church today, for better or for worse.

Confutatio Augustana (1530s)

In the early 1530s, the Lutheran Church created the Augsburg Confession, also known as the Confessio Augustana. This religious confession contained twenty-eight articles that covered the main Lutheran beliefs.[640] The Augsburg Confession is not used much in Lutheran sects today at the congregational level. However, it greatly impacted the Lutheran churches when it was first introduced.

The total original text of the Augsburg Confessional is about forty pages long, so we will not include it in this book. Readers can find a free link to the entire Confession here. Below is a list of the articles in the Confession:

1. God
2. Original Sin
3. The Son of God

---

[637] Mark, Joshua J. "Council of Trent."
[638] Mark, Joshua J. "Council of Trent."
[639] Mark, Joshua J. "Council of Trent."
[640] Britannica, T. Editors of Encyclopedia. "Augsburg Confession." *Encyclopedia Britannica*, November 8, 2021. https://www.britannica.com/topic/Augsburg-Confession.

4. Justification
5. The Ministry of the Church
6. The New Obedience
7. The Church
8. What the Church Is
9. Baptism
10. The Holy Supper of Our Lord
11. Confession
12. Repentance
13. The Use of Sacraments
14. Order in the Church
15. Church Usages
16. Civil Government
17. The Return of Christ to Judgement
18. Free Will
19. The Cause of Sin
20. Faith and Good Works
21. Of the Worship of the Saints
22. Of Both Kings in the Sacrament
23. Of the Marriage of Priests
24. Of the Mass
25. Confession
26. The Distinction of Foods
27. Monastic Vows
28. Ecclesiastical Powers[641]

---

[641] "The Augsburg Confession." Info Werke Martin Luther, 1530, https://infowerke.martinluther.us/augsburg_confession_1530.pdf.

Augsburg Confession
Moller, Reihold. World History Encyclopedia, CC BY-SA, January 26, 2022,
https://www.worldhistory.org/image/15199/augsburg-confession/.

The Catholic Church had mixed feelings about the Confession. The first twenty-one articles explained Lutheran doctrine to show that "they [dissented] in no article of faith from the Catholic Church." The final seven articles discussed abuses that had entered the Western church in the centuries before the Reformation.[642] This meant that the Catholics agreed wholly with the first twenty-one articles but disagreed entirely with the final seven articles.

Since there was so much disagreement, the Catholic Church met to create a confession of its own. This would later be known as the Confutatio Augustana, or the Roman Confutation. Like the Protestant version, the Catholic Confession also contained twenty-eight articles. Neither group was willing to change their stance on the final seven

---

[642] Britannica, T. Editors of Encyclopedia. "Augsburg Confession."

articles.[643] To this day, Protestant and Catholic churches tend to disagree on the items covered in these articles. However, individual Protestant sects may be more closely aligned with the Catholic Church than Lutherans were in the 1500s.

Elizabeth I's Excommunication (1570)

As Queen Elizabeth I inherited the English throne from her Catholic sister, Queen Mary I, she returned her country to Protestantism. This was something many common people, and even nobles, were happy with. However, the Catholic Church was not. As discussed in earlier chapters, under Mary I, the Catholic Church regained some of the power it had lost under King Henry VIII. Now, with Elizabeth I as queen, the Church had lost its power in England again.

To try to force the queen's hand, or the hands of her people, Pope Pius V declared Elizabeth I a heretic and excommunicated her in 1570.[644] By excommunicating Elizabeth I, the pope was saying that her rule was illegitimate and that she was condemned to Hell. The pope did this as a way to try to punish Elizabeth, hoping that her people would turn against her— especially England's Catholic population.

However, the pope's plan did not go as planned. The Catholics in England did nothing at all. Elizabeth was more religiously tolerant than most European monarchs at the time. Catholics could keep worshipping their way, and Protestants could worship in theirs. Whereas the pope hoped Catholics would be filled with rage and ready to wage rebellion, they were perfectly happy with the way things were. The majority of the populous did not care that their queen was excommunicated.[645]

It was unlikely that Elizabeth herself cared that she was excommunicated. As a Protestant, she would not have believed that the pope had the power to damn her to Hell.

All in all, it was a valiant effort by Pope Pius V to excommunicate Elizabeth I, but it had little effect in the long run. So far, the Catholic Church had not made much headway in its Counter-Reformation.

---

[643] "Roman Confutation (1530)" *Book of Concord*, n.d., https://bookofconcord.org/other-resources/sources-and-context/roman-confutation/.

[644] "Elizabeth's Excommunication 1570." BBC UK Bitesize, 2023, https://www.bbc.co.uk/bitesize/guides/zpy9fcw/revision/3.

[645] "Elizabeth's Excommunication 1570."

Battle of Lepanto (1571)

During the Counter-Reformation, the Catholics were fighting not only a metaphorical religious war but real battles. In the 1570s, the pope took on one of the most important battles of the Counter-Reformation—the Battle of Lepanto against the Ottoman Empire.

For the most part, the Ottoman Empire was made up of Muslims. Its rulers were sultans, who were almost always Muslim. While its population included Christians and Jews, these were in the minority and did not have much (if any) power within the Ottoman Empire and often faced discrimination.[646] This made the Ottoman Empire a great target for the pope. Of course, the pope was not out to pick a fight with the Ottoman Empire. However, when the Ottomans attacked, he was ready to fight back.

The Ottoman Empire was already powerful before the mid-1500s but got considerably more powerful as the century went on. The Ottomans proved to be a threat against monarchies in many parts of Europe. They decided to go to war by sea in the 1570s, first capturing Cyprus. As a direct result, Pope Pius V tried to rally forces against the Ottoman Turks. Together, along with Spain, Venice, Tuscany, Savoy, Urbino, Parma, Malta, and Genoa, the Christian Europeans formed the "Holy League." In total, they had a collection of over 50,000 men and hundreds of ships.[647]

The papal forces and their allies fought against the Ottomans, mostly by sea. They had several battles against the Ottomans but none as impressive as the Battle of Lepanto. Both forces met in the Gulf of Lepanto on October 7, 1571. The Europeans were led by Don John of Austria, brother of the King of Spain. They had almost twice as many guns as the Ottomans but only slightly more ships. However, the Europeans had fewer fighting men than the Ottomans. This was, in part, because the Ottomans had cushioned their numbers by using Christian slaves as sailors.[648]

---

[646] "The Ottoman Empire - Background." New Zealand Ministry for Culture and Heritage, April 26, 2023, https://nzhistory.govt.nz/war/ottoman-empire/background.

[647] Potter, Bill. "The Battle of Lepanto, October 7, 1571." Landmark Events, October 5, 2021, https://landmarkevents.org/the-battle-of-lepanto-1571/.

[648] Potter, Bill. "The Battle of Lepanto, October 7, 1571."

The battle ensued, with ships shooting at each other. The Europeans lost thirty-three ships and had about 23,000 casualties. The Ottomans lost a massive eighty-four ships and had over 25,000 casualties. The battle gave the Europeans a decisive victory over the Ottomans. It also crippled the Ottoman's navy, which would affect them for years.[649] However, even with the win, Protestants were not automatically drawn back to being Catholic. The damage had been done.

Conclusion

The Catholic Church gave its best shot at returning Protestants to the fold during the Counter-Reformation. Their efforts were not in vain, as they did regain some members. However, the Counter-Reformation was not as effective as they would have liked. The Protestant Church did not fall; instead, it continued to grow. Today, both the Catholic Church and Protestant sects operate around the world. They have made some changes since the Reformation but remain firmly Christian, believing in God, Jesus, and the Holy Spirit.

---

[649] Potter, Bill. "The Battle of Lepanto, October 7, 1571."

Conclusion

Today, Christianity is the most popular religion in the world, practiced by over two billion people. This includes all branches of Christianity: Catholicism, Eastern Orthodox, and Protestant denominations.[650] As of 2011, about 50 percent of all Christians were Roman Catholic, about 26 percent were Protestant, and around 11 percent were Eastern Orthodox Catholics.[651]

Even though there are over a billion Catholics on the planet, the Roman Catholic Church does not have the political power it once did. The Vatican (also called Vatican City) is an independent city-state that operates as its own country inside Italy. The head of the Catholic Church, the pope, resides here.

In centuries past, the pope had significant influence on other countries, namely those in Europe led by Catholic monarchs. Today, most countries are not so intrinsically tied to the Church. Because of this, the Catholic Church today acts almost solely as a religion and has much less to do with politics.

While most countries try to have a separation of church and state, religion still plays a big part in everyday life for people around the world.

---

[650] "Religion by Country 2023." World Population Review, 2023, https://worldpopulationreview.com/country-rankings/religion-by-country.

[651] "Global Christianity - A Report on the Size and Distribution of the World's Christian Population." Pew Research Center, December 18, 2011, https://www.pewresearch.org/religion/2011/12/19/global-christianity-exec/.

Many laws, especially in the United States, are based on Christian values.

However, while Christianity has healthy numbers, it is on the decline around the world. Fewer and fewer people are practicing Christianity. By 2050, Islam is expected to be the leading religion on earth. As of 2023, There are about two billion Muslims around the world.[652]

Why are people leaving Christianity? There is no one concrete answer. Only time will tell whether Christianity will prosper or if the number of Christians around the world will continue to go down. Missionary work around the world continues to add new people to the faith, but at the same time, people continue to leave for personal reasons.

That leaves one heavy question to ponder. Will Christianity live on forever, or will it eventually disappear and enter into mythology like so many ancient religions before it?

---

[652] "Religion by Country 2023."

Part 2: Medieval Knights

A Captivating Guide to the Knights of the Holy Sepulchre, Knights Hospitaller, Order of Saint Lazarus, Knights Templar, and Teutonic Knights

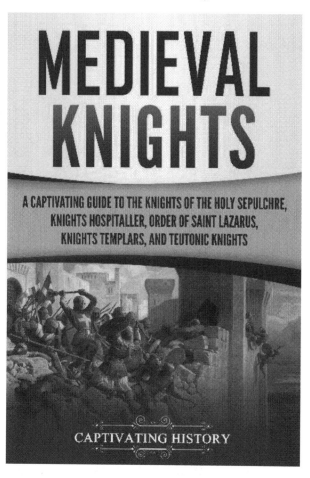

Introduction

The mention of medieval knights often evokes images of massive horses pounding over vast plains and sand-strewn deserts, horses and men alike swathed in armor, with battle flags flying high. Or some might envision a Grail Knight guarding the Holy Chalice, like in the Indiana Jones movie where the knight cautions Indy to "choose wisely." Or even further back to Robert Taylor's rendition of Sir Lancelot in *Knights of the Round Table*, filmed in 1954. Through the ages, the imagery of brave knights found in books and movies is romantic and chivalric yet not always realistic.

Knights were known to surge into distant and foreign lands with firm beliefs and dedication to their religion. Many fought in the Holy Land against the "scourge of the Muslim hordes," while others fought against Germanic invaders or the pagans of eastern Europe.

They were formidable warriors, some with families, some living monkish lives. They fought bravely and lived violent, bloody lives. The medieval knights and their secret and not-so-secret orders and societies no doubt played a huge role in history, but even so, some are still shrouded in mystery.

A few are well known, at least by name. Some knightly orders or societies were dedicated to protecting pilgrims and saving lives, yet they became known as the most ferocious fighters of all. They fought for the preservation of Christianity and set out on crusades into the Holy Land, where religious wars were fought. Many of their legends have been passed down from generation to generation, while the origins and exploits of others are still shrouded in mystery.

Yet the life of the medieval knight encompassed many aspects of society and beliefs of their time. These men fought when called upon to do so, but just as often, they lived relatively ordinary lives at home. Some came from lowly origins, while others were descended from nobility or belonged to wealthy and aristocratic families.

They spent years as pages and squires and then, if they were fortunate and considered brave enough, became knights. Many pursued knighthoods for the excitement of battles, much like today's modern warriors. But they would soon realize that war was a bloody and dangerous business. They might have envisioned themselves riding mighty steeds in full armor, but in truth, thousands of knights marched toward their destinies on foot. Many fought without the benefit of armored suits.

Knights surged forth with an often single-minded purpose or desire to fight those they believed to be heretics and pagans, but there were just as many who fought for a sense of justice and religious fervor. Others fought for simpler things, such as rewards of money, land, booty, or, sometimes even more importantly, their reputation and pride.

The medieval ages spanned a period of time lasting approximately nine hundred years, and while the knights within many of the Christian orders fought for a certain cause, they also served different masters and kings.

Who were these knights? What was expected of them, and why did they spend so many years of their lives journeying to distant lands, often never to return? What happened to these orders through the medieval ages? And who led the knights into battle?

In this book, we'll explore some of these knightly orders, from the Hospitallers to the Teutonic Knights to Knights Templar. These knights made history. Their reputation and exploits have been handed down for centuries, so there is much for us to discover. Join us on a journey of these knightly brotherhoods and how they lived and fought and bled for what they believed in a time of uncertainty, war, and domination.

Chapter 1: A Glimpse into the Middle Ages

Looking back through history, back through the centuries before the birth of Christianity, it seems as if mankind has always been fighting. They fought for land, sustenance, and their religions. Western Europe seemed to be constantly embroiled in war, and that did not change after the birth of Christianity.

The years from the 9th century (the 800s CE) through the 13th century (1200s CE) and beyond brought multiple and often violent clashes of nations, primarily between the Christians from western European countries and the populations to the east: the Magyars or Hungarian pagans, the Germanic hordes, and the Muslims from the deserts of the Middle East. Even western Europeans fought against one another, such as the English and the French; the squabbling often lasted generations.

Battles were waged near and far. Over time and over the multitudes of feudal wars that lasted for hundreds of years, castles were built, cavalries were formed, and warriors fought and died on hotly contested battlegrounds. Many of those mounted warriors who fought for one order or manor lord over another would today be called cavalry troops, but back in the day, they were known simply as mounted warriors before they became known as knights.

What made knights so special? They were often well trained, owned their own horses, and, if wealthy enough, were heavily armed and armored. Yet they were also known to be men who made vows of obedience, poverty, and chastity. It was a violent and bloody time to live, yet these knights were sworn to bravery, to serve others and a higher power, and to live by certain rules that are now known as the code of chivalry. History tells us they were polite, courteous, and sometimes even generous. Yet most of all, they personified the ideas of valor, gallantry, and bravery against all odds, ideas that have been passed down through the centuries that followed.

These warriors were honor-bound and loyal to the feudal system to which they belonged, but they fought not only for what they believed in but also in the hopes of providing honorable and loyal service that might enable them to earn a reward of land or a manor of their own.

Some of these men returned home to great acclaim, including Alfred the Great and Charlemagne. Eventually, the status of these mounted warriors, who later became known as knights, received special notice and honor. They belonged to what was otherwise known as a brotherhood—a brotherhood of knights serving one master or another. Their kings. Their religion. Their sense of justice.

For many centuries, noble and lowborn fought side by side, yet it was mostly the nobles or the wealthy who were found in these groups since they were able to afford the cost of fighting equipment and horses.

For a time, these knightly groups or orders were composed of those with elite status, such as members of wealthy households, landowners, or varying ranks of nobility. Eventually, that changed, especially in England. Nevertheless, these groups of men created a fraternity of sorts, representing valor, courage, honor, and duty. They were blessed by the church as defenders of the Christian faith. They believed that the battles they fought were not merely holy but also sacred, following the brave examples of the biblical David, Joshua, and Gideon who came before them.

Within three centuries after the death of Christ, the justification for such battles and wars was that they were noble and right. They believed in the words of Aristotle, the Greek philosopher, and the leaders of ancient Rome, who said that any war that attempted to recover a seized piece of property or territory or that defended one's beliefs was fought on God's authority. Knights became generally known as defenders of the faith and Christian warriors engaged in a holy war.

Christian fervor was found on many battlefields throughout the centuries, and artifacts from the time display Christian images on weapons, further justifying their fight to overcome paganism and vindicating their efforts to convert their enemies to Christianity and spread the faith. It was an era that sought greater protection for the church and the protection of the weak, meaning clergy, monks, and pilgrims. The knights wanted to promote the idea of justice not only in their native lands but also in foreign lands as well.

It was also a time of inner conflict for many of these knightly warriors in regard to their Christian faith. History tells us that even the soldiers who fought under William the Conqueror in the Battle of Hastings were required to perform penance for the blood spilled on the battlefield, even though they had fought valiantly under the papal banner.

The medieval ages, also known as the Middle Ages or the Dark Ages, encompassed the time between the fall of the Roman Empire and the Renaissance: in other words, from around 476 to the 16th century CE. This period is typically identified by three primary timeframes, known as the Early Middle Ages, the High Middle Ages, and the Late Middle Ages.

In essence, these centuries were consumed by bloody battles and religious fervor, with few developments or advancements in technology, literature, or art, hence the nickname the "Dark Ages." This era saw the bubonic plague, more commonly known as the Black Death, which started around 1346 and ended in 1353, although outbreaks continued to happen over the years. Nearly twenty-five million people died throughout Europe.

However, the medieval era was also a time that promoted the spread of Christianity from its origins in the Holy Land (the lands of Israel and Palestine). In eras past, these lands were known as the land of the Hittites. The term Asia Minor was coined to avoid confusion with the regions visited by the Apostle Paul.

Over a millennium before the fall of Rome, Alexander the Great conquered much of Asia Minor, but the region continued to be a land troubled by instability. After the fall of Rome around 476 CE, the region became known as the Byzantine Empire (although, at the time, the people living there considered themselves to be part of the Roman Empire).

Within a century after the decline of the Roman Empire, another religion swept through what is known today as the Middle East. This religion was Islam. Its followers, like the Christian knights who followed their faith, believed in the teachings of the Prophet Muhammad. Each group saw the other as infidels. What followed were centuries of fighting. It was a time of great upheaval in the Byzantine Empire, as the Muslims rose up and conquered lands, encompassing a huge area that on maps today incorporates the lands of Pakistan on their eastern border to the Moroccan region to the south and the current regions of Spain and Portugal, known as the Iberian Peninsula, to the west. During these years, Christianity also spread. The fighting continued, and the occupation of the Holy Land was hotly contested.

By the end of the 1st millennium, the German Empire was also in turmoil, with localized groups all vying for control. The Habsburg dynasty provided a vague sense of unity at the time, though princes throughout the land still fought one another for power. Yet, despite the infighting, Germany was a force to be reckoned with and used its growing power to influence countries around them to embrace Christianity. At the time, Germany had a huge influence that some historians have compared to that of ancient Rome.

During those years, thousands of Christians began to make pilgrimages to the Holy Land. They were sponsored by the church to visit and worship at holy sites and shrines throughout the region.

The Pilgrimages

Pilgrimages to the Holy Land turned, for all intents and purposes, into a tradition, a way for people to achieve a cleansing of their sins and souls. These pilgrims came from many different lands and made the journey to the holiest city of all—Jerusalem—in an effort to gain atonement for their sins and gain penance through the harsh sacrifices they endured during their journey. Most of these individuals came from higher classes of society because, quite frankly, they could afford it.

They came by the dozens and then by the hundreds and then often by the thousands. Men, women, children, and servants traveled through harsh and dangerous landscapes to prove to their priests and to their Lord that they were sorry for their sins and offenses to God and man alike. The journey to the Holy Land was only part of their penance, as they were also required to give money or aid to those less fortunate than themselves. Before they could even make the journey, they had to receive permission from their priest; otherwise, their pilgrimage wouldn't count, spiritually at least. After their return, the priest would pardon their sins.

By the dawn of the 2nd century, Jerusalem had become the primary destination for such pilgrimages, and by the 4th century (the 1300s), historical writings describe sizable Christian pilgrimages to the city of Jerusalem. Once in the Holy City, these pilgrims sought out famous sites mentioned in the Bible.

Constantine the Great (Roman emperor from 306 to 337 CE) is believed to have directed the building of churches and identified sacred sites, such as the reputed place of Christ's burial. There, Constantine directed the construction of the Church of the Holy Sepulchre in 325 CE.

However, during the height of the pilgrimages, the practice of Islam also began to spread, especially during the centuries following the death of their prophet, Muhammad, the founder of the Islam faith, in 632. They, like the Christians, believed they were fighting for what was right and sought to gain control of the Holy Land, which was also a sacred site to their faith.

Even before the years of the First Crusade in 1096, the expansion of Islam encompassed great swathes of territory, eventually spreading from the depths of the Middle East westward along the southern banks of the Mediterranean Sea to the west and north and east into the former Persian Empire, bordering the Caspian and Arabian Seas, and to the Byzantine Empire, nestled between the northern shores of the Mediterranean Sea to the Black Sea.

Land boundaries changed over the years, making the medieval era a time of conquests and migrations. Those of Slavic and Germanic nationalities migrated throughout Europe. The Goths played a large role in the Western Roman Empire's destruction and were also influential in the early years of the Middle Ages. The Goths were known as barbarians; they were seen as violent, uneducated, and unsophisticated. During the 4th century, the Visigoth leader, Athanaric, didn't much care for the "new Roman religion," otherwise known as Christianity, fearing that the religion would influence the Goths and make them abandon tradition.

During the Middle Ages, massive numbers of pilgrims ventured over land and sea to reach the Holy Land. For generations, making a pilgrimage as a form of penance and overcoming its hardships became a common practice. And who better to protect those pilgrims but brave knights? The men who joined the brotherhoods of chivalric knights were, perhaps like many throughout history, lured by the excitement of foreign lands and battles. Many of them lived like monks, vowing obedience, austerity, and even chastity. It was a brotherhood in the truest sense of the word. They ate together, slept together, fought together, and often died together.

During these turbulent years, numerous knightly societies or orders were founded. Some are more well known than others, such as, for instance, the Templars and the Hospitallers. They spanned a timeframe that encompassed numerous crusades or religious wars between Christians and Muslims with the goal of controlling sacred and holy sites throughout the regions of what is known today as the Middle East.

These orders were formed to protect and wrest the Holy Land from the Muslims, who had gained control of it toward the end of the Byzantine Empire. The orders also wanted to spread the message of Christianity to the pagans of Europe. While the vast majority of men who joined these orders were former cavalry soldiers or warriors, most were already knights. Many of these orders were known as religious military societies or orders, including the Hospitallers (originally a group of monks seeking to protect pilgrims journeying to the Holy Land), the Knights Templar, and the Teutonic Knights, all of whom had the same goals in mind.

Who founded these knightly societies and orders? Who were these men who fought for God and Christianity, and what happened to them?

Chapter 2: The Crusades: A Brief Overview

No history or glimpse into the lives of the medieval knights and their orders would be possible without providing a brief overview of the Crusades, which are primarily defined as religious wars that spanned centuries.

The major Crusades took place over a nearly two-hundred-year span of time. Different orders were prevalent during one or more of the Crusades, which resulted in thousands of lives lost, cities destroyed, and the nearly ongoing resentment from both sides.

These decades spanned empires and involved kings and emirs. Some of the major players came from the thrones of England, France, Germany, the Byzantine Empire, and the Islamic caliphates. These were years fraught with battles and skirmishes over land, the right to rule, and even infighting among groups from a varied number of countries.

The First Crusade: 1096–1099

Over time, Christians became divided between the Roman Catholics and the Eastern Orthodox Christians; this event was later known as the Great Schism of 1054. The divisions within the Catholic Church eventually provided the birth and growth of the Protestant Reformation, which, in turn, triggered several political and religious disagreements.

The First Crusade began at a time when a Byzantine general-turned-emperor by the name of Alexius Comnenus requested aid from Pope Urban II to help prevent the Turks from encroaching on the eastern

Byzantine provinces. What he really wanted was soldiers. The request came at an opportune time, as the pope at that time had been urging Christians throughout the west to support the Byzantines in their efforts to push back the Muslims, who had taken over many holy sites throughout the Middle East. The pope's goal was to recapture and control the Holy Land.

At that time, thousands of soldiers answered the call. Some went on foot or on horseback. Some of these armies were organized and led by experienced knights or those with military knowledge, while others were less organized, with some being led by clergymen or those seeking the glory of participating in a holy war. The politics of the regions and the allegiance of armies at the time were relatively fluid, and Alexius demanded that the armies arriving in his lands swear loyalty to him. He also insisted that he maintain control over any land won by the crusading armies. However, most of these knights declined to do so.

They fought together anyway, and by 1097, the Byzantines and their allies attacked Nicaea, which is today found in Turkey. The battle was important, as it was one of the first great battles that set the stage for the Crusades.

The Siege of Nicaea

The siege of Nicaea was where the soldiers of the Crusades first made a name for themselves. The city of Nicaea is an ancient Christian site; the first council of the Christian Church gathered there in 325. During this council, the Christian doctrine known as the Nicene Creed was agreed upon. For centuries, the city of Nicaea, which was less than one hundred miles from the city of Constantinople, had been part of the Byzantine Empire. The city fell to the Seljuk Turks in 1081.

At the time of the First Crusade, Nicaea was the capital of the Seljuk Turks, and as long as the capital remained in Turkish hands, the advance toward Jerusalem could not be achieved.

However, to think of the soldiers involved in the First Crusade as an organized, disciplined, and orderly army would be incorrect. They were highly disorganized, owing to the vast number of men involved, and their numbers were rife with rivalries, language and cultural barriers, and disciplinary issues, primarily because there was fighting and arguing among the lords and commanders who oversaw them.

Added to the cacophony were the civilians who accompanied the soldiers, non-combatants that included women and children. Some of the civilians were family members of the soldiers, while others were making pilgrimages or belonged to the clergy. Also joining the crusaders was a large force of Byzantine soldiers, approximately two thousand under the command of Tatikios, who had made a name for himself defending Constantinople against European peasants in 1096.

Yes, many were eager to make their devotion to God known, including the poor. The Peasants' Crusade (a rather unsuccessful effort by untrained peasants to help push back and defeat the encroaching Turks) saw tens of thousands of peasants make their way to the Holy Land; almost all of them died since they were not experienced in warfare or lacked the proper equipment.

The crusaders didn't arrive as one unified force at Nicaea. Among the first were knights under Godfrey of Bouillon and Robert of Flanders, a son of William the Conqueror. The final contingent of forces arrived under Robert of Normandy and Stephen of Blois by early June.

The crusaders managed to surround three sides of the city and settled in for an extended siege due to the fact they were unable to block the lake approach to the city (Lake Ascania), through which the enemy ensconced in Nicaea could receive supplies.

Early in the siege, the sultan of the Turkish state called Rum returned to the city from abroad, as he had been fighting another rival. He was apparently startled by the massive forces that had gathered at the capital. He quickly launched a surprise attack on one of the armies of Raymond of Toulouse, which turned out to be successful for the crusaders, especially after Godfrey of Bouillon sent reinforcements.

The siege of Nicaea lasted six long weeks, but the siege equipment was not capable of causing any real damage to the city walls. According to historical documents, a number of objects were catapulted over the walls, including beehives, rocks, detached heads of corpses, and flaming missiles. The more common goal of a siege is to starve the enemy out, but that would not happen due to the sultan's access to the lake.

Meanwhile, Emperor Alexius hoped that Nicaea would not be destroyed since his goal was to add it to the Byzantine Empire. So, he initiated an end run, to use today's American football parlance, and made secret negotiations with the Turks, promising them safety if they surrendered.

Imagine the crusaders' surprise when, in mid-June, upon their preparation to initiate a major attack on Nicaea, the crusaders spied the

Byzantine standard flying high above the walls. The Byzantine troops had already gained control of the city. The crusader leaders were likely quite frustrated, especially since the Byzantine troops only allowed small groups of crusaders into the city, making their "apologies" to the crusader commanders with gifts of jewelry, wine, and foodstuffs. Naturally, the knights were more than a little unhappy, as they had been planning to score some loot from the city.

In spite of infighting and increasing resentment between the Byzantine soldiers and their leaders and those of the crusaders, the united force went on to capture Antioch, a Syrian city, in 1098 and then headed for Jerusalem, which at the time was occupied by the Seljuks. The conflicts of this region felt as if they were never-ending (they actually continue to this day), but by 1099, the Christian crusaders forced the surrender of the Muslims occupying the city of Jerusalem. After this, the crusaders founded the Kingdom of Jerusalem, which would last for nearly two centuries.

After Jerusalem was captured, most of the knights and soldiers returned to their homes, leaving behind four primary settlements in the conquered region that were formed into what is known as the Crusader States or Outremer. These states remained under the tenuous control of the Christian crusaders from about 1098 to 1291. These states came to include Jerusalem to the south, Tripoli to the north, Antioch even farther north, and then Edessa, which was even farther north between the Euphrates and Tigris Rivers.

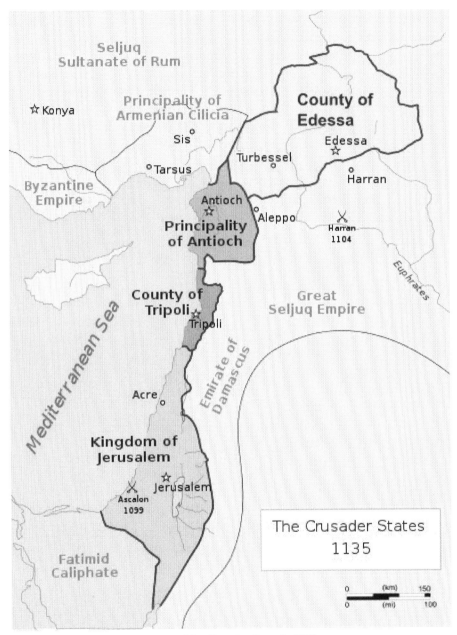

A map of the Crusader States in 1135.
Amitchell125, CC BY-SA 4.0 <https://creativecommons.org/licenses/by-sa/4.0>, via Wikimedia Commons; https://commons.wikimedia.org/wiki/File:The_Crusader_States_in_1135.svg

The First Crusade was over, and for nearly fifty years, an uneasy détente of sorts existed. Councils were constructed, and the area maintained a relatively peaceful existence until Muslim forces began a new jihad or holy war against the Christians in about 1130 CE.

In 1144, a Seljuk general by the name of Zengi recaptured Edessa, the northernmost state, and rumors of another crusade began to spread.

The Second Crusade: 1147-1149

The orders of knights, like the Knights Hospitaller and the Knights Templar, took part in the Second Crusade. Some orders, such as the Hospitallers, existed prior to the First Crusade but provided aid to the sick and gave care to traveling pilgrims making their way to the Holy Land.

The Second Crusade was overseen primarily by King Louis VII of France and King Conrad III of Germany. The primary objective of this crusade was to recapture Edessa. Once again, soldiers and knights rode off to war. Unfortunately, King Conrad's forces were decimated at a place known as Dorylaeum, which had been the location of a Christian victory in the First Crusade. After that defeat, the two European kings joined forces in Jerusalem and, with an estimated fifty thousand men, attacked Damascus, a Muslim stronghold at the time. The battle was yet another failure for the crusaders.

The Second Crusade, though short-lived, was a violent and bloody affair, yet when all was said and done, the crusaders had managed to win a number of battles within the Iberian Peninsula and Baltic regions. They successfully defeated the Muslims, even though the Muslims had called for aid from the ruler of Damascus (Syria) and Zengi's son and eventual successor, Nur al-Din, from Mosul (Iraq). Edessa remained in the hands of Nur al-Din.

However, in the years between the end of the Second Crusade and the beginning of the Third Crusade, Nur al-Din was not dormant. He eventually became the emir of Damascus. After having made a name for himself during the Second Crusade, he grew in might and power, and by 1154, he had absorbed Damascus into his own rapidly expanding empire.

The Third Crusade: 1189-1192

Nearly forty years passed between the end of the Second Crusade and the beginning of the Third Crusade. In brief, the Third Crusade was launched to regain control of the lands along the eastern shores and lands bordering the eastern Mediterranean region—the lands primarily claimed as Crusader States following the end of the First Crusade—and to protect their hold on Jerusalem

Conflicts continued to roil among the former forces of Nur al-Din, who had died in 1174. Saladin, who came from a family that had served Nur al-Din, made a name for himself on several military forays. Due to his prowess and despite his young age (he was just over thirty years old), he became the sultan of Syria and Egypt shortly after Nur al-Din's death.

While Nur al-Din had failed to gain control of Jerusalem in his lifetime, Saladin set his sights on capturing the city. By 1187, Saladin had gone on the offensive, wanting to drive the Christian crusaders from the Kingdom of Jerusalem once and for all. He nearly destroyed the crusaders at the Battle of Hattin (present-day Israel).

The Battle of Hattin and the loss of so many Christian soldiers led to the outbreak of the Third Crusade, which was led by King Richard I (Richard the Lionheart), Holy Roman Emperor Frederick Barbarossa, and King Philip II of France.

The German Crusader

Frederick I, better known as Frederick Barbarossa, which in Italian means "Red Beard," reigned as the Holy Roman emperor from 1152 to 1190. He partook in two crusades (the second and the third) but died during the Third Crusade. He drowned while crossing a river in what is now Turkey on his way to the Holy Land.

Frederick I gained a reputation as a great German ruler, and like others of his time, legends surround him. Some legends say he did not die and that he is simply sleeping in a cave in the mountains of central Germany to come forth when his native land needs him the most.

An image of Frederick Barbarossa, "Red Beard."
https://www.ancient-origins.net/history/frederick-i-barbarossa-megalomaniac-roman-emperor-crusade-power-008283

According to historical writings and legends, Frederick I was determined to restore the empire that had been established by Charlemagne. He managed to negotiate and encourage peace between numerous princes within his lands. He also took part in many campaigns, half a dozen of which were in Italy, in an effort to emphasize his imperial rights. During Barbarossa's first visit there in 1155, he ensured his coronation as Holy Roman emperor by Pope Adrian IV but was ultimately excommunicated in 1160 after legalities involving one of the church's lawyers and a hopeful pope, Alexander III, who desired to ensure a papacy that was independent of the Holy Roman Empire.

Over the following years, Frederick refused to recognize Alexander III as pope, and in 1167, during his fourth journey to Italy, where he intended to best Alexander, he was forced to give up on his goals since a plague (some sources say malaria) broke out. It wasn't until 1177 that Frederick recognized Alexander III as the pope.

When the Third Crusade broke out in 1189, Frederick I had taken up the cross and gathered a large army of Germans that is said to have been three thousand strong. They set out for the Holy Land and reached Constantinople in 1189. As Barbarossa captured one city after another, Muslims in the region grew increasingly concerned, especially Saladin, who gathered his own army to confront him.

Unfortunately for the crusaders, in early June 1190, Frederick fell from his horse while crossing the Saleph River and drowned. The exact cause of his death is unknown, but some believe that his armor weighed him down or that he experienced a heart attack caused by the shockingly cold water. Either way, he drowned, even though historical accounts state that the water was only waist-high.

At any rate, the Third Crusade was effectively over as far as his men were concerned. Many returned home, though others continued under the command of his son, Frederick of Swabia, who led them to join other crusaders at the siege of Acre on the northern borders of present-day Israel.

Some accounts relate that Barbarossa's son transported his body the entire way, hoping to bury him in Jerusalem. Apparently, Frederick of Swabia tried to preserve the body through the use of vinegar. Legend also has it that Barbarossa's decaying flesh was boiled from his bones and that the remnants of his army carried his bones all the way to Tyre, where he was ultimately buried.

Meanwhile, in the autumn of 1191, King Richard I's army defeated Saladin during the Battle of Arsuf, which, curiously enough, would be about the only large-scale battle that occurred during the Third Crusade. Most of the remainder of this crusade was relegated to skirmishes and clashes until Saladin signed a peace treaty with King Richard about a year later, in 1192. The peace treaty reestablished the Kingdom of Jerusalem under Christian rule but, oddly enough, did not include the actual city of Jerusalem. However, although the city would remain under Islamic control, Christian pilgrims were welcome to journey there.

The Fourth Crusade: 1202-1204

Peace in the region didn't last for long, as powers throughout western Europe to the Middle East and farther eastward played a tug-of-war for supremacy, though many of the issues that triggered conflicts existed between the European kingdoms and the Byzantine Empire. At the time, Pope Innocent III encouraged another crusade, but this time, it wasn't merely over religion but also the time-old concept of power and control over lands. And, of course, wresting Jerusalem from the grasp of the Muslims was at the top of the list.

The new crusade was answered, with many French barons being among the crusaders. They contracted with the Venetians for provisions and ships to take them to the Holy Land. The Venetians had their own grudges against the Byzantine Empire but agreed to supply the pope's army with a fleet of ships and enough provisions to last nine months. The crusaders faced a high cost and were further burdened by the Venetians' demand to receive roughly one-half of the plunder seized by the crusaders. Not all of the crusaders were able to make the journey, so when the crusaders made it to Venice, they realized they could not pay the Venetians what they owed.

The Venetians decided the crusaders could pay them back in a different way. They could attack ports along the coast, with Zara (located in modern-day Croatia) being the main prize. Even though Zara was a primarily Christian city, the Venetians wanted to gain it back, having lost it about twenty years prior. The pope learned about it and threatened the crusaders with excommunication if they attacked a Christian city, but they felt forced to proceed since they were obligated to pay off their debts.

Unfortunately, the sacking of Zara failed to provide enough loot to repay the Venetians. Constantinople was facing some difficulties, and the Venetians saw its trouble as a chance to gain funds. The crusaders initially arrived in Constantinople to help deal with the succession crisis. The aspiring emperor had promised them riches, but when he became emperor, he realized the treasury was dangerously low. He was unable to pay the crusaders what he promised. Tensions built up until the crusaders essentially rioted, destroying the city. The crusaders descended into lawlessness and abhorrent behavior and slaughtered many of the city's inhabitants.

The Significance of Constantinople

The significance of Constantinople (located in present-day Turkey) should not be underestimated. The city was located on a spit of land that connected Europe to the west with the landmass of Asia Minor to the east. The Black Sea was to the north, and the Aegean Sea just to the south, with the Mediterranean beyond that.

Since its founding in the 4th century by Constantine, the city of Constantinople was perceived as a symbolic rebirth of Rome. It became the center of clashes between the East and West and between Muslims and Christians. Following the Great Schism of 1054, the city became the most important city of the Eastern Orthodox Church. The Great Schism saw the splintering of the Christian Church into two factions: the Roman Catholic Church and the Eastern Orthodox Church.

Constantinople was engaged in a near-constant tug-of-war between various factions that included the Arabs, Bulgarians, and other European Christians. But in 1204, the crusaders plundered the city, drove the Byzantines out, and created a Latin state. In 1261, the Byzantines again took control of the city, and though it was no longer nearly as grand as it once had been, it was still a highly populated port city.

Eventually, the city again became the center of a tug-of-war for power, and in 1453, it was overtaken by Mehmed II for the Ottoman Empire. Once more, the city found itself under Muslim rule.

The fall of Constantinople in late May 1453 occurred after a fifty-five-day siege. Mehmed's success was primarily due to his use of gunpowder and cannons, which decimated the once-powerful city and its defenses.

The actual fall of Constantinople gives us a fascinating glimpse into the tenacity of an outnumbered force that fought valiantly to defend the great city, one that was subdued by the ongoing onslaught on its walls by Mehmed's artillery barrage.

During the following decades, the formerly Christian churches in the city were converted into mosques, except for the Church of Saint Mary of the Mongols. Perhaps surprisingly, Mehmed II tolerated a diverse religious population and is known to have encouraged those from different faiths and backgrounds to populate the city. From 1520 through 1566, the Ottoman Empire was ruled by Suleyman the Magnificent, who expanded the Ottoman Empire. Today, scholars often mark the fall of Constantinople as the end of the medieval or Middle Ages and the dawn of the Renaissance.

The Fifth Crusade (1217-1271)

Following the sacking of Constantinople during the Fourth Crusade, a number of crusaders marched into the Middle East and the Holy Land, with their goal now primarily being to engage in skirmishes and fights against any and all who were seen as "enemies of the Christian faith." Of course, Muslim forces felt the same way about the Christians, so it was a time of open conflicts that accomplished nothing much except bloodshed and the loss of men on both sides.

A proper crusade had to be sanctioned by the church, though. The Fifth Crusade again focused on recapturing Jerusalem, and in 1215, Pope Innocent III began to call upon knights and other able-bodied men to help achieve this by weakening the bonds that the Egyptian Ayyubid state had on the city and its surrounding lands. This time, though, the crusade was to be guided more directly by the church to avoid another major incident of crusaders going rogue, as had happened during the Fourth Crusade. However, by this time, many knights and soldiers were weary of near-constant warring, and interest was lukewarm at best.

The pope then called on the general populace and effectively "encouraged" them to join the crusade, promising them monetary rewards. Before that could be accomplished, Pope Innocent passed away, with his place being taken by Pope Honorius III, who then took over the organization of the crusade.

However, after gathering at Acre, the new group of crusaders, along with a number of French knights that bolstered their numbers, headed for Egypt. Their first goal was to take a city named Damietta, and then they would continue to Cairo. By the time they reached that city, they believed the Egyptian hold on the lands should be significantly weakened.

While the crusaders managed to drive the Egyptians from Damietta, their lack of knowledge of the area proved to be their downfall. They failed to take into account the season, and the Nile flooded. When they finally decided to turn back, they were attacked by the Egyptians, causing the loss of many crusaders.

Although there were other crusades, the Fifth Crusade was one of the last that really captivated the people enough to join. During the Sixth Crusade (1228-1229), Jerusalem would be regained. The last official crusade, the Eighth Crusade (1270), saw no advances made in the Middle East. About twenty years later, Acre fell, leading to the end of the Crusader States.

Numerous forays were made to the Holy Land during the Crusades, with one of the most unusual made by a surprising contingent of European citizenry.

The Children's Crusade

In 1212, something extraordinary happened, and while it isn't exactly considered an official crusade and did not include the medieval knights, it did include thousands of pilgrims vowing to march to Jerusalem. What was different about this crusade was that it was composed of thousands of young children. Today, it is called the Children's Crusade. According to historical documents, tens of thousands of people set out on the journey, even though rulers and the pope told them to return home. It wasn't only children and teenagers who joined in but also women, the poor, and the elderly. Basically, the outliers of society, the ones who were often rendered "invisible" from the wealthy or well-to-do of their times, were part of this crusade.

The group was led by twelve-year-old shepherd Stephen of Cloyes. Young Stephen held some sway over his followers and is believed to embody a boldness that likely took many by surprise. He even demanded to see the king of France (and did) to receive permission to conduct the crusade. But what was his goal? He wanted to reclaim the Holy Land for the Catholic Church and remove Muslims from Jerusalem.

Twelve-year-old Stephen of Cloyes was a unique young boy who gained attention and claimed to have experienced a vision that was divine in nature. Despite the king's warning not to proceed, young Stephen gained quite a following, and being a stubborn young man, he proceeded with his dream of accomplishing something great for Christianity. The mass of children and adults headed out, but they were ill-equipped, ill-provisioned, and mostly unarmed.

Little is known of their actual pilgrimage, and some historians today question the crusade's veracity. Since the crusade was not condoned by the pope, it was never declared an actual crusade. Nevertheless, the majority of historians believe it occurred. The group of children and adults ventured forward, but instead of carrying weapons, they carried crosses and banners. The youth must have been convinced that they could accomplish things the adults never could. They were convinced and very optimistic that once they reached the Holy Land, they would be able to convert the Muslims into Christians through divine intervention.

And it wasn't Stephen of Cloyes alone who led this crusade. Another group was also whipped into a frenzy of religious fervor, this one led by a young man named Nicholas of Cologne.

At any rate, the crusaders gathered in Marseille to prepare for the crossing of the Mediterranean before heading farther into the Holy Land. According to legend, they waited for the miracle that Stephen insisted would happen but didn't: the Mediterranean would part as the Red Sea did for Moses as he led his people to freedom. Many of his followers returned home. While Stephen of Cloyes's group waited on the banks of the Mediterranean for passage, the young German from Cologne took his group toward the Alps, also heading for Jerusalem.

What was unique about the Children's Crusade was its ability to gain attention not only from children but also from families in towns throughout western Europe. While their religious beliefs were no doubt firm, they were able to motivate the crowds like the popes had been able to do in previous crusades. As such, they might have been viewed less enthusiastically by the church, whose priests might have been somewhat concerned that they would lose some of their respect and control over the populace.

The church called these crusaders fanatics, and yet their very presence created curiosity throughout the land. These two child leaders of two different groups gave their sermons and spoke of miracles. They likely left their listeners spellbound.

Ultimately, both groups failed in their mission. Nicholas of Cologne and his followers did make it far, although they quickly ran out of food and became exhausted. They pressed on and finally managed to make it to Genoa, Italy. There, they were unable to communicate with the locals, who, as history tells it, weren't too thrilled with the sudden arrival of hundreds of starving children. As can be imagined, some of them met tragic fates. Some starved, some were forced to take local jobs to fund their return home, and some were sold into slavery. Others managed to gain passage on ships, with some of them being drowned at sea.

While the actual size and events of the Children's Crusade are difficult to historically verify, it does show the religious fervor of the times.

The first five crusades encapsulated some of the harshest years of the Middle Ages, but during these challenging times, the knights of old made their mark on history forever. However, not just anyone could become a knight. To do so required a unique character and a willingness to sacrifice. For some, this journey took years.

Chapter 3: The Journey to Knighthood

When one hears the words "medieval knights," the first thing that often comes to mind is men wearing armor, maybe with fancy plumes of feathers or perhaps a swath of horsehair trailing from atop their metal helmets. They sit on their mighty stallions, a long jousting pole tucked under one arm, the other tightly grasping his horse's reins as he charges toward an opponent at the tournament, determined to win the hand of a fair lady.

A number of myths about knights persist even today, such as those in full armor needing a crane-like contraption to be hoisted onto their mighty steeds. How awkward would it have been if they were knocked off their horse in battle?

Another myth is that knights were only those of noble birth. In the knighthood's earliest stages, more were from the aristocracy or nobility, but how could an order create an army of knights if only those with a certain pedigree were allowed? Men of lowly birth were often knighted following acts of valor or courage or for their loyalty to the knights they served. In some cases, their knighthood could be bought.

Not all knights donned full suits of armor; instead, some used bits and pieces of armor that were gathered as booty from a battlefield or won during a tournament. Armor, like anything manufactured today, was not always high-quality either. At any rate, it was more common for a knight to focus his need for armor on vulnerable body parts, such as the head, the hands, and the torso. Full suits of armor were constructed of metal strips that were attached with leather straps and movable links that allowed amazing freedom of joint movement. Heavy, yes, but they were not stiff and unwieldy.

The knight was supposed to personify chivalry and bravery, one who was duty- and honor-bound to defend not only the kingdom but also everyone in it. However, not every brave or chivalrous man had what it took to become a knight in the medieval ages. And as time passed, knights fell prey to corruption, seeking treasures instead of honor.

Perhaps most important of all, one who desired to become a knight was required to start at the bottom rung of the ladder, so to speak. They learned by doing. Typically, a future knight began his training as a young boy between seven and ten years of age. The boy would be charged with caring for a knight's horses. He was called a page, and he was an assistant of sorts to a knight. In the majority of cases, the page also came from an aristocratic family but not always. It was the page's duty to learn the ways of war, how to care for weapons, manners, and obedience.

During a page's daily activities, he might spend his time ensuring the cleanliness and readiness of the knight or nobleman's weaponry, caring for his horses, and even dressing the knight and aiding in the donning of his armor. After all, a complete suit of armor at the time weighed anywhere between thirty and fifty pounds (fourteen to twenty-three kilograms). Suits of armor were often cumbersome and difficult to don by oneself. The page was also responsible for ensuring that the leather straps and rivets that held the strips of metal together were kept in good condition.

Over time, the page was taught skills that would serve him well throughout life, such as hunting, horsemanship, and the wielding of weaponry commonly used by knights. Yet their days were not only filled with menial labor or learning how to fight. If the page was fortunate and had an educated knight as a mentor, he might also be taught a number of additional life skills, including reading and writing. He would also be taught what was expected in regard to behavior, courtesy, and manners in courtly environments. After all, the knight a page served might have to visit the royal court or receive orders from the lord of the manor, their feudal lord, or a fiefdom they served. In their spare time, pages might be taught subjects like music, art, and even poetry.

In return for their diligence and devotion, a page could expect to receive food, clothing, and shelter from the knight or nobleman they served. In some circumstances, and depending on the level of their service and dedication, a page might also receive a reward from the person they served, be it monetary or material.

After enough time passed, the page advanced to the next stage.

To Squire...

Typically, young boys could expect to serve a knight or nobleman as a page until they turned thirteen or fourteen, upon which they could be promoted to the position of squire. They would be required to spend about the same amount of time as a knight's squire.

Squires not only provided care for the knights they served but also for their lords of the realm, especially the lord that their knight served. Therefore, the squire not only assisted the knight when it came to tournaments or battle, but they also basically existed as servants in a manor house or castle if it were so desired by their lord.

Even after the conclusion of their seven years of serving as a squire, some of these young men continued to serve their knights or lords as squires well into adulthood. Some even served their entire lives because they never attained the rank of knighthood.

During tournaments, the squire was required to prepare the knight's horse and equipment, including his lance. A squire was supposed to always be ready to provide assistance. They learned how to handle common battle swords, as well as the heaviest two-handed swords, which could weigh as much as forty-five pounds (twenty kilograms), although most of the one- and two-handed swords often weighed anywhere between four pounds (two kilograms) and ten pounds (five kilograms).

In times of peace, they were taught what could be deemed daily activities, such as hunting, dancing, and some education in history. They enhanced their equestrian skills and learned how to joust. They were trained in numerous fighting styles, both with and without armor. Squires also served their knights during times of war and often accompanied them into battle.

By doing this, a squire was able to show he had the mettle to become a knight. This didn't happen overnight. The process could take years. If a squire proved his bravery and stoutness in battle and in service by having a good and obedient demeanor, he was often recommended for a knighthood. At this time, he would generally wear clothing and armor that identified him under the particular coat of arms of the knight he served. Some knights were able to earn great rewards, including lands and titles, depending on their performance and loyalty on the battlefield and their years of service.

One of the most important things taught to young knights was the concept of chivalry, which is basically a code of conduct. This was required of knights, squires, and pages. After being knighted, a knight promised loyalty to the feudal lord under whom he served. Of course, one of the most important traits a knight had to have was bravery. To not serve with bravery was to invite complete humiliation, not only by his peers but also by the general public as well.

The Idea of Chivalry as Epitomized by the Knights

The knights' code of conduct was not only related to bravery on the battlefield; it also emphasized service. Some codes of conduct stressed valor, bravery, generosity, and a willingness to serve others, not only through offering protection but also through their everyday actions and deeds. The code of conduct was not something that was recited from a piece of paper. It was a concept of behavior that was part of a young man's training as a page and squire.

The centuries of the medieval age encompassed a dark and bloody period of history. Yet, during those years, a knight was expected to be brave and gentle (primarily toward women and children). He was expected to offer protection for those who were defenseless or too weak to fight for themselves. They were sworn to protect their faith and their church, to live with honor, and to serve their feudal lords and kings without question.

Knights were also given codes of conduct by the feudal lords they served, which often included rules regarding positive characteristics, such as being prudent, truthful, and charitable. A knight was also expected to defend his church and his Christian faith. Not all knights during the Crusades belonged to orders; many fought for their feudal lords. It was assumed that if their lord joined an order, they would follow. During this time, knights were also encouraged to be ferocious in battles against the "infidels" and to always fight on the side of good and justice in defense of their people, the Christian faith, and their country.

The Legend of King Arthur

Today, many consider the fables of King Arthur and the Knights of the Round Table as nothing more than a fairytale, a legend that personifies the very idea of chivalry and bravery. Some might be surprised to learn that there was a King Arthur, and legends of this king and his brave knights were written about and respected throughout the medieval ages.

By the 11th century, the tales of King Arthur and his knights were popularly known, and in the 12th century, many sought his burial place on the island of fictional Avalon, believed to be an island in the sea just off the Cornwall coast, more commonly known as St. Michael's Mount, or perhaps a small island off the coast of Brittany. Very early in the 11th century, it was believed that Avalon was actually Glastonbury Tor, a hill near Somerset.

Rumors abound regarding King Arthur's final resting place, but today's historians believe that the actual King Arthur of legend might have been a Welsh prince who lived during the 5th or 6th century. The name Arthur is found in numerous accounts throughout the Middle Ages, harking back to the years of the many battles with the Saxons in the early decades of the 6th century.

Others believe that King Arthur was nothing more than a legend, a figure that encompassed the characteristics of soldiers at the time, and from there, the Arthurian legend was born, primarily following the publication of Geoffrey of Monmouth's *History of the Kings of Britain* around 1135.

By the year 1155, King Arthur's legend had grown, and his exploits were translated into French, with the French being among the first to define the Knights of the Round Table. One of the fictionalized accounts of Arthur's life, written by a French author, mentions a quest for the Holy Grail, the cup Christ is believed to have used during the Last Supper with his disciples. Allegedly, the cup was given to Joseph of Arimathea, who later brought the cup with him to Europe.

It was from these legends that the concept of knights living by a code of chivalry was born, as were the legends of his Knights of the Round Table, among them Sir Tristan, Sir Lancelot, Sir Galahad, and Sir Percival. All of these knights convey highly sought-after and honored qualities of knighthood, including their spirituality. During the Middle Ages, the symbolism of the Holy Grail was transformed into a literal object, a cup carefully guarded by what were known as Grail Knights or Grail Keepers, men who had been tasked with the lone objective of protecting the Holy Grail through the ages.

The ideals of honor, devotion, and dedication endured over the years as the concept of chivalry and knighthood evolved. Christian knights engaging in holy battles and acting as stalwart defenders of Jerusalem grew in popularity, leading to the growth of military orders. The search for King Arthur's verifiable resting place still continues today, and his legends endure, as do the histories and legends of many knightly orders.

Among these orders of knights were the Knights of the Holy Sepulchre, the Knights Hospitaller, the Order of St. Lazarus, and, perhaps the most well-known knightly societies in history, the Knights Templar and the Teutonic Knights.

Chapter 4: The Knights Hospitaller

The cross of the Knights Hospitaller.
https://en.wikipedia.org/wiki/File:Cross_of_the_Knights_Hospitaller.svg

A relatively lesser-known society of knights, at least in comparison with the larger, more well-known Knights Templar, was the Knights Hospitaller. This order consisted, for the most part, of single men who adopted an almost monastic way of life.

Many of them were monks and closely adhered to that way of life. They were typically simple men with strong beliefs. Some were illiterate, while others were educated. Regardless of their education, they devoted themselves and often sacrificed their lives in their service to the order.

Clothing of the Knights Hospitaller.
https://commons.wikimedia.org/wiki/File:Chevalier_de_Rhodes,_en_habit_religieux_(XVe_siecle)_et_en_armure_(XIVe_siecle),_d%27apres_des_pierres_tombales.jpg

While knights have a reputation for being noble warriors, many of the Hospitallers were not trained in war, nor did all of them come from royal lineages or places of wealth. They did not expect a comfortable existence and were often required to journey to places that were far from comfortable, safe, or even healthy.

These warrior monks lived by extremely strict rules, even limiting the number of days they were allowed to eat meat and then only to keep up their strength. The brotherhood required them to maintain silence during meal times, and some groups were not allowed to hunt. They were expected to don plain clothing made of wool. During their leisure time, they attended services, while the more literate among them led daily prayers or services. Others served as chaplains. They were all required to recite the Lord's Prayer—the *Pater Noster*—at certain times of the day. The rules were strict, and penalties for disobedience could be severe, from a beating to performing penance.

Though most came from humble beginnings, the ranks of the Knights Hospitaller were well respected. These knights earned their reputation and the respect of their peers and contemporaries. They were known for being highly disciplined and ferocious in battle and believed they were fighting for their own salvation. However, their origins were not steeped in blood on the battlefield; rather, they began as an order that sought to help pilgrims reach the Holy Land.

The Knights Hospitaller was founded sometime between 1070 and 1080. They eventually became known as the Knights of the Order of the Hospital of St. John of Jerusalem during the later years of the First Crusade and actually received the backing of Pope Paschal II in 1113.

One branch of the Knights Hospitaller that influenced history was the Knights of St. Thomas, formally known as the Hospitallers of St. Thomas of Canterbury at Acre. They made a name for themselves during the siege of Acre in 1191. This military order was only open to Englishmen, and their patron saint was Saint Thomas Becket of Canterbury.

Thomas Becket, an English archbishop, was murdered in Canterbury Cathedral in 1170, primarily because he had gained a reputation for being a somewhat rebellious priest. His reputation was garnered after he and King Henry II experienced differences of opinion when it came to the privileges of clerics. Tensions rose when Becket insisted that the church was not to be held to the English laws of the land.

Becket, who was initially the archdeacon of Canterbury, became lord chancellor in 1155. He served the crown as a diplomat and served the king. He even acted like a soldier at times, leading troops in France to reclaim the lands of Eleanor of Aquitaine, the king's wife.

Becket was ordained as a priest, and by 1162, the year he became archbishop of Canterbury, a number of disagreements and differences of opinion between Becket and the king had come to a head, not only regarding religious disagreements but also over political issues, including taxation and the responsibilities and rights of the church in general. Their differences convinced Becket to flee to France in 1164, and he did not return until early December 1170.

The history that follows is complicated, but eventually, after some of the dust settled, Becket returned to Canterbury Cathedral while King Henry was in Normandy. Apparently, the king was outraged by this and muttered a number of unfortunate words that were heard by some knights, something along the lines of when he might be relieved of the troublesome priest.

So, Becket's fate was sealed. On December 29th, 1170, four knights (William de Tracy, Hugh de Morville, Richard le Bret, and Reginald FitzUrse) took it upon themselves to provide a solution, and Becket was violently murdered in the cathedral. Within days, Pope Alexander III canonized Becket, and he became Saint Thomas.

The incident immediately gained Becket the sympathy of Christians throughout Europe, and he was deemed a martyr. In 1174, King Henry II was absolved of the incident after doing penance at Canterbury.

It is said that some routes the pilgrims took from various parts of England to Canterbury to honor the man can still be found at the location of where his shrine once stood until it was destroyed during the Reformation.

Origins

But how did they start? Well, the Knights Hospitallers can trace their origins further than the other orders, although they weren't officially established as a military order until 1099. The original hospital was founded by Italian merchants around 1023 to take care of the poor and sick. At that time, the hospital was manned by Benedictine monks who provided shelter for religious pilgrims who made their way to Jerusalem. This hospital was believed to be on the site of a church that was linked to the Apostle John, not far from the Holy Sepulchre.

Most scholars date the knight's origins to 1099, when the Benedictine monk Blessed Gerard founded the order. Others date the origin of the order much earlier to 1080 or even earlier to the time of the aforementioned Italian merchants from Amalfi.

The Hospitallers were officially known as the Order of Knights of the Hospital of St. John of Jerusalem. However, the hospital had existed long before they came around, even before the Italian merchants rebuilt it. The first known account of a hospital in Jerusalem was in 603 when Pope Gregory I commissioned a hospital to be built. However, in 1009, the structure was destroyed by the sixth caliph of Egypt, who deliberately ordered the destruction of many Christian shrines, including the Church of the Holy Sepulchre, which was built on the site believed to be where Jesus was crucified and buried. The hospital was rebuilt by the Italian merchants in 1023.

While there are disagreements over the exact timeframe of the creation of the hospitals and hospices in Jerusalem and the Hospitallers' presence there, history does confirm that they were there in the years prior to the arrival of the Knights Templar.

Suffice it to say that the hospital was devoted to providing care to traveling pilgrims. And it is fairly well agreed upon that from the time the brothers formed the order, they devoted themselves to living a life of chastity, obedience, and poverty.

Following the conquest of Jerusalem in 1099 by Christian forces, Gerard Thom (sometimes spelled Tum), a Benedictine lay brother, became the guardian of the hospital. He eventually came to be known as "Blessed Gerard" and is believed to be the founder of the Knights of St. John.

Blessed Gerard

Blessed Gerard, also known as Gérard de Martigues, was believed to have been born around 1040. History is unclear regarding his specific date of birth and birthplace, but he is believed to have been a Benedictine lay brother. The Benedictine monks were known to wear black robes and habits, giving them the nickname the Black Monks. Gerard was known to be a man of piety and practiced humility. Numerous legends have been written about the man.

As the years passed, the hospital in Jerusalem grew, and by the 1100s, the brothers cared for hundreds of patients, regardless of the religion they practiced or where they came from. Over the years, stories have been written that in times of need, the brothers would give up their beds and sleep on the floor to better care for their patients.

An image of Blessed Gerard.
Vertot abbé de, 1655-1735;Cavagna Sangiuliani di Gualdana, Antonio, conte, 1843-1913, former owner. IU-R, No restrictions, via Wikimedia Commons
https://commons.wikimedia.org/wiki/File:Gravure_de_Fra_Gerard_fondateur_des_Hospitaliers_de_Saint-Jean.jpg

Blessed Gerard was known to have traveled far and wide to gather support for the hospital and to raise money. He won over Pope Paschal II, who determined that the Order of the Hospitallers was to be subservient only to the papacy and not to the king of Jerusalem. The pope also exempted the order from paying church tithes.

Over the years, Gerard established hospitals along the routes typically taken by pilgrims to the Holy Land, and the order eventually became more than caretakers. The brothers provided pilgrimages with armed escorts along the more dangerous sections of their long journeys.

It wasn't until around 1113 that Pope Paschal II officially sanctioned the order, which was dedicated to Saint John the Baptist. At times, the hospital in Jerusalem is believed to have contained upward of two thousand patients.

Following the death of Blessed Gerard in 1120, the order slowly acquired more responsibilities in addition to taking care of the sick, and those responsibilities included military expectations. In 1121, Raymond du Puy stepped up to become the second grand master.

> **Note of interest: Relic**
>
> In the capital of Malta today, preserved in the convent of St. Ursula in Valletta, is a relic believed to be the skull of Blessed Gerard.

Raymond du Puy: The Second Grand Master of the Hospitaller Order (1121-1160)

Over the years following the origin of the hospital-based order that strictly followed Benedictine rules, the Hospitallers began to take on new roles. By the mid-1100s, they had been tasked to become defenders of the Holy Land. Over time, the rules regarding the behavior and actions of knightly orders changed according to circumstances, and the same is true of this order.

When Raymond du Puy, a French knight, became the second grand master of the Hospitallers around 1121, he revised expectations regarding the brotherhood. This list, called the Rule of the Order of St. John, contained the following:

1. How the brethren should make their profession
2. What the brethren should claim as their due
3. Concerning the conduct of the brethren in the service of the church and in the reception of the sick
4. How the brethren should go abroad and behave
5. By whom and how alms should be sought
6. Concerning the alms obtained in concerning the produce of the houses (they could not take land from collected alms, but they could take a third of food, including bread and wine, and the surplus could be given to the poor in Jerusalem)
7. Who and in what manner they should go abroad to preach
8. Concerning the clothing and food of the brethren

9. Concerning brethren guilty of fornication
10. Concerning brethren quarreling or striking one another
11. Concerning the silence of the brethren
12. Concerning brethren misbehaving
13. Concerning brethren found with private property
14. What office should be celebrated for the deceased brethren
15. How the things here detailed are to be firmly maintained
16. How our lords the sick should be received and served
17. In what manner brethren may correct brethren
18. How one brother should accuse another brother
19. That the brethren bear on their breasts the sign of the cross

A copper engraving of Raymond du Puy by Laurent Cars.
https://commons.wikimedia.org/wiki/File:%2BRaymond_du_Puy,_by_Laurent_Cars.jpg

Raymond du Puy guided the Hospitallers to become a group of brothers dedicated to providing for the sick, defending the faith, and fighting infidels. The eight-pointed star they wore on their robes symbolized their pledge to give their lives to their faith and to Christ and to follow the example of the martyrs who came before them.

The Hospitallers took part in battles in current-day Palestine and other places in the Holy Land, and they fought alongside other crusaders and mercenaries. It is said the Hospitallers were rarely captured as prisoners since there was no point in trying to ransom them or release them by encouraging them to deny Christ.

While Raymond du Puy was known as a devoted Christian and crusader, he was also known to be sensible and did not encourage wanton destruction in the aftermath of battles.

Several paintings depicting Raymond du Puy exist in Malta. There are also paintings of other saints of the order, including Blessed Gerard, in Valletta. (The painting of Saint John by Caravaggio in 1608 is also there.)

Raymond du Puy died around 1160 after leading the Hospitallers as their second grand master for thirty-three years.

What Happened to the Hospitallers?

Following the deaths of Blessed Gerard and Raymond du Puy, other grand masters stepped up to lead the order, first in Jerusalem until approximately 1187, after the city fell once again to the Muslims, then to Margat, and then to Acre in 1191. After the fall of Acre in 1291, they left the Holy Land and relocated to Cyprus, but the terrain wasn't fruitful enough to support them, so they relocated to Rhodes, which they were forced to take from the Byzantines. The Hospitallers ruled Rhodes from 1309 to 1522.

While their numbers rarely exceeded several hundred knights in the crusading armies, they were credited with aiding the evacuation of Acre in 1291 and protecting refugees escaping to Cyprus. They served as knights and medics on the battlefield.

In later years, they engaged in several campaigns in battles over the Ottoman Empire. The Hospitallers were part of the capture of Izmir in 1344 and took part in the attack on Alexandria in 1365.

The Hospitallers remained in Rhodes for just over two centuries until 1522, when they relocated to the island of Malta, where they remained until the late 18th century. In 1834, they became a permanent fixture of

Rome.

Today, the eightieth grand master of the Sovereign Military and Hospitaller Order of St. John of Jerusalem of Rhodes and of Malta (the Order of Malta, for short) resides over the order, which today is recognized as a religious order of the Roman Catholic Church, as well as a sovereign one according to international law. The order is still dedicated to helping the poor and defending the Christian faith. Today, the Order of Malta continues to maintain diplomatic associations and relationships with the Holy See and seventy-five other countries around the world.

Through the 1990s, membership required proof of noble lineage, but today, the order focuses primarily on international and humanitarian issues around the globe. They provide relief, aid, and support to the less fortunate, as well as aiding in natural disasters and providing support to countries devastated by war and epidemics. Today, members of the order focus on the pursuit of their humanitarian services, though they still wear white shirts with the emblem of a red shield with a white eight-pointed cross or similar emblems.

Chapter 5: The Knights of the Holy Sepulchre

The coat of arms of the Knights of the Holy Sepulchre.
Mathieu CHAINE, CC BY-SA 3.0 <https://creativecommons.org/licenses/by-sa/3.0>, via Wikimedia Commons; https://commons.wikimedia.org/wiki/File:GA_Ordre_du_Saint-S%C3%A9pulcre.svg

The Knights of the Holy Sepulchre was formed to protect the tomb of Christ in the Holy City, also known as Jerusalem. However, their story is perhaps not as well known as the other military orders, such as the Knights Templar, though their loyalty and devotion to their task were equal to none.

The historical origins of the Knights of the Holy Sepulchre differ slightly, as many of the histories and traditions of the order were passed down orally. However, the order is believed to have been founded during the First Crusade with the capture of Jerusalem in 1099.

Origins of the Knights of the Holy Sepulchre

The Knights of the Holy Sepulchre was conceived as an order under the leadership of a man named Godfrey of Bouillon, who is credited with helping to capture Jerusalem during the First Crusade (1096-1099), the first of many religious wars.

However, some historians trace the order as far back as decades after the crucifixion and death of Jesus Christ, with the order being tasked to protect his tomb. As one might expect, the history of the Knights of the Holy Sepulchre is bound up in legend and traditions that go back in time before Godfrey of Bouillon, stretching back as far as the first bishop of Jerusalem himself, Saint James the Just.

First Crusader Warrior: Godfrey of Bouillon

Godfrey of Bouillon hailed from France and was born around 1060. He was not only a nobleman but also a valiant leader during the First Crusade. Godfrey actually became the first ruler of Jerusalem, serving in that role from 1099 to 1100. He didn't want to be called a king; instead, he preferred to be called "an advocate of the Holy Sepulchre."

Godfrey's early history is mired in the vagueness of legends. However, by the age of forty, he took up the cross, something that nobles throughout the land were urged to do during the First Crusade. At the time, many nobles willingly joined, not only for religious reasons but also to procure lands or other material resources.

Statue of Godfrey of Bouillon, Brussels
https://en.wikipedia.org/wiki/File:Godefroy.jpg

During the First Crusade, Godfrey of Bouillon and his two brothers, Baldwin and Eustace III, Count of Boulogne, commanded a contingent of approximately forty thousand men (approximately ten thousand knights and thirty thousand foot soldiers) that set out from the area of Lorraine in northern France.

During the late summer of 1096, Bouillon and his men set out for Constantinople, taking a route that many pilgrims had taken before him through what is known as present-day Hungary and the Balkans, though at the time, it was known as the Byzantine Empire.

Godfrey of Bouillon partook in the siege of Antioch and then proceeded to Edessa. Legend has it that he prompted over 150 Turks to flee with only a dozen knights. He could reputedly cut a Turkish horseman in half with one mighty sweep of his sword.

In 1098, Godfrey of Bouillon journeyed to Jerusalem, arriving there in the early summer of 1099, though according to some sources, he lost nearly ninety percent of his men en route. He and his men were active in the siege of the Holy City. He is reputed to be among the first to enter the city, along with his brother Eustace, in mid-July of that year. According to legend, he made a vow (which he kept) following his entry into the city. It is said that he put down his arms and, wearing only his undergarments, rounded the ramparts of the city and then went to pray at the site of the Holy Sepulchre.

Godfrey was suggested to become and was ultimately elected the king of Jerusalem, although he refused to wear a crown, claiming that he refused to do so out of respect for Christ, who had been crowned in that very place with a crown of thorns. Godfrey accepted the position solely for his love of Christ.

It was Godfrey's responsibility to ensure the safety and survival of this new kingdom, which was a very uncertain prospect at the time, especially after a great bulk of the crusaders who had journeyed and fought with him eventually returned home. It is said that he was left with perhaps three hundred knights, a couple thousand infantry footmen, and no ships with which he could defend the city. A heavy burden had been placed on his shoulders, yet he managed to negotiate a number of treaties and truces with many surrounding cities and especially after defeating the Egyptian army in the Battle of Ascalon. The battle occurred in August of 1099, barely a month after he succeeded in capturing Jerusalem.

At the time, the secular order of the Knights of the Holy Sepulchre was charged with the protection of the holiest places of Jerusalem, including the tomb of Christ. It was not so much by design but rather a sense of duty that the knights in charge of defending the Holy Sepulchre became known as such. Therefore, it can be assumed that any knight who took up the sword in defense of such holy sites also took upon the identity of being a part of the Knights of the Holy Sepulchre.

Godfrey of Bouillon made a name for himself in history, as he was respected by many as a true protector of the church. Historical accounts of his demise differ, with some claiming that Godfrey fell victim to the plague in Caesarea not long before reaching Jerusalem the previous June. He never fully recovered and passed away in mid-July in 1100. Others claim that he had been struck by an arrow during the siege of Acre and endured an infection that gradually seeped into his bloodstream and eventually caused his death. Some accounts even propose that he had been poisoned by the emir of Caesarea.

Before Godfrey died, he named his brother Baldwin as his successor. He was buried in the Church of the Holy Sepulchre. Yet his legend continued to grow.

Following his death, Godfrey of Bouillon was portrayed as the epitome of a medieval knight. According to historical documents, he was similar to what the legends claimed: a man of courage, a Christian knight, tall, handsome, and courteous. He kept to his vows without question and at great personal cost.

Although Godfrey of Bouillon was among the first Christians to step into Jerusalem that July in 1099, he did not have long to enjoy the success of his long and arduous journey. However, he left behind a legacy of dedication and determination. Within one hundred years of his passing, Godfrey became a hero, and stories about him were told throughout the noble courts.

While myth and legend often develop about heroes and leaders of the past, it is important to remember, especially as it pertains to Godfrey of Bouillon, that he was a simple man, a man who fought hard and bravely for what he believed in. Whether all the stories passed down over the ages about him are true, one thing cannot be denied. He is still known as the defender of the Holy Sepulchre, and he certainly carried great influence and had an even greater impact on history, as he was the Christian knight who helped take back Jerusalem and become the first overseer of the Kingdom of Jerusalem.

The tomb of Christ continues to be a holy site, and pilgrimages to the believed site of the Holy Sepulchre have endured throughout the centuries.

Note of Interest: Godfrey of Bouillon and the Nine Worthies

Throughout the ages, civilization has often turned its attention to the "greats" of their times, such as the Seven Wonders of the Ancient World or the best fast-food places. During the Middle Ages, one of the most interesting of these lists was called the Nine Worthies. These are men who were purported to have been the most chivalrous and brave in all of history. These men were believed to have exemplified idealized virtues, especially dedication, loyalty, and service to their country and faith.

During the Middle Ages, this list included three Christians, three Jews, and three pagans. It is believed that each set symbolized aspects of heroism, devotion, and loyalty during the development of the concept of chivalry, as well as exemplified the efforts of mankind to accept and spread the divine will of God.

The three Jewish worthies are found in the Old Testament of the Holy Bible: David, Joshua, and Judas Maccabeus. Joshua became the leader of the Jews after the death of Moses. He was perceived as a general of the Israelites, who eventually conquered the Holy Land. David, the boy who fought Goliath and won, became the "anointed" man of God's family line and was instructed by God to lead his people to freedom and faith. Judas Maccabeus was a priest who ultimately led the Maccabees in a revolt against the Seleucid Empire to resist the spread of Hellenism in Judea and preserve the Jewish religion. He restored worship at the Temple of Jerusalem, which is still celebrated as Hanukkah every year.

Three pagan worthies were also recognized, among them Alexander the Great, Hector, and Julius Caesar, who represented Roman or pagan laws. Hector, a prince and also one of Troy's heroes, fought to defend his homeland, while Alexander the Great is no stranger to historians around the world. This great general is recognized as spreading Greek knowledge and wisdom throughout the Mediterranean and Persian regions. Julius Caesar was one of the most well-known rulers of Rome and sought to encourage peace following his conquests.

Three Christian worthies are recognized, including King Arthur, Charlemagne, and Godfrey of Bouillon. Perhaps combining fact and fiction, the legend of King Arthur and the concept of chivalry and his knights continue to this day, as he is known for his honor and desire to spread Christianity. As for Charlemagne, he is credited with the origin of the Holy Roman Empire and was crowned its king circa 800 CE. Charlemagne was known as the man who protected Christians and Christianity, especially the Roman papacy.

Godfrey of Bouillon was a contemporary of the Middle Ages, a French knight who led the First Crusade into the Holy Land and who became the brief ruler of the Kingdom of Jerusalem before his untimely death a mere year later. Godfrey epitomized the concept of the divine mission of chivalry, a mission that has endured for centuries and continues to this day.

What Happened to the Order of the Knights of the Holy Sepulchre?

The Order of the Knights of the Holy Sepulchre still exists today. It is one of the oldest orders in Catholic history. These knights may no longer wear the armor that they used to, but they continue to dedicate and devote themselves to the honor and preservation of the tomb of Christ in the city of Jerusalem.

In the 13th century, the Order of the Knights of the Holy Sepulchre was led by Franciscan missionaries. They were charged with maintaining the holy sites and establishing and protecting churches, hospitals, schools, and convents in the Holy Land. By the mid-1840s, the Latin patriarchate of Jerusalem, which was reestablished by Pope Pius IX, basically relieved the Franciscans of their duties.

Around 1496, the grand masters of the Order of the Holy Sepulchre were vested in the papacy. Just after the turn of the 20th century, in 1906, Pope Pius X took the role of grand master, and since then, the order has maintained four primary types of memberships, including knight, commander, commander with a star, and knight with a grand cross. Membership requires each of these knights to protect the tomb of Christ and other holy sites in Jerusalem. Since 1949, grand masters of the order have been cardinals and, as such, remain in their headquarters in Rome.

So, from the First Crusade until today, the Order of the Knights of the Holy Sepulchre is still devoted and dedicated to the protection and preservation of historical sites in the Holy City.

Chapter 6: The Order of St. Lazarus

The flag of the Order of St. Lazarus.
https://commons.wikimedia.org/wiki/File:Flag_of_the_Order_of_Saint_Lazarus.svg

Another lesser-known order of knights during the medieval ages was the Order of St. Lazarus of Jerusalem, which was founded around 1119, although some historians claim that the order was established around 1123. Regardless, this order was small; it was certainly smaller than the Knights Hospitaller, the Teutonic Knights, and the Knights Templar. Its mission was not all that unique from the other orders, as its members were also dedicated to caring for the pilgrims and soldiers who ventured to the Holy City, but the order was known for something unique.

The Order of St. Lazarus was dedicated to caring for lepers. In the Middle Ages, leprosy was greatly feared. Anyone who contracted it was literally shunned and driven from the community. In fact, any Knights Templar who contracted the dreaded wasting disease was required by Templar rules to transfer immediately into the Order of St. Lazarus. It is believed that the Templars helped train the medically focused brothers in the ways of the military.

Leprosy during the Middle Ages

From about the 11th to the 14th century, leprosy was a fairly common disease throughout Europe and the Middle East. It struck individuals of all ages and from all aspects of society, regardless of religion, country of origin, or status. There was no cure for leprosy at the time, and the disease carried a huge social stigma and prejudice. The disease physically alters human flesh, so back in the Middle Ages, it was believed that the disease was a punishment from God.

Lepers were greatly feared. They were outcasts, isolated and destined to live lonely and poverty-stricken lives until they died. Today, we know that leprosy is caused by a bacterium called *Mycobacterium leprae*, yet such knowledge was centuries away back in the medieval period. Those who contracted leprosy during the Middle Ages endured terrible changes to their bodies, especially their skin and eyes. Leprosy damages the inner organs and nerves and, in severe cases, causes facial and bodily malformations and transfigurations.

Leprosy has existed for millennia. The first mention of it has been found in the land known as India today, dating back to the year 2000 BCE, and it has also been written about in ancient Chinese and Egyptian writings. Documents talk of the existence of leprosy in the ancient kingdoms of Africa as well.

In the medieval ages, it was believed that leprosy first made an appearance in the Mediterranean region of Europe by troops led by King Alexander the Great. It was thought that the scourge might have been brought from India and then through Egypt around the 5th century BCE. However, references to leprosy are also found in the Old Testament and in the texts of Aristotle and Hippocrates, although the first detailed description of the disease was written by a Greek physician named

Aretaeus in about 150 CE.

The existence of leprosy is an important aspect of the history of the Order of St. Lazarus, and the fear and stigma of this disease during the Middle Ages cannot be overemphasized. Many people from numerous countries were terrified of the disease, which makes it even more impressive that the brothers of the Order of St. Lazarus dedicated their lives to providing aid and succor to individuals afflicted by it.

It is for this reason that the Order of St. Lazarus of Jerusalem came to be known as the "Leper Brothers" following its founding of a hospital for lepers around 1119. According to some sources, the founders of the order were knights suffering from leprosy and dedicated themselves and their order to care for those with the dreaded disease. Their patron saint was and continues to be Lazarus, who was raised from the dead by Christ in the Holy Bible.

It wasn't until 1255 that the Order of St. Lazarus gained the recognition of the papacy under the reign of Pope Alexander IV and enjoyed many of the same privileges as other knightly orders before them. The order received gifts of endowments from a number of European kings and emperors, including Louis VII of France, Holy Roman Emperor Frederick II, and King Henry II of England.

Historically, it is believed that the numbers of the Order of St. Lazarus grew, especially after 1262, when Pope Clement IV ordered priests to "confine" any leper (regardless of whether they were a man, woman, child, or layman) to the leper houses of St. Lazarus. Throughout these years, more than one leper house existed. Hundreds of them sprung up throughout Europe during the Middle Ages.

Over the years, the order became more militarized. Its brothers were likely trained by the Templars. However, the order's history is convoluted. Following the defeat of Jerusalem in 1187, the Order of St. Lazarus relocated to Acre, just as the Hospitallers before them. While they were known to engage in a few battles, such as the Battle of La Forbie (1244) and the Battle of Mansurah (1250), they were primarily known as a monastic military brotherhood after the fall of Acre in 1291, even though they had gained a reputation for being fierce warriors in battle and a trained force of highly disciplined men.

What Happened to the Order of St. Lazarus?

The historical timeline of the Order of St. Lazarus of Jerusalem provides a fascinating glimpse into the history of the times, especially in regard to the fear of lepers and their isolation, as well as the dedication of those who cared for them. While it is believed that the leper hospital in Jerusalem was founded sometime after 1098 and provided care to lepers in the Holy Land before the First Crusade, they didn't become known as a military order until later, taking part in some battles during the Second Crusade. In 1191, the leper hospital in Jerusalem was abandoned, and they maintained a new home base in Acre.

Approximately fifty years later, the order's historical timeline states that its men fought in the Battle of Gaza in 1244, where all the leper knights were killed. Throughout the decades, they continued to participate in a number of clashes until 1291. It has been said that all members of the order were killed in the unsuccessful defense of Acre.

Yet the Order of St. Lazarus survived to a certain extent, though by the mid-1400s, their raison d'être had faded since the scourge of leprosy was declining. Like the Knights of the Holy Sepulchre and even the Hospitallers, the Order of St. Lazarus faded somewhat, at least in their actions and reputations as mighty knights. However, new eras saw the order working quietly to support the sick and needy. Today, it continues to provide humanitarian and philanthropic aid around the globe.

Following the French Revolution, chivalric orders no longer enjoyed legalized recognition in France. The 1920s saw the reorganization of the former order, and in 1927, it was reorganized as the *Association Française des Hospitaliers de Saint-Lazare de Jérusalem*. In 1929, the order's statutes and rules were based on the 1841 Fundamental Statute of the Knights Hospitaller.

The Order of St. Lazarus of Jerusalem still exists today and is unique among the many Catholic orders since it allows non-Catholic members. The order has maintained a spirit of service, morality, discipline, and sacrifice that exemplify the knights of old and their dedication to helping others.

Today, the military and hospital order continues to focus on and care for members of society, including those living in poverty and the homeless. It claims to be an apolitical and non-denominational organization, with roughly four thousand members located across five continents, making it the smallest of the medieval military orders today. The organization continues to make pilgrimages to the Holy Land and dedicates itself to maintaining the history and purpose of the order.

Chapter 7: The Teutonic Knights

The coat of arms of the Teutonic Knights.
https://commons.wikimedia.org/wiki/File:Insignia_Germany_Order_Teutonic.svg

While it is often assumed that many of the orders of knights were English, several come to mind that were not. For instance, the Teutonic Knights were primarily of Germanic origin.

The Third Crusade was initiated by Pope Gregory VIII after the capture of Jerusalem by Saladin in 1187. For the most part, the crusade was composed of European nobility, but it was nearly abandoned following the drowning of the king of Germany and Holy Roman emperor, Frederick I Barbarossa, in 1190. Many of his troops, disheartened and grieving, returned to their native land, but others continued to partake in the siege of Acre, which concluded in the midsummer of 1191.

While the crusaders recaptured a number of cities throughout the region, Jerusalem was not destined to be one of them. In 1191, after the crusaders gained Acre, German merchants traveled to the city, where they established a hospital to provide care for those living there. They began calling it the Hospital of St. Mary of the German House in Jerusalem. The pope approved of the order, and thus, the Teutonic Knights were born.

The Teutonic Order can be defined as a type of Hospitaller order due to their original purpose in establishing the hospital. However, the Teutonic Order was independent of the Hospitallers. The primary focus of the Teutonic Knights' mission can be defined as "recapturing" stolen lands, not so much the conversion of the Arabs to Christianity. So, the Teutonic Knights and their goals differed from other orders that came before them.

Despite numerous attempts, the conquest of the volatile territories of the Middle East proved elusive, and the Teutonic Knights refocused their efforts toward the central and eastern portions of Europe, which eventually became known as Prussia. They were determined to convert the pagans to Christianity and accumulate more lands.

In their early years, the Teutonic Knights were accepted as a monastic brotherhood by the pope as simple men of simple means, but in 1198, with the approval of King Amalric II of Jerusalem, they were also recognized as a military order.

At the time of this recognition, approximately forty knights were inducted into the new order, and Heinrich Walpot von Bassenheim was made its first grand master. The primary requirement of knights in this fraternity mandated that they be of German birth, which made it unusual from other orders that had been founded in the Holy Land. Most of those knights came from noble classes or were related to other knights.

The Teutonic Knights were easily recognized by their white tunics or cloaks emblazoned with a black cross, and the Germanic brotherhood made their organization similar to that of the Knights Templar.

However, the Teutonic Knights were not nearly as large as the Hospitaller or Templar orders, but if one thing could be said of them, it was that they were intimidating, at least in regard to their power. As time passed, the Teutonic Knights became known as clever traders and political diplomats, with their reputation and control reaching from Prussia throughout Europe and as far as Sicily to the south and Lithuania to the east.

The First Grand Master

The first grand master of the Teutonic Knights was Heinrich Walpot von Bassenheim. He only served for a couple of years, from 1198 to 1200. Little is known about the man. It is believed he was born sometime between 1074 and 1094, although his date of death is unknown. Much of the history surrounding the man consists of myth, supposition, and plain old-fashioned guesswork. However, it is believed that he came from a rich family in the area of Mainz, and he is given credit for transforming the brotherhood into a military order.

It is believed that around 1199, he received a set of monastery rules from the grand master of the Knights Templar at the request of Pope Innocent III.

The grand master divided his knights into two primary classes: priests and simple knights. The knights were required to take vows, as other orders did at the time, of chastity, poverty, and obedience, as well as a dedication to fighting infidels and providing aid to the sick. However, and somewhat unusually, contrary to other orders of the time, the priests were *only* obligated to oversee and celebrate religious offices, such as administering the sacrament to the sick while they were in the hospital and to the knights themselves.

The priests were not allowed, at least in Lithuania or Prussia, to become commanders or masters of the military, although they were allowed to become commanders in their native land of Germany.

Brief Timeline of the Teutonic Knights

Following the death of Heinrich Walpot von Bassenheim, the Teutonic Order was led by Otto von Kerpen, who hailed from Bremen. However, it wasn't until around 1210, during the leadership of the fourth grand master, Herman von Salza, that the order's respectability and prestige were enhanced. Due to his ability to maintain peace between Holy Roman Emperor Frederick II and Pope Gregory IX in 1230, he gained the respect and trust of both, which led to an increase in wealth and possessions, including lands.

From about 1210 to 1239, the lives and struggles of the brotherhood of Germanic knights were by no means easy or without strife. Following the siege of Acre in the Third Crusade, the order turned its attention from the Middle East to central and eastern Europe. The Teutonic Knights' first forays into eastern Europe took them to Hungary in 1211 when King Andrew II asked them to help protect his Transylvanian borders and push back incursions by the nomadic Turks.

However, things didn't go so well for the Teutonic Knights in Hungary, especially after von Salza tried to gain authority and establish his own independent principality rather than following the Hungarian king. They were ultimately expelled from those lands in 1225.

Undaunted, the Teutonic Order persisted in its efforts to convert pagans to Christianity throughout the lands of central and eastern Europe. In 1226, under Herman von Salza, the knights agreed to fight against the pagan Prussians pushing against the borders of Poland. The bad blood between the Prussians and the Poles had been prevalent since 1221, when the Prussians launched their first crusade against Poland. Conrad of Mazovia, a Polish duke, requested the aid of the Teutonic Knights in controlling the pagan Prussians pushing at his borders. In 1233, the order proceeded with their intended conquest of Prussia.

In 1260, at the Battle of Durbe, the Teutonic Knights suffered a crushing loss, but they held out in the region while waiting for reinforcements, which didn't arrive until 1265. The Prussians were fairly unorganized and didn't take advantage of their position, nor did they have a strategy to use. Following the arrival of reinforcements, the Teutonic Knights pressed their advantage and came out victorious by 1274. By 1283, the knights had gained control over much of Prussia.

For nearly five decades, the Teutonic Knights fought, battled, and continually sought to convert the pagans to Christianity, and they primarily governed through pressure. In the intervening years, they built several fortress settlements, including one in Königsberg, which is now located in present-day Russia but at that time lay between Lithuania and Poland. Several other settlements were formed, but the conflicts between the Prussians and the Teutonic Order continued, with claims of brutality and torture on both sides.

During these years, the influence of the Teutonic Knights grew throughout Europe, including the outer regions of eastern Europe

(Romania at the time), Greece, and the outer edges of the Byzantine Empire. Numerous estates were given to the Teutonic Knights for their services, reaching as far north as the Netherlands and down into the lands of France and even as far south as Sicily and then eastward into Prussia.

Throughout the years of the early 13th century, the Teutonic Knights built numerous castles throughout the Middle East, as their main mission was to maintain and defend lands and fortifications that had been gained in previous years.

However, conflicts eventually arose between the Knights Templar and the Teutonic Knights, the latter of which made their headquarters at Montfort Castle in the northern region of present-day Israel in about 1220. The castle was located along the road between the eastern coastline of the Mediterranean and Jerusalem. By 1229, Montfort Castle was considered the home base of the grand masters of the Teutonic Order, as well as a place to store its archives and treasures.

During the beginning and middle of the 13th century, the entirety of Europe was under threat of Mongol invasions. By 1240, a huge swathe of the populace had been overrun by the Mongols. But despite the need for a united front against the Mongols, disagreements and infighting among the Teutonic Knights and the general populations of the lands they sought to control occurred.

At the same time, the Teutonic Knights made several attempts to expand their influence eastward, hoping to convert the Russians to the Roman Catholic faith. However, they were roundly defeated at the Battle on the Ice in 1242. The Teutonic Knights faced off against Alexander Nevsky, who is seen as one of the most important medieval figures in Russian history.

It was not an easy life for the Teutonic Knights. In 1244, Jerusalem fell into the hands of the Ayyubids of Egypt. In the Battle of La Forbie (located near Gaza), it is believed that approximately 437 Teutonic Knights were killed out of a force of 440. Over time, their forces were replenished, but the fighting was not over.

The knights repeatedly came under attack by the Mamluk sultan, Baybars. After initially driving him back, the knights found themselves once again fighting him five years later, in 1271. And after a week-long siege, the knights surrendered their castle at Montfort and returned to Acre.

Around 1283, the Teutonic Order primarily ruled from Prussia, where they had succeeded in converting a large number of the inhabitants of those lands to Christianity. However, their need for soldiers became desperate. They began to conscript locals, which ultimately led to rebellions against the Teutonic Knights, as the people resented their presence and demands that they convert to Christianity. In some cases, knights captured by the locals in the land now known as Lithuania were executed.

As such, by the time of the fall of Acre in 1291, the Teutonic Knights were not as strong as they should have been. They were forced to retreat to Cyprus and then to Venice, where they briefly regrouped before the brotherhood was again torn from within by quarrels and differences of opinion. The following centuries offered few victories for the Teutonic Knights, and they lost much of their autonomy.

Some historical writings claim that the knights often behaved unchristian-like. There were claims that the knights slaughtered Christians, ruined secular churches, engaged in trade with heathens, and interfered with conversions to Christianity. It is believed that many of the non-Christians in the region resisted conversion to Christianity because they didn't want to live under the control of the Teutonic Knights.

An investigation of their behavior was initiated by the pope in 1310, but nothing came of it, and it was ultimately determined that the rumors were being spread by enemies of the Teutonic Order.

Grand Master Conrad von Feuchtwangen ordered the Teutonic Knights to relocate to Venice, Italy, after the fall of Acre in 1291. In 1309, Grand Master Siegfried von Feuchtwangen (a relative of Conrad) again ordered them to relocate, this time to Poland and Malbork Castle. The order was successful in defending the castle after a two-month-long siege from Polish and Lithuanian forces, avoiding annihilation.

In 1386, one of Lithuania's dukes (Grand Duke Jogaila) was converted and baptized as a Roman Catholic Christian, and he married Poland's queen, automatically advancing him to the role of king. However, this union combined the forces of Lithuania and Poland at the time, creating a united force that threatened the Teutonic Knights and their control over the land.

At the same time, conversion to Christianity spread throughout Lithuania and Prussia, which didn't stop the bickering and feuds with Poland and Lithuania.

The knights also continued their conflicts against Poland. Even though the country converted to Christianity around 1387, the Lithuanians and the Poles united their forces and battled the Teutonic Knights a mere twenty-three years later and defeated them at the Battle of Grunwald during the Polish-Lithuanian-Teutonic War. Ultimately, the Germanic brotherhood conceded the territory to Poland.

By that point, a grand master of the order, Ulrich von Jungingen, and many of the order's higher-ranking members had been severely wounded or killed on the battlefield, leaving only a handful of the order standing.

A peace treaty was signed in 1411. While the Teutonic Order was able to retain much of its currently held territories, its reputation as nearly indestructible soldiers and knights was forever put to rest.

The Influence of the Teutonic Knights

The Teutonic Knights often came from noble or aristocratic families, with their numbers varying in size over the years. However, many of them joined for a sense of camaraderie of a specific purpose, food and shelter, a thirst for adventure, and ambition.

The number of men serving the Teutonic Knights was fluid and really depended on the political atmosphere of the time. All in all, it was considered a relatively small order, which history believes averaged no more than 1,300 men at any given time.

The Teutonic Knights followed the basic guidelines of other monastic orders, taking vows of obedience, chastity, and poverty, although many of them, like the other knightly orders, hoped that their services in the name of God, Christianity, and honor would gain them rewards, not only in the near future but also after they died.

The order, particularly at Malbork, created what can be likened today as a half-convent, half-castle, with soldiers, civilians, and others of non-combatant status relegated to serving as craftsmen and servants, otherwise providing the knights their daily needs, which included food, shelter, clothing, and so forth.

The men serving in the Teutonic brotherhood of knights benefited from booty taken from captured territories, including weapons, armor, and livestock. However, the Germanic knights primarily made a name for themselves as being excellent traders. In times of relative stability, they became landlords. In times of strife, when their numbers were large enough, they took on mercenaries, who were primarily paid by taxes incurred on local populations. As an added benefit, commanders often offered training services, shelter, and even lands where former members could live out their days.

The order wasn't only focused on war; it also created schools and hospitals. They built castles and churches. When not engaged in battle, they were required to follow a number of rules, even more so than some other military orders. They were required to maintain closely shorn hair but could grow beards. Gaudy or flamboyant equipment or clothing was discouraged. They were not allowed to display their personal coat of arms or seals and were not allowed to mingle with the knights of other orders or engage in any jousting activities or many types of hunting.

In the early decades of the 14th century, the Teutonic Knights reached the pinnacle of their power. They had supposedly (and this is still in question) been given permission by Holy Roman Emperor Louis IV to conquer the lands of Lithuania and Russian (Rus) holdings, and the Teutonic Knights gave it their best. Over the ensuing years and under the directorship of Grand Master Winrich von Kniprode (who maintained his position from 1351 to 1382), the knights made more of a name for themselves, gaining the attention of other crusaders and nobles throughout Christendom.

Changes on the Horizon

Following their failure to maintain their hold on their home base at Malbork Castle, the order disintegrated, and what followed were years of internal feuds and bickering. While the Teutonic Knights raised taxes on the lands they held, they didn't seem to have much interest in representing the populace, who held them in low esteem. Grand Master Heinrich von Plauen was forcefully removed from his position. The man who replaced him, Michael Küchmeister von Sternberg, also failed to restore order to the group. The Teutonic Knights suffered loss after loss.

As a final blow, in 1454, the Prussian Confederation rose up against the Teutonic Knights, initiating the Thirteen Years' War. Prussia wanted to get out from under the control of the Teutonic Knights. The war took a heavy toll on Prussia and the Teutonic Knights, but ultimately (and with great reluctance), the Teutonic Knights officially recognized Poland's rights over the lands of western Prussia. However, since their stronghold at Marienberg had been lost, the knights removed to Königsberg.

What followed was years of infighting and skirmishes. Throughout the centuries, the Teutonic Knights fought bravely, if somewhat recklessly. In 1525, Grand Master Elbert (Albert) of Brandenburg converted to

Lutheranism, so he could no longer be a member of the order. He was succeeded by Walter von Cronberg, who became the thirty-eighth grand master of the order.

The order managed to hang on to a large number of properties in Germany, and subsequent grand masters of the order often came from noble German families. By the mid-1700s, the Teutonic Knights held lands in Bohemia, Germany, and Austria. During those years, the knights were often called upon to command groups of mercenaries during the Ottoman wars.

At the dawn of the 19th century, Napoleon seized the order's holdings and dissolved the order in 1809. Yet just a few decades later, the Teutonic Knights reemerged in Vienna, and by the early 1830s, they primarily existed as an ecclesiastical group focused on charity work.

World War II

After the Teutonic Knights were, for all intents and purposes, disbanded during Napoleon's subsequent rule, the remnants of the Teutonic Knights took up in Austria. By 1834, it had regained its official title as a *Deutcher Ritterorden*, or German knightly order, with its members overseen primarily by members of the Habsburg dynasty until 1923.

By the end of the 1920s, the former warrior order of Teutonic Knights was living a primarily spiritual life. However, by the 1930s, war was once again on the horizon, with Nazi Germany annexing Austria in 1938. Adolf Hitler ordered the Teutonic Order to be abolished, although it would rise up again after the end of the Second World War in 1945.

However, the Nazis under Adolf Hitler assumed the imagery (the black cross on a white background) for war propaganda purposes, likely to instill fear in their detractors since the Teutonic Knights had a reputation for bravery on the battlefield. The Teutonic Knights were German-based, and Hitler sought to promote German nationalism as much as he could. He also pointed to the past expansionist efforts of the Teutonic Knights, believing it gave him credence for what he was trying to do.

During the years of the Second World War, the order managed to survive in Italy, only to be reborn again in Germany and Austria following the conclusion of the war and the destruction of the Nazi Party.

What Happened to the Teutonic Knights?

Following the conclusion of the Second World War, the Teutonic Knights maintained a presence in southern Europe, although they focused on providing charity, health care, and medical services. However, by the late 1990s, numerous sponsors enabled the order to engage in a number of archaeological excavations and curiosity-seeking tourism projects throughout the Middle East.

However, by the 2000s, the German chapters of the order officially declared insolvency and disbanded.

Today, the Teutonic Knights function on a relatively small but global scale with members that include priests and nuns who are fairly localized throughout central Europe, including the Czech Republic, Slovakia, and Slovenia, as well as throughout Austria, Italy, and Germany. They focus primarily on offering spiritual guidance and medical care for the elderly and ill.

So, in the end, the Order of the Teutonic Knights returned to its origins, providing care for sojourners to the Holy Land and seeing to the spiritual need of others. Today, a museum at their former Castle in Bad Mergentheim, Germany, the home base of the grand masters from 1527 through 1809, has been dedicated to the Teutonic Knights.

Chapter 8: The Knights Templar

The cross of the Knights Templar.
https://commons.wikimedia.org/wiki/File:Knights_Templar_Cross.svg

The Knights Templar is perhaps the most well-known order of knights, although there is still an aura of mystery surrounding it. Much but not all of its history has been found in historical records of the order and bibliographies; other aspects of this order have been passed down orally and have today become legendary.

Who were these knights, and what is it about the Knights Templar that has made their legacy survive the centuries? Why do they continue to be the most recognized order of knights over other knightly orders of the Crusades? These men weren't simply monks, soldiers, or warriors; they were men of their times, so their attitudes and actions cannot possibly be equated to those of modern man.

To know everything there is to know about this order of knights would require the reading of dozens, if not hundreds, of books, manuscripts, and documents. However, even a brief glimpse into their history is a fascinating journey into the past and into a different age, one that was surrounded and consumed by cultural and political battles and wars, not merely for the sake of land or kingdoms but also for personal salvation.

Discovering the truth about this order is challenging for historians, as the Templars' central archive in Cyprus was destroyed in 1571 by the Turks. However, records of the order have been found in libraries, private collections, and archives that contain information about the more mundane aspects of accounting, such as sheep farming. Some of these records have not yet been translated or further examined by historians or scholars, perhaps because they are scattered in countries throughout Europe.

The Knights Templar Stand Out

It can be said that the Knights Templar could be equated to the special forces today, elite military units that exist in many countries around the world. These knights were a different breed since they were expected to be trained in a different fashion than the "usual" knights of the realm.

Based on a letter written by Abbot Bernard of Clairvaux and received by the founder of the Knights Templar, Hugh de Payns, the Knights Templar were to be held to a higher standard than other orders of knights, especially the Knights Hospitaller, the undisputed rivals of the Knights Templar.

The abbot instructed that the Knights Templar should not only fight against heretics, heathens, and pagans but also drive back the invisible evils that plagued men's souls.

While the Knights Templar were not monks as we think of monks today, they were a dedicated and holy military unit that fought for Christianity. They were willing to forgo the temptations of the flesh and comforts of life to better serve God and their order.

While the Templars were not true monks, they are today often referred to as warrior monks. They were required to take vows of obedience, chastity, and poverty, similar to other knightly orders, but they were also formed to specifically provide military defense rather than the other way around. At the time, the concept of a knight was not one only engaged in a physical battle against the enemies of the church but also one who held a depth of spiritual devotion that might seem impossible to achieve. Over time, the Templars proved themselves capable of doing that very thing, and thus, the concept of a warrior monk was born.

In the medieval ages, the concept of knighthood was not a singular concept, such as the perceived ideals of the Knights of the Round Table of lore, nor even of secular knights who belonged to knightly fraternities. The Knights Templar was a new idea of knighthood, one that was born, specifically by Abbot Bernard, to turn knights away from behaviors that he considered unsavory, undignified, and unworthy. Such behaviors included playing games, storytelling, jousting, and gambling. He was displeased with the pride that many knights of the day displayed with their way of dress or the way they coveted material things. He believed that knights should set a higher example and live up to them.

Not all knights in the Knights Templar or in other orders were considered full knights. Only full Templar knights, known as knight-brothers, were given permission to wear the recognizable white mantle with the red cross emblazoned upon it. In many cases, full knights were limited to those who came from the upper echelons of society, but at the beginning of the order, knight-brothers were more of a separate society or caste to maintain this distinction.

Many knight-brothers already had the monetary wherewithal to pay for their horses, equipment, and clothing, such as their mantle or religious habit, which, depending on rank, was either white or black. During the early years of the order, they wore no mantle, instead opting to wear ordinary and simple clothes. Many of them were already trained in knightly skills, and after they were accepted into the Templars as a full knight-brother, they received additional weapons.

What about the lower echelons of the Knights Templar, those who were not considered full knights? Sergeants or lesser positions of authority were allowed to wear black tunics with the red cross emblazoned on the front and back of their mantles, which were either black or brown, contrary to the knight-brothers of the order, who were allowed to wear the white mantle with the red cross.

The Pilgrims and the Templars

Over the centuries, especially as pilgrims ventured to the Holy Land in the early 14th century, it became increasingly vital that they be protected. The pilgrimages of later crusade years became larger and included not only those among the "common masses" but also nobles, business owners, and others considered of higher status.

Pilgrimages before and shortly after the First Crusade had been spurred by the pilgrims themselves, who sought to make the journey as a penance of sacrifice and hoped for the forgiveness of a variety of sins. By the early 14th century, the journey was often considered *expected* of individuals by the church. One might even say required. Even so, like the centuries before, the journey was difficult and challenging.

During the early 14th century, the Knights Templar owned many ships and often granted hundreds of pilgrims passage on them for a great part of their journey to the Holy Land. Traveling by sea cut off many months of arduous travel by land. Even so, it could still take nearly a year for pilgrims from England to reach Italy before they stepped upon the shores of the Holy Land. Travel by boat over the Mediterranean Sea could take anywhere from four to six weeks, depending on weather and tides. So, they traveled by land and by sea to unknown destinations, crossing strange territories in the process. Pirates also preyed on pilgrims, but pirates likely stayed away from Templar ships when their banners or insignia were emblazoned on their sails. Still, it was a journey filled with uncertainty and fear. Many were never heard from again.

Pilgrimages to the Holy Land were strongly encouraged by the church. And pilgrims were not just men; women and even children were encouraged to travel to see the holy sites as well. To those at the time, a pilgrimage was seen as a badge of faith or a journey of the pious.

Of course, there were also those who were less pious among these groups, many of them criminals who were told to take the journey to atone for their crimes and sins. These criminal pilgrims or penitents had to take an oath before local authorities before they left, promising to purge their hearts and minds of evil thoughts and deeds. Only then were they given something known as a safe conduct document that displayed the crime for which they had been charged. The criminals had to show these documents and get them stamped or marked by a variety of religious authorities whenever they were asked for them. When they approached any holy city, shrines, churches, or religious landmarks, they had to show the religious authorities these documents before they were allowed to visit.

Also among the pilgrims were those who had been charged with heresy. To tell everyone apart, criminals were told to wear a chain somewhere on their body, sometimes around their neck or their waist. Heretics might be told to wear a black garment with a white cross emblazoned on the front and the back.

During the 13th century, pilgrimages had grown so large and were nearly constant that French authorities forbade pilgrimages to Rome for a while, fearing that their own population would decrease.

However, most of those individuals seeking to make a pilgrimage did so to pay their respects to the Christian saints and relics, particularly at sites found within the city of Jerusalem, the holiest of cities.

Note of interest: Badges

It became relatively common during the Crusades for "badges" to be created to demark a particular landmark, shrine, or destination, much like stickers can be found on cars or suitcases today to denote places a person visited.

In the days of the pilgrimages, these badges were unique to a specific location or shrine. Some pilgrims collected them as mementos or to verify that they had truly been to Rome, Jerusalem, or other important sites. For some, these badges became a symbol of their dedication.

For others, these badges were used as bragging rights. And like modern times, these badges were often falsely manufactured, traded, bartered for, and so forth. This was frowned upon. The Knights Templar knew of the practice, but they never designed or manufactured any badges for their assistance or transportation of pilgrims.

Templar Fortifications

Throughout Europe and the Middle East, churches and castles were erected by the Templars, many of which had been given to the knights with the purpose of protecting routes to Jerusalem and other holy cities. Over time, the Knights Templar were charged with the safety and protection of great spans of land, and they built garrisons and castles in places called Aragon, Chastel Blanc, and Ponferrada.

Some locations are more well known, such as the Templar holdings in Jerusalem (their quarters under Solomon's Temple) on the Temple Mount, believed to be the original site of the temple built by King Solomon. There was another Templar stronghold at Acre, where the knights fought the Saracens before staging a retreat to the island of Cyprus.

Pilgrim Castle today.

אסף.צ *at Hebrew Wikipedia, CC BY-SA 3.0 <https://creativecommons.org/licenses/by-sa/3.0>, via Wikimedia Commons; https://commons.wikimedia.org/wiki/File:Athlit_fortress_6.JPG*

Remnants of the castle known as Château Pèlerin, also known as Atlit or Pilgrim Castle, can be seen today in Haifa, a port city in Israel. This castle had only stood for just over seventy years prior to its abandonment by the Knights Templar following the loss of Acre to the Turks in 1291. It was a strong fortress that boasted it could hold four thousand knights

The ancient keep of Chastel Blanc in modern-day Safita, Syria, towers over a spit of land jutting into the Mediterranean Sea. The castle was destroyed in 1171, but one can still see remains of the keep today. The keep had officers' quarters, a garrison, and a chapel. It also boasted a warning bell tower that sounded an alarm upon sight of any suspected hostiles.

Art of the ruins of Ruad Fortress.
Michel Benoist, CC BY-SA 3.0 <http://creativecommons.org/licenses/by-sa/3.0/>, via Wikimedia Commons https://en.wikipedia.org/wiki/File:Cours_de_la_forteresse_d%27Arouad.jpg

An island fortress on Ruad Island in Syria is known to be the last stronghold of the Templars in the Middle East. It boasted infantry, knights, and archers. The story associated with this stronghold is a sad one. After a siege by the Muslims, a surrender was negotiated. The knights of the garrison were promised safe passage, but following the ceasefire, the negotiations were rendered null and void when the Muslims broke their word and executed the infantry and the archers. They banished the remnants of the Templar garrison to a prison in Cairo.

A keep on the island of Cyprus became the headquarters of the Knights Templar in the Holy Land. Other castles of the Knights Templar could be found in what is today Hungary, Croatia, Italy, Poland, and Switzerland.

Churches of the Templars sprouted out just about everywhere they trod, and their inspiration in design and structure mimicked the Church of the Holy Sepulchre in Jerusalem, especially the rounded sides that were popular throughout Europe at the time. One of these churches is known as the Church of the Holy Sepulchre, also known as the Round Church, which was built in Cambridge, England, around 1130. The London headquarters of the Templars in central London and the Temple Church still stand today.

The Templars' architectural acumen and skills are well displayed around the world, from round churches to those with a dozen sides (for example, the Safed castle built between 1240 and 1244, as well as Pilgrim Castle, which was built in 1218). Of course, other knightly orders, such as the Knights Hospitaller, also built churches and chapels in the round form.

The Rules of Templar Life

The Knights Templar gained a reputation fighting not only for Christianity and all it encompasses but also for their own order. Historically, the Knights Templar was a highly disciplined unit, but at the same time, the men often forgot about their own sense of unity for the sake of personal glory or vengeance. These knights were known for being incredibly brave, but they were still men who could be ruled by their emotions, making them reckless.

One of the most important documents that still exist about the Templars emphasizes what was expected of a Templar knight. This document is known as the Rule of the Templars. The Rule was not only a guideline of expectations regarding behavior; more importantly, it instilled a sense of obedience in the knights. As a code of conduct, it covered a variety of topics, including how they were to eat their meals, what their clothing was to look like, and a number of other restrictions regarding socializing and even sleeping arrangements.

Originally, the Rule included sixty-eight directives, but eventually, because of the growth of the Knights Templar, it ended up including several hundred. Punishment for not obeying the rules varied. Some of these rules were common sense, while others, at least by today's standards, were extreme and maybe even amusing.

It's impossible to list all of the rules here, but we will paraphrase some so you can get an idea of the Templars' standards.

The Knights Templar were allowed to eat meat only three times a week except under certain circumstances, such as All Saints' Day, Christmas Day, the day honoring the Feast of the Apostles, and the Day of Assumption. Back then, the common consensus among the order was that eating flesh (meat) had the potential to corrupt the physical body.

The habits or robes worn by the Knights Templar were to be of one solid color, either black, brown, or white. They were encouraged to wear white robes and cloaks to symbolize a life lived in purity. The color white also signified a bond with the lighter aspects of life rather than darkness to further strengthen their relationship with God.

Clothing and battle gear were to be as plain as possible since this was a sign of a humble life. Personal pride in fashion or battle adornments, for men or their horses, were discouraged. The knights were not allowed to wear pointed shoes or shoes that required shoelaces, as those were things that were perceived to be worn by pagans.

Head coverings were not encouraged, and even coifs were required to be worn over a cloth cap.

Horse trappings were to be as plain and humble as possible, and no Templars could adorn his horse's tack with fancy things like silver or gold. If there were any such adornments, they had to be tarnished so that neither the owner nor others who saw them could take any pride in or covet them.

Instructions in regard to women were also covered in the Rule.

Women were portrayed as dangerous. They were considered to be temptations that might lead a knight astray. Their attendance was to be discouraged in any Templar house to ensure the knights' vows of chastity.

The knights were strongly encouraged to avoid kissing any woman, whether it was a female relative or not. They were also encouraged to resist a woman's embrace, claiming that embracing her could, in some way, encourage them to turn away from the rules of the brotherhood. By avoiding any kissing, the knights could be assured that their hearts were dedicated and devoted to God, allowing them to maintain a clean conscience.

If any Templar was found to be with a woman in a "wicked" place or with a woman of ill repute, he was to be put in irons and lose his habit or robe. He could no longer participate in elections, especially the election of the grand master, and they were not even allowed to carry their banner.

When it came to women, the Templars were cautioned about talking with women about any carnal knowledge. If one of the men was on the recipient end of such a conversation, he was supposed to immediately fall silent, and if that didn't work, he was to walk away.

It should be noted that the primary focus of such guidelines was to encourage the knights to dedicate themselves wholly and completely to the order and brotherhood and in their dedication to God and Jesus Christ. However, the foundation of the Rule, as mentioned, was to instill strict and unquestioning obedience.

Among the Rule is also a number of directives that seem petty by today's standards and probably even to many of the knights of the brotherhood back then. However, their vows of obedience required them to follow the guidelines set before them. These rules could get quite extreme. We have included a few below as examples.

Asking permission was essential in the hierarchy of the Knights Templar. No brother was allowed to do just about anything without asking permission first. That included bathing, riding their horse, taking medicine, or venturing into town.

The brothers were not allowed to make even the smallest of changes to their horse tack, which means they couldn't change their saddles, stirrups, or bridles, without getting permission first. This also applied to their own weapons as well. That meant the brother couldn't adjust the belt bearing his sword (although he could adjust the buckle) or even shorten stirrup straps without asking first. He also had to ask permission to make repairs to his helmet, his armor, or his sword.

The grand master, the headmaster of the order, was allowed to gift one man's horse, armor, or whatever else he wanted to another brother or knight, and the knight whose items were taken was not allowed to get angry or frustrated. Doing so was considered by the grand masters to go against God's will.

No brothers were allowed to receive letters from relatives or anyone else without the permission of their commander or master. Even if they had permission, and if the commander required it, the letters had to be read to him.

It may be shocking to modern readers that the Knights Templar and other orders were required to obey such extreme rules, but the need to maintain discipline and obedience should not be underestimated. These rules were meant to encourage the right frame of mind and attitude, allowing Knights Templar to be obedient on and off the battlefield. It is easy to imagine that many were frustrated by these harsh rules, but the Templars dared not show it.

In a way, the Rule was meant to encourage the knights and brothers to avoid "normal" aspects of society, allowing them to adhere to a higher standard than the average person. The Rule also encouraged the Templers to live and die by their vows and to take their positions very seriously. These rules also included aspects of wealth.

A Templar was not allowed to keep or even carry money without the permission of his master, and if one borrowed money from another, he was required to buy only what he said he needed the money for and nothing else.

In cases where a brother or knight died and was found with money on his person, in a hidden pouch or otherwise, he was to be considered a thief. Such individuals were not allowed to be buried in hallowed ground, and prayers were not to be said over them.

Even guidelines about sleeping are found in the Rule.

Brothers were required to always have a candle or other light burning throughout the night so they would not become prey to wickedness as they dreamed.

Knights and brothers were encouraged to cover up at bedtime and to sleep in their stockings, shirts, and breeches. Shirts were to be belted.

The Rule also talked about how a knight should act in battle or during times of war.

It was forbidden for any knight to attack without the commander's permission. If a knight did so, and someone was harmed because of it, he could lose his habit. However, the rules differed slightly when it came to seeing a fellow Christian in peril. If a knight believed he could help that man, then he could do so.

However, if a fellow knight behaved in a reckless or foolish manner and an enemy attacked him with the intent to kill him, a knight could leave his squad to help that man without asking permission. Once he returned to his squad, he was not to boast about it.

There were rules about traveling. The Templars journeyed far on their crusades, but they were required to respect traveling and camp rules.

The Templars were not to stray from camp any farther than they could hear the ring of a bell without permission. They were not allowed to carry any additional belongings or bags on their horses without permission either.

The Templars were not typically able to hunt for food during their journeys except for fishing. They could forage for vegetables in fields. They could take a wild animal *only* if they knew how to do so without actually hunting it.

When it came to sharing food, a brother or knight was allowed to share his food with others but only with those close enough that he could reach them with an outstretched arm. The knight with the most food was always encouraged to invite the man closest to him to share if that man so desired.

In general, the Templars were required to present a certain character that exemplified their dignity and obedience. They were required to set examples for others and not do anything that spoke of less-than-stellar behavior at any time. In this way, they were perceived as not only honest but also humble in their devotion and dedication to their faith.

During certain eras, the knights were allowed to have up to three horses and a single squire. The rules also applied to the servants and squires. The knights were also not allowed to seriously injure any slaves without permission. (Some aspects of Templar business, like many societies throughout the Middle Ages, relied on the labor provided by captives, primarily from the steppes of Russia, taken by the Turks and Mongols.) They were allowed to beat them with leather straps if it was felt they deserved it, but care had to be taken not to maim them.

Gambling without permission was allowed as long as wagers were limited to candle pieces or a crossbow. The knights were not allowed to wager horses, weapons, or anything that cost themselves or anyone else any money.

Punishments for crimes were often severe. Here are a few examples:

Any knight or brother who failed to adhere to the house commandments could have his habits or robes taken away from him, and he risked being put in irons.

If any two knights or brothers exchanged blows, he risked losing his habit or robe, and if serious injury occurred, he could be put in irons.

Any knight or brother who struck another Christian, be it a woman or a man, with a staff, stone, or otherwise sharp weapon, especially if they intended the blow to maim or kill, could lose his habit or robe.

Any brother who left without permission (absent without leave, or AWOL in today's parlance) risked losing his habit or robe for one year and one day. If he happened to keep anything in his belongings that was forbidden for more than two nights, he ran the risk of being expelled from the house.

Conflicts with the Ideals of Knighthood

Idyllic knighthood has always represented the image of chivalry, devotion to one's faith, and a never-ending duty and obligation to defend and protect the weak. These guidelines and ideals were encouraged in a number of knightly orders, especially those of the monk warriors, including the Knights Templar.

One of the requirements of the Knights Templar was to take a vow of chastity and poverty, following the example of King Arthur's knight, Sir Galahad. This rule was approved in 1128 and recommended by the co-founder of the order, Hugh de Payns. A Templar would be frowned upon if they did not perform the duties expected of them by God and their society, such as defending the church, the poor, widows, and orphans.

However, the concept of chivalry didn't always equate to the realities of war, especially on the battlefield. In many cases, battles were fought to the death, especially when fighting against non-believers, such as pagans and infidels in the Holy Land or the Baltic region.

Many castle or fortification sieges of the time were conducted in a "gentlemanly" way. In many instances, military commanders allowed surrender up until the point where the opposing forces actually scaled the walls. They would often initiate a ceasefire to allow civilians or others who had sought refuge to exit without harm. Some of these people were even given money, food, and clothing by the attacking army.

However, when defenders of these keeps, fortresses, and castles refused such clemency and insisted on carrying on with the fighting, the invading armies could effectively collect whatever riches they could find inside the walls, except for places like churches or convents.

This type of behavior didn't always happen. In some cases, the knights grew uncontrollable, which is not necessarily surprising since many lived outside of the boundaries of the law. Some had agreed to fight in exchange for pardons. The concept of chivalry was not as important to "lower-class" knights as they were to noble knights, although there were surely times when even a noble knight succumbed to temptation.

As such, many knights did not follow the code of chivalry in battles, and during moments when emotion, fear, and bloodlust filled their hearts and minds, self-discipline eroded completely in those who sought personal glory.

Even so, the brotherhoods of knights, regardless of the order, required discipline, and this was especially true of the Knights Templar, one of the most memorable orders in modern history. For over seven centuries, the reputation and the deeds of the Knights Templar have been wreathed in historical truth, legend, and rumor. So, let's take a look at how it all began.

The Origins of the Knights Templar

The origins of the Knights Templar are generally perceived by historians to have been in the modern-day Champagne region of France, known as Troyes during its time. The order came about due to the desperate need for protection of large groups of Christian pilgrims to the Holy Land around the year 1119, following the First Crusade.

A 19th-century painting of Hugh de Payns.
https://commons.wikimedia.org/wiki/File:Hugues_de_Payens_(Versailles).jpg

History states that the Knights Templar was developed by two men: Hugh de Payns and a man by the name of Godfrey de Saint-Omer. It is said that these two men led a mere seven men to Jerusalem, where they took vows of obedience, poverty, and chastity.

Originally, this small group was known as the Poor Fellow-Soldiers of Christ and the Temple of Solomon, though today, they are known simply as the Knights Templar. The original nine knights, known as knight-brothers, came from noble families. In the early years of the organization, they received support and aid from the ruler of Jerusalem at the time, King Baldwin II, and the patriarch of Jerusalem, Warmund of Picquigny.

At the time, the small group of Templars became associated with the Hospitallers, which had been officially recognized by the church in 1113, although the Hospitallers didn't become known as a military religious organization until the late 1130s.

King Baldwin II accommodated the small group of Templars, allowing them to stay on a portion of his palace grounds known as the Lord's Temple, what today is called the Dome of the Rock. This was the site of Solomon's Temple.

The handful of Templars soon grew in number. Within a decade, it is believed the order increased quite dramatically. Historical documents state that in the 1170s, the group had grown to three hundred knights in Jerusalem alone. The dearth of historical materials doesn't give modern historians or readers much information about what the Templars did in Jerusalem during that time other than guarding the pilgrims venturing to the city, so the first decade of their presence in Jerusalem is sketchy.

However, by 1170, some historical documents show that the order was well organized and that the Knights Templar, as well as the Hospitallers and the Knights of the Holy Sepulchre, performed similar duties in regard to providing protection and aid to pilgrims.

The Grand Masters

Knightly orders were led by a grand master, and the same was true for the Knights Templar. The office of grand master was a powerful position and not only among the knights. The grand masters often influenced other aspects of society, including politics and religion.

A grand master was expected to fulfill the position for life. As such, he would be treated with the utmost respect by religious and secular leaders. During the time of the Crusades, the grand master was given the great distinction and honor of being able to have four horses and an entourage that included but was not necessarily limited to a chaplain, two personal knights, a sergeant, a clerk, a servant (to carry his lance and shield), and a cook.

Despite the power of the grand master position, he could not declare war, wage war, or negotiate in any way without first meeting with other high-ranking officials of the order. He also faced other limitations, especially regarding funds. However, the Templar grand masters were expected to lead by example, to personify the spiritual example of a devoted life, and to lead their men into battle.

By the middle of the 1100s, grand masters had accumulated great prestige and power. When Jacques de Molay achieved the rank of grand master in the late 13th century, he oversaw nearly one thousand Templar houses, outposts, and castles throughout western Europe and the Middle East. At that time, membership likely hovered around seven thousand individuals, not counting families or those who provided ancillary services. At its peak, there were twenty thousand members.

The Templar's First Grand Master

Hugh de Payns (often spelled Hugues de Payens) was the first grand master of the Knights Templar, although a number of historians and others believe he was in the Holy Land prior to the founding of the order during the years between 1104 and 1108. In his late teens, he accompanied his half-brother, Stephen de Blois, to the region.

During the early years following the First Crusade, the Christian presence in the Middle East was still limited. They were also effectively surrounded by the Muslims, mainly the Turks. Though the First Crusade had been won by the Christians, a trek to the Holy Land was still very dangerous for pilgrims, who were more often than not under constant threat by the Turks, who still inhabited much of the region. Between the port of Jaffa and overland to Jerusalem (a distance of just over thirty miles or fifty-four kilometers), pilgrims were often accosted, robbed, and sometimes killed.

While not much is known about the Frenchman Hugh de Payns, what is known is that he was a vassal of the Champagne region and might have been part of a group that visited Jerusalem in about 1104. In the Middle Ages, specifically in feudal societies that existed at the time, a vassal was someone who oversaw a fife given to them for services rendered to a lord or nobleman. Not all vassals received fifes or properties, as some lived as household knights within their lord's court.

A vassal was also expected to side with his overlord during times of strife. At a moment's notice, the lord could demand the services of the knight for any military or other purpose. In other words, the vassal not only promised but also owed loyalty to his lord, so his refusal to serve his lord was considered a felony. It was a breach of duty and something so offensive that they would be punished severely.

In some cases, fifes were passed down through generations, from eldest son to eldest son, although circumstances often changed. For example, upon the death of a vassal, his fife could be returned to the lord or nobleman who had given it to him.

Hugh de Payns was a vassal, and although he was believed to have taken part in some actions during the First Crusade, it is not known for sure. However, he was very much involved in the origins of the Knights Templar, as was Godfrey of Saint-Omer, Archambaud of St. Agnan, and André of Montbard (uncle of Bernard of Clairvaux). They pledged to provide protection to the Christian visitors coming to Jerusalem.

Over the years, Hugh de Payns spent much time encouraging and recruiting additional knights to join the order, and he was relatively successful in this endeavor, especially once King Baldwin II of Jerusalem became determined to set his sights on Damascus. Eventually, the Templars' reputation garnered attention from Europe's powerful clergy, politicians, and citizenry.

Historical accounts mention that within a decade of their founding, the order held properties throughout Europe, and its rise to power was nearly astronomical. As it is today, the more powerful one is, the greater the wealth generated, and as can be expected, new men who joined the ranks hoped to enjoy some of that power.

The Knights Templar reached its largest membership in the 12th century, but the Templars weren't just warriors. Many of them were advisors to kings, adept at banking and financial matters, and known for guarding valuable treasuries. They were exceptionally gifted as seafarers, traders, and business owners. They became known as experts in various fields of agriculture, trade, and commerce and eventually garnered a reputation of being one of the most powerful and wealthy organizations in Europe and beyond for their time.

Of all the knightly orders of the Middle Ages, the Knights Templar, perhaps due to their extraordinary financial acumen, continue to stand out, and their name continues to be recognized well into the 21st century.

Bernard of Clairvaux

Another person heavily involved in the origins of the Knights Templar was an abbot by the name of Bernard of Clairvaux. A number of legends are connected to him, especially in his somewhat eccentric views of the Christian religion. There are stories of him diving into freezing water to squelch his "carnal" instincts as a young man. Yet at the same time, he was recognized as someone who managed to connect with his audiences as he preached, so much so that his name traveled throughout Europe, especially in France.

It is commonly believed that upon his second return from the Holy Land, he became a co-founder of the Knights Templar and heavily influenced the reorganization of the Benedictine Order (also known as the Bernardines) and the creation of a new monastery. The piece of land was known as the Valley of Light (in French *Clairvaux*), which attracted people from throughout Europe.

Organization of the Knights Templar

The organization of the Templars was structured after the typical hierarchy of other military orders of the medieval age. The grand master was at the head of it all and typically resided in the headquarters of the Knights Templar in the Holy Land. Numerous officers under the grand master were chosen to oversee vastly large territories that were eventually divided into smaller areas or provinces. Each of these, in turn, was overseen by area commanders, who themselves oversaw masters, who were responsible for overseeing individual Templar houses in a given area.

Dozens of Templar houses were founded throughout various regions, primarily to establish their presence in a territory. The houses were equipped with adequate troops and manpower, equipment, and, of course, sources of money for those fighting in the Holy Land or farther east.

Some of the primary offices of the order included the following:

Grand Master – the leading authority who answered to no one but the pope

Seneschal – the grand master's advisor or co-pilot of sorts

Marshal – in charge of anything pertaining to battle or war

Draper – in charge of dispensing knight's clothing and in charge of making sure the knights were clothed in a manner that befitted the order. As such, the draper was considered to be above all the brothers in regard to status.

Of course, there were other commanders of the Templars who had responsibilities and specifically assigned regions, such as Antioch, Jerusalem, or Tripoli.

The *infirmarer* was in charge of hospitals or infirmaries, primarily providing care to elderly brothers. During the Middle Ages, most medical services, care for the poor and the infirm, and so forth fell to the Hospitallers and other similar orders. For this reason, the Templars were primarily known as warriors who were renowned for their fighting skills.

The grand masters of the Knights Templar made their headquarters in Jerusalem from the time of their founding in about 1119 until about 1190, following the fall of Jerusalem. They then made their headquarters at Acre in around 1191 through its fall in 1291. After that, they established their headquarters in Cyprus.

Other than the founder Hugh de Payns, one name truly stands out in regard to Templar grand masters, and that is Jacques de Molay, the grand master from 1293 to 1312.

Grand Master Jacques de Molay: The Beginning of the End

The twenty-third and last grand master of the Knights Templar was the leader from 1292 until the French king, Philip IV, decimated their ranks and dissolved the order in 1312. Jacques de Molay died in 1314 after he was burned at the stake. The demise of the Knights Templar is surrounded by lies, suspicions, torture, and bravery. As such, Jacques de Molay is one of the more well-known grand masters of the order.

Image of Jacques de Molay.
https://commons.wikimedia.org/wiki/File:JacquesdeMolay.jpg

Jacques de Molay was in his twenties when he joined the Knights Templar around 1265. He fought in several battles, earning himself a good reputation as an effective leader. His reputation followed him even after the defeat of the Christian forces in Acre in 1291, and it is said that even after that loss, he made huge efforts to recapture the city.

However, there is little known about his life over the next fifteen years prior to the flurry of arrests of the Templars in France in 1307. From then until 1312, hundreds of Templars were imprisoned, tortured, and forced to confess to all sorts of claims of heresy, anti-religious behavior, and other depraved acts.

Even Jacques de Molay, who was nearing seventy years of age by this time, confessed to a number of crimes against Christianity after he was forced to endure extreme torture. However, he and others recanted, publicly claiming coercion. And when he was sentenced to death in Paris, by burning at the stake no less, he loudly recanted, claiming that the knights and his order were innocent of the claims against them and that their honor and purity were beyond question.

But how did all of this come about?

By the autumn of 1307, the Templars' reputation had gone from heroes to scapegoats, perhaps some of it being generated by jealousy or a desire for power. A number of claims against them were believed to have been brought by King Philip IV of France. In the autumn of 1307, he presented his officers across France with sealed orders with the directive not to open the orders until the evening of October 12th. The reason for his orders and demands for secrecy? These orders stated his intention to arrest every Templar in the country.

But why would he do that? Basically, it boils down to greed.

King Philip believed that he should be the one benefiting from the wealth and power accrued by the Knights Templar, but there are some rumors that he believed the Templars owed him money. However, there are also rumors that it was King Philip who owed the Templars money and that he was angry that they refused to approve additional loans to him.

King Philip didn't care for the pope at the time, Pope Boniface VIII. History relates that some of King Philip's men had been ordered to kidnap and hold the pope hostage. Pope Boniface died a short time later, and a new pope, Clement V, took his seat. Clement V was perhaps intimidated by Philip and was more than willing to partake in Philip's efforts to destroy the Knights Templar.

Before Pope Boniface VIII's demise in 1303, he was believed to have greatly admired the Knights Templar. Once Pope Boniface died, the Templars realized how much they were in danger. The first arrest came early in the morning of October 13th (a Friday), and what followed was a vicious and bloody episode in the history of the Catholic Church.

Note of interest: Friday the 13th

Friday the 13th is often considered a day of bad luck. As mentioned, the first arrests of the Knights Templar occurred on the morning of Friday, October 13th, which certainly was a day of bad luck for the Templars. Some still equate the origin of modern-day beliefs of bad luck on Friday the 13th as being founded by the blitz attack on the Knights Templar on that blackest of days.

However, the concept of the number thirteen as being negative has existed for millennia, and many point to the fact that the Templars were not the only ones to face especially bad luck on Friday the 13th. It is widely believed that Christ was also crucified on a Friday, with some saying that the date possibly could have been the 13th. Although we don't know for sure what day Christ died, recent investigations claim that he died on Friday the 3rd.

The belief in unlucky number thirteen has persisted for centuries, and while the true origins of the concept of Friday the 13th is a mystery, the day is still considered to be filled with bad luck. Even today, many avoid stepping under ladders, breaking a mirror, or stepping on a crack. On Friday the 13th, people still might find it beneficial to throw salt over one's shoulder, not to cross paths with a black cat, and to keep one's home well-lit to reduce hiding places for bad spirits.

Whether King Philip chose that day to launch his attack against the Knights Templar because of the connotations with it will never be known, but the day remains one of infamy in the annals of history.

The Knights Templar were not the only targets of King Philip, as he also targeted French Jews and rich Italian merchants. At the time, Philip was filled with greed, seeking to increase his coffers. He targeted thousands of Templars who happened to reside in France at that time, including Grand Master Jacques de Molay, who had been summoned to the country from Cyprus by Pope Clement V around 1307 to discuss a potential new crusade.

Although the Knights Templar had taken vows of poverty, the order amassed great wealth through lands and their business dealings. By around 1300, few of the Templar Order were actually true knights. Many of their members were bankers or involved in finance. Historical documents state that noblemen, kings, and wealthy merchants left their riches with the Knights Templar for safekeeping. After all, no one would willingly mess with the Knights Templar.

So, how did the reputation of the Knights Templar decline so quickly? It was mostly due to rumors, much of it instigated by Philip and with the reluctant compliance of Pope Clement. In the early days of Philip's strategy against the knights, the Knights Templar was still revered and respected. The knights were feared for their might and prowess as soldiers and warriors.

Upon his arrival in France with sixty knights in the early months of 1307, Jacques spent several months engaging in discussions with the pope. Meanwhile, King Philip's men began to spread nasty rumors about the Knights Templar.

Rumors have a way of quickly becoming truths and overcoming doubt and disbelief. King Philip's spies also made attempts to insinuate themselves into the Knights Templar. Apparently, these spies created numerous charges against the Knights Templar. They not only made some of it up but also used complaints or disgruntled murmurs from former members of the order. Some people whispered that the Knights Templar engaged in black magic and horrible rituals regarding sex. Whether any of the rumors King Philip started were true or not remains a mystery, but due to the king's hatred of the Knights Templar, it can be supposed that most of them were false.

And once the people were disgruntled enough, the king pounced and sent out his orders of arrest against the Knights Templar. Unfortunately, any Templar arrested was not only to be imprisoned but also questioned. If the knight refused to tell the truth (which was really the "truth" Philip wanted to hear), he would be tortured until he did or died. This persecution was extreme, and it is believed that one of the truths that King Philip wanted to hear and obtain a confession regarded the rumor that the Knights Templar secretly renounced their belief in Christ. It was even said that they spat on the cross.

The Templars were imprisoned, isolated, and put on a diet of bread and water, all the while enduring torture. Some of the torture was quite extreme, including one method of tying a man's hands behind his back and then suspending and lifting him into the air by a rope slung over a beam with the intention of dislocating the shoulder joints. Men were tortured on the rack, a torture device also intended to dislocate joints, and some were tortured by having their feet coated with oil and then held over a fire.

Unfortunately, these torture techniques resulted in many of the Templars confessing to false charges, some sooner than others. Among those who confessed to the false charges was the grand master himself, the elderly Jacques de Molay.

Unfortunately, it wasn't just the knights who were arrested and condemned. Farmers, bankers, and other support staff were also targeted. These men were accused of a number of offenses that included but were not limited to devil worship, spitting on the cross, homosexuality, fraud, heresy, and financial corruption.

It is believed that Pope Clement V had no idea that things would go so far and was terribly shocked. Yet, at the same time, he was afraid of retribution from the Templars who had not yet been captured. However, the so-called "confessions" of the knights required him to respond to their heresy. As such, it can be said that Pope Clement V was caught between a rock and a hard place.

Ultimately, he gave papal orders to kings throughout western Europe to arrest any Templars living on their properties. While many outside of France refused to do so, the fall of the Knights Templar had effectively begun when a vast number of them were arrested in France.

The trials and hearings of these unfortunate knights took place between 1307 and 1314, the year Grand Master Jacques de Molay died. Some historical documents state that while King Philip and Pope Clement V had discussed the possible arrests of Templars in France, the pope claimed that he had not been informed about the arrests going forward, hence the questions about whether the pope had actually approved of King Philip's actions.

Because King Philip required Pope Clement's "approval" for the hunting down, capture, torture, and even death of the Templars for legitimacy, he placed pressure on the pope until he finally agreed to allow the king to proceed. Still, the pope "interfered" by insisting that all proper procedures be followed, delaying the process for years.

It is perhaps not surprising that many of the Templars who confessed to these salacious claims later recanted their confessions, including Jacques de Molay, since those confessions had been given under torture. As a result, additional trials and hearings were conducted, which dragged on for some time. However, most of these prisoners were kept in dungeons and jail cells for years before King Philip, perhaps as a last slap in the face, had roughly fifty of them burned at the stake in 1310, with Pope Clement V apparently looking the other way, perhaps fearful of King Philip's wrath being directed at him next.

In 1311, the pope met with cardinals and King Philip at the Council of Vienne. While the Order of the Knights Templar was declared not guilty of the charges that had been brought against it, the pope believed its reputation had been so badly damaged that it would no longer be able to defend Christendom. However, it was determined that the leaders of the order could still be charged guilty.

In 1312, Pope Clement officially dissolved the Order of the Knights Templar. In total, roughly 127 charges had been brought against the Knights Templar, and while none of the charges were verified, and the order was found not guilty, their leaders paid the price of King Philip's resentment and greed.

Four of the leaders of the Knights Templar, including Jacques de Molay and Geoffrey de Charney, were brought before a small group of French cardinals and religious theologians and condemned to life imprisonment. At this time, de Molay and de Charney denied any confessions they had made. Nevertheless, their fate was sealed, as they were charged as being relapsed heretics. They were turned over to King Philip, who, without consulting the pope, sentenced them to death by burning at the stake.

So, in the early months of 1314, Grand Master Jacques de Molay, an elderly man, was burned at the stake in Paris, France, along with other Templar leaders. The might of the Knights Templar faded, but the order's story has not.

The riches, lands, and money of the knights living in France were taken by King Philip. Although he kept some of the riches, most of the vast wealth of the Knights Templar was given to the Knights Hospitaller. Many remaining Templars fled France, while others joined orders, such as the Hospitallers. The rest faded into history.

Rumors and myths

Numerous rumors and myths regarding the Knights Templar exist today, including one that suggests these knights were the first to sail across the Atlantic Ocean to the New World after the initial voyages of the Vikings. The rationale for this rumor is that numerous gravestones with Templar insignia were found in Nova Scotia.

Note of interest: Roger de Flor

One Templar by the name of Roger de Flor made quite a name for himself as a naval commander in the late 13th century. He led mercenaries and mounted knights from Catalan. He gained the reputation of being a fierce and powerful commander, especially on the high seas. In fact, after he married into a Byzantine royal family, he actually held the title of Caesar, which was quite impressive in those days.

In Roger's earlier years, he served as a shipmate on a Templar ship in Marseille, France. By the time he was twenty years old, he had served as a sergeant-brother in the Knights Templar and had taken part in several battles. He also took part in the evacuation of the Templars at the Battle of Acre in 1291. At the time, the young man appeared to have been tempted by some of the riches that were being evacuated from the city and took it upon himself to appropriate some of them for his own use. Unfortunately, Grand Master Jacques de Molay learned about it and not only denounced Roger but also expelled him from the order.

Ultimately, Roger de Flor fled. Because he was so gifted at sailing, he became a successful pirate in the later medieval ages. As such, a legend blossomed that the well-known black pirate flag with the skull and bones upon it, nicknamed the Jolly Roger, was named for him. Whether truth or fiction, it is a rumor that has followed the privateer over the centuries.

Over time, a number of conspiracy theories have been born regarding the Knights Templar, such as rumors of secret societies and missions. There is no doubt that a number of rumors damaged the reputation of the Knights Templar, such as the claims made against them by King Philip, which led leading to their eventual downfall.

Even today, centuries after the remaining Knights Templar went into hiding following the debacle in France, it is believed that some traveled across the oceans and seas, some to the far reaches of Europe and some as far north as Scotland. Tunnels with Templar emblems have been found under Scottish castles.

Rumors continue to endure even after the demise of the Knights Templar. One of those rumors was that they hid a number of priceless artifacts and treasures during the early months of their persecution. Some of these treasures have become myths and still encourage treasure hunters to this day. You also might hear of these treasures in popular movies and books.

Supposedly, the Knights Templar possessed the Holy Grail, the cup Jesus sipped during the Last Supper with his disciples before his crucifixion. Another religious relic the Templars supposedly hid was the Ark of the Covenant, the wooden chest that held the original Ten Commandments, the stone tablets that had been brought down from Mount Sinai by Moses himself. Such rumors have not been substantiated yet, but many hope to be able to prove their veracity.

Historical accounts, even while the Templars retained their might, specify a number of relics revered by the knights. The Templars are believed to have carefully stored precious objects and guarded them carefully within the walls of monasteries, cathedrals, and shrines. These relics could have included a piece of the True Cross, the bones or clothing of saints, or items closely associated with the crucifixion, such as the nails or the crown of thorns.

It is believed and historically written that a number of sojourners and crusaders returning from the Holy Land brought a number of religious objects with them, so the Templars were far from the only ones to do. The Hospitallers also have a history of being in possession of such relics.

Even the Rule of the Knights Templar mentions the protection of a revered piece of the True Cross that was carried with them on their crusades and how it was to be guarded and protected. However, it is believed that the order's True Cross was ultimately captured during the Battle of Hattin in the year 1187 by the Ayyubids. One legend surrounding this event claims that a Templar knight escaped with it and buried it quickly in the sand, but when he returned to find it later, he could not remember exactly where he had buried it. Others say the Ayyubids sent it to Damascus, placing it upside down on a lance.

The order made it known that it possessed the crown of thorns, and on Holy Thursday, the priests of the order brought it out for all to see.

Unfortunately, no historical documents have provided any indisputable evidence that the Knights Templar ever possessed the Holy Grail, the Ark of the Covenant, or the Shroud of Turin, the burial shroud of Christ. However, it is believed, based on historical documents and the Rule, that they might have owned a piece of the True Cross, a piece of the crown of thorns, and even a small vial of Christ's blood. Of course, none of this is known for sure. Some historians believe these legendary artifacts were never in possession of the Templars. They believe it made a nice story after the Templars' downfall and further added to the Templars' mystique.

It is also believed that some testimony regarding ownership of these relics cannot be verified because of the torture the knights faced during the later years of the order's existence. However, King Philip II of France ordered that Templar relics, documents, and archives, along with their land and properties, should be given to the Hospitallers, though he kept some of that wealth for himself. The Templar archives were destroyed in 1571 following the Turkish attack on Cyprus. It is likely some things about the Templars will forever be shrouded in mystery.

Conclusion

The Knights Hospitaller, the Knights of the Holy Sepulchre, the Order of St. Lazarus, the Teutonic Knights, and the Knights Templar were not the only orders of knights that existed during the Middle Ages. Some are better known than others, but regardless, these military orders, which saw action in many of the Crusades, live on today. In fact, many of the orders continue to exist.

These crusaders evoke an image of bravery and valor, of dedication to a cause and the willingness to sacrifice for that cause. Some crusades and their leaders are well known and written about in history books, but there are also numerous smaller battles, wars, and crusaders that will likely never get the attention they deserve.

The legacy of these brothers-in-arm endures, as do many of their missions. Their leaders and their reputations have been passed down for generations, and the concept of chivalry is still epitomized by envisioning these knights of old.

Numerous books have been written about many of these knightly orders, some with more historical documentation to rely on than others. Still, much of their history is wreathed in an aura of mystery and intrigue. Not everything can be found in the annals of history, such as all of the disagreements between kings and popes and the seemingly never-ending disputes of men.

Whether the knights of old took upon the mantle for religious reasons or pride is debated, but there is no doubt that many felt it was their duty to serve. The legends and histories of many of these knights maintain their place in history. They lived in troubled, dark, and uncertain times, and they followed their beliefs, many of them until their bloody and violent deaths.

Part 3: The Inquisition

A Captivating Guide to the Medieval, Spanish, Portuguese, and Roman Inquisitions

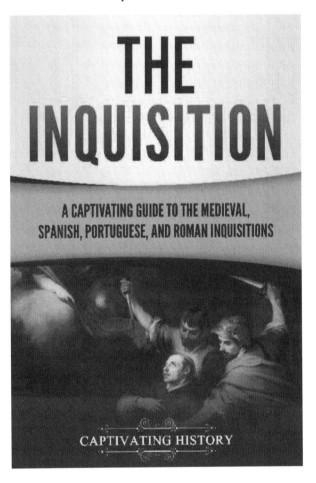

Introduction: Asking Too Many Questions

It is somewhat ironic to think that religion—a mode of human experience that has its origins in asking big questions—can, at times, morph into a dogmatic shutdown of freedom of expression and thought. After all, religion comes about as part of humanity's quest to figure out who we are, how we got here, and what the ultimate purpose of existence is.

Religious experience begins with the deep thoughts of people and dreamers, those thoughts that make us ask important questions. Different religions reach different conclusions from this soul-searching, but it is from a deep yearning and questioning of the human experience that religion is ultimately derived. So, yes, it is indeed ironic that this religious search for meaning often reaches a point in which a religion's adherents decide that the deep thinking and questioning phase is over and that only officially sanctioned answers by religious officials will suffice.

The primary impetus for any religious inquisition is not to ask questions about the meaning of life but to ask questions about those who are asking too many questions. Inquisitions are designed to make sure that everyone believes the same official dogma and do not go off into their own abstract beliefs, which could potentially cause a rift in the religion. The whole point of an inquisition is to shut down any and all questioning of officially accepted dogma.

As far as religious officials are concerned, the time for searching and questioning the origin of the cosmos is over; it is time for the people to simply adopt the official strain of thought and be done with it. Those who are naturally free-spirited and inquisitive can find such constraints frustrating. If you talk to someone who has grown up in an organized religion, you might find yourself being given blank looks or even openly hostile stares from asking fairly basic questions. There is strong pressure in organized religions to stick to the official script.

Even the great Saint Augustine of Hippo once joked about the fate of those who ask too many questions regarding religion. He once spoke of how some occasionally mused about what God might have been doing before creation. The human mind might naturally wonder what God might have been up to during the infinite eons of eternity before human beings were even thought of. Augustine, with his wry wit, quipped that God was "preparing hell for people that asked too many questions."

Of course, Augustine was joking; this great theologian was just as inquisitive as the best of them. But for the grand inquisitors who were intent on shutting down the discussion of ideas and thoughts that went against the grain, such an answer took on a whole new reality. In Portugal, Rome, and Spain, people were set ablaze and burned at the stake for simply asking too many questions.

Let us discover their stories and find out what drove the Catholic Church to expunge these inquisitive minds for good.

Chapter 1: La Convivencia — Religious Tolerance and Coexistence before the Inquisition

"The European wars of religion were more deadly than the First World War, proportionally speaking, and in the range of the Second World War in Europe. The Inquisition, the persecution of heretics and infidels and witches, they racked up pretty high death tolls."

-*Steven Pinker*

Most today subscribe to religious tolerance. Today, even the most diehard of the faithful of any given religion would most likely agree to disagree with those of other faiths. Of course, there are always exceptions to the rule, but for the most part, the days of folks despising others simply because they have different religious beliefs are over.

For example, zealous Christians may still think that an agnostic or someone from another religion is destined for hell because they do not believe in Jesus. But they most likely keep those thoughts to themselves since they have been conditioned to realize that they are not entitled to force their opinion on others, although they are certainly entitled to have their own ideas. At most, they will share their Christian experience with the "wayward sinner" and pray for them, but they likely would not persecute them!

Most societies around the world, except for a few rare exceptions (such as in Iran or North Korea), practice some degree of religious tolerance and coexistence in the modern age. Interestingly enough, just prior to the Inquisition, there was a fairly great degree of tolerance being practiced as well. To see this religious tolerance in practice, all one has to do is look at what religious life was like in the Iberian Peninsula (Spain and Portugal) from the 8th century to the 15th century, just prior to the Spanish (and then Portuguese) Inquisition.

Spain had been conquered by Muslim armies, which had surged into the peninsula from North Africa. This kickstarted a centuries-long struggle between the holdout Christian kingdoms in northern Iberia and the Muslim principalities. The struggle would be known as the Reconquista. And as bloody and violet as this struggle was, religious violence (at least on the scale of the Inquisition) was largely absent.

During this period, religious tolerance of multiple faiths was the norm, whether it was a section of Iberia controlled by Muslims or a section controlled by Christian or even Jewish rulers. However, it must be noted that although religions were tolerated in the sense that those who practiced faiths contrary to the rulers were not outright expelled, those who believed in things contrary to the rulers were typically treated as second-class citizens.

Perhaps the best example of this was what happened under Muslim rule. One must keep in mind that the notion that Christians and Jews are fellow people of the book, yet in error to the true light of Muhammad, is baked into the Quran. The Quran specifically teaches Muslims to tolerate Christians and Jews but also recommends applying restrictions to them and even instituting a special religious tax called the jizya on them.

Yes, if you were a Christian or Jew under Muslim rule, you could agree to pay for your faith, wear distinctive garb, and be banned from certain aspects of society but still be allowed to keep your beliefs intact. We would look at such things in utter horror today, but in reality, these practices were much more tolerant than what was ultimately practiced during the Spanish and Portuguese Inquisitions. There is no question that the Inquisition that took place in Iberia was an act of sheer and absolute intolerance for any deviation from the accepted faith.

During the Inquisition, if a person did not stick to the official religious script, there was no tax one could pay (with the exception of the Portuguese tax leveled against Hindus of the Far East) or compromise one could make. You would either be expelled or killed.

Although much of the premise is still debatable, the whole notion that Muslims, Christians, and Jews lived in relative harmony prior to the Inquisition has been dubbed the period of La Convivencia. That is Spanish for "living together." The term itself is a relatively new one; it was first used in the 20th century by Spanish historian Américo Castro.

As historians occasionally do, Castro sought to reinterpret traditional views of history. From his perch in the 20th century, when it was just coming into vogue to criticize everything the West ever stood for, he sought to paint a more sympathetic picture of Muslim rule in Spain. Many have since criticized his efforts, referring to it as an attempt to mythologize Muslim rule and make it seem more benevolent than it was.

However, there is still no denying that under Muslim rule, Iberia saw a period of relative harmony (at least relative as it pertains to the medieval period), which lasted for nearly four hundred years during the Moorish occupation of Spain. During this period, Christians, Jews, and Muslims were neighbors and hammered out a unique social compact in which they could all live their lives. Treatment was not always equal, but varying degrees of religious tolerance were indeed practiced.

A great cultural exchange took place against the backdrop of this relative harmony and stability of La Convivencia. Since the various groups were not constantly at each other's throats, they were able to work together and learn from each other. This proved quite pivotal when it came to saving ancient works and translating them into multiple languages. The relative openness between groups allowed Spain to maintain the light of ancient learning while most of the rest of Europe had gone into a "dark age."

The rest of Christendom would ultimately benefit from the learning of Spain, and this is perhaps no better demonstrated than through the development of one, two, three, and four. Yes, the numeral system that we all know and love today was alien to much of Christian Europe at the time. The medieval European West did not know the value (literally and metaphorically) of the numerals that had been developed in the East. Instead of these familiar numbers, the Christian kingdoms of Europe relied upon unwieldy Roman numerals.

The mathematical number system that we currently appreciate is actually an import from India. The Indians had a tremendous lead in mathematics, even developing the complex notion of the number zero. It sounds simple to us today, but the development of zero was absolutely groundbreaking. Without zero as a placeholder, you would not have numbers like 2,024 or 2,025. Instead, you would have 2.24, 2.25, or some other unsightly placeholder. (It must be noted that the Maya first developed the concept of zero; however, that knowledge did not travel to Europe.)

More importantly, without these innovations, it would also be quite impossible to do complex math. If you do not believe it, just try a simple division problem such as 445/12 as CDXLV/XII. Needless to say, 445 over 12 is much more easily done with Indian numerals than it would be with Roman numerals. The Muslim conquest of India brought Indian mathematics into the Islamic world, and these ideas would eventually arrive in Muslim Spain and then reach the minds of Christian Europe.

Interestingly enough, it was none other than Pope Sylvester II who first realized just how valuable this new number system was. Prior to becoming pope, Sylvester lived in a monastery in Spain's Pyrenees mountain range, which was nestled right at the border between what was then Christian and Islamic Spain. Here, he was able to gather much data on the state of learning in Muslim Spain and ultimately picked up the newfound number system.

Pope Sylvester II learned how to use these numbers and subsequently wowed those around him with his ability to do complex math. Some were so amazed they likened him to a wizard, but this pope was not a wizard; he just knew how to do math! And he was passionate about it. Pope Sylvester II actually went as far as to introduce a new way to calculate the abacus in the year 999. It was fairly new to him and his peers, although non-Westerners had been using the abacus for centuries. The abacus itself is an ancient Near Eastern invention. It is believed to have originated from Mesopotamia (ancient Iraq) as early as 2500 BCE.

Pope Sylvester II perished a few years later, in 1003, and it would take some time for what he had learned to become commonplace in Christian Europe. But as commerce and trade began to grow, the number system advocated by this pope would become prominent.

But perhaps the most obvious benefit of this period of togetherness was the robust architecture, which still stands in some places as a testament to this rich period of civilization and learning. Al-Andalus (Muslim Spain) boasted complex canals, aqueducts, and even full-fledged underground sewer systems!

The city of Córdoba was said to have had nine hundred public bathhouses, as well as six hundred mosques, fifty hospitals, and seventy libraries. The libraries themselves were of note because they are said to have been jampacked with all kinds of books loaded with ancient and more recent aspects of learning. The city was even advanced enough to be lit at night with a series of street lamps.

Of course, these were not electric street lamps. They obviously ran on gas, oil, or some other sort of flammable substance and were lit up with an open flame, but they must have been an impressive sight at the time nonetheless. Yes, when much of western Europe was still crawling out of a "dark age," Spain served as a shining example of what humanity's potential was. The region shined through the bleak dreariness and exemplified the possibilities for greater enlightenment.

Even so, despite the many benefits of learning from the rich Muslim culture, the Christian rulers of northern Iberia were not pleased that their hegemony and monopoly over the Iberian Peninsula had been denied to them. They were the original ideological rulers of the peninsula, and even after centuries had passed, they desired to retake what they believed to be theirs.

So, the Reconquista of Iberia would continue until that fateful year of 1492. That year, the last great enclave of Moorish Spain—Granada—was eliminated under the orders of King Ferdinand II of Aragon and Queen Isabella I of Castile, both of whom were staunchly Catholic. On the heels of their successful reclamation of all of Iberia, the inquisition into who was a Christian and who was not began in earnest.

As we will see later, much of the push to interrogate others and figure out "who was who" was borne out of people's grave and uncompromising fears. The Christian kings had just concluded centuries of bloody struggles to retake Iberia, and they wanted to make sure that the region would not slip from their grasp again. Their worst nightmare was a perceived "fifth column" of false converts to Christianity, as the Christians feared they would aid and abet future enemy incursions.

Not all of the Iberian powers were eager to carry out this zero-sum game against their own subjects. Queen Isabella—one-half of the ruling power couple of Ferdinand and Isabella of Spain—was initially hesitant to bring the hammer down on the so-called Conversos of Spain.

She had received many reports of suspicions over the behavior of Conversos in the region of Seville. But it was only after being reportedly petitioned by clergy there that she moved toward an investigation into the religious leanings of these converts.

There were charges that the Conversos were not only insincere but that many of them were plotting with outside forces (such as the Muslim Moors of neighboring Morocco) to topple Spanish authority. This push to investigate these growing suspicions would ultimately lead to the Inquisition.

Having said that, perhaps the best argument that can be made about the Muslim rule of Spain being more benign than Christian rule was the fact there was no Islamic version of the Inquisition. Surely, Muslim rulers must have dealt with the same fears and suspicions of betrayal at the hands of religious "others."

There were indeed plenty of opportunities for Christians within al-Andalus to betray the Muslim rulers and link up with the Christian kingdoms in the north. Yet, even so, there was no call to round up or expel Christians and Jews. This alone is perhaps the greatest testimony to the relative tolerance of this period of interfaith togetherness.

Chapter 2: The Hunters and the Hunted: The Roles Are Established, and the Inquisition Takes Shape

"Though I do regard the Inquisition in general and the burning of Giordano Bruno in particular as blots on the history of the Roman Catholic Church, I am far from being actuated by hatred of that church, and in fact cannot imagine that European civilization would have developed or survived without it."

-Louis MacNeice

Who were the inquisitors who carried out the Inquisition? This might seem like a simple question, but those who were charged to make forceful inquiries into the lives and characters of millions were themselves many and varied. But by the middle of the 15th century, some key characters had begun to emerge. First and foremost, of course, is the looming figure of Tomás de Torquemada.

Much has been said about this larger-than-life figure, but there is still much that is not known. Furthermore, through the sands of time, it has become increasingly difficult to ascertain what aspects of his historical memory are true and what aspects are figments of someone else's imagination.

Tomás de Torquemada is believed to have been born around the year 1420 in the vicinity of Valladolid, which was then a part of the Kingdom of Castile. When Torquemada entered his teenage years, he made the fateful decision to join the ministry by dedicating himself to becoming a Dominican monk. It is believed that Torquemada came from a Jewish background, with some of his family members being "Conversos," people who had been pressured to convert to the Christian faith.

Some have pointed out this fact to illustrate the tragedy of how a man whose own ancestors were likely persecuted for their faith would ultimately become a leading persecutor himself. Others have speculated about Torquemada's Jewish ancestry and have gone as far as to suggest that perhaps his burning desire to conceal this fact made him such a vociferous opponent of the Jewish faith. Much has already been written in regard to this, but at the end of the day, such musing and theorizing amount to nothing more than mere speculation.

At any rate, Tomás de Torquemada's first major posting of note was as the prior of a monastery in Santa Cruz. While serving in this capacity, Torquemada became acquainted with the princess (and future queen) of Castile, Isabella. Torquemada became a great mentor to his royal charge, and he would ultimately be instrumental in helping to facilitate her marriage to Ferdinand of Aragon. The union would establish one of the greatest power couples in history: King Ferdinand and Queen Isabella of Spain. Although they were never officially titled as the rulers of Spain, the country as we know it today began to form during their reign, so they are often referred to as such. In fact, after King Ferdinand and Queen Isabella solidified their control over Spain, they tapped Torquemada to begin leading inquisitions into the faiths of others.

As the stage began to be set for the hunters and the hunted during the Inquisition, Tomás de Torquemada was made the chief of all inquisitors, gaining the title of inquisitor general. On the surface, Torquemada lived the life of a humble monk, wearing worn-out and weather-beaten clothes, but behind the scenes, he was gathering a large number of funds. He used this money to renovate his old monastery and build new ones.

Torquemada always had a keen interest in architecture. He not only enjoyed financing building projects but also had a habit of hanging around the work crews who built them. Torquemada seemed to genuinely enjoy their company. As hard as it might be for us to imagine, Torquemada cast off much of his pride and pretense around "the simple workmen" who labored to complete the grand buildings he had commissioned. It is easy to view every person who does terrible things as being rotten to the core, but the truth is, these people are not demons but humans who do terrible things for a reason, whether that is money, power, or for one's faith. This is not brought up to make you feel sympathy for Tomás de Torquemada; we just want to illustrate the point that many people back then would have seen him in a much different light than what he is remembered for today.

Although Tomás de Torquemada would later be in the business of tearing down people, he enjoyed nothing better than raising up new churches and other ecclesiastical structures. Thanks to Torquemada, the Monastery of St. Thomas at Avila was built, and several other buildings were commissioned as well.

At any rate, upon being commissioned as the inquisitor general, Torquemada became quite serious about the task at hand. He sought to remake the already established rules of the Inquisition into his own image. His efforts to reform the Inquisition led to him compiling twenty-eight new articles for what would be referred to as his own special "Instructions" on how the Inquisition should be carried out.

The first article concerns the exact modus operandi to be used when an inquisition is being made for the first time in a new location. The article laid down instructions to have all of the locals brought to church on a Sunday or holiday, a day when it would have been common for them to gather. A sermon would then be delivered, which would be tailor-made to support the Inquisition that was about to take place.

The sermon would praise the virtues of the pending Inquisition and condemn those of suspected deviance. In essence, this was a massive exercise in brainwashing and propaganda. And it was carried out well, setting the stage for the next major drama to come: the *auto-da-fé*.

On February 6th, 1481, the first *auto-da-fé*, or "act of faith," took place. These so-called "acts of faith" were actually shorthand for "public penance" of all kinds, including burning folks at the stake or any other manner of public execution.

During these instances, it was believed that if those who were condemned were innocent of their charges that they would be miraculously spared. Perhaps the wood would not burn? Or perhaps the rope used to hang the condemned might snap? Whatever the case may be, if the execution was deemed to have been supernaturally thwarted, it would be called off.

This sort of superstitious rationalizing would later be made famous during the witch trials. Those believed to be witches were routinely tossed into bodies of water to see what might happen. However, these instances came with a strange twist. If someone miraculously survived drowning, they were deemed to be a witch, whereas those who perished were proclaimed innocent!

The pope often inflamed superstitions with his remarks. For example, Pope Innocent VIII issued a bull in 1484 in which he matter-of-factly stated his opinion that, among other things, women might be secretly cavorting with demonic entities or that witches could be putting hexes on farms, resulting in bad harvests. Life was hard back then, and folks were looking for people to blame; making such statements only played right into the urge to scapegoat others for the problems people faced.

Then again, it must be noted that some popes demanded at least some level of measured restraint. Pope Innocent VIII's immediate predecessor, Pope Sixtus IV, made it a point to urge caution during the Inquisition. In particular, he demanded better treatment of the hunted and hounded Conversos of Iberia.

Tomás de Torquemada, the grand inquisitor himself, oversaw a massive *auto-da-fé* held in Toledo, Spain, in March of 1487. This grim event is said to have led to over a thousand deaths. It must be explained that such a major onslaught did not occur overnight. The Inquisition into these supposed heretics was a lengthy process.

And when we say "heretics," the reference can be both broad and narrow in scope. In a narrow sense, the Inquisition had its usual suspects of Conversos, Jews, and Muslims, but in the broader sense, a heretic could also be a lifelong Christian whose family had been in the faith for generations. Even if one came from a Christian family that had practiced the religion for several generations, if the person had been deemed to have somehow stepped outside the bounds of what was considered acceptable by the Catholic Church, they could be burned at the stake just as easily as anyone else.

According to standard procedure, those suspected of being in error were given a thirty-day grace period. During this time, the accused had a chance to recant, and the accusers had time to gather supposed evidence against the condemned. Confessions during the thirty-day grace period were greatly encouraged, and leniency was promised for those who did so. Those who confessed to trespasses did not typically receive serious punishment. The harshest measures were reserved for those who refused to confess on their own and were instead accused by others.

More often than not, those who were doing the accusing were actually the neighbors of the condemned. Neighbors were in a prime position to report anything they deemed to be unusual or even just slightly off.

For example, if neighbors noted that someone did not have any chimney smoke on a Saturday, this was ample grounds to accuse one of being a Converso who was secretly practicing Judaism since no chimney smoke on a Saturday could be suggestive of one observing the Sabbath. Another commonly purported piece of evidence was the instance of a neighbor suddenly buying a bunch of feed immediately before a Jewish or Muslim holiday. If someone was seen doing this, they could be accused of secretly making preparations to celebrate banned religious holidays.

Such things are petty in the extreme, and considering how neighbors often grow to dislike each other, one can only imagine hostile neighbors flinging flimsy accusations at each other out of pure and simple malice. And it was often the pettiest of accusations that got the wheels of the Inquisition turning.

The truly scary thing is that after a person was brought before a panel of inquisitors on baseless accusations, they could have immense pressure applied to them, including torture, to force them to admit to things they had never done. Those who refused to make a false confession would suffer an even worse fate.

They were not necessarily killed, but they were most certainly in for a grueling process of being interrogated over and over again. And the more they were interrogated, the more potential there was for some kind of "error" to be found. As charges racked up against someone, a death sentence became increasingly likely.

After the first "act of faith" ran its course, several had been burned to ashes. However, it is important to note that not all of these spectacles resulted in executions. Theologian and historian Elphège Vacandard researched the history of the Inquisition and came to the conclusion that death was much rarer than many contemporary portrayals had let on.

He looked all the way back to the Medieval Inquisition, which directly preceded the Spanish Inquisition. The Medieval Inquisition was actually a series of inquisitions that began in the late 12th century. These included the "Episcopal Inquisition" that took place from 1184 and lasted until the 1230s. The Medieval Inquisition was aimed at rooting out supposed errors in the doctrine.

Cathars were largely targeted in the Medieval Inquisition. They were viewed as heretical by Catholics because of their beliefs. For instance, Cathars believed that the human spirit was actually an angel trapped on this plane by an angry god. Cathars believed in a form of reincarnation and two gods (the good God was the God depicted in the New Testament, while the evil God was the one from the Old Testament). It is easy to see why the Catholics back in the medieval ages would have persecuted the Cathars, as these beliefs would be seen as heretical by many Christians today!

Vacandard pointed to the example of French inquisitor Bernard Gui. Inquisitor Gui oversaw several inquisitions. According to Elphège Vacandard, the most elaborate processions over which Bernard Gui administrated often did not end in death. Typically, the most severe penalty was some time allotted in prison.

According to Vacandard, although the threat of death as punishment was always there, for the most part, Bernard Gui's Medieval Inquisition was much more theatrical than forceful, with a solemn sermon as a warning for the accused and others of what might happen if they transgressed against the teachings of the Catholic Church.

Vacandard's theory about the Inquisition having fewer deaths than believed is an accurate statement for the Medieval Inquisition. Yes, people died, but they likely did not die in the tens of thousands. However, the Spanish, Portuguese, and Roman Inquisitions would become a much more formidable institution than its medieval predecessor. The Spanish Inquisition, in particular, would become notorious for the number of lives that would be lost during it. The exact number is not known, although some estimate that the death toll was in the tens of thousands. Others have suggested there were hundreds of thousands of deaths, and still others are of the opinion that millions died as a result of the Spanish Inquisition, especially when considering all of the vigilante justice that occurred from everyday citizens.

The Vatican released a report in 2004 about the Inquisition, saying that the number of deaths in the Inquisition has been greatly exaggerated over the years. However, the report only looked at deaths that were decided by church tribunals. It did not take into account other tribunals that were not sponsored by the church. Although these tribunals did not have the backing of the Catholic Church, they operated on the same principles as the church-sponsored ones, namely on the fear that subversives would cause chaos and bring down Christianity.

As dreadful as all of this is, one might naturally wonder what was in it for the inquisitors themselves. Some were, no doubt, diehard religious zealots who were led by their own (however misguided) belief that they were serving a greater good by rooting out non-Christians. Others were not motivated as much by religion as they were by monetary gain. There was always the opportunity for an inquisitor to receive a lot of money or other goods if they targeted rich people. If one were found to be a heretic, all of their property and fortune were forfeit.

Many of the Conversos who were so ruthlessly targeted in the first phase of the Spanish Inquisition were wealthy. Many were merchants or doctors or served in some other capacity that brought them an affluent position. However, all it took was a random accusation for all of their assets to be taken from them and divvied up by the inquisitors and their helpers—the so-called familiars who served as guards and enforcers for the inquisitors.

There are even cases in which the familiars—the harsh taskmasters of the inquisitors—were given immunity. This essentially allowed the familiars to run roughshod over communities and commit all manner of offenses without fear of any repercussions.

But even when the inquisitors and their cronies were found guilty of outright extorsion, nothing came of it. The absolute corruption of the Inquisition as an institution would create a lot of pain and sorrow for those who fell in its crosshairs. For them, there was no recourse. These hunted and hounded individuals would be at the full mercy of the Inquisition and its grand inquisitors.

Chapter 3: The Spanish Inquisition

"The decent moderation of today will be the least of human things tomorrow. At the time of the Spanish Inquisition, the opinion of good sense and of the good medium was certainly that people ought not to burn too large a number of heretics; extreme and unreasonable opinion obviously demanded that they should burn none at all."

-Maurice Maeterlinck

The Spanish Inquisition, which was officially called the Tribunal of the Holy Office of the Inquisition, came about during the reign of King Ferdinand and Queen Isabella of Spain. It first came into being in 1478. These measures had been approved by Pope Sixtus IV. The pontiff had given the go-ahead to the Inquisition due to growing concerns over newly converted Christians who were believed to be secretly practicing a different faith.

The tribunal was created toward the end of the Reconquista, and the initial impetus for establishing it was out of a desire to establish a universal Catholic presence in Iberia. Iberia had previously been largely a multi-faith dominion. As mentioned previously, it is a myth to say that all faiths were treated equally, but even so, people of different faiths did tolerate each other, at least for the most part.

But as the Reconquista came to a close, King Ferdinand and Queen Isabella wished to consolidate the lands of Iberia and ensure the people believed in Catholicism. They had no desire for interfaith coexistence;

instead, they yearned for an entirely Christian dominion.

Multiple theories have been pushed for this fateful decision to aggressively re-Christianize Spain. The simplest and most obvious would be that the king and queen, like many in their day, were zealous Christians and simply felt it was their duty to make sure that Christianity reigned supreme. But such an explanation is insufficient when considering the fact that many Christian kings of Iberia had shown a small degree of tolerance to other faiths in the past.

So, it is more likely these monarchs were not just motivated by religion but also by pragmatic politics and military strategy. Yes, they had just reconquered the Iberian Peninsula, but their grip on it was far from secure. North Africa was still under complete Muslim dominion, and Muslim corsairs filled the waters of the Mediterranean. It was feared that the Muslim population of Spain, as well as some Jewish population centers, could unite and provide support and cooperation for another major Islamic advance into Iberia.

The deep suspicion that was held for the Jews must be mentioned since the early phases of the Inquisition heavily persecuted the Jews. Those who practiced Judaism were not viewed as being loyal to a Christian kingdom in the same way that practicing Christians would be, so Jews were constantly viewed as suspect. Many Christians feared that it would not take much for Jewish communities to switch sides and aid a Muslim invasion.

We may not agree with such stereotyping of groups of people today, but things were seen in a different light back then. Thus, the main purpose of the Inquisition was to root out supposed subversives from Iberia, lest they help facilitate the next major Islamic incursion and completely undo all of the gains of the Reconquista.

And as mentioned, during the first phase of the Inquisition, the Jewish community was targeted in a major way. Besides fears that Jews could collaborate with outside forces to overthrow the kingdom, there was widespread concern that recently converted Jews, known as Conversos, were susceptible to being pulled back to Judaism.

King Ferdinand and Queen Isabella became determined to expel practicing Jews from Iberia. In 1483, the first major expulsions occurred in Córdoba, Cádiz, and Seville. As these expulsions began, sensational charges were leveled against Jews in Toledo, alleging that they had ritually sacrificed a Christian child. No solid proof of this has ever been found, but the Christian mobs in Toledo were caught up in such a frenzy that a group of Jews and Conversos were apprehended, interrogated, and killed over these wild charges. Torquemada oversaw these happenings and made sure that the punishment was severe.

It was only after the Reconquista was complete, with the final conquest of Grenada in 1492, that total expulsion was recommended. The notion that all Jews who refused to convert would be expelled is almost unbelievable; it is hard to even fathom that such a thing could happen. But it has been recorded for posterity that the Spanish monarchs issued an infamous edict on March 31st, 1492, which stated that the Jews of Spain had two choices: become Christians or leave the country.

Some did accept the offer to convert, thereby becoming lumped in with all of the other so-called "Conversos." But many steadfastly refused to give up their ancestral faith. Their only option was to sell everything they owned, save a few things they could carry, and leave the country for an unknown land.

The first of the grand inquisitors—Tomás de Torquemada—perished in 1498. Unlike many of those upon whom he had made his inquiries, he did not die a terrible death. He passed away from natural causes. Immediately after his passing, a popular theologian by the name of Diego de Deza was tapped to take his place.

Diego de Deza, who just so happened to be good friends with Christopher Columbus, who had made his famous voyage of discovery just a few years prior, was a known figure in the Spanish court. Rather than tamping down the Inquisition, Diego de Deza actually ramped it up—and he ramped it up considerably. In 1500, just a couple of years after he was inaugurated as the chief inquisitor, Diego de Deza took on one of his most infamous cases.

A woman said to be a Converso started a popular following in some remote corner of Spain. She and her followers claimed to have been imparted with divine visions. Normally, such a thing would not have been too troubling for the Catholic Church—that is, as long as it fell along the usual lines of Catholic teaching and belief—but this supposed prophetess and her followers claimed to have seen things that were not on the typical Catholic script.

The prophetess and her followers were allegedly transported to another realm and saw indescribable things; whatever it was that they swore they saw was not palatable for the church. As such, an *auto-da-fé* was held. She and her hundreds of followers were held to account for their actions.

Ironically, the pagan oppressors of early Christians, the latter of whom claimed to have seen and witnessed incredible things, and the inquisitors, who persecuted Iberian mystics (whether Converso or Morisco), are really one and the same. The early Christians and the Iberian mystics both had a mystical experience that was deemed contrary to the popular dogma of the day. In both instances, their willingness to go against the grain of the accepted narrative ultimately made them targets of persecution. At any rate, not one but two *autos-da-fé* were held in the spring of 1501 to take care of these supposed heretics.

Not all inquisitors would have a free hand, and there were cases when some were deemed to have gone just a bit too far, as was the case with Grand Inquisitor Diego Rodríguez Lucero of Córdoba. Diego created much dread and anguish through his bizarre fears of a Converso conspiracy to supplant Christianity with Judaism.

His paranoia was entirely unfounded, but he would take the weakest of accusations and suspicions to persecute whole communities. Many prominent and well-known figures who were either Conversos or simply had a distant relative who was one found themselves in his crosshairs. The onslaught became so terrible that Diego's own subordinates eventually turned on him and pleaded with the pope to intervene.

One official complaint read, in part, that the "Captain of Córdoba" was "able to defame the whole kingdom, to destroy a great part of it without God or Justice, slaying and robbing and violating maids and wives, to the great dishonor of the Christian religion." By this point, Queen Isabella had passed (doing so in 1504), and the nominal governance of Castile was replaced by her daughter, Joanna, and her husband, Philip.

Both monarchs took an interest in the situation and wanted to investigate for themselves. Unfortunately for them, the abrupt passing of Philip and the subsequent mental distress of Joanna proved to derail their efforts. It was not until the surviving King Ferdinand II of Aragon gained control of the situation that the mad inquisitor's campaign of terror was brought to a halt in 1507.

Ferdinand did not just punish the "Captain of Córdoba" but also went straight up the ladder of command to his boss and fired Inquisitor General Deza. Deza was replaced with a much more benign (at least benign as far as inquisitors go) inquisitor by the name of Ximenes (also known as Francisco Jiménez de Cisneros). He served as inquisitor general for the next ten years (from 1507 to 1517).

Ximenes would prove to be much more careful and thorough in his inquests than his predecessors had been. He also cleaned house. In addition to the dismissal of Lucero, the whole inquisitorial deck was reshuffled.

In the middle of Ximenes's administration as inquisitor general, the most affected regions of the Inquisition—Aragon, Catalonia, and Valencia—let their displeasure be known. These regions staged a conference of sorts in 1512 where they aired all of their complaints for Inquisitor Ximenes in person.

As a result of these complaints, a decision was made between King Ferdinand and Ximenes to curtail inquisitions to instances that involved blatant heresy; the Inquisition would no longer focus on mere suspicions and unfounded claims. It has been said that the very day before Ferdinand passed away in 1516, he made it a point to enjoin his heir, Charles I (who later became Charles V of the Holy Roman Empire; we will refer to him as Charles V, his better-known title, to avoid confusion), to seek out "God-fearing and conscientious" men of faith to take part in the holy tribunal of the Inquisition.

In 1518, Charles V received a petition from locals that further indicated how tired the people were of the Inquisition. They hinted that they thought the Inquisition was a corrupt practice cloaked in religion used merely for engineering the personal gain of a few by orchestrating the oppression of others. The petition also called for an end to the practice of secret accusations, which were the plaything of many aggressive inquisitors.

The whole notion of "secret accusations" was a common practice among the lay people, who were eager to accuse others to save their own hide or show their loyalty to the church. It was also a protocol for the inquisitors. Ever since the days of Torquemada, it had been stipulated that under no circumstances should the accused be told what they were actually accused of. This was done in the hopes that those who were being interrogated would openly admit to what they were charged with without having to be told. The strange, convoluted logic behind this was that the accused would make better (and more honest) confessions if their supposed crimes were not aired by the inquisitors.

But it also created a bizarre and tragic situation in which people were routinely hauled before the inquisitors with no idea what they had been accused of and with no way to figure it out. There were many accounts of the condemned screaming and shouting under torture for someone to let them know what their crimes were so they could confess and be done with it. But under the hard gaze of the inquisitors, there would be no such luck for these tortured souls. Pretty early on, people realized how ridiculous this situation was, which was why the 1518 petition that was sent to Charles V made mention of it.

Pope Leo X also sought to minimize the Inquisition and issued a bull urging the inquisitors to be more merciful in their pursuits. At this point, Charles V began to push back. He apparently began to have his own suspicions of subversive behavior in his realm and increasingly came to view the inquisitors as serving a vital role in weeding out dangerous elements from his kingdom.

Considering the stance that Charles V took and his view of the inquisitors as being vital in rooting out subversives, it could be said, in many ways, that the inquisitors served as an early form of a secret police. Similar to many totalitarian regimes, the inquisitors dealt with religious affairs and acted as the guardians of the status quo. They were ready and willing to call out anyone daring to step out of bounds.

In this manner, the inquisitors and the tribunal could be likened to the KGB. They were an intelligence gathering outfit empowered to not only spy on others but also take action against them if deemed appropriate. Charles V went as far as to defy the pope, refusing to publish his papal bull calling for increased tolerance.

In the meantime, the Catholic Church would be rocked by the theological eruption of the Reformation, which had been kickstarted in late 1517 by a German monk named Martin Luther. As much as the Inquisition had been trying to prevent alternate beliefs and interpretations of faith, thanks to Martin Luther and his fellow Protestant reformers, there was suddenly a wide variety of viewpoints contrary to Catholic teachings sprouting up all over northern Europe.

While northern Europe became increasingly Protestant, the Catholic stronghold of southern Europe clamped down in the midst of its own Counter-Reformation. The Inquisition would be ramped up once again, as the strong-armed agents of the church wanted to make sure that the Catholic faithful toed the line as it pertained to the official doctrine of the

Roman Catholic Church.

Charles V played a pivotal role in all of this; after all, he was not just the ruler of Spain but also the head of a conglomerate of central and western European territories known as the Holy Roman Empire. And his realm was indeed deeply affected by the Reformation. Charles was actually in attendance during Luther's debate at the Diet of Worms. A diet was an imperial assembly of the Holy Roman Empire in which crucial matters of policy were discussed and deliberated.

The Diet of Worms of 1521 is well known for the moment when Martin Luther stood toe to toe with Catholic theologian Johann Eck, Archbishop of Trier. During the course of the debate, all of Martin Luther's writings and previous statements about reforming the Catholic Church were called into question. Johann insisted that Martin Luther had no right to try and alter Catholic tradition because of his own interpretation of the scripture. Martin Luther had already been excommunicated from the church by this point, so the Holy Roman emperor branded him a heretic and banned the people from talking about or spreading Luther's ideas.

The only reason Luther was not faced with the Inquisition himself was due to his German benefactor, the elector of Saxony. Holy Roman emperors were actually elected; they did not automatically inherit the throne. Electors were stationed throughout the Holy Roman Empire, and without the support of the elector of Saxony, Charles V would likely have faced problems. To win the throne, all he needed was a majority of electors, but he likely feared that if the elector of Saxony was not on board, other electors would decide to defect. It was a political game of chess, and Charles did not want to lose. This was a fear that both Charles V and the pope shared. So, although Luther was excommunicated from the church for his "heretical" beliefs, he remained physically unharmed.

Nevertheless, the turbulence of the Reformation clearly had an effect on Charles V and his decision to clamp down and use the tools of the Inquisition under his jurisdiction. When Charles V lay on his deathbed, he passionately enjoined his son and successor to the Spanish throne, Philip II, to wholeheartedly pick up the Spanish Inquisition where he had left off.

And for the most part, Philip did just that. Philip II made sure that the dictates of the 1545 Council of Trent were enforced. The Council of Trent was largely prompted by the eruption of the Protestant

Reformation and the subsequent Counter-Reformation. The council sought to reaffirm what the church believed in the face of the rumblings of the Reformation. It also sought to address what would be considered heretical and how such heresies should be addressed. In essence, these were clear and updated guidelines for the inquisitors.

In light of the Council of Trent, Philip II largely let the machinery of the Inquisition run its course as planned. Even so, there were times when even Philip II was aghast at how quickly things could get out of control. For instance, in the aftermath of the Council of Trent, an esteemed theologian, Friar Luis de León, quickly found himself in the crosshairs of the Inquisition. Friar Luis and some other theologians discussed the merits of a new translation of the Bible. The translation purportedly went back to the original Hebrew of the Old Testament for a more accurate rendering of the text.

Friar Luis applauded these efforts only to find himself condemned since the Council of Trent had declared the Latin Vulgate translation should be held as the ultimate authority. Luis's championing of the new translation was, therefore, deemed to be heretical according to the guidelines that had been laid down at the council. As a result, Luis came very close to being burned at the stake for his remarks.

He was only saved by a last-minute intervention from Philip II himself in 1576. If Philip II had not stepped in, this friar most likely would have died.

The most dangerous thing about the Inquisition was its snowball effect. The lines were so finely drawn that the merest perceived deviation could set the dreaded machinery of the Inquisition in motion. There were clearly those who knew that what was happening was wrong, but once the wheels started to spin, they proved almost impossible to stop.

Philip II would be succeeded by his son, Philip III, in 1598. Under Philip III, the Spanish Inquisition would reach another new low (although it was likely seen as a high back then) when it was decided that a massive expulsion of Moriscos was in order. As mentioned earlier in this book, the Jews were expelled from Spain in 1492. Now the inquisitors turned their attention toward the Moriscos.

The Moriscos were Muslims who had converted to Christianity. This conversion was done under intense pressure from the Crown, and even once they converted, other Christians often suspected them of being "false converts." This, of course, demonstrates the irony of what the

Catholic authorities sought in Iberia. Catholic leaders pressured Jews and Muslims to convert, and once they did, many Christians subsequently refused to believe that their conversion was sincere. Inquiries were then demanded to test the sincerity of their faith.

Although the Moriscos were routinely accused of various heresies, for the most part, they had escaped massive, wholesale retribution. There were a few reasons for this. For one thing, the Moriscos, unlike the Conversos, tended to live away from city centers in more rural and remote regions that were often out of the reach of inquisitors. The Moriscos also tended to be self-sufficient farmers. They did not have much valuable wealth that could be readily seized (tomatoes and goats were not as attractive as silver and gold), thereby eliminating a monetary motive to go after them. Moriscos were also less integrated into Christian society, which, paradoxically, seemed to spare them.

The Conversos, on the other hand, were wealthy, lived right in the middle of urban centers, and did everything they could to fit in with the "Old Christians." Yet, no matter how hard they tried, they were only continuously investigated.

Although much attention was paid to the Conversos, the Moriscos were the ones who would have presented a real threat to the status quo. Due to their close familiarity with the culture of neighboring North Africa, it does not take much imagination to consider Morisco communities occasionally lending aid to Moorish incursions coming from the North African coast.

At any rate, it was really only after the persecution of the Conversos had fully run its course that the Moriscos were scrutinized. The notion of expelling them outright had become a popular course of action by the time of Philip III, although some of his officials continued to advise against it. The debate continued over the next few years, with Philip III's own confessor officially coming out against it in 1602.

The confessor expressed his disgust that any baptized Christians, whether they were Morisco or not, would be expelled to Muslim-controlled North Africa. Nevertheless, on April 4th, 1609, the long-discussed plans were finally executed when Philip III officially decreed that the expulsion would indeed go forward. It was a sad and sorry sight that involved Spanish troops rounding people up and hauling them away to the nearest ports to be shipped to North Africa.

The Moriscos were apparently just dumped in North Africa with no consideration at all over where they would go or what they would do. Some were welcomed by local communities and treated well, but many more were ruthlessly preyed upon. As Philip III's confessor had feared, the Moriscos largely met an unpleasant fate.

In the midst of this tragedy, some exceptions were made. Moriscos in good standing who had parish priests who could readily vouch that they were "good Christians" could gain an exemption from the expulsion. Allowance was also made for children under fourteen years of age as long as their parents agreed to give up any right to them.

One can only imagine the hard decisions that many Morisco parents ultimately had to make. It might have been nearly unbearable to give up their children, yet at the same time, they probably knew they would likely fare far better in their native-born Spain than to be sent to an ancestral homeland in North Africa that they knew practically nothing about.

All in all, it is said that around twenty-five thousand Moriscos were able to stay in Spain. Those who were expelled numbered somewhere in the hundreds of thousands. It seems that after the expulsion of the Moriscos, much of the Spanish Inquisition turned inward. The so-called "Old Christians" would largely be targeted with routine inquiries as to whether they were true Christians or not.

Even though exact numbers remain elusive, the estimates of those who are believed to have been killed or exiled during the course of the Spanish Inquisition are staggering. Some estimates come up with the figure of 300,000, which is not as bad as the estimates that put the death toll in the millions. Regardless, 300,000 people is still a shocking number. Populations were typically much smaller back then, so to consider 300,000 people perishing by steady, systematic executions instead of war or disease is rather difficult to contemplate.

Chapter 4: The Portuguese Inquisition

"A prisoner in the Inquisition is never allowed to see the face of his accuser, or of the witnesses against him, but every method is taken by threats and tortures, to oblige him to accuse himself, and by that means corroborate their evidence."

-John Foxe

So much historical emphasis has been placed on the Spanish Inquisition that it is quite easy to overlook the Inquisition that was simultaneously taking place within the borders of Spain's closest neighbor—Portugal. The two main players in the Portuguese Inquisition were King João III of Portugal (King John III) and his little brother Henrique (Henry), who just so happened to be a prominent priest in the Catholic Church.

King João III officially kicked off the Portuguese Inquisition in 1536. Although the Inquisition was initially limited to just Portugal, it would soon spread to Portugal's growing overseas territories. Portuguese colonies in South America, Africa, and Asia would all be fair game for the Inquisition.

Henrique would become the first inquisitor general for Portugal in 1539. Henrique was a colorful character and was able to rise to the upper echelons of the Portuguese elite. Born a prince and brother of King João III, he would go on to become archbishop before becoming a cardinal. He then became an official papal legate and ultimately the king of

Portugal, all while retaining his title and role as inquisitor general.

Henrique's unique status within the church and the state would ultimately allow him to make use of the levers of power perhaps more than any other inquisitor. Upon becoming king of Portugal, practically any previous check on his power had been removed. One could not complain to the state apparatus about the measures used by this inquisitor general since he wielded all of the power of the state in his own hands.

Around this time, the Jesuits came to prominence in Portugal. Interestingly, one of Henrique's predecessors, King João III, requested that the Jesuits march themselves to the front lines of the Portuguese Inquisition in 1550. This request was ultimately declined by none other than the founder of the Jesuits, Ignatius of Loyola.

Nevertheless, the Portuguese Inquisition would really heat up by 1560 when the green light was given to launch a major inquisition in the Portuguese overseas territory of India. The Portuguese had oppressed residents of different faiths in the region for some time. India is traditionally Hindu. The Muslims had also invaded and made inroads in the southwest long before the Portuguese arrived in the area.

The Muslim invasion/occupation created large pockets of Muslim faithful in what today constitutes Pakistan. But besides that, India predominantly remained a Hindu-believing nation. The Portuguese arrived on the scene in the 16th century, famously proclaiming that they were in search of spices and Christians. The fact that the Portuguese reached India at all was astonishing. The road to India had long been shut down, ever since Turkish Muslims conquered the previous Greek Christian powerhouse of the Byzantine Empire.

The capital of the Byzantine Empire, Constantinople (now Istanbul), was overrun in 1453, and the old roads to the East were effectively shut off. The only way to reach India was by water. However, the Muslim powers had a monopoly over land routes and the traditional waterways. It was relatively easy for a Muslim fleet to sail from the eastern Islamic-controlled ports across the Persian Gulf to India.

The Portuguese, on the other hand, had to face a much harder trek. Their water voyage would have them sailing from western Europe and then south all the way to the southern tip of Africa. After rounding the tip, they would take a northeasterly route to India. Considering what a long and hard journey that must have been, those who saw the Portuguese were indeed astonished that they had even attempted the trip. They were then further perplexed when asked for spices and Christians.

The spices might not sound all that strange, but sailing to India just to find Christians might seem a bit odd. But as strange as it might sound, it was the truth. It had long been rumored that there were pockets of Christians in the Far East, perhaps even in India. The Portuguese did find a small minority of Nestorian Christians living in India, but the Portuguese were greatly depressed at how small and limited the group was.

Nevertheless, the Portuguese set up shop in Goa and eventually created a powerful outpost. They began to control this fledging colony with an iron fist. Even before the Inquisition, the Portuguese began to throw their weight around with their non-Christian subjects. They shut down Hindu temples and mosques, insisting that only churches remain open. They also banned the worship of idols and the display of other non-Christian symbols.

These acts set the stage for the Inquisition, which would erupt in Goa in the year 1560. The Hindus, in particular, were targeted, as their religious beliefs were often greatly misunderstood and perceived as being diabolical, even demonic. Considering some of the idols used in Hinduism, such as an elephant with many heads, it is not hard to understand why the Portuguese might have thought as much.

However, Hinduism, which is itself a monotheistic faith just like Judaism, Christianity, and Islam, is still greatly misunderstood to this day. Hindus believe in just one all-powerful god or "Brahman." But they also believe that everything in the universe, in one way or another, is a manifestation of this supreme being. All of their many "gods" are merely a manifestation of this supreme source of consciousness.

Hindus view the supreme being as a kind of dreamer whose very thoughts manifest as all of creation. Rocks, trees, humans, and even the supposed Hindu gods are said to be manifestations of this divine source. However, the Portuguese did not appreciate this complex theology and attempted to shut it down in the colony they administered.

The original conversion process of the local population of Goa was a complicated process. The first "converts" were the wives of the Portuguese settlers. Portuguese men who settled in the region began marrying local women and settling down with them shortly after their arrival. These women and their children would have been considered new converts to Christianity.

As this small base of Christians grew, financial and political incentives for those who converted to Christianity became clear. It has been said that in the first phase of Christianization, many locals converted willingly because of these special privileges.

However, if you were a new convert to Catholicism during the time when the Inquisition ramped up, many inquiries might be made into the true nature of your faith. And similar to what happened with the Conversos of Spain, the locals in India who did convert were subjected to intense scrutiny, with their every action and motivation being called into question. In all, it is estimated that over sixteen thousand local converts faced the wrath of the Portuguese Inquisition from 1560 to 1774.

Some of these converts were killed, and many were tortured. Others had their lives greatly disturbed by all of the incessant questionings of the inquisitors. At times, whole villages were punished, and in some cases, they were even burned to the ground on the mere suspicions of a few individuals.

In another bizarre twist, the Christian Portuguese took a page out of the playbook of the Muslim conquerors who had passed through the region before. In a move that was similar to the Islamic tax on non-believers—the jizya—the Portuguese issued their own discriminatory tax, which they referred to as the Xenddi, against Hindus. Even those who were already Christians were not immune. Even though the Indian Nestorian Christians were nominally of the Christian faith, they were not of the Catholic faith. That alone was enough for them to be suspect.

The same could be said for Portuguese relations with Ethiopia during this period. For the Ethiopians, relations with Portugal would become a bit of a mixed bag. It is true that the Portuguese rushed in to help defend Ethiopia from an Islamic invasion in the 1540s. If the Portuguese had not done so, Ethiopia (at least the Christian variation of it) likely would have been destroyed.

However, Ethiopians were Orthodox Christians, and it was not long before they were pressured by the Portuguese to become proper Catholics. Under the Portuguese Inquisition, Hindus, Nestorians, and Orthodox Christians were all targets. Buddhists were also in the Inquisition's crosshairs.

In 1540, the Portuguese enacted penal laws in their possessions in Southeast Asia, which expressly forbid the public profession of Buddhism, Hinduism, and Islam. In the Portuguese-controlled Canarim region of southern India, the Portuguese tried their hand at making inquiries into the religious lives of the local Buddhist population. The most astounding of these encounters was when the Portuguese actually seized Buddha's tooth.

To be clear, no one knows if the relic really was Buddha's tooth or not, but it was revered by the locals as such. And yet the Portuguese wanted to destroy this sacred artifact that the Buddhist community held so dear. The king of Pegu even declared that he would pay a huge amount of money if the relic was returned, but the Portuguese refused to hand it over. Instead, the Portuguese took the relic out in a public place for all to see and smashed it to dust. This was indeed the legacy of the Portuguese Inquisition in the Far East.

Even more disturbing was how the Portuguese carried out the practice of forcibly converting the local children in their far-flung territories. In Gao, the Portuguese did not actively force conversion upon adults, but they did force all orphans into the fold.

Such efforts were backed by the Portuguese royal authority under a direct order issued in 1559. The decree stated, "All children of heathens in the city and island of Goa who are left without father and without mother, and without grandfather or grandmother or any other forbears, and who are not yet of an age when they have a proper understanding and reasoned judgment should forthwith be taken and handed over to the College of Sao Paulo of the Company of Jesus in the said city of Goa, in order that they may be baptized, educated and catechized by the Fathers of the said College."

As much as the local priests may have liked to take these orphans under their wing to indoctrinate them at a young age, surviving relatives were not always so keen to allow such a thing to happen. It was reportedly common for relatives to gather up these orphans and "smuggle" them to territories outside of Portuguese control just so they could avoid being subjected to such a fate.

Monetary persecution was just as bad for the so-called "New Christians" who had fallen under suspicion of the Portuguese Inquisition. Beginning in the year 1563, Cardinal Henrique requested and was granted permission to seize the lands of those who were suspect; anyone could have just about anything taken from them at any time.

In what was little more than a strange twist of fate, Henrique became king. He was essentially a last resort due to a lack of descendants. In

1578, this cardinal king was crowned. It was a short-lived intermission of sorts since Henrique would perish in 1580. But during that brief span of time, the Portuguese Inquisition took on dramatic proportions, as the state and religious inquisitors became one and the same.

All of this drama came to a close with Henrique's passing in January 1580. Unlike many of his predecessors, who often preferred to live in the moment, the forward-thinking Henrique had the presence of mind to consider what might happen after he was gone. Since he was a priest, he obviously was not going to have a natural heir, so he made careful arrangements for what should happen upon his passing.

Henrique made provisions for Portugal to be governed by a board of five administrators until a proper successor could be chosen. And after Henrique perished, this legislative body had to figure out who would take the throne. Most of the people favored Philip II of Spain. The notion of a union between the Spanish and Portuguese crowns had been spoken of by the Spanish and Portuguese elite for some time. Many wondered if Philip II would be the one to finally achieve such a feat.

However, not everyone welcomed such an idea, and there would be considerable pushback against the unification of Iberia. A faction developed in opposition to Philip II led by a man named António, who was the illegitimate grandchild of the former Portuguese King Manuel I. António's claim was weak, but he was willing to roll the dice. After gathering a force of about twenty thousand loyal troops, he marched on Lisbon.

Things came to a head at the Battle of Alcantara, which saw António's forces crushed. António was forced to flee, and he lived out the rest of his life as a fugitive in exile.

All of this paved the way for Philip II to take the throne of Portugal for himself, with no further opposition to the merger of Spain and Portugal. And with the merger of Spain and Portugal would come the merger of the Spanish and Portuguese Inquisitions.

Their enemies also merged into one as well, which was indicated when Spain's archnemesis began to assault the Portuguese. Who was the archnemesis of the Spanish (and subsequently Portuguese) Empire at this time? The Ottoman Turks? The Barbary pirates of the Mediterranean? No. Their archnemesis was their Protestant rivals, the Dutch.

There are many reasons the Dutch turned their guns on the Iberian Union. Ideologically, they were at arms since the Dutch, many of whom embraced the teachings of John Calvin, were viewed by Catholics as heretics of the worst sort. There were also political and military consequences to consider. Philip II of Spain had been battling the Dutch over dominance of the Netherlands since 1568.

As both the Spanish and the Dutch expanded their dealings overseas, they would come to challenge each other on just about every level. And as soon as the Portuguese united with the Spanish, the Dutch essentially viewed them as fair game. Unfortunately for the Portuguese, their possessions in the Far East were far more vulnerable to Dutch encroachment, and as such, they became frequent targets of the Dutch from that point forward.

Throughout this period of hostility, the Inquisition would wax and wane at various intervals until it petered out in the 18th century. Although the exact date of the Portuguese Inquisition's termination is not known, it can be said that the Portuguese Inquisition was greatly curtailed after Portugal regained its sovereignty. The Iberian Union ultimately came to an end in 1640.

Various power struggles would ensue, leading to the infamous Pombaline dictatorship in 1755. Under Pombal, the Portuguese Inquisition really ran out of gas. Pombal did not have the religious zeal of his predecessors, so he put a stop to inquisitors applying pressure on Conversos and other religious suspects. He instead used the apparatus as his own form of secret police against his political opponents. Although there is no clear endpoint, the Portuguese Inquisition had lost sense of its original purpose and would become entirely meaningless as a result. It is estimated that several thousand local inhabitants were negatively impacted in one way or another as the Portuguese Inquisition ran its course.

Chapter 5: The Roman Inquisition

"You find this curious fact, that the more intense has been the religion of any period and more profound has been the dogmatic belief—the greater has been the cruelty and the worse has been the state of affairs. In the so called age of faith, when men really did believe the Christian religion in all its completeness, there was the Inquisition, with its tortures; there were millions of unfortunate women burnt as witches; and there was every kind of cruelty practiced upon all sorts of people in the name of religion."

-Bertrand Russell

Both the Portuguese and the Spanish Inquisitions had characteristics that were unique to the lands from which they originated. For those who viewed the happenings of these twin Inquisitions from the outside, though, these distinctions were not always clear. Regardless of one's own personal religious convictions, much of what was taking place was easily confused with political conditions on the ground rather than being solely a result of religious feeling. In the meantime, in other Catholic strongholds, especially the northernmost Catholic regions, those who were deemed to be heretics were largely at the mercy of regional governors rather than some grand inquisition.

As it pertains to Rome of the 16th century, which, of course, was the very heart of Roman Catholicism, there were many more factors in play. Looming largest of all was the Reformation that kickstarted in 1517. The Roman response to the Reformation did not create a vast inquisition comparable to that of Spain or Portugal, but it did ignite a more regional variant of religious inquiry into who was really a Christian.

The fact that the Italian Peninsula, of which Rome was a part, was still divided among various powers at this point played a big role in the relative disunity and regional nature of the Roman Inquisition. Italy itself would not become a unified country until the 19th century, and the regional nature of the Roman Inquisition largely reflects this reality. Under the Roman Catholic Church's immediate control were the Papal States and a few other obscure territories.

It could be said that the most well-defined divergences of approach between the Spanish, Portuguese, and Roman Inquisitions could be found within the confines of the Eternal City—Rome itself. Due to the Reformation, much of Christendom had been split between Catholic and Protestant, and there were many divergences between the two major groups of religious thought.

The effects of the Reformation were further inflamed by the Catholic response, as the church declared the Counter-Reformation, of which the Roman Inquisition was a part. There was also the Council of Trent, which was a series of meetings between 1545 and 1563. The decisions made at the council would have quite a bit to do with ideological thought.

A few years prior to the start of the Council of Trent, the Roman Inquisition officially began. On July 4th, 1542, Pope Paul III issued a bull that, among other things, authorized Rome's own version of the Inquisition. Unlike the inquisitions in the Iberian Peninsula, there was no grand inquisitor. Rather, there was a group of six cardinals handpicked by the pope. These cardinals were all dubbed inquisitor generals and given equal power to make inquiries into alleged instances of deviation from the faith.

These inquisitors also had the power to deputize others and essentially make them inquisitors. They could deputize inquisitors outside of Rome if it was deemed appropriate. That same fateful year of 1542, the Roman Inquisition, along with looking for heretics, compiled a list of so-called heretical books, which were then subsequently banned.

The list was further revised in 1559 under the comprehensive heading of the "Index of Prohibited Books and Authors." The list would again be updated in 1564, right after the conclusion of the Council of Trent.

It has been said that the Roman inquisitors basically worked from the same script as their peers in Iberia, but one big difference was the fact that their inquiries were largely kept from the public eye. In contrast to the humiliating public spectacles, which ironically were quite reminiscent of the Roman Games held in Roman coliseums, the Roman Inquisition of the 16th century was a much more muted affair. It largely took place behind closed doors and away from the public. All hearings were carried out according to well-worn manuals that the inquisitors had at their disposal, such as the aptly named *Directorium Inquisitorum*, which was compiled by an Aragon inquisitor named Nicholas Eymerich in 1376.

The work was edited and revised in 1578 to better meet the situations in which Roman inquisitors found themselves. Much of this editing involved the deletion of sections that pertained to instances found only in Aragon. Other sections were revised to be more appealing to Rome. It is important to understand that while the Spanish and Portuguese inquisitors were largely influenced by the Reconquista and the continuing question of how to handle those Christians who were suspected of having alternate allegiances, Rome was much more interested in rooting out Protestants.

Ironically, Italy was often a place of refuge for those same souls fleeing the Spanish and Portuguese Inquisitions! Italy was the go-to place of asylum for many Jews and Conversos during the height of Iberia's Inquisition.

Only after it was certain that the Protestant threat had been subdued, the inquisitors of Rome began to turn their attention to the more subtle matters of theological differences within the Catholic Church itself. Many of the charges being sent to the inquisitors were of instances of local superstition and magical beliefs. Those accused of such were not necessarily entirely at odds with Christianity; they were simply accused of using unauthorized addendums to the faith of which the Catholic Church did not approve.

The phenomenon of locals attaching their own superstitions to Catholic beliefs was by no means a new phenomenon. Ever since the pagan cultures of Europe first embraced Christianity, there were always instances of local superstitions being incorporated into their new faith. All one has to think of is Ireland's patron saint, Saint Patrick, being adorned with the Celtic good luck charm of the four-leaf clover, and one immediately understands how such things came into being.

Local communities all over the world had more than their share of homegrown superstitions, and many of these indigenous superstitions remained even after being overlaid with Christian beliefs. The more rural regions of Italy, which Rome sought to either outright control or at least influence, were no exception. Due to the splintered nature of regional government in the Italian Peninsula during this time, it could even be convincingly argued that Italy had even more local superstitions than Spain or Portugal.

These alternative practices that ran contrary to official church teachings were often referred to as the "popular religion" of the local people. In consideration of this, it is important to note that since the Roman Inquisition was highly decentralized and left up to regional officials, this allowed for fewer chances of gross misunderstandings. Those appointed to make inquiries into a specific region likely had experience with that region and, therefore, were well aware of the local people's beliefs.

The inquisitor would be much more understanding of and sympathetic to those who were charged, likely resulting in a more lenient and merciful result. For example, if a local had some peculiar practice of shoving a crucifix into the ground and dancing around it to facilitate the growth of their crops, a stranger unaware of the practice might have become so revolted that they felt compelled to order the superstitious local dragged before a tribunal on the spot. An inquisitor who was well versed in local superstitions would have immediately understood this was a local practice and that the person who carried it out meant no harm. The accused would have been viewed as ignorant rather than a criminal, and efforts would have been made to reeducate them rather than punish them.

This was indeed one of the purposes of the Council of Trent: to have inquisitors develop enough discretion among them to be able to determine true heretics from those who were simply uninformed. And the inquisitors of Rome knew full well that in remote regions of the surrounding Italian countryside, there were plenty of well-meaning souls who simply had not been properly informed of standard Catholic protocol. Throughout the Roman Inquisition, at least as it pertained to these misguided souls, there was much leniency.

However, if someone was blatantly practicing witchcraft or some clearly anti-Christian form of mysticism, action was taken. A 17th-century work was used to determine who was a witch and who was not. This inquisitorial guide entitled "Instruction for conducting trial procedure in case of witches, sorcerers, and injurious magicians" was authored by Cardinal Giovanni Garcia Mellini and was first published in 1625.

The title might sound fairly ironic to us today, but it was a clear attempt by those in charge of the Roman Inquisition to lay out some benchmarks when it came to distinguishing the mildly superstitious from those who were considered far more dangerous. Part of the reason behind all of this was the fact that there were some in Rome who actually became concerned that the Roman inquisitors in more remote backwater regions were being a bit too lenient. Some feared that real witches and warlocks were slipping through the fingers of these more moderate Roman inquisitors. Therefore, this text sought to set the record straight so that there would be no chance for confusion between who was a real threat and who was practicing their ancestral superstitions.

As evidence of the slow-moving nature of the Roman Inquisition, witchcraft was not made a capital offense until 1623. The inquisitors of Spain and Portugal had been putting many people to death on charges that were far less criminal than openly practicing witchcraft.

However, one must realize that the Roman Inquisition was a process that evolved during its duration. The centralized power of Rome also had far less control over regional inquisitors, and it would take many instances of reproach to redirect them.

In the same vein as the Spanish and Portuguese Inquisitions, the Roman Inquisition began with an initial onslaught against a certain threat. In Iberia, the threat had been alternate religions, such as Islam and Judaism. For Italy, the main threat was Protestantism. However, in all three inquisitions, after the initial threat, whether it be Judaism, Islam, or Protestantism, had been alleviated, the focus of the Inquisition turned toward local Catholic believers. For regions farther afield and out of Rome's reach, such as Venice, which at that time was its own autonomous republic, the pope could only hope to use his massive influence to have an impact on how the Venetians carried out their own form of the Inquisition.

Perhaps most distressing to authorities in Rome was the fact that the Venetians seemed to give refuge to Protestants from time to time. The Venetians usually saw things differently and often took umbrage to what they saw as meddling in their internal affairs. Nevertheless, by the early 1600s, the Venetians began to comply with the edicts of Rome more readily and routinely consulted with the Roman inquisitors as to the best practices to be employed for their own inquiries.

This was perhaps most notably demonstrated during the 1633 inquiry of the astronomer Galileo Galilei. Galileo had stoked the wrath of religious officials by having the gall to declare that the earth revolved around the sun rather than the sun revolving around the earth. Such things are laughable today, but it was considered a serious error at the time.

One of the reasons that such a belief might have been frightening for theologians of the day was due to the fact that the Book of Joshua records a great miracle in which the "sun stood still." During this celebrated biblical event, the sun miraculously stood still in the sky, allowing more daylight for Joshua to carry out his battle. The discovery that the earth revolves around the sun rendered such a feat seemingly impossible.

Fortunately for Galileo, he was allowed to give a simple (although not sincere) apology and was spared the worst of what the Inquisition could have meted out. The Roman advisors, who allowed for leniency, were owed some small thanks for this.

However, not all who fell under the scrutiny of the Roman Inquisition were that fortunate, as was clearly indicated in the case of Giordano Bruno, a Dominican friar. This friar found himself accused of trespassing key Catholic foundational beliefs in regard to the Trinity, the nature of Christ's divinity, and the matter of transubstantiation (the act of turning the wine and bread during Communion into Christ's blood and flesh).

Bruno was also accused of developing some more mystical views, such as ones hinting at pantheism and even the transmigration of souls. Pantheism refers to the belief that the entire universe is a manifestation of God and that there is some essence of God in everything. Those who subscribe to pantheism believe that even the most average of average Joes is actually God and does not even know it.

According to a pantheist, it is only when this average Joe's physical form expires that he wakes up to the reality of his true nature. It could be compared to waking up from a dream, as this person would essentially return to reality and realize they had actually been God all along. They had just temporarily tricked some small aspect of themselves into thinking they were a mortal, finite human being.

These beliefs are complicated, but they are the sort of far-reaching concepts in which pantheists believed. And somehow or other, Bruno had come to believe such radical notions. He also considered the validity of the transmigration of souls or, as it is perhaps better known, reincarnation as a real possibility.

In light of such beliefs, Galileo's suggestion that the earth revolved around the sun could be overlooked as an error of ignorance, but Bruno's beliefs could not be viewed as anything other than heretical and an outright trespass against Catholic teaching. He would end up paying a high price for his views. He was interrogated, found guilty, and burned at the stake in 1600.

Interestingly, Bruno, like Galileo, made some rather forward-thinking assertions about the nature of cosmology. Bruno is widely viewed as one of the first to make the connection that every single star in the sky is actually a sun no different from the earth's own sun. Bruno realized that these suns simply look smaller in the nighttime sky because they are so far away.

Bruno also hypothesized that every one of the stars has planets like Earth revolving around them. The first exo-planet or extrasolar planet around another star system was not officially discovered until the early 1990s. Giordano Bruno was certainly a forward thinker.

But the Catholic Church was apparently not as concerned about these notions. It could be that such ideas were so far removed from the normal thought of the day that the scientific discoveries went over the heads of the Roman inquisitors. One can imagine an inquisitor thinking, "Stars are suns? That is patently absurd!" and then moving on to more conventional grounds for charges of heresy.

Bruno's death would have some unforeseen consequences and create significant blowback for the Roman Catholic Church. The Roman arm of the Inquisition had previously prided itself on its relative tolerance and had sought to "persuade" rather than "punish."

However, Bruno refused to be persuaded, and the inquisitors felt they had no choice but to punish him for his contrary beliefs. Bruno had contacts outside of the Catholic domain and was well known in Protestant circles. Bruno seems to have known that the whole world was watching, and it is said that he even warned the inquisitors as much.

When his death sentence was handed down, he supposedly stated, "You may be more afraid to bring that sentence against me than I am to accept it." And it was indeed with a heavy heart that Cardinal Robert Bellarmine, who was in charge of Bruno's inquisition, authorized Bruno's final punishment.

Several years later, when Galileo came under the scrutiny of the Inquisition, Bruno's case was front and center. It could be argued that the case of Bruno and the blowback it received made inquisitors tread more carefully when trying Galileo for his heretical beliefs.

Another interesting thing about the Inquisition and the suppression of supposed heretical beliefs involves Venice. Venice had a robust printing press, which greatly concerned the Roman Inquisition. The Roman Inquisition wanted to prevent the spread of Luther's ideas, so Venice's printing press worried the Roman Church. Remember, Martin Luther galvanized the Reformation by printing anti-church tracts on German printing presses, so the church's fear was well founded.

The Catholic Church was equally fearful of what might be coming out of Venice's printing press. During this period, Venice produced roughly half of all published works in Italy. If the presses in Venice began printing material contrary to church teachings, it would be a very big problem for the Roman Catholic Church. The Roman authorities had plenty of reasons to keep a close eye on what the Venetians were up to.

The authorities of Venice, for their part, cooperated with the pope. Venice was staunchly Catholic and shared much of the same values as Rome, but its cooperation came with some conditions. Venetians resented anything that would have been viewed as an overreach by Rome, and they most certainly did not want the Roman Inquisition to interfere with their lifeblood: trade.

Venice had long been a trading and merchant city. Since Venice was deeply entrenched in trade with so many parts of the world, the city routinely welcomed visitors of a wide variety of beliefs. As such, Venice was a frequent stomping ground of the Protestant faithful. The fact that Venice openly harbored Protestants stood at odds with much of the Catholic world, but it seems that throughout much of the Inquisition, Venice was allowed to be an exception to the rule.

Since these visitors were crucial to the Venetian economy, the Venetian authorities were not about to hand them over to the Inquisition. Instead, the Protestant visitors were typically given the green light to practice their faith how they saw fit as long as they did not interfere with the status quo.

In Venice, like much of the rest of the Italian Peninsula (Rome included), the Inquisition would ebb and flow to some degree until it was ended by the Napoleonic Wars in the early 1800s. By the end of the 18th

century and the dawning of the 19th century, events in France would prove to be disruptive for the Roman Inquisition.

First, there was the French Revolution, which rocked the Catholic world. This uprising was not only indifferent to the Inquisition's efforts; it was also initially outright hostile to the Catholic Church. It was not until the rise of General Napoleon Bonaparte as dictator or emperor of France that the church was welcomed again. The crafty Bonaparte realized the church's political power and restored friendly relations with Rome.

Even so, Napoleon saw to it that the Inquisition was either curtailed or eliminated altogether in most of the regions where he held sway, including Rome itself. After 1814, papal authority over such matters was restored. The Inquisition would start up again but largely in name only, with very little teeth to its religious inquests.

Then, in 1860, when efforts to unify Italy into the nation-state that we know it as today began in earnest, the inquisitors' abilities were diminished even further. The Inquisition focused only on inquiries in the Papal States.

Interestingly enough, one of the last vestiges of the Roman Inquisition was the index of banned books. It was not rescinded until 1966, when it was officially absolved by Pope Paul VI. Although the Roman Inquisition was milder and more regulated than its predecessors, it could be said that the legs of this Inquisition were the longest of them all.

Like the other inquisitions, there are no firm numbers of how many died in the Roman Inquisition. It was likely in the thousands, but it is not known if it was in the tens of thousands.

Chapter 6: Crime and Punishment during the Inquisition

"It is in the name of Jesus, himself become God, that fanaticism ignominiously condemned to the stake men like Giodano Bruno, Vanini, Etienne Dolet, John Huss, Savanarola, and numerous other heroic victims; that the Inquisition ordered Galileo to belie his conscience; that thousands and thousands of unfortunates accused of witchcraft were burnt alive in popular ceremonies; it was the express benediction of Pope Gregory XIII that the butchery of St. Bartholomew drenched Paris in blood."

-Camille Flammarion

The subject of crime and punishment is, of course, always of great importance when talking about any society. All societies have rules, and there has to be some sort of consequence for those who break them. Thus, rules and consequences were of great importance during the time of the Inquisition as well.

Of course, during the Inquisition, what could be considered a crime often depended on who was doing the interpreting. Many things that might not be considered a crime today were considered terrible crimes back in the days of the Inquisition. Some of the crimes inquisitors focused on were rather common, such as theft, forgery, smuggling, and even pure and simple disrespect of authority figures. Most of these are crimes today. But other crimes, such as witchcraft, are not considered crimes today, at least for the most part. However, this was not the case during the Inquisition.

There was also something referred to as ecclesiastical laws. This was a set of laws that had to do with the religious code of conduct rather than the state's legal code.

One of the most interesting aspects of the Inquisition that is often missed or overlooked is that a large part of it consisted of those who openly confessed to just about any perceived infraction. As the Inquisition continued its course, it naturally created a climate of paranoia and fear. It was well known that those who confessed to transgressions were more likely to get off easy than those who stubbornly insisted they did nothing wrong. After all, torture was reserved for those who insisted they had committed no transgression.

In many ways, considering the climate of the time, when an inquisitor came to a local community, it often provided an opportunity to clear the air. There were many instances in which townspeople would approach an inquisitor and begin openly confessing to some milder transgressions. For instance, in Spain, a man by the name of Gonzalez Ruiz had been heard boisterously declaring during a game of cards that even if God was on his opponent's side, he still would not be able to beat him.

The account does not specify whether the man won his card game or not, but it does recall him groveling at the feet of an inquisitor while declaring himself guilty of uttering such a sacrilegious statement. This man likely would not have mentioned anything if it were not for the fact that he feared someone else would tattle on him. Instead, with great relief, he openly confessed to his supposed transgression. The inquisitor was pleased with the man's confession and penance and moved on to make further inquiries.

However, there were some who actually ended up making repeat confessions, some to the worst crimes. Perhaps the people had actually transgressed and felt a heavy weight on their hearts, or maybe these people suffered from some sort of neurotic condition. Regardless, those who repeatedly confessed put themselves under terrible scrutiny and faced harsh punishments.

But the most dangerous aspect of the whole thing by far was when the actual accusations were kept secret from the accused. Yes, that is right. A person would be accused of something, hauled before an inquisitor, and then be denied the basic right of knowing what they were accused of in the first place. It is because of terrible moments like these in history that the US Constitution guarantees citizens the right to know what crimes they are accused of and who did the accusing.

At any rate, the records of the Inquisition are full of accounts of people being subjected to the rack, water torture, or some other terrible punishment. People were more than ready to confess due to the pain; however, they had no idea what they were supposed to confess to. There are direct quotes of these miserable souls crying out, "Please tell me what I did, and I will confess to it! Please! Anything to end this pain!"

And yet these torturers, hoping to get the accused to confess on their own without any prompting, remained silent as the excruciating torture session continued. Even without applied torture, the guessing game of trying to figure out what one was being accused of was ridiculously excruciating in itself. This was evidenced by a case in Córdoba, Spain, in 1528. A man by the name of Diego de Uceda was accused of being a closet Protestant simply because of a conversation he had with some random stranger he had just met.

However, Diego had no idea that this random encounter was what had brought him to the inquisitors. He spent several months attempting to argue against all manner of other intrigues and supposed grievances. If he had simply known what it was that he was being accused of, he could have saved everyone a lot of time and energy.

Those who knew what they were likely to be accused of could beat the inquisitor (as well as any nosy neighbors) to the punch by denouncing themselves. And these people were likely better off for it.

Ultimately, the punishments for those who found themselves on the wrong side of the Inquisition fell into three distinct categories. Those categories consisted of those who were either "absolved," given instructions for "penance," or were "relaxed."

For the lucky few who found themselves in the absolved category, they were essentially absolved of any guilt and sent on their way. However, most fell into the category of penance. They were expected to take on some sort of punishment for their perceived errors.

The "relaxed" category is sinisterly deceptive. At first glance, we might think this category would have been a good and fortunate thing. There is nothing better than a little rest and relaxation, right? But people back then were not granted some sort of relaxing vacation, at least not in how we would think of it. Those who were relaxed were those destined to be burned at the stake!

The most common punishment was penance. One of the most common forms of penance was for someone to wear the infamous sackcloth called the *saco bendito*. The term literally means "blessed sack." Wearing a sackcloth as a punishment dates back to the 13th century. During the height of the Albigensian War, the sackcloth was forced onto the shoulders of the heretical sect known as the Cathars.

The practice was subsequently revised and brought into practice by Tomás de Torquemada. During the Spanish Inquisition, the inquisitor would give someone an exact sentence or period of time to wear this miserable and unsightly sackcloth. The garment was meant to mark those who wore it as sinners and served the express purpose of humiliating them among their peers in the community.

In today's world, we often take umbrage to any form of shaming. The internet is dedicated to combating instances of body shaming, hobby shaming, political shaming, and just about anything else you can think of. During the Inquisition, however, shaming was not considered a bad thing at all.

On the contrary, shaming was considered a necessary punishment. And the whole community was encouraged to take part in it. Just imagine being forced to wear this unsightly get-up called the *saco bendito* and having folks openly jeer at you as you walk to the market. It would not have been fun, but, of course, that was the whole point.

Being forced to wear this garment of shame may have been viewed as a more lenient punishment than being burned at the stake or tossed onto the rack, but the psychological damage must have been immense all the same. Having to wear this garish, sheep-skin coat, rain or shine, was probably enough to make one lose all sense of their original identity and purpose in life.

Prior to being forced to don the *saco bendito*, someone may have been a proud banker, a merchant, or an apothecary. After being forced to wear the *saco bendito* for a prolonged period of time, all of this would change. They were no longer known as the merchant down the street but rather the horrible sinner who had been marked to do penance. No matter how high their station was before, they were brought low. They were deemed to be one of the most wretched and undesirable members of the community.

And on some rare occasions, the person was sentenced to wear the garment for life. But in almost all instances, this sentence was commuted, as such a thing would have been clearly ridiculous and impractical to impose for the duration of one's entire lifetime.

Another, albeit much more devastating, form of penance was to have the penitent serve on a galley. Just think of a bunch of people chained to oars on a boat, forced to continually row, and you get the idea of the kind of grueling and tedious existence a person faced.

During the Inquisition, crime and punishment were a harsh, hard-edged affair, and the exact retribution one might face often hinged on the inquisitor's whim. However, the greatest spectacle of crime and punishment during the Inquisition was the *auto-da-fé*. The *auto-da-fé* could be perhaps best summed up as a kind of elaborate show trial in which the whole community was encouraged to take part.

As mentioned earlier in the book, there was a great and concerted psychological lead-up to the main event of the *auto-da-fé*. First, the inquisitors would have the whole community meet at the local church. They would be delivered a full-blown sermon in which the merits of the Inquisition were lauded. Recriminations were made against those who might be under suspicion.

There were usually no direct accusations at this point, but there was a general condemnation of whatever happened to be the suspected evils of the community. Just imagine someone standing before a congregation and railing against those who drink too much and play cards late into the night. There may not have been any direct names called out at this point, but the stage was being set for those who would later be condemned.

Whether any actual crimes were being committed, these fire and brimstone sermons had the effect of making everyone feel somehow guilty. The thirty-day grace period would then be enacted, giving those with a guilty conscience time to confess. It also gave those who wished to point fingers the opportunity to rat out their family and friends.

There were many instances of children accusing their parents of committing various trespasses. Torquemada set down provisions that granted children a certain amount of immunity when they leveled accusations against their parents. One can only imagine the toxic atmosphere that such a thing would have created. If a youngster was diabolical enough, they could use the Inquisition as an excuse to get revenge on their parents for simply making them do too many chores. As unlikely as such a thing might seem, Torquemada's approach certainly opened the door to the possibility.

This toxic environment, which pitted neighbor against neighbor and even children against their parents, is reminiscent of what would later happen in communist China during Mao Zedong's Cultural Revolution in the 1960s and 1970s. It was a different time and a different place, but the phenomenon was remarkably similar. China's Cultural Revolution, just like the Spanish Inquisition before it, sought to redefine what a crime against the state was. And the way that Mao empowered teenagers in his Red Guards as minders was similar to how Torquemada empowered the youth during the Spanish Inquisition.

Mao had youth brigades going around China bullying adults who were deemed not "communist enough" in the same way children were being empowered by Torquemada's inquisition to rat out their parents for not being "Christian enough." Somehow, you just know that society has gone completely haywire when normally respectable adults are being bullied into submission by a bunch of kids. Society was turned upside down to the point that the very notion of crime and punishment had been subverted and twisted into something almost altogether unrecognizable.

Perhaps one of the clearest signs of justice run amok during the Inquisition was that it was common practice to dig up a dead person who had been tried and convicted of crimes. Of course, the dead were unable to participate in the justice system, but they were nonetheless dug up and put on trial. After they were found guilty (which, as you might surmise, happened more often than not), their bones would be burned. This is contrary to how most modern courts operate.

In most modern legal systems, the dead cannot be convicted because they are unable to attend their trial. For example, in modern America, even in cases in which killers are more or less proven through DNA evidence, if the alleged killer dies before being brought to trial, there is no posthumous conviction. But that was not the case during the Inquisition. Even the dead were not too far removed from the grand inquisitor's reach!

However, the most scandalous crimes that Torquemada had to tackle during his tenure often involved fellow church members. Torquemada became aware of a rather embarrassing trend among some lustful priests to take advantage of people in the confessional while they confessed their sins. Torquemada knew of several instances in which priests actually stained the confessional booth itself by having sinful relations with parishioners inside of it.

Due to the implications of such scandalous scenes playing out right under the pope's nose, this was no easy matter for Torquemada to address. Then, just as all too often the case now, the Catholic Church wished to keep such matters quiet. Torquemada was able to address the problem and mete out punishment to wayward priests, but it was done quietly and behind the scenes. There was no great *auto-da-fé* of condemnation. Instead, the priest was likely given some minor form of penance or perhaps just shuffled off to another location in the hopes that time and distance would correct his sinful behavior.

The greatest travesty of all was the fact that victims of predatory priests were often punished far greater than those who had preyed upon them. Writer and historian Jean Plaidy spoke of this in her epic work on the Inquisition and described the account of Father Joseph Peralta, who was accused of molesting a fourteen-year-old boy. The priest in question was given a slap on the wrist and was moved to a monastery where he was expected to quietly contemplate his actions. The boy, on the other hand, was publicly humiliated.

He was made to march through the streets while being jeered at by crowds of people and given the lash. It is said that the shock of this punishment was just too much for the child, and he perished shortly after. Such things are appalling to us today but were standard practice back then and were very rarely questioned. In the corrupt two-tiered legal system of the Inquisition, the clergy were given the benefit of the doubt and received a merciful sentence—two very important indulgences that the average person at the time did not get.

Perhaps the most psychologically frightening aspect of the Inquisition was the way people were occasionally snatched up by inquisitors in the middle of the night. There was no warning whatsoever, just a knock on one's door and a quick conveyance to the nearest dungeon. The accused were not allowed to question their captors, and if they made even the slightest disturbance, they were outfitted with a primitive sort of gag.

This medieval-styled gagging device was designed like an oblong pear, which was shoved into the protesting soul's mouth. If anyone has ever endured painful teeth x-rays at the dentist that involves biting down on a sharp instrument known as a bitewing, they have had a small taste of the prolonged pain of having a metal "pear" shoved into their mouth.

Such a comparison is slightly facetious, but it is perhaps the closest that any of us today might get to the feeling of having a hard object abrasively jammed against our gums and teeth. The dentist, of course, relieves us of this "torture" after a few minutes, whereas the inquisitors would keep such a device in place for several hours. And if they felt that it was not muffling their charge well enough, they would literally "turn the screws" to open the pear, applying even more pressure to make sure their charge would not be able to make a sound.

Those charged with heresy were bidden not to resist, and if they so much as cried out in protest, they would be brutally shut down. Once they were deemed sufficiently compliant, the accused were presented to the inquisitor, who then promptly proceeded to ignore them.

For the first few minutes, as the accused stood, shaking and trembling in fear, the inquisitor typically shuffled papers at his desk, pretending to be too absorbed in the charges to even look up. This behavior was no mere happenstance but pure and simple theater designed by Torquemada himself. Torquemada suggested this tactic in the first user manual he compiled.

All of this theater was perpetuated to increase the accused's apprehension and fear. As they stood there being completely ignored by the inquisitor and watching him shuffle through cracked pieces of parchment, the accused could only wonder what it was he was sifting through. Was there some diabolical charge already written up about them that the inquisitor was consulting? Or was it a list of punishments that he was contemplating?

After letting the frightened accused sit there with their thoughts for a moment, the inquisitor would look up, address the accused, and then bluntly ask them if they knew why they had been brought in. This was not because the inquisitor wanted to inform the accused and help clear things up. On the contrary, this was the beginning of the guessing game of demanding that the accused confess to whatever mysterious thing of which they had been accused.

In most modern societies, it is of the utmost importance for anyone accused of a crime to be promptly informed of what it is that they have been accused of. But once again, as it pertains to the Inquisition, all of these things had been entirely turned on their head. Instead of informing the accused of what they had done, the inquisitor was in the business of forcing the accused to come up with satisfactory admissions of guilt.

Yet this charade of a legal procedure would continue. After the accused were made to stand before the inquisitor, struggling to figure out why they were even there, the inquisitor would begin a round of what initially seemed to be rather innocuous questions. The accused would be asked simple things, such as whether they attended church services regularly. Most people in this situation would obviously answer, "Oh yes, quite regularly!"

But the inquisitor was seeking to lay a trap and would rattle off more specific questions about who their confessor was and the last time they went to confession. Many in this nerve-wracking condition might forget the name of their confessor, and most of them would certainly have a hard time recalling the last time they went to confession. And if they were found to have any inconsistencies at all, it would be used as ammunition against them.

Even though there was no direct physical torture at this stage, the interrogation was made to be as excruciating as possible. Furthermore, as per Torquemada's specific instructions, the inquisitors were to remain absolutely unmoved by the plight of the accused. If the accused were to break down and cry, pleading that they were a good Christian and had done nothing wrong, the inquisitor was to remain unfazed.

If the accused laid it on thick about how their family would suffer should something happen to them, the inquisitor was not to lend a sympathetic ear. Instead, he was supposed to view the accused as a kind of con artist of the worst kind, someone who would pretend to be in distress merely to get out of their just penance. It remains a bit hard to fathom how the inquisitors could have really believed such things considering the very real pain and sorrow that was likely expressed by those who stood before them.

Then again, the whole premise of the Inquisition was to find those who were supposedly deceptive enough to be Christians in name only while practicing heretical acts and beliefs in private. In their minds, they thought that if someone could pretend to be a Christian, then they could pretend to be in pain. At any rate, the inquisitor hoped that this first phase of fear tactics would be enough to break the suspect.

Those who were strong enough to resist these machinations would be taken off to be subjected to various physical tortures. There were many occasions when the torture served its purpose in quickly eliciting confessions, but problems were sometimes compounded when those who were tortured confessed to things other than what they were being charged with. Again, since accusations remained secret, it was a guessing game for those who decided to confess.

The main methods of physical torture were the rack, the hoist, and water torture. Of these, the hoist was perhaps the most terrifying method since it consisted of binding one's hands behind them before attaching the bound hands to a hoist, which could be slowly raised by a pulley that *hoisted* the victim up into the air.

Although this torture was typically not lethal (it could be if it was used for too long), being lifted up like this would be excruciatingly painful and would likely damage the joints of a person's arms and shoulders, perhaps even permanently. While some might have had their lives spared by making a last-minute confession, they very well might have left those torture chambers with their arms wrecked beyond recognition, leaving them permanently maimed for the rest of their life.

Water torture was not any better. During these horrid episodes, a suspected heretic was laid flat upside down on a ladder of sorts, which was propped up in a sloping position. This ensured that the subject had their feet at an angle higher than their heads. While they were in this precarious position, a metal contraption was put in the mouth, which ensured that it was left pried open, and wooden bits were stuffed up the person's nose.

This meant the only way this person could breathe was through their mouth. And while the subject was stuck in this state, a piece of cloth was draped over their open mouth. They could still breathe through the cloth, albeit slightly uncomfortably. Matters would soon get worse, though, as the torturers would dump water over the cloth. This would have the inevitable effect of the victim breathing in the damp cloth, giving them the sensation that they were being smothered.

If this sounds strikingly similar to the infamous waterboarding episodes conducted in modern times against suspected terrorists at the US military installation located in Guantanamo Bay, Cuba, you are not mistaken. Many parallels have been drawn between the two practices.

At any rate, punishments during the Inquisition were certainly not a pretty sight. But even so, there was a certain measure of restraint put on the inquisitors.

Although popular imagination often depicts these torture sessions as murder, the goal was not to inflict a grisly and terrible death. The goal was to get the accused to confess to being a heretic and perhaps even implicate others with accusations of their own.

No one was to die unless they were actually found guilty. Those who were ultimately deemed to be guilty and worthy of being burned at the stake were usually those who refused to give in to the pressure and continued to proclaim they were innocent. If someone was accidentally killed during the process of torture, the inquisitors involved were instructed to immediately cease and desist and head to the nearest priest to make a confession for their own sin of murder.

Even in the corrupt world of the Inquisition, it was not deemed acceptable to kill supposed heretics until the inquisitorial process had run its course. Inquisitors found to have overreached in this manner were made to step away from the process altogether in what essentially amounted to administrative leave.

As it pertained to the Inquisition, death was normally only meted out after the inquisitorial process had run its course and if the individual was found guilty. But as mentioned, the biggest problem of the accused was often the fact that they simply did not know what crime they were even being accused of.

At times, the supposed crime was not even really a crime itself but merely how the thought police of the Inquisition might have interpreted the supposed motives behind someone's actions. For example, someone deciding to take a rain check on eating a ham sandwich should not have been anything to get excited about. But in the eyes of the Inquisition, such a simple decision could be interpreted as a person refusing to eat pork on religious grounds.

This might seem like a silly example. What if the person simply had a stomach ache or just was not hungry at the time? But there were those willing to use such a silly assumption to inquire further into the people's lives. And this scenario actually happened in the 16th century. A Spanish woman by the name of Elvira del Campo declined to eat pork on a Saturday, and the next thing she knew, she was being reported to the Inquisition. However, as was standard procedure, she was not told the reason she had been brought in.

The situation escalated to torture, with ropes being tied around Elvira's arms. The ropes were pulled back until she cried out in pain. Elvira was more than willing to cooperate, but she did not know what was expected of her. The meticulous records of her inquisitors record her saying, "Señors, tell me what I have to say. I do not know what I have done. Loosen me, and I will tell the truth. I do not know what you wish me to say, but only tell me, and I will say it."

Yet, bizarrely enough, since the inquisitors required a "true confession," the torture continued. It seems that at some point, one of the inquisitors must have eventually given Elvira enough of a hint. According to the records, she confessed to having relapsed to Judaism and requested full "reconciliation to the Holy Catholic Church."

When the subject of refusing pork came up before, she simply said she did not like pork, but suddenly she was on the record saying she had been secretly practicing Judaism. This is likely because one of her inquisitors eventually felt sorry for her and coached her as to what they expected her to say. Willing to do anything to end the pain, she gladly agreed to confess; whether there was any truth in that confession or not is impossible to say.

Interestingly enough, the inquisitors were apparently not blind to the fact that innocent and God-fearing Christians might be wrongly tortured and condemned at their hands. One might think this would be enough to give them pause and reconsider what they were doing. But on the contrary, it was a common argument by the inquisitors that even if a few good Christians were condemned and even killed, their efforts were worth it to protect Christianity as a whole.

It was argued that Christians who were falsely accused and needlessly consigned to the flames had died a martyr's death. They had died for their faith and would be handsomely rewarded in heaven. These inquisitors seemed to live in their own little world of twisted logic and skewed ideals, and at times, they seemed to be making it up as they went along.

During the Inquisition, if there were no crimes, one was gladly created. If there were no heretics to be found, one was coached on how to be one. Those who told the truth were punished, and those who readily lied and gave false confessions were rewarded. This was indeed the sad state of affairs as it pertained to crime and punishment during much of the Inquisition.

Chapter 7: Papal Involvement

"The world calls for, and expects from us, simplicity of life, the spirit of prayer, charity towards all, especially towards the lowly and the poor, obedience and humility, detachment, and self-sacrifice. Without this mark of holiness, our word will have difficulty in touching the heart of modern man."

-*Pope Paul VI*

If one were to consider the full impact of the Inquisition, it is hard not to acknowledge the role that popes played during the process. After all, the popes were the greatest authority of Christianity at the time. It is true that the Spanish and Portuguese Inquisitions, in particular, had the potential for rogue actors, but at the end of the day, the popes had to at least give their tacit approval on what was being carried out.

In regards to the Inquisition, the main popes that come to mind are Pope Lucius III, Pope Sixtus IV, Pope Sixtus V, Pope Alexander VI, Pope Julius II, and Pope Leo X. In this chapter, we will take a closer look at the lives of these popes and their own personal involvement with the Inquisition that they presided over as heads of the church.

Pope Lucius III held the papal office a few centuries prior to the start of the official Inquisition in Spain and Portugal. Born in 1097, Lucius hailed from the Italian city of Lucca. He joined the clergy as a young man and steadily rose through the ranks, becoming a cardinal in 1138. In 1159, he was serving as an official papal legate before being promoted by Pope Adrian IV to the position of cardinal bishop of Ostia and Velletri. Lucius was also placed in charge of the Sacred College of Cardinals as its dean.

After many years of service, Lucius would become pope in September of 1181. He would take a strong stand against supposed acts of heresy. In 1184, he issued his infamous papal bull *Ad abolendam*, which declared that "counts, barons, rectors, consuls of cities and other places" must join in the fight against heresy.

Many have come to view this early call to take a stand against perceived heretics as an early push toward what would ultimately become the Inquisition. It must be noted that although the groundwork was laid, this pope did not officially make the Inquisition church policy. That would be left up to Pope Gregory IX in 1234. Gregory became pope in 1227 and started out as both an activist and a reformer.

In 1231, he issued the bull *Parens scientiarum*, which stipulated how to handle the University of Paris strike, which had occurred in 1229. The strike was in response to the previous handling of a riot that had erupted. Rowdy students were celebrating on the day before Ash Wednesday (this would have been essentially Mardi Gras or "Fat Tuesday"). During the course of the festivities, the students got into an altercation with a tavern owner.

The following day, on Ash Wednesday, the students regrouped and broke into the tavern. They badly beat the owner and damaged his property. University authorities were hesitant to punish the rabble-rousers, but after a great outcry, they dropped their hedge of protection. The city guardsmen were allowed access to the riotous students. Several of the students were killed. Even back then, people considered this as harsh.

The strike was carried out in protest of what had happened. The papal bull *Parens scientiarum* was issued, which sought to give clear guidelines on how to handle such disagreements in the future. The bull declared that the university should be revered as the "Mother of Sciences" and should be held apart from the local authority. Instead, it would be under the direct patronage of the pope himself. A few years later, in 1234, Gregory set the ball in motion to start the official Papal Inquisition. These efforts were made to pick up where his predecessor Lucius had taken off.

Lucius's efforts were largely viewed as scattershot and chaotic. Gregory took it upon himself to create a much more refined, systematic approach. Lucius had made inquiries into heresy, but they often had very little basis. Gregory sought to create a procedure that would ensure that accusations had some merit and were not wild, superfluous ramblings with no basis in reality.

Gregory's emphasis on procedure served him well, considering the fact that he had a legal background as a learned lawyer. His many efforts would result in his compilation of the *Nova Compilatio decretalium*. This was his creation of a set legal standard regarding procedures on how to find and interview those who were accused of heretical acts.

The inquisitors handling the persecution of Conversos (Jewish converts to Christianity) would draw many precedents from Gregory's actions. Pope Gregory took the advice of a Converso named Nicholas Donin and instituted an inquiry into practitioners of Judaism. Donin informed the pope of the nature of Jewish writings in the Talmud and claimed that this work disparaged Christianity.

We are entering controversial grounds while speaking of these events. To be clear, just about nothing is considered certain in regard to them. As much as Donin claimed that the Talmud disparaged Christianity and Christ, there are plenty who say that Donin was either purposefully lying or was, at the very least, gravely mistaken.

Diving into this minefield of controversy, let us first discuss what the Talmud is. The Talmud (also known as the Babylonian Talmud) is rabbinical work that was composed in the 5th century by rabbis stationed in Iraq (hence Babylon). The mere fact that the Talmud was written in the 5th century (at least some four hundred years after Christ) at a time when Christianity was already dominating much of the Mediterranean world makes it at least possible that the Talmud could mention Jesus.

The controversy comes from Donin, who claimed that the Talmud mentions the story of Jesus, but instead of describing him as a holy man, the text disparages him as a wicked magician. It also states that Jesus was the illegitimate child of a Jewish woman and a Roman soldier named Pantera, who was stationed in Israel/Palestine at the time. According to the Talmud, the woman later made up stories about the divinity of her illegitimate child. A terrible story from the Christian perspective, right?

Well, according to experts on the Talmud, the passages that Donin refers to are not even referring to Jesus Christ; it speaks of a Yeshua (Jesus), but not *Jesus*. According to most Talmudic experts, Yeshua was an entirely different person and not at all a reference to the biblical Jesus. Even so, the Catholic Church was all ears to Donin's claims and used it as an excuse to ban the Talmud and persecute Jewish people.

The most dramatic instance of this persecution and book burning occurred in 1240 in France when all copies of the Talmud were seized and consigned to the flame. Anyone who attempted to prevent this confiscation was subject to the death penalty. All of these events can be seen as a lead-up to the Inquisition, which would be officially instituted under Pope Sixtus IV with his papal bull entitled, *Exigit sincerae devotionis affectus*, which was issued in the year 1478.

This led to the official institution of the first leg of the Spanish Inquisition in Castile. It must be said that this was passed under considerable pressure from King Ferdinand II of Aragon since he suggested that he would withdraw military aid in the pope's ongoing struggles in Sicily unless the bull was issued. Sixtus was leery of the persecution that might erupt under the blanket order to make wholesale inquiries into who was a Christian and who was not.

Sixtus would go on to condemn much of what went on in the early stages of the Inquisition and would ultimately urge restraint. His successor, Pope Innocent VIII, would greatly disagree. He made sure that the Inquisition continued in force and with great vigor. He also expanded inquiries to include claims of witchcraft. This pope would go on to institute the infamous papal bull known as *Summis desiderantes affectibus*.

In this official bull, Pope Innocent VIII declared, "It has recently come to our ears, not without great pain to us, that in some parts of upper Germany, Mainz, Koln, Trier, Salzburg, and Bremen, many persons of both sexes, heedless of their own salvation and forsaking the Catholic faith, give themselves over to devils male and female, and by their incantations, charms, and conjuring, and by other abominable superstitions and sortileges, offences, crimes, and misdeeds, ruin and cause to perish the offspring of women, the foal of animals, the products of the Earth, the grapes of the vines, the fruits of trees, as well as men and women, cattle and flocks and herds and animals of every kind, vineyards also and orchards, meadows, pastures, harvests, grains, and other fruits of the Earth."

Some pretty heavy stuff, for sure, but it largely has to do with local superstitious beliefs. Just imagine local villages steeped in Christianity and also ancestral practices that predated their conversion. They would go to a shaman and have them bless their fields or, even worse, curse the fields of someone else. These were primarily the superstitious activities that were afoot. At any rate, this bull is important because it added another dimension to the Inquisition, allowing for the prosecution of the alleged practice of witchcraft.

Shortly after this bull was issued, Pope Innocent officiated Tomás de Torquemada as Spain's grand inquisitor. He would be in charge of overseeing the Spanish Inquisition in its entirety.

Innocent was succeeded by Pope Alexander VI. Alexander VI largely stuck with the status quo. He is most notable for being the pope who witnessed the first Spanish forays into the New World. He issued the papal bull entitled, *Inter caetera* on May 4th, 1493, which gave the Spanish the green light to make what would ultimately become the Americas their own.

Alexander was succeeded by Pope Leo X. Leo was largely an arbiter of the status quo, but the most consequential incident of his tenure was the eruption of the Protestant Reformation in 1517. Pope Leo X would ultimately excommunicate Protestant reformer Martin Luther. He would also set the groundwork for future inquisitions to focus on Protestant musings within Catholic lands. And when we say "Catholic lands," we are referring to the staunchly Catholic bloc of southern Europe.

Northern European regions, such as the German principalities and Scandinavia, might have been slipping away, but this pope sought to tighten his grip on those who remained loyal to ensure that they remained loyal.

Now, let us fast forward to the administration of Pope Sixtus V and consider his unique contributions to the Inquisition. But first, a little background on this important pope. Pope Sixtus V began his papacy in 1585 when the Inquisition was in full force. He would only be pope for five short years before he perished of malaria, but within that time, he played a vital role in the inquisitions that had taken root, especially the Roman Inquisition. In this pope's stomping grounds of Rome, one of the most interesting stories of his career occurred.

There was apparently a local property owner who was making quite a bit of money by charging people to see a wooden statue of Christ that was said to be miraculously bleeding. Many assumed this was a miraculous sign of the divine. But Pope Sixtus V was not so easily convinced. Already on the lookout for heresy and witchcraft—even in regard to religious icons—he went and took a look for himself.

He came equipped with an ax, and it is said that he took one look at the wooden statue and declared, "As Christ, I worship you; as wood I break you!" He then landed a heavy blow of the ax right on the statue, and it broke into bits. It was revealed that a sponge drenched in blood had been hidden inside. A string that was all but invisible to the naked eye was attached to the sponge.

This shifty local had apparently set up the statue with the bloody sponge inside. All he had to do was pull on the string to make blood ooze out of it. After this superstitious charade had been dispelled by Pope Sixtus V, the man responsible for it was hauled in by the Inquisition and subsequently given a death sentence. Whether we agree with the brutality of the Inquisition or not, you have to hand it to Pope Sixtus V for being such a stern officiator of events.

Now that we have relayed some of the histories of the most influential popes of the Inquisition, let us consider how the office of the papacy held sway over the day-to-day operations. It must be noted that the pope—and the pope alone—could excommunicate an inquisitor. It was highly unlikely that a pope would exercise this right; as long as the inquisitors kept up their quota of supposed heretics and did not cause any trouble for the intricate political wranglings of the Roman Catholic Church, then there was no cause for alarm.

Relations between the popes and monarchs—even staunchly Catholic ones—were often a mixed bag of loyalties, and it served the pope well to have powerful ears and eyes on the ground through the inquisitors, who had jurisdiction over various realms of Catholic Europe. The inquisitors themselves were further protected by their so-called "familiars," who essentially served as armed guards.

The inquisitors were protected on high by the pope and on the ground by their own loyal guards, so it is not hard to understand why the inquisitors held such power and why they held it for as long as they did. As long as they stayed in the pope's good graces, they were virtually untouchable. If it were not for the abiding power of the popes, the Inquisition would not have gone forward.

Chapter 8: The End of the Inquisition

"I read with great delight the inquisitors' manual, and I am angry at myself because [I had] Candide kill only one inquisitor. My brothers—I thank you in the name of humanity for having sent me the manual of the inquisition. It is a great pity that the philosophers are not numerous, zealous, or rich enough to destroy by fire and flame these enemies of the human race, and the abominable sect that has produced such horrors; [reading] the pretty jurisprudence of the inquisition has had on me the same effect as the sight of the bloody corpse of Caesar had on the Romans. Men do not deserve to live as long as there is enough wood and fire that they do not use to burn these monsters in their infamous lairs. [I embrace] the worthy brother who has made this excellent work. May it be translated into Portuguese and Castilian as well. The more we are attached to the holy religion of our savior Jesus Christ, the more we must abhor the abominable use of his divine law that men make every day."

-Voltaire

The Inquisition was such a massive enterprise that it is, at times, hard to determine exactly when it ended. There are definitely markers of when the Inquisition was curtailed, paused, or went into decline. But there is no definite time that the Inquisition actually came to an end. One could, for example, easily point to the French Revolution and the resulting Napoleonic Wars as a definite starting point for the end of the Inquisition.

In many of the regions that Napoleon Bonaparte controlled, which included Rome (Italy), Portugal, and Spain, the pause button was pressed on the Inquisition that had been carried out within those dominions. The Inquisition that had been taking place in Venice, for example, was brought to an end by Napoleon's official decree in 1797. It was subsequently enforced in its entirety by 1806 when the Inquisition in Venice was officially abolished.

Even before Napoleon toppled the traditional Spanish monarchy and placed his brother, Joseph Bonaparte, on the throne, the Spanish Inquisition had already been greatly curtailed under King Charles IV. An influential Spanish minister named Manuel Godoy was a very vocal critic. He viewed the Inquisition as nothing more than a form of censorship that stifled innovation.

This was the same criticism that many others had of the Inquisition, both then and now. Many humanist writers who hailed from France made many condemnations of the Inquisition prior to the French Revolution. Godoy wanted the Inquisition stopped. And consequently enough, he had his wish fulfilled. Once the Napoleonic takeover happened in 1808, the Inquisition was suspended.

The Napoleonic Wars, which lasted from 1803 to 1815, directly led to declarations of independence in many of Spain's former colonies in Latin America. These colonies made known their desire to end any and all inquisitions being carried out in their regions. The end of the Napoleonic Wars would see the return of the traditional Spanish monarchy and a return of the Inquisition. The final death attributed to the Spanish Inquisition is said to have taken place in 1826.

This last gasp of the Inquisition consisted of the execution of a local teacher for allegedly debating the merits of Deism in a local school. Perhaps such things were a pushback against the French since Deism was the popular religion of the French Revolution. At any rate, the Inquisition was officially banned in Spain in 1834 under Queen Maria Christina.

The Roman Inquisition returned in 1814 toward the end of the Napoleonic Wars and the restoration of the pope. Although the Inquisition would never again return in force, it existed in name and would slowly trundle on as an artifact of the church until it was reorganized as the Sacred Congregation of the Holy Office in 1965.

The Portuguese Inquisition's story is a bit more complicated. Portugal, like Spain and Rome, was seized by the forces of Napoleon. The

Inquisition had already been greatly curtailed under the Pombaline dictatorship in the 1770s before Napoleon came along. The Portuguese Inquisition had been reduced so much that it was not even a pressing issue for Napoleon. Nevertheless, after the Napoleonic Wars ended and Portugal regained autonomy, Portugal's assemblies moved to officially abolish the Inquisition in 1821.

As mentioned, the French Revolution and the subsequent Napoleonic Wars had quite a bit to do with sending the Inquisition into decline. But also, as previously mentioned, even prior to the French Revolution, there were thoughts reverberating in nearby France that had a direct impact on the Spanish, Portuguese, and Roman Inquisitions. It is often overlooked, but a French writer by the name of Pierre Bayle penned a work in the late 17th century that would be quite influential on religious tolerance and the Inquisition.

Pierre Bayle, who lived from 1647 to 1706, grew up in a religious minority called the Huguenots. They had been relentlessly persecuted by French authorities. Despite the hardship of his youth, Pierre was sharp and a quick learner. Upon reaching adulthood, he became a tutor, training others while he continued his own education in literature and philosophy.

Religious persecution would wear thin on Pierre Bayle, and he would ultimately run away from France to seek refuge in Rotterdam in 1681. Pierre took a modernist view of religious persecution and sought to demonstrate how ridiculous it all was.

Considering the modernization of the Enlightenment, it becomes rather convincing that both the Inquisition and the Reformation were inevitable results of the growing freedom of thought. The Inquisition can be seen as a direct backlash to the growth in freedom of thought and expression. After all, the Catholic Church had kept an iron grip on doctrine for well over a thousand years, and anyone who strayed off the official script would face dire consequences.

As the masses became more educated and more prone to think for themselves, dissent was almost inevitable. The more knowledgeable people became, the more ridiculous it seemed to be punished for merely having a different opinion over scripture. Being burned at the stake for believing in a different method of Communion, for example, just seemed utterly absurd in the wake of the growing intellectual freedom that learned scholars such as Pierre enjoyed. And Pierre was great at expressing this growing sense of absurdity.

As Pierre Bayle himself once wrote, "The communion of Rome has never permitted anyone to contradict her, without exterminating by iron and fire anyone who dared to assume such a liberty. It made great efforts to establish everywhere the Tribunal of the Inquisition, the most infernal, and the most shameful instrument for the maintenance of its authority that was ever displayed by the human spirit, and which was never practiced even by the most abominable religions of paganism, even by those which used to sacrifice human victims to their idols."

This is a pretty stern rebuke of the Inquisition, and it is also one that uses the full reasoning and logic of the Enlightenment to highlight (at least in Pierre's view) how silly the whole thing was. Thoughts like these would eventually lead to the irreverence of another great French writer, Voltaire, who used the relative freedoms at his disposal to assail church oppression at every turn.

The thoughts of these French writers were ultimately at the forefront of the intellectuals of the French Revolution as well. Even though the French Revolution turned into a terrible nightmare, in which those who claimed to bring freedom ushered in a spate of some of history's most awful oppression, it all sprang from this general, growing disdain of the Inquisition.

Perhaps one of Pierre's greatest points was when he likened Apostle Paul to a reformed inquisitor! Pierre described how prior to Paul's dramatic conversion to Christianity, he was a relentless persecutor of the faith. Similar to a grand inquisitor, Paul would go around making inquiries and branding others as religious heretics (except in Paul's case, he sought heretics of Judaism).

For those who are unaware of the story, Paul had a miraculous conversion to Christianity on the road to Damascus, and upon becoming a follower of Christ, his inquisitions ceased. Pierre argued that if Paul could cease and desist his own inquisition, why couldn't the Catholic Church? Pierre Bayle would further argue that true conversion would never come by the sword but only through one's own conscious decision to convert.

Pierre argued that if one was pressured to convert under duress, such as was the case for the Conversos in Spain, it should come as no surprise if they ended up lapsing in their "faith." In his opinion, faith should be a personal decision made by one's own conscience; if one is forced to proclaim something that they do not really believe in the first place, then no one should be astonished to find that their commitment to this faith is rather limited.

And that was precisely what the Spanish Inquisition did. It was as if the church was setting up people to fail. Jews were forced to convert and then had their lukewarm (or perhaps non-existent) faith tested by the inquisitors. And when they failed to live up to the inquisitors' standards of what a true believer should be, these forced converts were forced to pay the price.

Pierre, who wrote in the late 17th century, boldly and unapologetically called out all of these absurdities for what they were. All of his arguments would culminate in his 1696 work, the *Historical and Critical Dictionary*, which, despite its rather boring title, holds powerful arguments on what Pierre viewed as the illegitimate nature of state-enforced persecution of religious beliefs. Pierre Bayle, whether he knew it or not, was essentially laying out some of the groundwork for what would become the concept of the separation of church and state.

Pierre argued that whether one is a Christian, Muslim, Jew, or even an atheist, their personal religion should be none of the state's business. He insisted that the state should only be concerned with regulating behavior and not religion. As long as everyone is following the state's civic laws and not out killing and robbing people, they should be considered good citizens, regardless of their personal religious beliefs.

It might sound like common sense to most of us today, but back in Pierre's time, when most nations had religions enforced by the state itself, such statements were revolutionary. By the time Pierre passed away in 1706, his thoughts had crystalized into what would grow into a revolt against the coercion of religious beliefs. These thoughts would be echoed and revised by the next generation of philosophers, including Montesquieu and Voltaire.

Montesquieu, in particular, made a great point of further highlighting the absurdity of the inquisitors by speaking of how it was usually only those who proclaimed innocence who were condemned. Montesquieu wrote, "It is one of the great abuses of the Inquisition of Spain that, of two persons accused of the same crime, the one who denies it is condemned to death, and the one who confesses it avoids punishment. This difference derives from monastic ideas, according to which anyone who denies the [charge of heresy] is impenitent and damned, while one who confesses appears to repent and is saved."

Yes, it was quite common for those who made a "confession" to be spared the wrath of the Inquisition while those who insisted on their innocence were condemned. As mentioned earlier in this book, it eventually got to the point where folks were openly confessing to just about everything under the sun to avoid punishment.

In such an atmosphere, one has to assume that the people who refused to admit any guilt had an incredibly high moral standard, as they would not admit to things that they did not do. Ironically enough, the Inquisition, which supposedly sought to seek out sinners, forced people to commit the sin of lying to save their own skin. As more and more writers soberly pointed out the absurdity of the Inquisition, it was perhaps inevitable that a great writer like Voltaire would turn this absurdity into sheer comedy through his many satires.

In consideration of the excesses of the Inquisition, Voltaire was capable of making one shudder and laugh all at the same time, as was demonstrated in his 1759 work entitled *Candide*. One passage, which reads almost like a news report from *The Onion* (a modern American satirical newspaper), describes an infamous *auto-da-fé* in Portugal. The passage declares, "After the earthquake had destroyed three-fourths of Lisbon, the sages of that country could think of no means more effectual to prevent utter ruin than to give the people a beautiful auto-da-fé; for it had been decided by the University of Coimbra, that the burning of a few people alive by a slow fire, and with great ceremony, is an infallible secret to hinder the earth from quaking."

With his light-hearted humor, Voltaire sought to use the "illumination" of the Enlightenment to shine a spotlight on the dark misery that the Inquisition had unleashed. Perhaps the greatest reproach anyone could have given the authority figures who perpetuated the Inquisition was a rhetorical roasting of their own. No greater punishment was more fitting for the foreboding bogeyman—the grand inquisitor—than to have people laughing in his face.

But as well intended as such things were, and as much food for thought that French writers and philosophers gave us, this same humanist discourse would have some unintended consequences of its own. The native French homeland of so many of these great philosophers and thinkers would find itself in the grip of abject terror in the aftermath of the French Revolution.

And this terror was not perpetrated by the promulgators of religion. Rather, enlightened humanists had run amok. The tables turned, and suddenly it was the Catholic Church and other traditional institutions that faced terrible persecution. Knowing full well that two wrongs do not make a right, Bayle, Montesquieu, Voltaire, and others probably would have been rolling over in their graves.

It was not until the despotic peace of Napoleon descended upon the chaotic French Revolution that the Catholic Church was spared, and it was only spared because Napoleon viewed it as a useful political tool to keep people in line.

These same strains of thought also found their way to the North American colonies and factored into their rebellion against Britain. The resulting United States of America made sure religious freedom was one of the major foundations of the Constitution. The Founding Fathers likely considered the Inquisition and the writers and philosophers who railed against it and wanted to ensure that such a thing did not happen in the United States.

During Napoleon's occupation of Spain, as terrible as it was to be occupied by a foreign power, the average citizen was probably relieved to finally be free from the terrible paranoia that the Inquisition had inflicted over the past few centuries. And for once, the intelligentsia of Spain was able to voice complaints about the disbanded practice.

Demonstrating how tight of a grip the Inquisition had on all aspects of Spanish life prior to Napoleon's takeover, even an idle complaint against the Inquisition could see someone being hauled off to a dungeon somewhere. But when Napoleon took over, the free-thinking minds of Spain were able to voice their disgust over the Inquisition. Furthermore, even before the French were pushed out of the Spanish government, the intelligentsia made it clear that they did not wish to see the Inquisition return.

Those who did wish to have the Inquisition reinstituted were primarily among the top leadership of the Catholic Church and perhaps the government. Their reasons for wanting the Inquisition were not so much out of religious zeal as it was out of wanting to have the benefit of control and surveillance.

In many ways, the Inquisition behaved as a secret police force that could keep tabs on what the general public was thinking and stay vigilant for any signs of dissent. It was difficult for the elite to let such a powerful tool slip from their grasp. As such, after Napoleon was finally defeated in 1815, the Spanish elite attempted to bring the Inquisition back, but this new form of the Inquisition was largely procedural and did not have any real teeth.

Tribunals were set up, and trials took place, but the efforts were lukewarm at best. There was never any real effort to enforce the Inquisition on a wide scale.

In the meantime, the Spanish intelligentsia remained emboldened and continued to openly criticize the practice, ensuring that 19th-century Spain would not return to the horrors of the 16th century.

Even so, the Inquisition attempted to clamp down and push back against this popular resistance. In 1826, Cayetano Ripoll was executed on charges of being a Deist. The execution of Cayetano Ripoll did not have the effect the administrators of the renewed Inquisition had hoped to have. Instead of scaring everyone into submission, the people rose up as one to express their outrage. Instead of keeping the Inquisition going, this overreach ensured that it would come to an end. Queen Maria Christina officially decreed the end of the Spanish Inquisition in 1834.

Chapter 9: Impact and Legacy of the Inquisition

"It is pure illusion to think that an opinion that passes down from century to century, from generation to generation, may not be entirely false."
  -Pierre Bayle

In the end, the legacy of the Inquisition devolved into an utterly absurd spectacle mocked by philosophers, social commentators, and satirists alike. By the early 1700s, it was already well enough entrenched to become a popular source of speculation for historians and writers of fiction, especially satirists looking for some good dark comedy for their latest works.

The practice of the Inquisition, even though not as lethal by the 18th century in comparison to a couple of centuries prior, was viewed as archaic. The Inquisition was seen as a holdover from the darkness of the Middle Ages, whose horrors were being fully revealed by the Enlightenment. And even if mass burnings at the stake had become rare, the great thinkers of the Enlightenment could not help but see the institution of the Inquisition as a great drag on the freedom of thought, so they naturally railed against it.

But strangely enough, as critical as many of these modernists were, many were also intrigued by a culture and regime they found so alien to their own dispositions. Many of the critics of the Inquisition were as drawn to it as they were repelled by it, and there are many accounts of critics paying visits to Spain, Portugal, and Rome.

They were there to find firsthand material on the subject, but they also enjoyed their extended stays in these realms that were steeped in their own unique ways and culture. Edgar Allan Poe, for example, referenced the Inquisition more than once to enhance his fictional portrayals. After all, the true horror of the Inquisition was enough to make even his spookiest of narratives pale in comparison.

The horrors of the Inquisition were many and complex. And they did not just involve the most obvious trespasses, such as killing others because of their religious beliefs. The Inquisition had a deep impact on just about every aspect of society.

For example, in Spain and Portugal, there had traditionally been a large number of Jewish and Muslim doctors. It was fairly common for rich families to employ learned doctors who just so happened to be adherents of either Judaism or Islam. Once the Inquisition (as well as its subsequent expulsions) kicked into high gear, such doctors could no longer be employed. Thus, learned physicians were scarce and in short supply.

The Inquisition also had a deep impact on the economy of Iberia for similar reasons since many skilled members of the workforce were excised, leading to a general brain drain of the Iberian Peninsula. But even beyond those who were expelled and pushed out of Spain and Portugal, the Inquisition could be downright devastating for business, even for Christians.

Just imagine yourself being a prominent Christian businessman who is owed a large sum of money by a debtor. You expect to collect what you are owed, but then your crafty debtor gets wise and turns you over to the Inquisition. It does not matter what for; the mere fact that you were accused gets you thrown into a dungeon, and your debtor's debt is rendered null and void as a consequence. This situation is convenient for the debtor but absolutely horrible for you.

Such travesties of justice occurred throughout the Inquisition, often turning society upside down on the merest of whims and the most distorted of falsehoods. In short, the Inquisition, although initially targeting specific groups of supposed heretics, was bad news for just about anyone. The Inquisition was a terrible blight on society and cast a dark shadow on just about every aspect of life for those who lived underneath it.

A great testament to the effect the Inquisition had was its stifling of the sciences in Iberia. It is indeed ironic that Spain, which had once been the most enlightened part of the European continent, would become shrouded in the darkness of the Inquisition.

Just consider how many great discoveries might have been stifled. When Galileo pushed the envelope by insisting that the earth orbited the sun rather than the other way around, all hell broke loose. Rather than thanking Galileo for his groundbreaking discovery, he was forced to apologize for it!

This sort of forced ignorance was one of the worst and most terrible impacts the Inquisition inflicted, and it would lead to a lasting and unnecessary legacy of stifled and stunted growth in what otherwise should have been robust societies. Spain and Portugal forged huge global empires, but due to corruption and chronic stagnation, their empires disintegrated, and both nations ended up being quite behind their peers in Christian Europe.

The nature of this decline was noted as early as 1837 when William Prescott published his epic work *History of the Reign of Ferdinand and Isabella*. Prescott lays out the ultimate impact and legacy of the Inquisition for all to see. Prescott wrote, "Folded under the dark wing of the Inquisition, Spain was shut out from the light which in the sixteenth century broke over the rest of Europe, stimulating the nations to greater enterprise in every department of knowledge. The genius of the people was rebuked, and their spirit quenched, under the malignant influence of an eye that never slumbered, of an unseen arm ever raised to strike."

Prescott's words were certainly prophetic. Portugal, Spain, and Italy would spend time ruled by dictators and despots. Spain would fight a bloody civil war in the 20th century and be ruled by a fascist dictator named Francisco Franco until his death in 1975. In many ways, Spain, Portugal, and Rome are still trying to recover from the Inquisition.

The Roman Catholic Church managed to officially rebuke the Alhambra Decree that initiated the traumatic expulsion of the Jews in 1492. This edict had lingered on the books for centuries, only being officially disbanded in 1968. It must be noted that Jewish believers had returned and openly practiced their faith in Iberia for well over a century prior to this (largely symbolic) overturning of the edict.

The official scratching out of this horrid decree was primarily a symbolic overture of repentance on the part of church authorities. It was a tepid attempt to come to grips with the terrible legacy that the Inquisition still manages to invoke any time it is mentioned. There are very few who would come right out and say that the Inquisition was a good thing.

However, there are some apologists who maintain that it was not all bad and was perhaps even somehow a necessary and natural development of the time and place in which it transpired. There are also those who point out that the worst excesses of the Inquisition have been greatly exaggerated.

There probably is *some* truth in these assertions. Protestants were often the primary critics of the Inquisition, and they certainly had no motive to sugarcoat or hold back any of the gory depictions of what took place. There could be some merit in the idea that the Inquisition was often presented in the worst possible light. Even so, the Inquisition, even on its best day, was still not anything to praise.

Chapter 10: An Intermission of the Inquisition: Historiography Through Multiple Lenses

"From the Crusades, to the Inquisition, to American politics—the name of Jesus had been hijacked as an ally in all kinds of power struggles. Since the beginning of time, the ignorant had always screamed the loudest, herding the unsuspecting masses and forcing them to do their bidding. They defended their worldly desires by citing scripture they did not understand. They celebrated their intolerance as proof of their convictions."

-Dan Brown

Modern writers of history have struggled to reconcile traditional mythologies and legends of the Inquisition from the actual historical record. Modern historians also have to sidestep some of the pride and hubris of previous historians who condemned the Inquisition's dark superstitious motives without addressing the fact that many of these irrational fears are still very much a part of the societies in which they lived.

It was all well and good for Voltaire to point his finger at the absurdities of Spain, Portugal, and Rome until the French society utterly collapsed and the worst abuses of mob mentality and human ignorance took hold. Modern historiography (the study of history itself) attempts to take a closer look at the root causes of the Inquisition and the negative factors that still lurk in any social grouping of humans.

It is not that we, as human beings, have vanquished the darkness of the Inquisition, but rather, we have just succeeded in keeping it at bay. The current historiography of the Inquisition is perceived in light of this more modern view of the need for constant vigilance to keep back the worst of humanity. If modern historians need any reminder to just how easily human society can regress, all they have to do is look at the two world wars and even religious extremism currently ongoing in the Middle East.

In the early 2010s, Islamic extremists known as **ISIS** very nearly created their own dystopian, religious fundamentalist society in Syria and Iraq. The leaders of this so-called Islamic caliphate instituted their own version of the Inquisition, killing anyone who did not conform to their specific religious beliefs. If it were not for outside intervention, these madmen would have thrown the entire Middle East into a new dark age.

This brings up another point. In previous historiographies, there was a tendency to be highly critical of the Catholic Church while holding up those they persecuted as noble victims. While it was certainly terrible what the Catholic Church exacted in the name of the Inquisition, to focus on the mere fact that it was Catholics perpetuating these abuses misses the point. These things are not unique to any time, group, or place. Just about any human religion or sociological construct has the potential of devolving into abject darkness and brutality if certain factors are in play.

As it pertains to the Inquisition, there is no point in labeling "good guys" and "bad guys" when diving into its historiography. These terrible actions are universal in scope and come from deep within the human soul itself. Any social grouping of humans is capable of inflicting such terror if the proper guardrails are not in place to prevent such abuses from happening.

Acclaimed writer Arthur Miller, who survived the modern-day witch hunt of McCarthyism—the US congressional inquiry into who was a communist and who was not—would later reflect on how he previously read up on things about the Salem witch trials and the Spanish Inquisition with detached distaste. He likely thought that what happened was terrible but could never happen in the modern day and age.

However, Miller became caught up in a congressional inquiry—a congressional inquisition, if you will—to figure out whether he had communist leanings. As such, the lens through which he viewed the Inquisition became altered. Miller realized that nothing had changed since the days of witch hunts and the Inquisition. The same people were still there, with the same dark motives lurking just underneath the surface.

These modern-day inquisitors are just waiting for those aforementioned guardrails of society to drop long enough so that they can have the chance to unleash their inquisitorial fury on the rest of us. As Arthur Miller put it, "It was not only the rise of 'McCarthyism' that moved me, but something which seemed much more weird and mysterious. It was the fact that the political, objective ... Capable of creating not only terror, but a new subjective reality, a veritable mystique which was gradually gaining resonance. I had known of the Salem witch hunt for many years before 'McCarthyism' had arrived, and it had always remained an inexplicable darkness to me. When I looked into it now, however, it was the contemporary situation at my back, particularly the mystery of handing over my conscience, which seemed to me the central informing fact of the time ... I saw accepted the notion that conscience was no longer a private matter but one of state administration."

Arthur Miller had endured a modern version of the Inquisition in which his own ideological beliefs were forced to be laid bare. The trauma he sustained was no different from what the Conversos of Spain had faced during the Inquisition.

And both the Spanish Inquisition and the modern-day US Congress's witch hunt had something else in common—they were inspired by fear. Ferdinand and Isabella were convinced that there was a secret Jewish cabal seeking to link up with Islamic insurgents to undo the Reconquista. Similarly, the US Congress of the 1950s feared an enemy within. Americans were scared of communists or even those with the slightest of communist sympathies infiltrating the country. No matter how flimsy the accusations leveled at these alleged subversives were, they were still hauled before congressional committees, where their dirty laundry was laid bare.

It was 1492 all over again—the cast, characters, dialogue, and location may have changed, but the plot was the same. Even seen through multiple lenses, we would ultimately get the same result. This is the greatest lesson that can be learned from the historiography of the Inquisition: human society is not immune to these abuses; they are just currently in remission. At best, we are merely in a brief intermission between the next historical incidence of a brutal and altogether ugly episode of the Inquisition.

Conclusion: Make Way for the Grand Inquisitor

The Inquisition is still a thought-provoking event. One can hardly consider the abuses that were meted out and remain unaffected by them. Humor is perhaps the best medicine when dealing with darkness like this. It is for this reason that Voltaire, the great writer from the Enlightenment, chose to use satire to describe the worst of the Inquisition. Because, quite frankly, the Inquisition was so terrible that if one did not outright laugh about its excess, one just might cry.

So, what is the ultimate legacy of the Inquisition? What are we to make of it all? The Inquisition, by and large, was put in place as a religious and political tool, and it was hellbent on keeping the status quo after the Reconquista. The methods of the Inquisition then spread to Portugal and Rome, regions in which the precepts of these religious inquiries were carried out to greater and lesser degrees.

However, if we are to consider the bigger picture, the Inquisition was more or less just a symptom of a disease, the chronic illness of intolerance that has plagued humanity from the beginning.

Perhaps theologian, historian, and writer Elphège Vacandard describes this phenomenon best. Vacandard states, "Intolerance is natural to man. If, as a matter of fact, men are not always intolerant in practice, it is only because they are prevented by conditions born of reason and wisdom. Respect for the opinion of others supposes a temper of mind which takes years to acquire. It is a question whether the average man is capable of it."

Yes, sadly enough, intolerance of different beliefs seems to come naturally to the average person. The guardrails of society that have been forged are tested from time to time. However, tempered wisdom (wisdom often learned the hard way) should keep societies in check and prevent society from transgressing into outright intolerance.

The Founding Fathers of the United States had egregious trespasses, such as the Inquisition, in mind when they baked the separation of church and state into the Constitution. They put sturdy and strong guardrails in place to make sure that no one would go out of bounds and into the realm of complete intolerance.

The guardrails of modern societies are often taken for granted, but if they were to slip—even just for a moment—we most likely would not like what we would see as a result. If mob mentality were to rise to the surface, with the inflamed, paranoid passions of the moment taking hold of the masses, it might not be long before we would once again see the likes of the grand inquisitor coming our way.

Here's another book by Captivating History that you might like

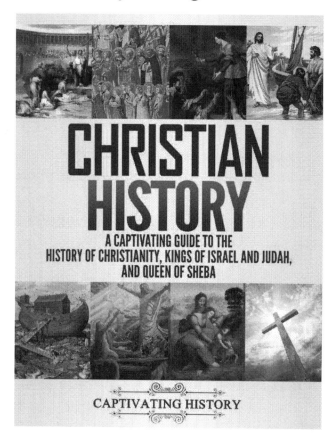

Free Bonus from Captivating History (Available for a Limited time)

Hi History Lovers!

Now you have a chance to join our exclusive history list so you can get your first history ebook for free as well as discounts and a potential to get more history books for free! Simply visit the link below to join.

Captivatinghistory.com/ebook

Also, make sure to follow us on Facebook, Twitter and Youtube by searching for Captivating History.

Bibliography

Abbey, Ian. "Taifa." World History Encyclopedia, May 16, 2022, https://www.worldhistory.org/Taifa/.

Adams, John P. "Sede Vacante 1565-1655." CSUN, October 15, 2015, http://www.csun.edu/~hcfll004/SV1566.html.

Adams, John P. "Sede Vacante 1591." SCUN, July 24, 2015, http://www.csun.edu/~hcfll004/SV1591.html.

Adams, John P. "Sede Vicante 1655." CSUN

Ames, Tom. "6 Key Changes During the Reign of Henry VIII." History Hit, January 11, 2021, https://www.historyhit.com/key-changes-during-henry-viiis-reign/.

Armistead, Samuel G. and Gerli E. M. *Medieval Iberia*. Taylor and Francis: London, 2003.

Arnold, Jack L. "The Roman Catholic Church of the Middle Ages: Reformation Men and Theology, Lesson 1 of 11." *IIIM Magazine Online* 1, no. 1 (March 1-7, 1999). https://www.thirdmill.org/newfiles/jac_arnold/CH.Arnold.RMT.1.html.

Ashbridge, Thomas S. *The First Crusade: A New History*. Oxford University Press, New York, 2004.

Bachrach, Bernard S. "A Reassessment of Visigothic Jewish Policy, 598-711." *Oxford University Press*, February 1973, https://www.jstor.org/stable/1853939.

Baird Rattini, Kristin. "Who was Constantine?" *National Geographic*, February 25, 2019, https://www.nationalgeographic.com/culture/article/constantine?loggedin=true.

Baldwin, Philip B. *Pope Gregory X and the Crusades*. The Boydell Press: Suffolk, UK, 2014.

Barber, Malcolm. *The Crusader States.* Yale University Press: New Haven, Connecticut, USA, October 23, 2012.

Barraclough, Geoffrey. "History of Feudalism." History World, n.d., http://www.historyworld.net/wrldhis/PlainTextHistories.asp?ParagraphID=eny#:~:text=Although%20feudalism%20develops%20as%20early,the%20entire%20continent%20is%20Christian.

Beck, Elias. "Eighth Crusade." History Crunch, November 17, 2019, https://www.historycrunch.com/eighth-crusade.html#/.

Beck, Elias. "Ninth Crusade." History Crunch, June 22, 2021, https://www.historycrunch.com/ninth-crusade.html#/.

Beck, Elias. "What is the Holy Land in the Crusades?" History Crunch, June 22, 2021, https://www.historycrunch.com/what-is-the-holy-land-in-the-crusades.html#/.

Becker, Rachel and Sullivan, Nate. "The Dark Ages - Definition, Causes, & History." Study, October 11, 2021, https://study.com/learn/lesson/the-dark-ages.html.

"Bell of St Patrick and its Shrine." National Museum of Ireland, 2022, https://www.museum.ie/en-IE/Collections-Research/Collection/Resilience/Artefact/Test-5/8e122ba9-6464-4533-8f72-d036afde12a9#:~:text=This%20bell%20is%20reputed%20to,the%20principal%20relics%20of%20Ireland.

Beuck, Charles. "718/722: The Battle of Covadonga as the Beginning of the Reconquista in the Iberian Peninsula." *Medium*, January 3, 2021, https://medium.com/traveling-through-history/718-722-the-battle-of-covadonga-as-the-beginning-of-the-reconquista-in-the-iberian-peninsula-e3fae9a8942b.

Bhullar, Julian. "The Roman Emperor Majorian on Protecting Pagan Temples in Late Antiquity." *Medium*, March 26, 2022, https://medium.com/flavius-claudius-julianus/the-roman-emperor-majorian-on-protecting-pagan-temples-in-late-antiquity-20686bbceb85.

Biography.com Editors. "Saint Patrick Biography." A&E Television Networks, Biography, April 20, 2021, https://www.biography.com/religious-figure/saint-patrick.

Blakemore, Erin. "The Disastrous Time Tens of Thousands of Children Tried to Start a Crusade." History. A&E Television Networks, April 8, 2019, https://www.history.com/news/the-disastrous-time-tens-of-thousands-of-children-tried-to-start-a-crusade.

Bouwsma, W. J. "John Calvin." *Encyclopedia Britannica*, July 6, 2023. https://www.britannica.com/biography/John-Calvin.

Brill, E.J. *Encyclopedia of Islam: A Dictionary of the Geography, Ethnography, and Biography of the Muhammadan Peoples.* Ed 1., Vol. 1. BRILL, 1913.

Britannica, T. Editors of Encyclopedia. "Adrian VI." *Encyclopedia Britannica*, February 26, 2023. https://www.britannica.com/biography/Adrian-VI.

Britannica, T. Editors of Encyclopedia. "Al-Andalus." *Encyclopedia Britannica*, July 9, 2019. https://www.britannica.com/place/Al-Andalus.

Britannica, T. Editors of Encyclopedia. "Augsburg Confession." *Encyclopedia Britannica*, November 8, 2021. https://www.britannica.com/topic/Augsburg-Confession.

Britannica, T. Editors of Encyclopedia. "Baldwin I." *Encyclopedia Britannica*, January 1, 2023. https://www.britannica.com/biography/Baldwin-I-Byzantine-emperor.

Britannica, T. Editors of Encyclopedia. "Baldwin I." *Encyclopedia Britannica*, March 29, 2022. https://www.britannica.com/biography/Baldwin-I-king-of-Jerusalem.

Britannica, T. Editors of Encyclopedia. "Baldwin II." *Encyclopedia Britannica*, July 28, 2022. https://www.britannica.com/biography/Baldwin-II-king-of-Jerusalem.

Britannica, T. Editors of Encyclopedia. "Baldwin III." *Encyclopedia Britannica*, February 6, 2022. https://www.britannica.com/biography/Baldwin-III-king-of-Jerusalem.

Britannica, T. Editors of Encyclopedia. "Clement VII." *Encyclopedia Britannica*, August 18, 2023. https://www.britannica.com/biography/Clement-VII-pope.

Britannica, T. Editors of Encyclopedia. "Clement VIII." *Encyclopedia Britannica*, March 1, 2023. https://www.britannica.com/biography/Clement-VIII-pope.

Britannica, T. Editors of Encyclopedia. "Council of Trent." *Encyclopedia Britannica*, July 14, 2023. https://www.britannica.com/event/Council-of-Trent.

Britannica, T. Editors of Encyclopedia. "Godfrey of Bouillon." *Encyclopedia Britannica*, July 14, 2022. https://www.britannica.com/biography/Godfrey-of-Bouillon.

Britannica, T. Editors of Encyclopedia. "Gregory XV." *Encyclopedia Britannica*, July 4, 2023. https://www.britannica.com/biography/Gregory-XV.

Britannica, T. Editors of Encyclopedia. "Guillaume Farel." *Encyclopedia Britannica*, January 1, 2023. https://www.britannica.com/biography/Guillaume-Farel.

Britannica, T. Editors of Encyclopedia. "Innocent IX." *Encyclopedia Britannica*, July 16, 2023. https://www.britannica.com/biography/Innocent-IX.

Britannica, T. Editors of Encyclopedia. "Innocent X." *Encyclopedia Britannica*, May 3, 2023. https://www.britannica.com/biography/Innocent-X.

Britannica, T. Editors of Encyclopedia. "Lucius Verus." *Encyclopedia Britannica*, January 1, 2022. https://www.britannica.com/biography/Lucius-Verus

Britannica, T. Editors of Encyclopedia. "Marcellus II." *Encyclopedia Britannica*, May 2, 2023. https://www.britannica.com/biography/Marcellus-II.

Britannica, T. Editors of Encyclopedia. "Maximian." *Encyclopedia Britannica*, January 1, 2022. https://www.britannica.com/biography/Maximian.

Britannica, T. Editors of Encyclopedia. "Nūr al-Dīn." *Encyclopedia Britannica*, May 11, 2022. https://www.britannica.com/biography/Nur-al-Din.

Britannica, T. Editors of Encyclopedia. "Paul V." *Encyclopedia Britannica*, January 24, 2023. https://www.britannica.com/biography/Paul-V.

Britannica, T. Editors of Encyclopedia. "Piero di Lorenzo de' Medici." *Encyclopedia Britannica*, January 1, 2023. https://www.britannica.com/biography/Piero-di-Lorenzo-de-Medici.

Britannica, T. Editors of Encyclopedia. "Saint Francis of Sales." *Encyclopedia Britannica*, December 24, 2022. https://www.britannica.com/biography/Saint-Francis-of-Sales.

Britannica, T. Editors of Encyclopedia. "Sixtus V." *Encyclopedia Britannica*, August 23, 2023. https://www.britannica.com/biography/Sixtus-V.

Britannica, T. Editors of Encyclopedia. "Urban II Summary." *Encyclopedia Britannica*, March 5, 2003. https://www.britannica.com/summary/Urban-II.

Britannica, T. Editors of Encyclopedia. "Urban VIII." *Encyclopedia Britannica*, July 25, 2023. https://www.britannica.com/biography/Urban-VIII.

Britannica, T. Editors of Encyclopedia. "Wars of Religion." *Encyclopedia Britannica*, June 1, 2023. https://www.britannica.com/event/Wars-of-Religion.

Britannica, T. Editors of Encyclopedia. "Zangī." *Encyclopedia Britannica*, January 1, 2022. https://www.britannica.com/biography/Zangi-Iraqi-ruler.

Broussard, Karlo. "Is Baptism Necessary for Salvation or Not?" Catholic Answers, 2023, https://www.catholic.com/qa/is-baptism-necessary-for-salvation-or-not

Butler, Alban, Rev. *The Lives of the Fathers, Martyrs, and Other Principal Saints*. James Duffy, Dublin, Ireland, 1866.

Cameron, Averil, and Peter Garnsey. *The Cambridge Ancient History*. 13. Vol. 13. Cambridge University Press, 1970.

Cameron, Euan. "Six Articles, Act Of." Oxford University Press, 2019, https://www.encyclopedia.com/history/encyclopedias-almanacs-transcripts-and-maps/six-articles-act.

Cameron-Smith, Ray. "Jacques Lefevre: A Reformer Before the Reformation." Banner of Truth, Oct 31, 2018, https://banneroftruth.org/us/resources/articles/2018/jacques-lefevre-a-reformer-before-the-reformation/.

Carr, K. E. "Who were the Arians?" Early Medieval Christianity, Quatr.us Study Guides, October 22, 2022, https://quatr.us/romans/arians-early-medieval-christianity.htm.

Cartwright, Mark. "Council of Clermont. *World History Encyclopedia*, October 22, 2018, https://www.worldhistory.org/Council_of_Clermont/.

Cartwright, Mark. "Crusader States." *World History Encyclopedia*, November 1, 2018, https://www.worldhistory.org/Crusader_States/.

Cartwright, Mark. "Feudalism." *World History Encyclopedia*, November 22, 2018, https://www.worldhistory.org/Feudalism/#:~:text=Origins%20of%20Feudalism&text=The%20system%20had%20its%20roots,and%20receive%20service%20in%20return.

Cartwright, Mark. "Fifth Crusade." *World History Encyclopedia*. September 6, 2018, https://www.worldhistory.org/Fifth_Crusade/.

Cartwright, Mark. "First Crusade." *World History Encyclopedia*. July 9, 2018, https://www.worldhistory.org/First_Crusade/.

Cartwright, Mark. "Knights Templar." *World History Encyclopedia*, September 28, 2018, https://member.worldhistory.org/Knights_Templar/.

Cartwright, Mark. "Reconquista." *World History Encyclopedia*, October 5, 2018, https://www.worldhistory.org/Reconquista/.

Cartwright, Mark. "Saladin," *World History Encyclopedia*, August 30, 2018, https://www.worldhistory.org/Saladin/.

Cartwright, Mark. "Seventh Crusade." *World History Encyclopedia*, September 12, 2018, https://www.worldhistory.org/Seventh_Crusade/.

Cartwright, Mark. "Sixth Crusade." *World History Encyclo*pedia, September 10, 2018, https://www.worldhistory.org/Sixth_Crusade/.

Cartwright, Mark. "Third Crusade." *World History Encyclopedia*, August 27, 2018, https://www.worldhistory.org/Third_Crusade/.

Cavazzi, Franco "Emperor Honorius." The Roman Empire, 2022, https://roman-empire.net/people/honorius/.

Cavazzi, Franco. "Emperor Julius Nepos." The Roman Empire, 2022, https://roman-empire.net/people/julius-nepos/.

Cavazzi, Franco. "Emperor Majorian." The Roman Empire, 2022, https://roman-empire.net/people/majorian/.

"Celtic High Cross Sculptures (c.750-1150 CE)" Visual Arts Cork, n.d., http://www.visual-arts-cork.com/irish-sculpture/celtic-high-cross-sculptures.htm.

"Charlemagne: King of the Franks." Students of History, 2022, https://www.studentsofhistory.com/charlemagne-the-holy-roman-empire.

Chakra, Hayden. "Battle of the Frigidus 394 AD - Clash Between the East and West." About History, September 14, 2021, https://about-history.com/battle-of-the-frigidus-394-ad-clash-between-the-east-and-west/.

Chery, Fritz. "Catholic vs Orthodox: 14 Major Differences to Know." Bible Reasons, November 12, 2022, https://biblereasons.com/catholic-vs-orthodox/.

"Children's Crusade 1212: The Strange & Confusing Children's Crusade 1212." *Medieval Chronicles*, 2023, https://www.medievalchronicles.com/the-crusades/childrens-crusade/.

Chinazzi, Ernesta. *Sede Vacante per la morte del Papa Urbano VIII Barberini e conclave di Innocenzo X Pamphili*. Rome, 1904.

Claxton, Miguel A. III. "The Islamic Iberian Peninsula: Cultural Fusion and Coexistence." Young Historians Conference, February 29, 2016, https://pdxscholar.library.pdx.edu/cgi/viewcontent.cgi?article=1082&context=younghistorians.

"Clonmacnoise - History and Significance." Enjoy Irish Culture, n.d., https://www.enjoy-irish-culture.com/Clonmacnoise.html.

Collier, Theodore F. "Sixtus." In Chisholm, Hugh (ed.). *Encyclopedia Britannica*. Vol. 25 (11th ed.). Cambridge University Press, 1911.

Comyn, Robert B. *The History of the Western Empire: From Its Restoration by Charlemagne to the Accession of Charles V*. W.H. Allen & Company: Oxford, 1841.

Connell, Timothy J. and Rodriguez, Vicente. "History of Barcelona." *Encyclopedia Britannica*, n.d., https://www.britannica.com/place/Barcelona/History.

Constable, Giles. "The Second Crusade as Seen by Contemporaries." *Traditio 9* (1953): 213-79. http://www.jstor.org/stable/27830277.

Conti, Alessandro. "John Wycliffe." *Stanford Encyclopedia of Philosophy*. Retrieved June 3, 2019.

Corkery, James; Worcester, Thomas. *The Papacy Since 1500: From Italian Prince to Universal Pastor*. Cambridge University Press, 2010.

Christiansen, Eric. *The Northern Crusades*. Penguin Books: London, 1997.

Csorba, Csaba; Estok, Janos; and Salamon, Konrad. *The Illustrated History of Hungary*. Magyar Konuvklub, Hungary, 1999.

Cusack, Margaret A. "Mission of St. Palladius." Library Ireland, 1868, https://www.libraryireland.com/HistoryIreland/Mission-St-Palladius.php.

Da Silva, Bridgette. "Saint Patrick, the Irish Druids, and the Conversion of Pagan Ireland to Christianity." *Strange Horizons,* July 27, 2019, http://strangehorizons.com/non-fiction/articles/saint-patrick-the-irish-druids-and-the-conversion-of-pagan-ireland-to-christianity/.

Davies, Norman. *The Isles: A History.* Pan Macmillan: London, 2008.

Davis, G. R. C. *Magna Carta.* London, British Museum. January 1, 1985.

"Death of Pope Julius II." Italy On This Day, February 21, 2016, https://www.italyonthisday.com/2016/02/death-of-pope-julius-ii-san-pietro-in-vincoli-rome.html.

Department of European Paintings. "List of Rulers of Europe." In Heilbrunn Timeline of Art History. New York: The Metropolitan Museum of Art, 2000-. April, 2007, http://www.metmuseum.org/toah/hd/euru/hd_euru.htm.

Dhahabui, Muhammad A. *The Lives of Notable Figures: Volume 21.* Al Resala Publishers, Beirut, 2014.

"Differences Between Peter and Paul's Message." Grace Ambassadors. Grace Ambassadors Ministry, 2022, https://graceambassadors.com/midacts/list-petervspaul.

"Discover how Johannes Gutenberg's printing press increased the literacy and education of people in Europe." *Encyclopedia Britannica,* Inc., n.d., video, https://www.britannica.com/video/171689/history-printing-press-work-discussion-Johannes-Gutenberg.

"Dividing the Roman Empire into Each & West." Students of History, 2022, https://www.studentsofhistory.com/division-of-the-empire#:~:text=In%20286%20CE%2C%20the%20Emperor,Roman%20life%20and%20government%20forever.

Duggan, Anne J. *Queens and Queenship in Medieval Europe.* The Boydell Press: London, 2002.

Editors of Encyclopedia Britannica. "Iconoclastic Controversy." *Encyclopedia Britannica,* September 4, 2020, https://www.britannica.com/event/Iconoclastic-Controversy.

Editors of Encyclopedia the Britannica. "Michael Cerularius." *Encyclopedia Britannica,* January 17, 2022. https://www.britannica.com/biography/Michael-Cerularius.

Eighth Crusade Timeline." *World History Encyclopedia,* 2023, https://www.worldhistory.org/timeline/Eighth_Crusade/.

"Elizabeth's Excommunication 1570." BBC UK Bitesize, 2023, https://www.bbc.co.uk/bitesize/guides/zpy9fcw/revision/3.

"Elizabeth I's Religious Settlement." Royal Museums Greenwich, n.d., https://www.rmg.co.uk/stories/topics/elizabeth-religious-settlement.

Evert, Jason. "Why Can't Women Be Priests?" Catholic Answers, January 1, 2002, https://www.catholic.com/magazine/print-edition/why-cant-women-be-priests.

Favorito, Rebecca. "The Magna Carta and Its Legacy." *Origins*, January 2015, https://origins.osu.edu/milestones/january-2015-magna-carta-and-its-legacy?language_content_entity=en

"Fifth Crusade Timeline." *World History Encyclopedia*, 2023, https://www.worldhistory.org/timeline/Fifth_Crusade/.

"Fourth Crusade Timeline." *World History Encyclopedia*, 2023, https://www.worldhistory.org/timeline/Fourth_Crusade/.

Frakas, Catherine. "Biography - Pope Gregory XIV - The Papal Library." Saint Mike, March 17, 2021, https://saint-mike.org/blogs/papal-library/gregoryxiv-biography.

"France During the Reformation." Lineage, 2023, https://lineagejourney.com/read/france-during-the-reformation.

Freed, John. *Frederick Barbarossa: The Prince and the Myth*. Yale University Press: New Haven, CT, 2016.

Freeman, Evan. "Byzantine Iconoclasm and the Triumph of Orthodoxy." Khan Academy, 2013, https://www.khanacademy.org/humanities/medieval-world/byzantine1/beginners-guide-byzantine/a/iconoclastic-controversies.

Fuhrmann, Horst. *Germany in the High Middle Ages: c. 1050-1200*. Cambridge University Press: Cambridge, UK, 1986.

Fulton, Michael S. *Artillery in the Era of the Crusades*. Brill Publications: Paderborn, Germany, 2018.

Garcia-Arenal, Mercedes. "Granada." *Encyclopedia of Islam, Three*. Union Academy International: Brill, 2014.

Gibb, H. A. R. *The Damascus Chronicle of the Crusades: Extracted and Translated from the Chronicle of Ibn Al-Qalanisi*. Dover Publications: Garden City, NY, November 24, 2011.

Gibbon, Edward. *The History of the Decline and Fall of the Roman Empire*. Edited by David Womersley. London, England: Penguin Classics, 1996.

Gildas, Marie. "St. Bernard of Clairvaux." New Advent LLC, 1907, https://www.newadvent.org/cathen/02498d.htm.

"Global Christianity - A Report on the Size and Distribution of the World's Christian Population." Pew Research Center, December 18, 2011, https://www.pewresearch.org/religion/2011/12/19/global-christianity-exec/.

Görich, Knut. *Friedrich Barbarossa: Eine Biographie*. Germany: C. H. Beck, 2011.

Grousset, Rene. *History of the Crusades and the Frankish Kingdom of Jerusalem II*. L'equillbre, Paris, 1935.

Hamilton, Bernard. "Spreading the Gospel in the Middle Ages." *History Today* 53, no. 1, January 2003, https://www.historytoday.com/archive/spreading-gospel-middle-ages.

Herrmann, Joachim. *Die Slawen in Deutschland*. Akademie-Verlag GmbH: Berlin, 1970.

Hill, J. H. and Hill, Laurita L. "Bohemond I." *Encyclopedia Britannica*, June 10, 2020. https://www.britannica.com/biography/Bohemond-I.

Hillgarth, J.N. *The Spanish Kingdoms: 1250-1516. Volume II: 1410-1516, Castilian Hegemony*. Clarendon Press, Oxford University Press: Oxford, 1978.

"Historical Figure: Alessandro Farnese." Histouring, n.d., https://www.histouring.com/en/historical-figure/alessandro-farnese/.

History.com Editors. "Charlemagne." A&E Television Networks. History, July 22, 2022, https://www.history.com/topics/middle-ages/charlemagne.

History.com Editors. "Council of Nicaea Concludes." History. A&E Television Networks, July 28, 2019, https://www.history.com/this-day-in-history/council-of-nicaea-concludes.

History.com Editors. "Goths and Visigoths." History. A&E Television Networks, April 3, 2019, https://www.history.com/topics/ancient-rome/goths-and-visigoths#:~:text=The%20Thervingi%20were%20the%20Gothic,the%20next%20decade%20or%20so.

History.com Editors, "Huns." History. A&E Television Networks, April 5, 2018, https://www.history.com/topics/ancient-china/huns.

History.com Editors. "Islam." A&E Television Networks. History, March 11, 2022, https://www.history.com/topics/religion/islam.

History.com Editors. "Knights Templar." History, A&E Television Networks, August 23, 2022, https://www.history.com/topics/middle-ages/the-knights-templar#:~:text=Around%201118%2C%20a%20French%20knight,simply%20as%20the%20Knights%20Templar.

History.com Editors. "Magna Carta." A&E Television Networks. History, October 21, 2021, https://www.history.com/topics/european-history/magna-carta

History.com Editors. "Who Was St. Patrick?" History. A&E Television Networks, March 15, 2022, https://www.history.com/topics/st-patricks-day/who-was-saint-patrick#:~:text=St.-,Patrick%20Was%20Never%20Canonized%20as%20a%20Saint,the%20era%20he%20lived%20in.

Holt, Edward L. "Out of Many, One?: The Voice(s) in the Crusade Ideology of Las Navas de Tolosa." Medievalists, 2010, https://www.medievalists.net/2011/05/out-of-many-one-the-voices-in-the-crusade-ideology-of-las-navas-de-tolosa/.

Holt, James. "Quarrel with the Church of John." *Encyclopedia Britannica*, n.d., https://www.britannica.com/biography/John-king-of-England/Quarrel-with-the-church.

Holt, P.M., Lambton, Ann K. S., et al. *The Cambridge History of Islam: Volume 2A: The Indian Sub-Continent, South-East Asia, Africa, and the Muslim West.* Cambridge University Press: Cambridge, 1977.

Hughes, Philip. *History of the Church: Vol. II: The Church in the World: The Church Created: Augustine to Aquinas.* A&C Black: London, 1979.

"Illuminated Manuscripts (c.600-1200)." Visual Arts Cork, n.d., http://www.visual-arts-cork.com/cultural-history-of-ireland/illuminated-manuscripts.htm.

"Islam Timeline." *World History Encyclopedia*, 2022, https://www.worldhistory.org/timeline/islam/.

"Is Purgatory Mentioned in the Bible?" Watch Tower Bible and Tract Society of Pennsylvania, 2022, https://www.jw.org/en/bible-teachings/questions/is-purgatory-in-the-bible/.

"John Calvin on Predestination." Theologians & Theology, 2013, https://www.theologian-theology.com/theologians/john-calvin-predestination/.

"John Calvin Timeline." *World History Encyclopedia*, 2023., https://www.worldhistory.org/timeline/John_Calvin/.

Johnson, Ben. "The History of the Magna Carta." Historic UK, n.d., https://www.historic-uk.com/HistoryUK/HistoryofEngland/The-Origins-of-the-Magna-Carta/.

Jones, Terry, and Alan Ereira. Crusades. Facts on File, 1995.

"Julius II Ca. 1445-1513 Pope." Encyclopedia.com, 2019, https://www.encyclopedia.com/humanities/encyclopedias-almanacs-transcripts-and-maps/julius-ii-ca-1445-1513-pope.

Kedar, Benjamin Z. *Urbs Capta: The Fourth Crusade and its Consequences.* Lethielleux: Paris, 2005.

Kelly, J. N. D., and Michael J. Walsh. *A Dictionary of Popes.* Oxford University Press, 2010. https://www.oxfordreference.com/view/10.1093/acref/9780199295814.001.0001/acref-9780199295814.

Kilcrease, Jack. "Katharina von Bora Luther." Lutheran Reformation, December 20, 2016, https://lutheranreformation.org/history/katharina-von-bora-luther/.

King, Laura. "The Book of Kells." Virginia Commonwealth University, 2004, http://www.people.vcu.edu/~djbromle/color-theory/color04/laura/bookofkells.htm.

Kongstam, Angus. *Historical Atlas of the Crusades.* Facts on File: New York, USA, 2002.

Lataste, Joseph. "Pope St. Pius V." *The Catholic Encyclopedia.* Vol. 12. New York: Robert Appleton Company, 1911.

Levron, J. "Louis IX." *Encyclopedia Britannica*, January 13, 2023. https://www.britannica.com/biography/Louis-IX.

Lightfoot, Christopher. "The Roman Empire (27 B.C. - 393 A.D.)" Department of Greek and Roman Art. *The Metropolitan Museum of Art*, October 2000, https://www.metmuseum.org/toah/hd/roem/hd_roem.htm.

Lock, Peter. *The Routledge Companion to the Crusades.* Routledge, 2006.

Löffler, Klemens. "Pope Leo X." *The Catholic Encyclopedia.* Vol. 9. New York: Robert Appleton Company, 1910. 17 Aug. 2023 <http://www.newadvent.org/cathen/09162a.htm>.

Logos Staff. "How Martin Luther Accidentally Sparked the Reformation." Word by Word, Logos, October 8, 2021, https://www.logos.com/grow/luther-how-he-accidentally-sparked-the-reformation/.

Loud, G. A. *The Crusade of Frederick Barbarossa: The History of the Expedition of the Emperor Frederick and Related Texts.* Ashgate Publishing: Surrey, 2010.

Loud, G. A. "The German Crusade of 1197-1198." White Rose Research Online, 2015, https://eprints.whiterose.ac.uk/82933/.

Loughlin, James. "Pope Adrian VI." *The Catholic Encyclopedia.* Vol. 1. New York: Robert Appleton Company, 1907. 17 Aug. 2023 <http://www.newadvent.org/cathen/01159b.htm>.

Loughlin, James. "Pope Blessed Eugene III." New Advent LLC, 2021, https://www.newadvent.org/cathen/05599a.htm.

Loughlin, James. "Pope Paul III." *The Catholic Encyclopedia.* Vol. 11. New York: Robert Appleton Company, 1911. Accessed August 21, 2023, <http://www.newadvent.org/cathen/11579a.htm>.

Loughlin, James. "Pope Paul IV." *The Catholic Encyclopedia.* Vol. 11. New York: Robert Appleton Company, 1911. August 22, 2023 <http://www.newadvent.org/cathen/11581a.htm>.

Luther, Martin. *Dr. Martin Luther's Catechism with Explanation and Bible History.* The Apostolic Lutheran Church of America, 1996.

Lyons, M.C. and Jackson, D.E.P. *Saladin: The Politics of the Holy War.* Cambridge University Press, Cambridge, UK, 1982.

Maalouf, Amin. *The Crusades Through Arab Eyes.* Schocken Books: New York, USA, 1984.

MacEvitt, Christopher. *The Crusades and the Christian World of the East: Rough Tolerance.* University of Pennsylvania Press: Philadelphia, USA, 2010.

MacMillian, Amanda. "What Influences a Baby's Sex?" Health, June 9, 2023, https://www.health.com/condition/pregnancy/do-these-5-things-really-influence-a-babys-gender.

Madden, Thomas F. *The Fourth Crusade: Event, Aftermath, and Perceptions: Papers from the Sixth Conference of the Society for the Study of the Crusades and the Latin East in Istanbul, Turkey.* Routledge: London, 2008.

"Magna Carta: Muse and Mentor." Library of Congress, 2014, https://www.loc.gov/exhibits/magna-carta-muse-and-mentor/executive-power.html.

Mark, Joshua J. "Council of Trent." *World History Encyclopedia,* June 16, 2022, https://www.worldhistory.org/Council_of_Trent/.

Mark, Joshua J. "Diet of Worms." *World History Encyclopedia,* December 8, 2021, https://www.worldhistory.org/Diet_of_Worms/.

Mark, Joshua J. "Huldrych Zwingli." *World History Encyclopedia,* January 13, 2022, https://www.worldhistory.org/Huldrych_Zwingli/.

Mark, Joshua J. "Huns." *World History Encyclopedia,* April 25, 2018, https://www.worldhistory.org/Huns/.

Mark, Joshua, J. "Johannes Gutenberg." *World History Encyclopedia,* July 25, 2022, https://www.worldhistory.org/Johannes_Gutenberg/.

Mark, Joshua J. "Martin Luther." *World History Encyclopedia,* November 30, 2021, https://www.worldhistory.org/Martin_Luther/.

Mark, Joshua J. "Odoacer." *World History Encyclopedia,* September 20, 2014, https://www.worldhistory.org/Odoacer/.

Mark, Joshua J. "The Goths." *World History Encyclopedia,* October 12, 2014, https://www.worldhistory.org/Goths/.

Mark, Joshua J. "The Medieval Church." *World History Encyclopedia,* June 17, 2019, https://www.worldhistory.org/Medieval_Church/.

Markseken, Susan F., Surgone, Lambert M., and Timpledon, Miriam T., ed. *Zengi.* ZDM Publishing, 2010.

"Martin Luther and the Protestant Reformation." Trinity Lutheran Church, n.d., https://trinitylutheranchurch.360unite.com/martin-luther.

"Mary I (r.1553-1558)." The Royal Household, n.d., https://www.royal.uk/mary-i.

Masci, David and Lawton, Elizabeth. "Applying God's Law: Religious Courts and Mediation in the U.S." Pew Research Center, April 8, 2013, https://www.pewresearch.org/religion/2013/04/08/applying-gods-law-religious-courts-and-mediation-in-the-us/.

Mayer, Hans E. *The Crusades*. Oxford University Press: Oxford, UK, 1972.

McClintock, Alex. "8 Ways Magna Carta Still Affects Life in 2015." ABC News, October 9, 2016, https://www.abc.net.au/news/2015-06-15/magna-carta-800-years/6538364.

McGinness, Frederick J. "Paul V (Pope) (Camillo Borghese; 1552–1621; Reigned 1605–1621)." *Europe, 1450 to 1789: Encyclopedia of the Early Modern World*. Encyclopedia.com. August 23, 2023. https://www.encyclopedia.com/people/philosophy-and-religion/roman-catholic-popes-and-antipopes/paul-v#3404900846

"Medieval Illuminated Manuscripts." Minneapolis Institute of Art, n.d., https://new.artsmia.org/programs/teachers-and-students/teaching-the-arts/five-ideas/medieval-illuminated-manuscripts.

Meyer Everts, Janet. "The Apostle Paul and His Times: Christian History Timeline." *Christianity Today*, 1995, https://www.christianitytoday.com/history/issues/issue-47/apostle-paul-and-his-times-christian-history-timeline.html.

McIntosh, Matthew A. "The Early Medieval Hiberno-Scottish Missions." Brewminate, January 31, 2021, https://brewminate.com/the-early-medieval-hiberno-scottish-missions/.

"Michael I Cerularius." Hellenica World, n.d., https://www.hellenicaworld.com/Byzantium/Person/en/MichaelICerularius.html.

"Monasticism, Early Irish." *New Catholic Encyclopedia*. Encyclopedia.com, 2019, https://www.encyclopedia.com/religion/encyclopedias-almanacs-transcripts-and-maps/monasticism-early-irish.

Morrill, J. S. "Edward VI." *Encyclopedia Britannica*, July 2, 2023. https://www.britannica.com/biography/Edward-VI.

Morrill, J. S. and Elton, Geoffrey R. "Henry VIII." *Encyclopedia Britannica*, June 30, 2023. https://www.britannica.com/biography/Henry-VIII-king-of-England.

Murphy, Michael. "The Moors - 711 CE." History Tree, 2022, https://www.historytree.net/world-history/the_moors_711_ce.

Murray, Alan V. *Crusades: An Encyclopedia*. ACE-CLIO: Santa Barbara, 2006.

Murray, Alan V. *The Crusader Kingdom of Jerusalem: A Dynamic History 1099-1125*. Occasional Publications of the Unit for Prosopographical Research: Oxford, UK, 2000.

"Muslim Spain (711-1492)" BBC, September 4, 2009, https://www.bbc.co.uk/religion/religions/islam/history/spain_1.shtml#:~:text=In%20711%20Muslim%20forces%20invaded,1492%20when%20Granada%20was%20conquered.

National Geographic Society. "Jul 16, 1054 CE: Great Schism." *National Geographic* Society, May 20, 2022, https://education.nationalgeographic.org/resource/great-schism.

Nicolle, David. *The Second Crusade 1148: Disaster Outside Damascus.* Bloomsbury USA: New York, January 20, 2009.

Norman, Jeremy M. "The Book of Darrow, One of the Earliest Surviving Fully Decorated Insular Gospel Books." Jeremy Norman's History of Information, 2022, https://www.historyofinformation.com/detail.php?id=1468.

Norwich, John J. *A Short History of Byzantium.* Vintage Books: New York, 1997.

Nutter, Nick. "Muslim Invasion of Hispania 711 AD." Visit Andalucia, March 18, 2022, https://www.visit-andalucia.com/muslin-invasion-hispania-711ad/.

Oehring, Chris. "King Henry II." Historic UK, n.d., https://www.historic-uk.com/HistoryUK/HistoryofEngland/King-Henry-II-of-England/.

O'Neil, Sam. "Earliest Days of the Roman Christian Church." Learn Religions. Dotdash Meredith, June 25, 2019, https://www.learnreligions.com/the-early-church-at-rome-363409.

O'Nell, Brian. "Monasteries in Ireland." Your Irish Culture, March 2, 2020, https://www.yourirish.com/history/christianity/monasteries-in-ireland.

Ott, Michael. "Pope Julius II." *The Catholic Encyclopedia.* Vol. 8. New York: Robert Appleton Company, 1910. August 17, 2023 <http://www.newadvent.org/cathen/08562a.htm>.

Ott, Michael. "Pope Julius III." The Catholic Encyclopedia. Vol. 8. New York: Robert Appleton Company, 1910. August 21, 2023 <http://www.newadvent.org/cathen/08564a.htm>.

Ott, Michael. "Pope Leo XI." *The Catholic Encyclopedia.* Vol. 9. New York: Robert Appleton Company, 1910. September 1, 2023.

Ott, Michael. "Pope Sixtus V." *The Catholic Encyclopedia.* Vol. 14. New York: Robert Appleton Company, 1912, August 30, 2023 <http://www.newadvent.org/cathen/14033a.htm>.

Pacaut, M. "Philip II." *Encyclopedia Britannica*, August 17, 2022. https://www.britannica.com/biography/Philip-II-king-of-France.

Painter, Sidney. "II. The Third Crusade: Richard the Lionhearted and Philip Augustus," *A History of the Crusades, Volume 2: The Later Crusades, 1189-1311*, edited by Robert Lee Wolff, Harry W. Hazard and Kenneth Meyer Setton, 45-86. Philadelphia: University of Pennsylvania Press, 1962.

https://doi.org/10.9783/9781512819564-009.

Pastor, Freiherr L. *The History of the Popes.* Legare Street Press, 2022.

Pernin, Raphael. "Visitation Order." *The Catholic Encyclopedia*, Vol. 15, New York: Robert Appleton Company, 1912. Accessed August 14, 2023, https://www.newadvent.org/cathen/15481a.htm#:~:text=The%20nuns%20of%20the%20Visitation,Jane%20de%20Chantal.

"Peter the Hermit: 1050-1115." Heritage History, 2023, https://www.heritage-history.com/index.php?c=resources&s=char-dir&f=hermit3.

Petruzzello, Melissa. "The Seven Sacraments of the Roman Catholic church." *Encyclopedia Britannica*, February 6, 2018. https://www.britannica.com/list/the-seven-sacraments-of-the-roman-catholic-church.

Petry, Carl F. *The Cambridge History of Egypt, Vol I: Islamic Egypt, 640-1517.* Cambridge University Press: Cambridge, 1997.

Phillips, Jonathan. "Troyes, Council (1129)." World History, February 9, 2015, https://www.worldhistory.biz/middle-ages/23710-troyes-council-1129.html.

Pirie, Valerie. *The Triple Crown: An Account of the Papal Conclaves From the Fifteenth Century to the Present Day.* New York: G.P. Putnam's Sons, 1936.

Pohlsander, Hans A. *The Emperor Constantine.* New York, NY: Routledge, 2004.

"Pope Clement VIII." Pope History, 2023, https://popehistory.com/popes/pope-clement-viii/.

"Pope Gregory XIII." Papal Artifacts, 2021, https://www.papalartifacts.com/portfolio-item/pope-gregory-xiii/.

"Pope Gregory XIII." Pope History, 2023, https://popehistory.com/popes/pope-gregory-xiii/.

"Pope Gregory XIV." Pope History, 2023, https://popehistory.com/popes/pope-gregory-xiv.

"Pope Gregory XV." Pope History, 2023, https://popehistory.com/popes/pope-gregory-xv/.

"Pope Innocent X." Pope History, 2023, https://popehistory.com/popes/pope-innocent-x/.

"Pope Julius III (1487-1555) - a dream about the power of ... a family." Roma Non Per Tutti, n.d., https://roma-nonpertutti.com/en/article/417/pope-julius-iii-14871555-a-dream-about-the-power-of-a-family.

"Pope Leo X." Pope History, 2023, https://popehistory.com/popes/pope-leo-x/.

"Pope Leo X (Giovanni de' Medici)." The Medici Family, October 31, 2022, https://themedicifamily.com/pope-leo-x.

"Pope Paul V." Pope History, 2023, https://popehistory.com/popes/pope-paul-v/.

"Pope Pius IV." Pope History, 2023, https://popehistory.com/popes/pope-pius-iv/.

"Pope St. Leo IX." Pope History, 2022, https://popehistory.com/popes/pope-st-leo-ix/.

"Pope Urban VII." Pope History, 2023, https://popehistory.com/popes/pope-urban-vii/.

"Pope Urban VIII." Pope History, 2023, https://popehistory.com/popes/pope-urban-viii/.

Potter, Bill. "The Battle of Lepanto, October 7, 1571." Landmark Events, October 5, 2021, https://landmarkevents.org/the-battle-of-lepanto-1571/.

Renee, R. "When Was Tithing Instituted in the Church?" The Tithing Hoax, 2022, https://thetithinghoax.com/when-was-tithing-instituted-in-the-church/.

Reeves, Marjorie. *The Influence of Prophecy in the Later Middle Ages: A Study in Joachimism.* Oxford University Press, 1969.

Riley-Smith, Jonathan. *Atlas of the Crusades.* Facts on File: New York, 1991.

Rodocanachi, Emmanuel. *History of Rome: The Popes Adrian VI to Clement VII.* Paris, Hacette, 1933.

"Roman Confutation (1530)" Book of Concord, n.d., https://bookofconcord.org/other-resources/sources-and-context/roman-confutation/.

"Roman Empire (27 BC - 476 AD)." Rome.net. *Civitatis,* n.d., https://www.rome.net/roman-empire.

"Romulus Augustulus." Imperium Romanum, June 9, 2019, https://imperiumromanum.pl/en/biographies/romulus-augustulus/.

Runciman, Steven. *A History of the Crusades, Vol. II: The Kingdom of Jerusalem and the Frankish East, 1100-1187.* Cambridge University Press: Cambridge, UK, 1952.

Runciman, Steven. *A History of the Crusades, Vol. III: The Kingdom of Acre and the Later Crusades.* Cambridge University Press: Cambridge, UK, 1954.

Russia Beyond. "7 Main Differences Between Catholicism and Orthodox Christianity." *Russia Beyond,* June 1, 2022, https://www.rbth.com/lifestyle/335081-7-main-differences-orthodoxy-catholicism.

"Saint Palladius." Newman Ministry, 2022, https://www.newmanministry.com/saints/saint-palladius.

Schrader, Helena P. "The Knights Templar and the Emperor: The 6th Crusade." Defender of Jerusalem, n.d., https://www.defenderofjerusalem.com/kt---6th-crusade.html.

Schroeder, Steven. "Christianity in the Roman Empire." Khan Academy, n.d., https://www.khanacademy.org/humanities/world-history/ancient-medieval/christianity/a/roman-culture#:~:text=Rome%20becomes%20Christian&text=The%20result%20of%20this%20council,religion%20of%20the%20Roman%20Empire.

Schurb, Ken. "Martin Luther's Early Years: Christian History Timeline." Christian History Institute, Originally published in *Christian History*, Issue 34, 1992, https://christianhistoryinstitute.org/magazine/article/martin-luthers-early-years-timeline.

Setton, Kenneth. *A History of the Crusades, Vol. VI.* University of Wisconsin Press: Madison, 1969.

Setton, Kenneth. *The Papacy and the Levant, 1204-1571. Volume IV: The Sixteenth Century.* Philadelphia: American Philosophical Society, 1984.

"Seventh Crusade Timeline." *World History Encyclopedia*, 2023, https://www.worldhistory.org/timeline/Seventh_Crusade/.

Simkin, John. "Mary and Elizabeth: Catholics and Protestants." Spartacus Educational, January 2020, https://spartacus-educational.com/U3Ahistory12.htm.

"Sixth Crusade Timeline." *World History Encyclopedia*, 2023, https://www.worldhistory.org/timeline/Sixth_Crusade/.

"Skellig Michael." Monastic Ireland, 2014, http://monastic.ie/history/skellig-michael/.

Smitha, Frank E. "More Crusades and Heretics, 1144 to 1212." F. Smitha, 2018, http://www.fsmitha.com/h3/eu09.htm.

Smail, R. C. *Crusading Warfare 1097-1193.* Barnes & Noble Books: New York, 1995.

Stacey, John. "John Wycliffe." *Encyclopedia Britannica*, August 4, 2023. https://www.britannica.com/biography/John-Wycliffe.

Starkey, David. Six Wives: The Queens of Henry VIII. Harper Perennial: New York, 2004.

Strathern, Paul. *The Medici: Power, Money, and Ambition in the Italian Renaissance.* New York, Pegasus, 2016.

Sullivan, Nate. "The Dark Ages: Definition, History & Timeline." Study, September 7, 2015, www.study.com/academy/lesson/the-dark-ages-definition-history-timeline.html.

Taylor, Pegatha. "Moral Agency in Crusade and Colonization: Anselm of Havelberg and the Wendish Crusade of 1147." *The International History Review* (2000): 772.

The Anne Boleyn Files and Tudor Society. "May 12 - Martin Luther's Books are Burned in London." May 11, 2019, video, https://www.youtube.com/watch?v=bI9d8GhvZMo&t=186s.

"The Augsburg Confession." Info Werke Martin Luther, 1530, https://infowerke.martinluther.us/augsburg_confession_1530.pdf.

"The Conquest of Granada." The Spanish War History, 2012, https://www.spanishwars.net/15th-century-conquest-of-granada.html.

"The Creeds and Confessions of the Lutheran Church." Our Savior Evangelical Lutheran Church, n.d., https://havasulutherans.org/catechism-explanation/creeds-confessions/.

"The Cross of Cong." National Museum of Ireland, 2022, https://www.museum.ie/en-IE/Collections-Research/Irish-Antiquities-Division-Collections/Collections-List-(1)/Early-Medieval/The-Cross-of-Cong.

The Editors of Give Me History. "Christianity in the Middle Ages." Give Me History, November 17, 2022, https://www.givemehistory.com/christianity-in-the-middle-ages.

"The Five Pillars of Islam." The MET, 2022, whttps://www.metmuseum.org/learn/educators/curriculum-resources/art-of-the-islamic-world/unit-one/the-five-pillars-of-islam.

"The List of Popes." *The Catholic Encyclopedia.* Vol. 12. New York: Robert Appleton Company, 1911. Accessed 17 Aug. 2023 <http://www.newadvent.org/cathen/12272b.htm>.

"The (Original) Nicene Creed of 325." Christ the Savior OCA, 2020, https://christthesavioroca.org/files/2020-Resurrection-Classes/The-Nicene-Creed-of-325.pdf.

"The Ottoman Empire - Background." New Zealand Ministry for Culture and Heritage, April 26, 2023, https://nzhistory.govt.nz/war/ottoman-empire/background.

"Theodosius I (378-395 A.D.)" Roman Emperors - An Online Encyclopedia of Roman Rules and Their Families

Thurston, Herbert. "Pope Clement VII." *The Catholic Encyclopedia.* Vol. 4. New York: Robert Appleton Company, 1908. 18 Aug. 2023 <http://www.newadvent.org/cathen/04024a.htm>.

Van Cleve, Thomas C. "The Crusade of Frederick II." Library at the University of Wisconsin-Madison, 1969, https://images.library.wisc.edu/History/EFacs/HistCrus/0001/0002/reference/history.crustwo.i0026.pdf.

Van Cleve, Thomas C. *The Emperor Frederick II of Hohenstaufen, Immutator Mundi.* Clarendon Press: London, 1972.

Vernet Gines, Juan and Viguera, Maria J. "Muslim Spain." *Encyclopedia Britannica*, 2023, https://www.britannica.com/place/Spain/The-Almoravids.

Visceglia, Maria A. "A Comparative Historiographic Reflection on Sovereignty in Early Modern Europe: Interregnum Rites and Papal Funerals." *Cultural Exchange in Early Modern Europe*. Cambridge University Press, 2006.

"Visigoth Wars." Heritage History, 2020, https://www.heritage-history.com/index.php?c=resources&s=war-dir&f=wars_visigoths.

Wasson, Donald L. "Battle of Adrianople." *World History Encyclopedia*, August 26, 2019, https://www.worldhistory.org/Battle_of_Adrianople/.

Wasson, Donald L. "Sack of Rome 410 CE." *World History Encyclopedia*, September 23, 2019, https://www.worldhistory.org/article/1449/sack-of-rome-410-ce/.

Weber, Nicholas. "Pope Innocent IX." *The Catholic Encyclopedia*. Vol. 8. New York: Robert Appleton Company, 1910. August 30, 2023 <http://www.newadvent.org/cathen/08020a.htm>.

"What is the Filioque Clause/Controversy?" Compelling Truth, n.d., https://www.compellingtruth.org/filioque-clause.html.

"What the Early Church Believed: Filioque." Catholic Answers, August 10, 2004, https://www.catholic.com/tract/filioque.

"Who We Are." Wycliffe Global Alliance, 2023, https://www.wycliffe.net/about-us/.

Wieja, Estera. "10 Places Where Jesus Walked in Israel from Scripture." Fellowship of Israel Related Ministries, October 22, 2020, https://firmisrael.org/learn/10-places-where-jesus-walked/.

Williams, George L. *Papal Genealogy: The Families and Descendants of the Popes*. McFarland & Company, 1998.

Wilson, Stephen D. "The Magna Carta & the Rise of Religious Liberty." Baptist Press, June 15, 2015, https://www.baptistpress.com/resource-library/news/the-magna-carta-the-rise-of-religious-liberty/.

Wooden, Cindy. "Heavenly Hosts: Popes Aren't Automatically Saints." Catholic News Service, May 3, 2011, https://web.archive.org/web/20130518205656/http://www.catholicnews.com/data/stories/cns/1101685.htm.

Woolf, Greg. "The Tetrarchy." Wellesley College, 2012, http://omeka.wellesley.edu/piranesi-rome/exhibits/show/basilica-of-maxentius-and-cons/the-tetrarchy#:~:text=The%20Tetrarchy%20was%20established%20in,districts%20and%20each%20ruled%20separately.

"Religion by Country 2023." World Population Review, 2023, https://worldpopulationreview.com/country-rankings/religion-by-country.

Knights Templar Encyclopedia. Ralls, Karen, Ph.D. 2007, Career Press, Franklin Lakes, NJ

The Illustrated History of Knights and Crusades. Phillips, Charles, 2010, Anness Publishing, UK

"Blessed Gerard (the Rules of Raymond du Puy)." http://blessed-gerard.org/bgt_rule.htm

"Blessed Raymond du Puy." http://www.smom-za.org/saints/raymond.htm

"The Becket Story: Archbishop Thomas Becket." https://thebecketstory.org.uk/pilgrimage/st-thomas-becket

"The Great Schism." https://education.nationalgeographic.org/resource/great-schism

"Knights of the Holy Sepulchre." https://cnewa.org/magazine/knights-of-the-holy-sepulchre-30042/

"World History Encyclopedia – Medieval Knight." https://www.worldhistory.org/Medieval_Knight/

"The First Crusade – World History.org." https://www.worldhistory.org/First_Crusade/

"History.com – The Middle Ages." https://www.history.com/topics/middle-ages/middle-ages

"The Hospitallers of St. John of Jerusalem." https://www.ewtn.com/catholicism/library/hospitallers-of-st-john-of-jerusalem-10553

"The Order of Malta." https://www.orderofmalta.int/about-the-order-of-malta/knights-of-malta/

"Catholic Answers/Encyclopedia: Knights of the Holy Sepulchre." https://www.catholic.com/encyclopedia/knights-of-the-holy-sepulchre

"Godfrey of Bouillon." https://www.newadvent.org/cathen/06624b.htm

"World History – Visigoth." https://www.worldhistory.org/visigoth/

"PubMed – Mycobacterium leprae: A Historical study on the origins of leprosy and its social stigma." https://www.ncbi.nlm.nih.gov/pmc/articles/PMC8805473/#:~:text=Treatment%20of%20leprosy%20has%20undergone,Guy%20Faget%20of%20Carville.

"Military and Hospitaller Order of Saint Lazarus of Jerusalem." https://stlazarus.onmessagecomms.co.uk/sites/default/files/media/files/history_key_dates_leaflet_0420_final.pdf

"Fall of Constantinople." https://www.history.com/topics/middle-east/constantinople#fall-of-constantinople

"Knights Templar – Important Castles and Churches." https://www.knighttemplar.org/single-post/2018/03/16/knights-templar-s-important-castles-and-churches

"The Templars' 'curse' on the King of France." https://blog.nationalarchives.gov.uk/templars-curse-king-france/

"April 3, AD 33: Why we believe we can know the exact date Jesus died." https://cbs.mbts.edu/2020/04/08/april-3-ad-33-why-we-believe-we-can-know-the-exact-date-jesus-died/

"Teutonic Knights." https://www.worldhistory.org/Teutonic_Knight/

"Teutonic Knights." https://www.newworldencyclopedia.org/entry/Battle_of_Tannenberg_(1410)

"Teutonic Knights." https://www.newworldencyclopedia.org/entry/Teutonic_Knights

"Frederick 'Barbarossa.'" https://www.britannica.com/place/Italy/Institutional-reforms

"Knights Templar Rules." https://www.history.com/news/the-knights-templar-rulebook-included-no-pointy-shoes-and-no-kissing-mom

"The Nine Worthies." https://www.ancient-origins.net/history-famous-people/nine-worthies-are-these-most-chivalrous-men-history-007416

"Templars Being Burned at the Stake." https://www.carmichaeldigitalprojects.org/hist447/items/show/132

Anderson, James. *Daily Life during the Spanish Inquisition*. 2004.

Peters, Edward. *Inquisition*. 1989.

Plaidy, Jean. *The Spanish Inquisition: Its Rise, Growth, and End*. 1994.

Vacandard, Elphège. *The Inquisition: A Critical and Historical Study of the Coercive Power of the Church*. 1907.

Made in the USA
Middletown, DE
21 March 2025

73039780R10236